the
Psalms
&Proverbs
Devotional *for* WOMEN

edited by

Rhonda	Dorothy
Harrington	Kelley
Kelley	Patterson

PUBLISHING GROUP

NASHVILLE, TENNESSEE

978-1-4627-5120-4

Published by B&H Publishing Group
Nashville, Tennessee

Dewey Decimal Classification: 242.2
Subject Heading: WOMEN \ SPIRITUAL LIFE \ DEVOTIONAL LITERATURE

2 3 4 5 6 7 8 9 • 24 23 22 21 20

Contents

Introduction

What does God say to a woman in the twenty-first century? God's Word provides all you need for living life to the fullest and honoring the Lord Jesus in the process. The *Psalms and Proverbs Devotional for Women* is prepared directly from the text of Scripture by a multi-generational team of God-honoring, spiritually-gifted women. This inspirational tool will guide you through a careful reading of Psalms and Proverbs each month. Your study and meditation on the message of these beloved books will change your life by providing biblical solutions for life's problems.

The *Psalms and Proverbs Devotional for Women* features relevant discussions on various topics relating to the challenges you face every day. Each day's message includes application and encouragement for you as the Lord writes His truths on your heart, molding you into His image and using you as a conduit for glorifying Him in every aspect of your life.

The single and married women who have written these daily commentaries come from different seasons of life and various geographical areas. We have several generational groups—a mother, daughter, and granddaughter from one family; several mother-daughter duos; and a mother-in-love and daughter-in-love. We have a teen in high school, college and seminary students, young mothers, and grandmothers. Their names are found with the devotionals, together with brief information about each in the list of contributors. All are committed to woman-to-woman ministries.

The *Psalms and Proverbs Devotional for Women* has a reading for every day but is undated. You can pick it up and begin your spiritual journey any day of the year. You can turn to the numbered day of your annual calendar or start with "Day 1" on any day you choose to begin. Each devotional stands alone. You can read the extended passage, or you can simply read the focus verse(s), printed for you as the devotional unfolds. The brevity of the passage enables you to savor its words and meditate upon its message, perhaps even memorizing the verse(s).

Use the guided prayer pattern to approach the throne of grace with your own petition and praise. Make your personal notes in the space for "Personal

Reflection." Perhaps you will note somewhere on the day's page the date (day/month/year)—make your own "stones of help" along the way as reminders in days and years to come of what God has been doing in your life. This *Psalms and Proverbs Devotional* is not planned as a one-time experience; rather, we think you will want to come back, whether in successive years or return after skipping a year or two, and work through its pages again, seeing what God has already done in time past and looking afresh for His Word to you.

This journey through the Psalms and Proverbs will touch you in whatever your life situation. Whether you are looking for answers to challenging questions, inspiration for spiritual nurture, direction for your life journey, renewal in your heart and spirit, or just conversation with the Lord—this *Psalms and Proverbs Devotional for Women* is prepared to be your companion and guide. Packed with insights from Scripture and practical applications, each day's reading will touch your life, perhaps speaking to your heart's deepest needs, your family challenges, or your service for Christ.

When you come to God's Word with an open heart, ready to hear God speak, willing to respond to Him in obedience, you will find yourself in His story—your place in His master plan. He will teach you; He will conform you to His image; He will then use you in ways you could never have imagined except that you have spent time with Him!

A Pattern of Personal Quiet Time

The commitment to building personal intimacy with the Lord Jesus is personal—not something anyone else can build into your life. Whether a child, teenager, young adult, or mature woman—whether you are new in your faith journey or spiritually strong and disciplined in your faith, you must initiate genuine, heart-felt communication with the Lord and establish your own pattern for sustaining the relationship you have established with the Lord Jesus.

Women throughout history—from Bible times to the current generation—have been marked by such a commitment. The maidservant of Naaman's wife was taken from her parents into captivity at a young age (2 Kin. 5:1–3); yet she had already developed a relationship with the living God. She kept her faith; she shared it. Her strength did not come because of many years of spiritual training but because she started at a young age and refused to let earthly circumstances destroy a heavenly commitment.

The Moabitess Ruth had no witness to the true God until after she married, but she observed her mother-in-law Naomi and learned spiritual disciplines, which brought her into a relationship with the living God and introduced her to the joys of serving Him. Mary of Nazareth, the mother of our Lord, as a young woman had been introduced to Yahweh God and taught His Word through her childhood years so that when she was faced with what seemed humanly impossible, she humbly bowed herself before God the Father and willingly accepted His assignment.

These "spiritual sisters" were characterized by a commitment to hearing and knowing God's Word, then living it out in practical ways (see Matt. 7:24). That commitment thrives and blooms in the presence of the Lord—reading His Word, listening for His voice, sharing your innermost fears and petitions, spending quality as well as quantity time with Him.

Women more than anything else need a word from God. The written Word of God was prepared in "the fullness of time" (Gal. 4:4) and continues to speak to women in this generation with the same authority and clarity as it did in centuries gone by, and that Word will continue to speak to generations to come.

Scripture does not speak in detail to every situation in life, but the Bible records timeless principles that continue to be timely solutions to all of life's challenges.

Let this volume be a tool for you to return to **Bethel** (Hb., "house of God"). Pursue with purpose and passion, putting yourself in the presence of the Lord for a time of prayer and reading His Word. Let these woman-to-woman devotionals add an inspirational thought or instructive moment to your time with the Lord.

In addition to the devotionals, you will find a Bible Reading Plan, which leads you through a reading plan for the books of Psalms and Proverbs every month, prepared by Kim Whitten. Nothing will enrich your life so much as systematic and purposeful reading of the Word of God. Rhonda Kelley's article sets forth clearly how you can come to know Jesus Christ as your personal Savior.

Join Rhonda and me in a "Bethel" year. Let us make our way, not merely on a whim of urgent need or as a perfunctory happenstance or even a passing fad, into the presence of the living Lord—sitting at His feet, reading His Word, meditating on its application to life, pouring out our praise and petition to Him! Do this every day, and consider making a commitment to work through the entire year with a pattern of personal quiet time devoted to pursuing the Lord—not through an ordinary ritual but rather establishing an extraordinary life discipline that will carry you through life with purpose and praise.

This time for personal intimacy with the Lord is yours to establish. The psalmist speaks of calling out to the Lord "morning, noon, and night." Surely you can select one time—even brief minutes—during the twenty-four-hour cycle you are given to devote uninterrupted and focused minutes to the Lord. Start today!

Dorothy Kelley Patterson

The Christian Life

Are you a Christian? A Christian is anyone who has received by faith the salvation God has provided in Jesus Christ. **Salvation** is necessary because all have sinned against God (Rom. 3:23). Salvation begins with **repentance**—turning away from sin and turning toward God, who alone has the power to save. You cannot earn salvation by doing good works, for it is a gift of grace from God, accomplished through the death of His Son, Jesus Christ (Eph. 2:8–9). When Jesus died on the cross, He paid the price to forgive all sin (John 3:16; Rom. 5:8; 1 John 2:2). Romans 6:23 says, "For the wages of sin *is* death, but the gift of God *is* eternal life in Christ Jesus our Lord." God's free gift of salvation—the exchange of your sin for His righteousness—must be accepted by faith (Rom. 10:9–10). When you accept God's gift of salvation, you become a new creation (2 Cor. 5:17). Salvation changes everything—your past, your present, and your future:

- **Justification** may be considered the past tense of salvation. Justification is God's declaration that you are righteous through the blood of Christ (Rom. 4:3–25).
- **Sanctification** is the present tense of salvation, the process of growing in faith and in holiness since you are set apart by and for God (1 Cor. 6:11).
- **Glorification** is the future tense of salvation. Glorification is the perfection of God's image and character in you when you enter His presence in heaven (2 Cor. 3:18).

If you are a Christian, you are promised security in your salvation, but what is your present "new creation" life supposed to look like? What responsibilities do you have in maintaining a vibrant relationship with your Savior?

The Beginning. Your Christian life begins the moment you turn away from sin and, by faith, receive the salvation God has provided in the crucifixion and resurrection of His Son Jesus Christ. At that moment, the Holy Spirit makes Himself at home in your life, immediately beginning the remodeling

process necessary for Christ to be seen in every aspect. Just as the Christian life does not begin when you are born, when you become a church member, or when you mistakenly think you have earned God's approval for doing good, so it does not continue on the basis of who you are, whom you know, where you go to church, or what you do. Just as there is nothing you can do to get rid of your sin and restore your relationship with God—Jesus sacrificed Himself to provide the forgiveness needed, so you cannot "live the Christian life" on your own terms. Relinquishing ownership and control of your life to Christ is just the beginning of the total life makeover.

The Ongoing Story. From that point on, your salvation is secure. Regardless of how sin-stained or sin-wrecked your life is when you entrust it to Christ, all is forgiven. However, you have a ruthless enemy (Satan), who is determined to thwart God's renovation plans for your life by any means possible and keep you from telling anyone else the Good News. In Christ you have freedom from the addiction to sin and from consequent death (i.e., eternal separation from God). No longer are you the enemy's slave to do his bidding, but he strives to convince you otherwise. Scripture often talks about this war in terms of light and darkness. Christ's message is that "God is light and in Him is no darkness at all" (1 John 1:5). Speaking to authentic Christians about their changed status, Ephesians 5:8 says, "For you were once darkness, but now *you are* light in the Lord," and commands, "Walk as children of light."

The power to "walk in the light as He [Jesus Christ] is in the light" (1 John 1:7a) is available in the Holy Spirit who is always with the Christian. Living the Christian life—walking in the light—is only possible by continually agreeing with the truth He reveals and letting Him exchange, change, and rearrange however He sees fit. The truth is found in the Bible. The power to obey the truth is in the Holy Spirit. The Christian whose mind is Scripture-saturated and whose will is Spirit-directed is equipped to grow in Christlikeness, but this growth also requires staying connected to the body of Christ, the local church. The Christian life is nurtured in your personal devotional life of Bible study and prayer but expressed in your relationships—both with your brothers and sisters in Christ and with non-Christians.

The Eternal Promise. Until Jesus returns, the physical lives of Christians will end but not without hope. Jesus' resurrection validates His promise of eternal life to those who follow Him. The Christian life is best lived with the end (as described in Scripture) in mind (see 2 Pet. 3), not only looking forward to God's justice and the rewards of endurance but also looking for opportunities to proclaim the gospel (see 1 Pet. 4). From confession of faith into eternity, the Christian life is a reflection of Christ Himself, an extension of His work in the world, and a witness of salvation to those who are unsaved.

Blessings,
Rhonda Kelley

Prosper in the New Year

Psalm 1:1–3

*"He shall be like a tree
Planted by the rivers of water . . .
And whatever he does shall prosper." (v. 3)*

Happy New Year! As one year ends and another begins, Christians often take time to reassess their lives and make resolutions. Have you determined your resolutions? Do not get ahead of God; turn to His Word before you start planning. The Bible is the source of guidance for those who seek to follow God's will. So, consider God's Word as you make your plans for the future.

King David begins the book of Psalms with wisdom that could help with your resolutions. He contrasts the way of the righteous and the end of the unrighteous, describing their action plan. He clearly identifies the blessings of the godly life and gives directions for prosperity. To accomplish God's will and receive His blessings in the New Year and every day, believers must:

- delight in the law of the Lord (v. 2);
- meditate on His law day and night (v. 2); and
- plant themselves firmly by the rivers of water (v. 3).

Total commitment to God's Word is necessary to bear fruit and prosper in life. A Christian grows and produces fruit when she seeks wisdom and guidance from God's Word. She can experience great joy in learning the truths of God. She must study the Bible regularly and meditate on it throughout the day. When planted firmly in God's Word, a believer has a continual supply from the Lord to flourish in life and ministry.

As this new year begins, I will make personal resolutions after I evaluate my progress during the past year. I will set several goals in each of these six

areas: spiritual, physical, mental, social, family, and financial. I will seek to define goals that are specific and measurable. As a Christian, I will pray for wisdom and guidance from the Lord so my goals will help accomplish His purposes in and through my life. The study of His Word clarifies my path and keeps me firmly grounded in His will. I am so grateful for His continual supply of wisdom.

Do you want to prosper in the new year? Do you pray that your family and friends will prosper? If so, you must delight yourself in the law of the Lord. Find more joy in God's Word than any other source. Meditate on His truth day and night, so that His Word is a conscious part of your life. Encourage those you love to plant themselves by His rivers of water, the Word of God, so they can also experience the blessings of God. What a joy to know you can prosper and be fruitful in the New Year!

Rhonda Kelley

Prayer: *Take time in prayer and Bible study as you make resolutions for a new year. Allow God's Word, not the world, to guide and direct you.*

Personal Reflection: ....

....

....

....

....

Lord, Help Me!

Psalm 3:1–8

"But You, O LORD, are a shield for me,
My glory and the One who lifts up my head.
I cried to the LORD with my voice,
And He heard me from His holy hill. Selah" (vv. 3–4)

The world is a mess! News agencies broadcast the violence, corruption, and terrorism in the world as well as our own communities. Loved ones face trouble—illness, loss, and death. At times, we ourselves suffer with physical, emotional, or spiritual problems. Some of these crises impact relationships with God and others. Christians are not exempt from the daily challenges of living. Life happens, but the Lord helps!

In Psalm 3, David cries out to the Lord in his personal despair. The king's life was torn apart by family turmoil and civil unrest. As a consequence of his adultery with Bathsheba and the murder of her husband at the king's command, problems began with David's family (2 Sam. 12:9–12). His son Absalom attempted to usurp the throne and caused David to flee from Jerusalem (2 Sam. 15:13–37). In his despair, King David wrote the words of this song.

Many people opposed him, but David had confidence in God: He clung to the promises of God to be his **shield** (Ps. 3:3), his **strength** (v. 3), his **sustainer** (v. 5), and his **salvation** (vv. 7–8). David knew the importance of a shield for a warrior's protection from an enemy. He had experienced the strength of God in battle to lift him up and restore energy. David had depended on the Lord throughout his life and knew He would help again. Ultimately, he believed that salvation was a grace gift of God to rescue sinners from themselves and their enemies.

Have you ever been attacked by other people? Has someone been critical of you because of different opinions? Relationships in life can often become tense. Like King David, you may feel at war even with those you love. In your

frustration and despair, call out to God for protection and guidance. I have learned the lesson personally. When the people closest to you are critical of you or your husband, it hurts! Call out to the Lord for help. He hears and heals and gives hope. The problems do not always disappear, but the Lord is your shield of protection and lifts up your head to give you strength. God has always been my present help in times of need!

God's promise to David is your promise today: God is with you, to protect you and give you strength. Cling to the promises of God. Call out to Him for help. And, give Him the glory for your salvation. You can be confident in the Lord's provision when you call out to Him: "Lord, help me!"

Rhonda Kelley

Prayer: *Ask the Lord to forgive you of your sin and protect you from your enemies. Claim the promises of God to be your shield, strength, sustainer, and salvation.*

Personal Reflection: ....

....

....

....

....

....

Take a Deep Breath

Psalm 4:1–5

"Be angry, and do not sin.
Meditate within your heart on your bed, and be still. Selah
Offer the sacrifices of righteousness,
And put your trust in the LORD." (vv. 4–5)

Do you trust God to hear your cries and answer your prayers? David expressed his faith in God in Psalm 4, expecting God to hear and extend mercy. The king knew that even though he was the ruler, he needed the intervention of Almighty God in his life. Despite his own personal failures and relentless opposition by his enemies, David had been set apart by God to be king. Because of his anointed position, his life and leadership needed to be characterized by godliness.

In Psalm 4:4–5, David issued a fourfold command for godly living to himself and his people: (1) "Be angry, and do not sin"; (2) "Meditate within your heart, and be still"; (3) "Offer the sacrifices of righteousness"; and (4) "put your trust in the LORD." What profound wisdom for yesterday and today! People who follow these guidelines will live godly lives and give God glory.

An interesting word punctuates verse 4. The Hebrew word *Selah* appears here and seventy other times in the book of Psalms as well as three times in Habakkuk. While the exact meaning is unknown, this term is thought to have musical significance in singing the psalms. *Selah* most likely indicates a pause for silence or a period of interlude. It may also provide helpful guidance for dealing with the tensions of life—when you are angry, take a breath. A pause for silence is good in singing and in life.

Do you ever get angry at yourself or others? If you are alive, you have inevitably experienced anger. Some of us control our anger more effectively than others. All of us can handle our anger with the help of the Holy Spirit. David's

inclusion of *Selah* in his psalms instructs us to take a breath when our emotions swell. Allow the Lord to calm your spirit and guard your tongue.

I am usually patient with others though impatient with myself. In the first year of marriage, I became furious when I could not mash my undercooked potatoes with my hand mixer. My sweet husband innocently walked into the kitchen as my anger exploded, and I flung potatoes across the room. In an effort to calm my anger, Chuck gave me a very nice electric mixer, which he says saved our marriage. As a young bride, I was embarrassed by my behavior and disappointed by my husband's practical gift of an appliance for the first Christmas in our marriage. I have learned to control my emotions with the help of the Lord and a deep breath.

What about you? Do you sin by becoming angry? If so, take a deep breath and meditate within your heart. *Selah*. When you put your trust in God, He tempers your emotions and encourages righteous living.

Rhonda Kelley

Prayer: *Spend a few moments crying out to God. Confess to Him any anger or other sin. Be still and meditate in your heart as you renew your trust in Him.*

Personal Reflection: ....

....

....

....

....

A Countenance of Joy

Psalm 4:6–8

"You have put gladness in my heart,
More than in the season that their grain and wine increased.
I will both lie down in peace, and sleep;
For You alone, O LORD, make me dwell in safety." (vv. 7–8)

One rainy Monday in New Orleans, I needed to run my errands. So, I donned my rain slicker and rain boots as I headed out with my list. I popped into the card store and greeted the clerk: "Happy Monday morning!" She immediately asked why I was smiling on such a miserable day. Without hesitation, I replied, "The weather doesn't determine my mood; the Lord does. He has given me joy despite the rain." My joyful countenance and positive words gave me an opportunity to be a witness on an otherwise miserable day.

In the last three verses of Psalm 4, King David petitions the Lord to reveal the light of His countenance. The word *countenance* is not a popular word in contemporary vernacular, but it is an important biblical word. Several Hebrew and Greek expressions are translated in the Bible with the noun *countenance*. The term has a deeper meaning than outward appearance. It actually reflects inward character and feelings of the heart. David asked the Lord to reveal His nature, to radiate His very being for all to see. Created in the image of God, believers should look like Him, reflecting His likeness. Christians are to be like Him and look like Him.

How can you have a godly countenance? How can your love of God and true character be reflected in your face? King David explained the source of his joy in verses 7 and 8. God put gladness in his heart. In times of harvest or famine, David could sleep in peace because he was safe in the presence of the Lord. You can have a heart of peace and a countenance of joy despite the circumstances when you trust in the Lord.

14

Take a look in the mirror. Is your face a joyful reflection of the peace you have in God? Do your eyes sparkle with hope and your lips smile with love? When you trust in God and depend upon Him, your face and tone of voice should express your confidence in Him despite the circumstances. Be conscious of the power of your feelings. Inward joy should be reflected outwardly.

Your countenance matters because you may be the only Bible some people will ever read. The first impression of your facial expression can speak more loudly than your words as you relate to others. So, witness with your face. Have a joyful countenance and a face of faith.

Rhonda Kelley

Prayer: *Lift your head up to the Lord and ask Him to show you His glory. As you receive His joy and rest in His peace, you will be secure in His arms and be a testimony of His grace.*

Personal Reflection: ....

....

....

....

....

....

15

Go to God for Guidance

Psalm 5:1–3

"My voice You shall hear in the morning, O LORD;
In the morning I will direct it to You,
And I will look up." (v. 3)

To whom do you go for guidance? Women today turn to many different sources for help—television, magazines, books, friends, and even themselves. While some helpful counsel is offered by these people, God is the most accurate and reliable source of guidance. His wisdom is available through prayer and the study of His Word. Daily pursuit of God can keep you on the right track.

Psalm 5 is David's prayer for guidance. It is one of the consecutive psalms of David written to be performed under the leadership of the "chief musician" or "choir director" (Pss. 4; 5; and 6). Each of the three psalms begins with an imperative verb demonstrating confidence in approaching God in prayer or song. Whether performed in public or prayed in private, this psalm voices confidence in God and commitment to His will.

The first stanza of this song seeks God's attention to the words and the heart of the soloist (Ps. 5:1). King David cries out to the King of kings and Lord of lords for guidance (v. 2). Despite his power and position, David needs the wise counsel of the one true God. He begins the day in prayer, talking directly to God. "In the morning" is mentioned twice in verse 3, emphasizing the importance of daily guidance and renewed hope.

I am not a morning person, so I have always struggled with scheduling my quiet time early in the morning. In fact, I confess to reading several translations of the Bible before finding one that uses "earnestly," or "eagerly," instead of "early" in Psalm 63:1, "Earnestly I seek you" (NASB and ESV). I do understand the necessity of starting each day in prayer so God will guide me.

Morning brings with it newness and hope. At daybreak, each person has the opportunity to begin again. The promise of a new day begins, and only God knows how the minutes will unfold. David knew his need to seek God every morning, though at times he did take matters into his own hands and go ahead of God. In Psalm 5, King David renews his commitment to go to God for guidance every day. All Christians should pray his prayer and sing his song.

Rhonda Kelley

Prayer: *Renew your own commitment to seek God's guidance as each new day begins. Listen to Him, not others, for direction in life.*

Personal Reflection: ....

....

....

....

....

....

....

Trust in God and Rejoice

Psalm 5:11–12

"But let all those rejoice who put their trust in You;
Let them ever shout for joy, because You defend them;
Let those also who love Your name
Be joyful in You." (v. 11)

Psalm 5 begins with David's personal pursuit of God's guidance. Then, like many songs, this psalm changes its timbre. This chapter is the first of several imprecatory psalms, which invoke a curse or call on God to bring misfortune and disaster on one's enemies (see also Pss. 11; 17; 35; 55; 59; 69; 109; 137; and 140). They are included in the book of Psalms to remind us that God knows our hearts completely.

How can God, who teaches His children to love their enemies, respond to their prayers for retribution? David struggled to love those who opposed him while also seeking their destruction. God wants His children to bear their souls to Him while trusting Him for divine justice.

How can believers today understand these imprecatory psalms, which are divinely inspired yet seemingly inconsistent with the love of God? Keep these biblical truths in mind:

- Scripture never contradicts Scripture.
- Expression of human emotion honestly to God in prayer is always acceptable.
- Vengeance belongs to the Lord.
- The wicked will ultimately be judged by God.
- God loves His children and will act in their best interests.

David obviously felt confident in expressing his deepest emotions to the Lord. He did not tell God what to do; he asked the sovereign God to judge the unrighteous. After his passionate plea in Psalm 5:9–10, the king resumed his song of praise. He called on all who trust in God to rejoice, shout for joy, and be joyful in Him (v. 11). He knew God would bless the righteous with His favor and protect them with a shield (v. 12).

Who are the righteous? Simply speaking, the righteous are those who live in right relationship with the Lord. The Bible clearly teaches that God alone is all righteous (Ps. 119:137). Jesus was the only human being to live without sin and be fully righteous (2 Cor. 5:21). And, the Bible states firmly that human beings cannot achieve righteousness in their own efforts (Rom. 3:20). People receive righteousness through faith in Jesus Christ and seek to become more righteous through the power of the Holy Spirit. Repentance of sin is necessary for righteousness (1 John 1:9); it is not the result of good works. While on earth, believers should seek to become righteous. When in heaven, every believer will be wholly righteous in the presence of the Holy God.

David had every reason to rejoice! He trusted in God with his whole heart. You can rejoice today in the presence of your enemies, when you trust in God. Cry out to the Lord to do what is right; do not give Him directives to follow.

Rhonda Kelley

Prayer: *Ask God to forgive you of your own sin and deal justly with your enemies. Trust Him by faith and rejoice in His blessings.*

Personal Reflection: ....

....

....

Lord, Have Mercy on Me!

Psalm 6:1–5

*"Have mercy on me, O LORD, for I am weak;
O LORD, heal me, for my bones are troubled." (v. 2)*

Psalm 6 is a first of seven psalms considered to be penitential in nature. In these songs, the psalmist admits moral failure and prays for forgiveness. Psalm 51 is probably the most well-known psalm of penitence as David emotionally confesses his sin to God and passionately pleads for forgiveness. Repeatedly, sinful man must approach the Holy God, seeking His grace.

While Psalm 6 contains no explicit confession of sin or petition for forgiveness, David implies an admission of guilt: "O LORD, do not rebuke me in Your anger, Nor chasten me in Your hot displeasure" (v. 1). The psalmist does not beg the Lord to withhold correction and punishment but pleads for mercy (v. 2). He acknowledges his own weakness and responds in fear. The imagery of his bones being troubled or trembling conveys a sense of panic and alarm as the inevitable punishment is exacted.

Do you identify with the fear of David? I do personally. I have trembled in the face of judgment. As a child, I was a people-pleaser. So, when I did something wrong, I was brokenhearted and fearful of the consequences. I often cried out in confession before my mother could learn of my misdeed. While I understood the serious nature of my offense, I begged for mercy and grace. I find myself responding in a similar way as an adult. When I confess my sin to God, I ask for His mercy, knowing He is a just judge.

In the early church, penitential psalms were traditionally sung on the liturgical holiday of Ash Wednesday. This primarily Catholic observance is the first day of Lent and always follows forty-six days before Easter. Ashes from the burned palms of the preceding year's Palm Sunday, are often placed on a parishioner's forehead as a symbol of repentance and self-examination. Lent is the

time to recognize the death and resurrection of Jesus Christ. In New Orleans, Ash Wednesday follows Fat Tuesday, or Mardi Gras. Carnival celebrations that begin on January 6—the Epiphany (Three Kings Day)—culminate on Mardi Gras Day. The Lenten season begins with fasting and prayer. New Orleanians often say: "Live it up on Mardi Gras; give it up on Ash Wednesday." Though this religious tradition has become a secular celebration, it is a reminder to God's children to pursue righteousness.

Why did David write penitential psalms? Why should Christians today confess sin to an all-knowing God and seek forgiveness from an all-loving God? God knows your sin and still loves you. He wants you to acknowledge what He already knows as He forgives and forgets your sin. So cry out: "Lord, Have mercy on me!" Then, be confident that He will hear and answer.

Rhonda Kelley

Prayer: *Thank God for His mercy and grace! Ask Him daily to forgive your sin; then receive His forgiveness.*

Personal Reflection: ....

....

....

....

....

God's Goodness in our Grief

Psalm 6:6–10

"I am weary with my groaning;
All night I make my bed swim;
I drench my couch with my tears.
My eye wastes away because of grief;
It grows old because of all my enemies." (vv. 6–7)

In the early 1600s, William Shakespeare wrote, "Give sorrow words; the grief that does not speak. Whispers the o'er-wrought heart and bids it break" (*Macbeth* IV. iii). Thousands of years before Shakespeare penned these words, the psalmist understood this timeless principle. Grief requires our honest words.

At times the human experience expects more from you than your heart can hold. Anyone who has walked through the deep heaviness of a wounded soul understands that grief does not always follow a trajectory or plan. It can strike at unsuspecting moments. Grief is not linear, but it should be vertical. It should always drive us back to the One who holds our pain in the palm of a nail-scarred hand. No matter how you are hurting, Jesus has already been there. Hurt may have cycles or seasons or stages, but the only thing that relieves the weight of your grief is taking it to Christ, who has "carried our sorrows" to the cross (Is. 53:4).

David is not describing a sniffle here. His hurt is gut-wrenching. This pain is so deep that the bed is swimming and the couch is drenched with overwhelming heartache. David is brave enough to voice what so many of us have experienced. When the diagnosis is read, when the vow is broken, when the casket is closed, when the dream is shattered, even in the midst of God's own holy discipline, be certain that the Lord wants honesty from you. We have a God who is not afraid of our tears. He is the God who climbs into our pain with us.

God is also good to us in our grief. You will not find the psalmist being reprimanded for pouring out his sorrow to the Lord. While the goal is never allowing our emotions to lead us, we must notice the honesty of David's relationship with Yahweh God. Here is where I stop to ask myself, and encourage you to do the same: Does my relationship with the Lord reflect this level of honesty even in the midst of my grief? If there are any areas of sorrow that you have not laid at the feet of the Savior, I encourage you to take the time to do that today. Lean in to our loving Father. His comfort will meet you in your grief.

Kim Whitten

Prayer: *Confess to the Lord that He is still God. He understands your pain; so trust Him with your wounds and allow His Word to heal your hurt. Ask the Lord to show you how to walk in integrity even when you feel like you cannot take another step. Thank Him for being a gracious God, even in your grief.*

Personal Reflection: ....

....

....

....

....

....

23

The Crescendo of Praise

Psalm 7:1–17

*"I will praise the LORD according to His righteousness,
And will sing praise to the name of the LORD Most High." (v. 17)*

When I was a freshman, I joined the chorus at my high school. Despite the uncomfortable black taffeta dresses that we girls were forced to wear, I loved the community of singing with those young men and women. I remember the year our chorus took on the lofty goal of performing Handel's *Messiah*. What an exquisite piece! I must admit that to this day I still get lost somewhere in the midst of those magnificent hallelujahs. My breath catches every time the ending of the Hallelujah Chorus is sung with those four giant resonating "hallelujahs" followed by a dramatic pause. I believe that the crescendos make the ending so powerful. Each hallelujah is sung with increasing intensity, followed by the final four-note expression. It brings me to tears every time!

The concluding verse of Psalm 7 appears to serve as a great crescendo to the ending of this dramatic poem. Full of prayers for justice and deliverance, David capsizes a great rush of indignation with the resolve of praise. He definitively states, "I *will* praise the LORD." The psalmist states with no uncertainty that he *will* praise the LORD. What resolve!

There are plenty of days when we do not want to praise the Lord. There are uncountable moments when circumstances do not fit the bill for shouts of joy or exultation. When your husband gets sick, does that seem like a time of praise? When your finances are upside down, does that warrant joy? When your job is on the line, is your automatic response to worship the Lord? If I were honest, more times than not, my response would be no. But praise should rise beyond your personal circumstances. Praise is not based on the one giving the praise but on the one receiving the praise. The worthiness lies within the recipient. There is no one more worthy of our praise than God.

In the midst of David's righteous anger concerning wickedness, his concluding epilogue is that of praise. Take notice of what the psalmist identifies as the reason for his praise. He cites the righteousness of the Lord Most High. Praise is a response to the character of God. It is based on His value and not our own. There are so many attributes of God that are worthy of the great crescendo of our praise. Would you take some time today and identify some of those characteristics of God and praise Him for who He is?

Kim Whitten

Prayer: *Let praise be your response to who God is and not dependent on your individual circumstances. Recognize the greatness of God and respond with a heart of gratitude. Let your life reflect praise to Him.*

Personal Reflection: ....

....

....

....

....

....

....

Who Am I?

Psalm 8:1–9

"When I consider Your heavens, the work of Your fingers,
The moon and the stars, which You have ordained,
What is man that You are mindful of him,
And the son of man that You visit him?
For You have made him a little lower than the angels,
And You have crowned him with glory and honor." (vv. 3–5)

I am not a morning person and have always admired those who wake up before the sun rises. Maybe that's you. Maybe you enjoy the stillness before the day-break, the smell of fresh coffee, or those few quiet moments before life calls out its endless to-do list. Others of us would be happy with mornings that start at 10 a.m.! For me, there is something special about the end of the day. Wrapped on my couch with tea in one hand and a good book in the other, my mind comes alive. I have stood outside on many a starry night and stared out at the expanse of heaven with the same question that David voiced. When I look at the overwhelming wonder of God's creation, I cannot help but wonder: *Who am I*?

This psalm was written by David. He may have still been a shepherd boy, lying in an open field. Perhaps he was a king, standing on the rooftop of a palace. But I have imagined him staring up at a black and white speckled sky, then looking down at his own sandals and marveling at the distance between the two. When you look at the work of God's fingers, do you ever wonder where you fit in this great expanse of God's handiwork? The Creator God in His infinite wisdom made man and woman as image-bearers of His own likeness.

The author gives us a theology lesson. Not only have we been made a little lower than the angels, but the Lord Himself has crowed us with glory and honor. The astounding part of this revelation is that God is great enough to share His own glory! The fact that God would crown His creation with glory and honor

does not take away from His glory. It is still His alone. We are merely the representations of God's glory here on earth. If you are a believer in Jesus Christ, then you are also a witness of the Good News of salvation that has come to the world. How are you doing with that? Have you had an opportunity to share the glory of the Lord with a neighbor, a friend, a colleague, or a family member who does not know the Lord? The next time you peek up at a star-studded sky and quietly ask yourself: *Who am I?* be reminded that you are His. As His daughter, you are an ambassador of His glory to the entire world!

Kim Whitten

Prayer: *Thank the Lord with your whole being for allowing you the privilege of being His daughter. Thank Him that His majesty is displayed as faithfully as the moon rises each night. Ask the Lord to give you an opportunity to share His glory, His name, and His fame with someone.*

Personal Reflection: ....

....

....

....

....

....

The Rightful Place of Praise

Psalm 9:1–18

"I will praise You, O Lord, with my whole heart;
I will tell of all Your marvelous works.
I will be glad and rejoice in You;
I will sing praise to Your name, O Most High." (vv. 1–2)

Did you grow up with a nickname? My father assigned each one of his children a fun nickname that was a play off our given names. We instantly knew upon hearing these names that he was calling because these names were reserved for us. We often smiled as our playful pet names were called. However, I had a friend whose household was different than my own. The nicknames assigned in her family were not good-natured or playful. They were hurtful and insensitive, tearing at the very fabric of self-worth. I remember cringing as I heard one of her family members use this spiteful identity-marker. The names we use for people matter. They mark not only identity but also the relationship between two people.

As we read this psalm of praise, focus on the names that the author uses to address God. The descendants of Abraham had a reverent name for God—one considered so holy that it was not to be spoken aloud. The Hebrew word, *YHWH*, or Yahweh is translated in most English Bibles by the proper name Lord. The psalmist begins by directing his praise in humble reverence to the high and holy Lord. Understanding God's awesome and holy nature allows us to praise Him in an appropriate way, acknowledging that He is greater than we are. The praise becomes more than just a happy song or joyful declaration; it is a revelation of the nature of God which makes our praise all the more poignant.

The author goes on to reference God as *Elyon* or "Most High." David is acknowledging God as preeminent or the authority over all things. David attributes God to His rightful place as the ruling authority with songs of glorious

praise. Where does the Lord rank in authority within your own life? Does God Most High have jurisdiction over every area of your existence? It can be all too easy for us to sing with our lips songs of praise that others have prepared, while still holding on to control of our lives.

Are you giving God the authority to make decisions about your future? Are you willing to be submissive when it comes to your finances? May the Lord change your plans for His glory and your good? Today, would you call on the name of the high and holy "LORD" and ascribe to Him the supreme authority over every area of your life?

Kim Whitten

Prayer: *Put the Lord Most High, in the rightful place in your life, as the authority over everything. Relinquish your own control to His rightful rule. Identify any areas of your life that you have not fully surrendered to Him. Place the Lord on the throne of your heart.*

Personal Reflection: ....

....

....

....

....

....

I Will Trust In You

Psalm 9:9–20

"The LORD also will be a refuge for the oppressed,
A refuge in times of trouble.
And those who know Your name will put their trust in You;
For You, LORD, have not forsaken those who seek You." (vv. 9–10)

Trust is not an easy commodity to secure. We still find ourselves reluctant to fully put our trust in a perfect God. The Lord is our "refuge" (Hb. *misgav*)—a high place, stronghold, or place of security. When oppression and trouble strike at the low-lying levels of your life, you can trust that your place of security is found in God.

Verse 10 is a cry for those who know the name of the Lord. My first and most urgent question to you is: Do you know the name of the Lord? Do you have a relationship with Him? Can you call Him *your* Lord? Can you say with sincerity that there has been a time in your life when you have surrendered your all to the God of heaven and called on the name of the Lord for your salvation?

You may be one who is seeking to know God. You may want and sincerely hope for these things the psalmist has written here to be true. If you have been seeking, God can be sought and found. If you do not have a personal relationship with the God of the universe and call Him *your* Lord, I have good news for you today! You can put your faith and trust in Jesus Christ alone and be saved. If you confess Him, He will be your God. You may find yourself under the oppression of your own sin. The cross of Christ is the payment for that sin. Confess Jesus Christ as your Savior.

If you are a believing sister in Christ, I encourage you to place your full confidence and trust in the Lord despite the oppression or trouble you see

around you. Be confident in Him as your stronghold, for He will not forsake you.

Kim Whitten

Prayer: *Affirm to the Lord that He is God. Know that He is trustworthy. Admit that your sin has kept you from Him. But acknowledge that the penalty for that sin was paid on the cross through the work of Jesus Christ! Trust that work, and put your faith in Jesus Christ alone.*

Personal Reflection: ....

....

....

....

....

....

....

....

Father to the Fatherless

Psalm 10:1–15

"But You have seen, for You observe trouble and grief,
To repay it by Your hand.
The helpless commits himself to You;
You are the helper of the fatherless." (v. 14)

In this series of psalms David cries for help in his suffering. His enemies have chased him and brought defeat. In this verse, David recognizes that God has seen the situation and that He is the one who will repay the enemies for their deeds.

At that time, being fatherless meant having no property or rights of any kind. The "fatherless" were desperate for someone to provide for them. David recognized that when we are helpless, God is standing by to help.

Have you been in a state of complete helplessness when you had no one to help? How did you respond? Did you give up in despair or stand on the truth of God's presence and provision?

When I was teaching on one of our seminary campuses hundreds of miles from home, a family crisis occurred. All I could do was pray and release the situation into God's very capable hands. Not really knowing even how to pray, I just called on the name of Jesus. When I did, an unbelievable peace washed over me. And it was enough to carry me until I could get home the next day. There was no other way to actually sleep that night and then teach the next day before getting on a plane for home. God was enough!

The psalmist understood that God Himself knew trouble and grief, God knew the enemy, and He had capable hands in which to hold David and relieve his fears. The psalmist could trust his Father to take care of his "trouble" because He is the perfect Father, ready to provide all that was needed by the helpless.

What situation are you in now? If you are facing a challenge, the enemy, or just a tough season, will you allow the Lord to hold you safely in His hands, will you trust Him to work regardless of how the present situation looks?

The Lord knows the trouble and grief in our world. He understands the work of the enemy. He sees you right where you are today. He protects His children and provides exactly what they need as they allow Him to do His work in their lives.

Chris Adams

Prayer: *Confess to the Lord your own helplessness. Choose to trust that He sees you, knows exactly what is happening, and is right beside you. Call on His name and stand firm in your faith. While you may be helpless, you are not fatherless! God is your Father. Commit yourself and your situation to Him and rest in His presence and provision.*

Personal Reflection: ....

....

....

....

....

....

But God

Psalm 10:16–18

*"The Lord is King forever and ever;
The nations have perished out of His land." (v. 16)*

Why do the wicked seem to prosper while I am struggling to make ends meet? Why is my family dealing with severe health issues while those who are cruel to others are healthy and hearty? Why does it seem that the harder I seek to know Christ, the more problems I face; whereas the one who does not even want to hear the name of Jesus seems to have it all?

Have you ever asked those questions? Maybe you have not voiced such murmuring out loud, but have you even wondered about it? David may have felt the same way. At times he was hounded constantly by his enemies. He faced defeat as he sought to follow God.

Yet, David came to the "but God" stage. When I am faced with a difficulty that appears overwhelming and without solution and yet as I trust Him, the Lord moves me from hopelessness to the truth of who God is and what He has promised. All else fails, "but God" will never leave me, always choosing what is best, bringing glory to Himself, working all things together for my good as I follow His will (Rom. 8:28).

David reminds the reader that the Lord is King forever, no matter what the situation is. He hears the humble cries of His people. David reminds us that the Lord will bring justice to the fatherless, to those who are helpless. One day the wicked will not be able to oppress God's people anymore.

Not too long ago, I was falsely accused of saying something I did not say. Even when I denied saying it, my words were ignored. The accusing person was one with whom I had a history, and she knew I had never lied to her. It caused a painful and continuing break in our relationship. But each time I begin to feel the stab of pain, I am reminded of God's sovereignty and ability to work good

out of this situation. I choose to pray and trust God when I want to cry out about the injustice and unfairness I am facing.

You may feel as though God is absent when others oppress you, betray you, break your heart; but be reminded that Jesus is King. He is your strength when you face injustice. He is sovereign, and He will triumph.

Chris Adams

Prayer: *Does it hurt when someone falsely accuses you? Perhaps it appears that some people get away with evil while those who follow the Lord face oppression. Ask the Lord to remind you daily of His sovereignty in your life and ultimately over all of life.*

Personal Reflection: ....

....

....

....

....

....

....

What Can We Do?

Psalm 11:1–7

*"If the foundations are destroyed,
What can the righteous do?" (v. 3)*

Some days I feel as though the foundations of my life are being destroyed. I look around and wonder how I got to this place. My life is not the way it is supposed to be. Sometimes I feel like the devil has trapped me in a place I am not supposed to be.

Perhaps the politics of the day are discouraging to you. Maybe you despair at the way the morality around you is diminishing. Maybe you have suffered a great loss and cannot even think straight. You wonder how life will ever be normal again.

Christians can respond in different ways. We can fret and become depressed. We can give up and just stop trying. We can complain and become cynical. Or, we can follow the example of the psalmist.

David claims, "In the LORD I put my trust" (v. 1). These are not just spoken words; they are cries from the very depths of our souls. We must stand on our faith in Christ even when it does not even make sense.

Although David was surrounded by his enemies, he knew his God. He even claimed, "For the LORD is righteous, He loves righteousness; His countenance beholds the upright" (v. 7). David knew that in the midst of crisis and fear, God is righteous and that His righteousness would be made known. David's foundations had been destroyed, but he stood on the truth of God's character.

Do you need to stand on the foundation of Christ right now? What foundations in your life seem as though they are about to shatter or maybe they have already been shattered? Keep in mind, God is never shaken by the circumstances in your life or in the challenges of your world.

Take refuge in our righteous Lord as did the psalmist David. Faith in God keeps us from losing hope. God is so much bigger than any enemies or situations that appear to be planned by the enemy to keep us from walking in victory. Because of His righteousness, we are victorious. Let's not just bide our time until eternity; let's walk in victory today.

Chris Adams

Prayer: *Are you struggling to find God's presence in some situation in your life? When you do not even know the direction to turn, choose to turn to the Lord. Do not give in to fear and despair. Choose to trust that God and His righteousness will reign supreme in your life and in your world. Along with David, put your trust in the Lord. Stand on the truth of who He is and let Him be glorified through your life.*

Personal Reflection: ....

....

....

....

....

....

Speaking Pure Words

Psalm 12:1–8

"The words of the Lord are pure words,
Like silver tried in a furnace of earth,
Purified seven times. You shall keep them, O Lord,
You shall preserve them from this generation forever." (vv. 6–7)

How often do you find yourself using words that are less than kind? A "bit" dishonest? Maybe somewhat self-serving? Unthoughtful? Unkind? Evil? Why is it so easy to use our mouths for speaking something other than what is holy and good?

Often I say something without truly thinking about my words, and then I wish so much that I could have a "re-do" in that conversation. Once in a car with others, I said something that could almost be considered a racial slur by some. I truly did not mean it that way and was *so* embarrassed by my comments I wanted to slink out of the car and drop in a hole somewhere. I just did not think about how I expressed my thoughts. I have never forgotten that, but I pray the others in the car have not remembered my comment.

Psalm 12 contrasts human words with God's words. David relates the flattering and idle words to the proud who say:

Who have said,
"With our tongue we will prevail;
Our lips are our own;
Who is lord over us?" (v. 4)

God wants us to submit our words as well as our thoughts to Him daily. We must confess pride when we choose to say whatever feels good at the time, even if what we say is an outright untruth!

In contrast, the words of the Lord are pure. The purity of God's words is demonstrated through the purity of silver, which must go through the fire multiple times to be truly pure metal. God's purity ought to be our model in conversation.

Though we often want our words to disappear or at least be forgotten by those who heard them, God's pure Word will *never* fade away. His promises are true and permanent. He preserves His words throughout all generations.

I love Psalm 33:11, which also affirms this timeless truth: "The counsel of the LORD stands forever, The plans of His heart to all generations." Because His Word is of such value, generation after generation will know it!

Are you asking the Lord to use your words for His glory? If not, make that request part of your prayer each day. Are you teaching those following behind you to use their words wisely? Teach them about the holiness of God's eternal words, which are true, beneficial, loving, and eternal. Model and teach the importance of being in His Word continually, seeking to apply each truth He reveals in the Bible. Let's pray that we will speak words to be remembered and appreciated!

Chris Adams

Prayer: *Let the pure words of God penetrate your heart. Learn to speak with truth and sincerity today and every day. Share the truth of who God is so that future generations will know His Word.*

Personal Reflection: ....

....

....

....

How Long, Lord?

Psalm 13:1–4

"How long, O LORD? Will You forget me forever?
How long will You hide Your face from me?
How long shall I take counsel in my soul,
Having sorrow in my heart daily?
How long will my enemy be exalted over me?" (vv. 1–2)

Think of the last time you prayed over and over and over for something. Several times in my life a situation has been so big and lasted so long that some days I wondered why I still prayed for resolution. But I did! Did you? Or did you get weary of praying and just stop?

Imagine David, faced with enemies over and over. He sought to obey God's assignment, but he still continued to face war, betrayal, and discouragement as his enemies seemed to get the victory over David. But his cry in this psalm was repeated: "How long, how long, how long, how long?" David never gives up. He continues to cry out to God until he receives God's answers.

This "keep asking" theme is repeated in Luke 11:9–10. Jesus tells His disciples, "So I say to you, ask, and it will be given to you; seek, and you will find; knock, and it will be opened to you. For everyone who asks receives, and he who seeks finds, and to him who knocks it will be opened." The emphasis in Scripture is to keep asking.

As I have persisted in asking God for answers, at times I cried because it hurt. Sometimes I rejoiced because I knew He was sovereign and could still work miracles. At other times I rested in peace, knowing that He knew better than I did how to take care of the situation. But like David, I never gave up.

David's faith sustained him when the journey got hard. His hope in a loving God kept him seeking answers from Him. When you read the rest of this psalm, you will see how he was able to keep trusting:

But I have trusted in Your mercy;
My heart shall rejoice in Your salvation.
I will sing to the LORD,
Because He has dealt bountifully with me. (Ps. 13:5–6)

Can you hear the testimony of his faith? David's faith will challenge and encourage you and me as we face a need that takes a long time to be filled.

Chris Adams

Prayer: *Have you asked the question: How long, Lord? When you have a heavy burden on your heart, be assured that God knows the situation even better than you do. Ask the Lord to increase your faith and help you to "keep on knocking" as you wait patiently, and sometimes not too patiently, for Him to resolve your situation. Continue to pray and trust God's timing and wisdom.*

Personal Reflection: ....

....

....

....

....

....

41

Sing Anyway

Psalm 13:5–6

*"I will sing to the LORD,
Because He has dealt bountifully with me." (v. 6)*

I love this verse! David begins the psalm with repeated questions about how long God will delay His response to his needs. But David chooses to praise God anyway. And seemingly he is able to praise Him because of all God has done for him prior to this current situation.

One of the beauties of walking a long time with the Lord is having history with Him that you can remember. Because He is forever faithful, your history with the Lord will always be one of His faithfulness even if you were not always faithful to obey Him.

This year I retired from a ministry position I held for twenty-two years. All through the year, God continued to affirm the decision and gave me the sweetest year. During the year, I have been able to "sing to the Lord because He has dealt bountifully with me." As I enter retirement, ministry may look different; there may be days of confusion and even concern. But when I look back on my last years of formal service, I will be assured of God's provision for the future because of how He has continued throughout the year to affirm this new season of ministry.

Over my life and fifty-plus-year journey with Christ, a history has developed to which I can always look back when I face an unknown and maybe even critical situation. Because I have seen His consistent love and faithfulness, I do not have to doubt His faithfulness in new challenges.

David loved God and trusted Him to handle the current attacks from the enemy. Even though he was honest in his questions and frustration because of God's delay in providing the answer, David knew that God would answer. He had

a history with God that gave him the ability to look beyond the present situation and focus on his faith in his faithful God.

How about you? Can you recall times when God came through in a tough situation? You knew that He had your best and His glory in mind when He answered, even if not the way you expected. Can you in your current situation focus on His faithfulness rather than on your fear, pain, or disillusionment? If not, ask the Holy Spirit to change your heart from doubt to the assurance of God's love and faithfulness. He cannot be something He is not. God is love. God is faithful. God will deal bountifully with His people.

Chris Adams

Prayer: *Are some of your days overwhelming? As David did, sing to the Lord and praise Him anyway. Remember that God has always been nothing less than totally faithful to you, even when you have not been faithful to Him. Thank the Lord for His constant love and care. Trust Him today because you see how faithful He has always been.*

Personal Reflection: ....

....

....

....

....

....

Foolish or Wise?

Psalm 14:1–9

"The LORD looks down from heaven upon the children of men,
To see if there are any who understand, who seek God.
They have all turned aside,
They have together become corrupt;
There is none who does good,
No, not one." (vv. 2–3)

Life is about choices. God did not make us robots; He has given us hearts and brains to use for making choices. The question is: What kind of choices are we making?

These verses contrast a foolish choice to one that is wise. A fool does not base choices on healthy spiritual discernment from God's truth. "The righteous," who love the Lord, do "call on the LORD" and seek His wisdom.

Verse 1 indicates that a fool says: "There is no God." A foolish woman chooses to do whatever she wants, her way, not regarding the commands of the Lord. Her choice and her life are all about her. But women who seek God's will, God's heart, and God's truth, become wise and discerning. Wise choices then are based on what God wants, not personal, self-serving desires.

This passage indicates that God, who knows everything happening on earth, is searching for the women who understand the importance of knowing God. Yet God cannot find women like that. How terribly sad! Does that break your heart to hear that not one person who is good can be found?

The truth is: We are *all* guilty before God. We have all sinned. Our only hope is salvation through Christ. He alone can take the morally and intellectually bankrupt and give wisdom to those who receive His forgiveness.

So, in contrast to fools who deny that God exists, those who "call on the LORD" for salvation from sin are to continue to grow in His wisdom and to honor

His desires for their lives. Discipleship is all about growth in wisdom. Until we breathe our last, we are to grow to become more and more like Christ every day. Then we can teach "the children of men" to know and grow in Him as well (v. 2).

The Father's heart breaks to see a generation who has turned away from Him and said: "There is no God." Will you take the steps needed today to know Him, to be wise with His wisdom, and to share Him?

Chris Adams

Prayer: *Seek to walk with the Lord more closely each day, following His truth and His wisdom. Ask Him to use you to share that wisdom with those around you today.*

Personal Reflection: ....

....

....

....

....

....

....

God's Family Rules

Psalm 15:1–5

"LORD, who may abide in Your tabernacle?
Who may dwell in Your holy hill?" (v. 1)

I had not been married long when I commented to my father-in-love, Jack, how surprised I was at the warm reception and extraordinary service I received at a favorite local business. He responded, "They know our family and you are part of the family now. Since you are a Stovall, they immediately know what kind of person you are." I got the message that Jack, being a man of few words, was sending. I had chosen to take my husband's name. Now, as part of his family, certain expectations applied to those who carried the family name. How we interacted with those around us was a big part of those expectations. I saw these expectations as the family rules.

Psalm 15 starts with a question. The psalmist asks the Lord: Who can live with, settle down in, and be under the care and protection of the Master? The response to that question gives us God's family rules and His expectations of one who claims to be a member of the family of God. As women who are followers of Christ, fully embracing our adoption as daughters of the King and taking on the name of Christ, there are expectations for how we are to conduct our lives. According to Psalm 15, we are to be women

- who act and speak rightly (v. 2);
- who relate to people with integrity, not saying or doing anything that harms those around us (v. 3);
- who demonstrate wisdom and discernment, doing all the good we can do (v. 4); and
- who do not seek fortune or gain unfairly (v. 5a).

Interestingly, all these rules have to do with the way we relate to and interact with others. How we behave tells those around us what kind of person we are and to whose family we belong. They do not see our hearts, but they do see our actions and hear our words.

I have never forgotten that admonition from my father-in-love, grasping the responsibility that came with the name I now shared with this godly family. This understanding was an unspoken admonition never to do anything that would bring shame to the family. Likewise, as I claim to carry the name of Christ and proclaim my acceptance into His kingdom through salvation, I want to live my life daily per God's family rules, so that, as I face each day, I will never bring shame to my Savior. I "shall never be moved" (v. 5b) as I continually abide under the protection and care of the Father.

Terri Stovall

Prayer: *Ask the Lord to help you live a life of integrity that reflects the name of Christ. Confess where you may have not treated or responded to others in the spirit of being a Christ-follower. Renew your heart and desire to live each day following God's family rules.*

Personal Reflection: ....

....

....

....

....

Whatever My Lot

Psalm 16:1–11

"The lines have fallen to me in pleasant places;
Yes, I have a good inheritance." (v. 6)

My life was all planned. I would earn a college degree, have an extremely successful, high-powered career, eventually find a good man to marry, give birth to two children, live in a big house, and experience a perfect life. Honestly, I was certain I would have the perfect family and take over the world all at the same time. But then, life . . . but then, God!

I did get that college degree and then some. I did find a good man to marry. What I thought would be a super, high-powered career was redirected into a life of service and ministry. My husband and I live a comfortable life in the same home into which we moved in our first year of marriage, and the rooms we thought would be filled with children remain empty. There are days I feel like Superwoman, and there are days when I wonder if I even make a difference.

Looking back on those young-hearted dreams, I realize that so much was wrapped up in the world's picture of a perfect life—life focused on me, self-fulfillment, and stuff that I believed would guarantee happiness. Many women today continually seek elusive contentment, trying to chase dreams wrapped in man-made standards.

Psalm 16 contrasts the life of one who is wholly devoted to the Lord and those who still have an eye on the world with its enticements. We are reminded that embracing the things of the world brings multiplied sorrows and cravings that are never fully satisfied because apart from God, nothing is truly good (v. 2).

As followers of Christ, we are called to trust, worship, and focus on God and God alone. As we gladly accept God's parameters for our lives, we can trust that those "lines have fallen . . . in pleasant places," and we can proclaim that looking to the days ahead, we "have a good inheritance."

Today, I cannot imagine what my life would be like if I had continued to chase those early dreams, shoving God's call to the side. I would not have the hundreds of spiritual daughters I have today or the ability to rest in the deep, fulfilling goodness that comes from God alone. Just between us, there are days I do feel like Superwoman, changing the world one life at a time. But it has not been easy because it looks so different than I expected. As I have struggled to embrace fully the lot God has given me and to release those early, world-focused dreams, I have had to reach the point of believing at the core of my soul that God was enough and to trust Him completely. Today, I proclaim with full-hearted devotion that whatever my lot, it is well with my soul. I would have it no other way.

Terri Stovall

Prayer: *Ask the Lord to help you keep your eyes fully on Him and not on the world. If there are areas of your life where you are struggling to be content, ask God to help you gladly accept the parameters He has placed around you in order that you may be truly satisfied in Him and Him alone.*

Personal Reflection: ....

....

....

....

....

3 a.m. Heart Trials

Psalm 17:1–15

"You have tested my heart;
You have visited me in the night;
You have tried me and have found nothing;
I have purposed that my mouth shall not transgress." (v. 3)

Do you ever wake up in the middle of the night, perhaps about 3 a.m., and your mind immediately begins to race? You think through all the events of the day, the things you should have done, the other things you should have done better. You may think about a conversation that was hurtful or a difficult situation that remains unresolved. Many women experience this sleep interruption on a regular basis. The middle of the night seems to be the time when the house is quiet and the family is asleep, so we let down our guards and the true concerns of our hearts spill forth.

Psalm 17, the first psalm in the book of Psalms to be identified as a prayer, finds David praying for vindication and deliverance from the Lord. He was a hunted man as King Saul relentlessly pursued, seeking to kill David. Fighting was going on all around him, fear rose within him, and in the middle of the night God tested his heart.

As David cries out to God for help and as he searches for God's vindication of his innocence, his focus begins to shift. David declares God's lovingkindness, salvation, protection, and righteousness. David turns his fear and focus on vindication to a prayer of confidence in the Lord. Even though the enemy still surrounds him, he does not allow his mouth to sin but remains secure in the presence of the Lord.

When these times of anxiety, fear, and concern occur in the middle of the night, talk to the Lord about them. He hears your cry and truly listens. In these times, let the Lord test your heart, instead of rehashing your case against those

who have hurt you or complaining about situations that you can do nothing about from your bed in the middle of the night. Rather, use this middle-of-the-night trial to let your mouth purposefully call upon the name of the Lord with confidence. Middle-of-the-night encounters with the Lord at 3 a.m. will be good evidence of the integrity of your heart.

Terri Stovall

Prayer: *Confess to the Lord those areas of anxiety, fear, and concern you may have. Ask the Lord to test your heart and to reveal any transgression in your own heart. And as you do, begin to turn your prayer from seeking vindication to a prayer of declaring the lovingkindness, protection, and righteousness of your Savior.*

Personal Reflection: ....

....

....

....

....

....

....

God Hears

Psalm 18:1–15

"In my distress I called upon the LORD,
And cried out to my God;
He heard my voice from His temple,
And my cry came before Him, even to His ears." (v. 6)

The little girl in the grocery store was trying her best to get her daddy's attention. She must have been about five or six years old, but this young girl apparently believed that she had something urgent to tell her father. I watched her from a distance as she first patted his arm, then began pulling his pant leg, all to no avail. He was distracted with the task at hand, the people around him, and probably the burdens of day-to-day life that encumber many parents. As she continued to seek his attention, she became more distressed that her cries were not reaching his ears. Finally, she stopped in her tracks, placed her hands on her hips, and when her father turned around to face her, she yelled in a loud voice: "Daddy, I need you to listen to me right now!"

Psalm 18, written by David, is a song of thanksgiving and deliverance recounting all the Lord did to rescue David from the hands of Saul. The first few verses of the psalm emphasize the relationship David has with God, and he exalts God with some direct comparisons. God was David's rock, fortress, deliverer, strength, shield, salvation, and stronghold.

In verses 4–6, David gives his readers a glimpse into the overwhelming anguish he experienced. He looked around and saw nothing but death and pervasive ungodliness, which seemed to be suffocating. David was afraid and he cried out to God. He needed the Father to hear him, and God heard.

David cried out to God from the depths of his soul. But, unlike the little girl in the grocery store, David's cries were not ignored. Not only did God hear, but also He listened. David's cries reached "even to His [God's] ears."

I do not know what was so important for that little girl in the store to tell her father. Perhaps her distress came more from his not stopping to listen than from what she needed to say. Thankfully, as God's daughters, we do not have to take drastic measures to get God's attention when we cry out to Him. In our distress, our cries reach "even to His ears."

Have you ever found yourself at a point when you are desperate for the Father to hear you? Perhaps you are looking around right now and you are overcome with death, ungodliness, or difficult circumstances, and you are afraid. Cry out to God and He will hear. For though the circumstances may drive you to prayer, God will not turn a deaf ear upon His child. Rather, He will take pity and comfort His daughter. Take heart; God hears.

Terri Stovall

Prayer: *In your distress, cry out to God, sharing your fears and concerns with Him. Instead of being overcome by the storms that surround you, ask God to give you the confidence to know that He hears.*

Personal Reflection: ....

....

....

....

....

God Delivers

Psalm 18:16–27

*"He also brought me out into a broad place;
He delivered me because He delighted in me." (v. 19)*

Large crowds and gatherings can mark joyous occasions for communities as they celebrate accomplishments, cheer heroes, and mark milestones. However, if too many people are in one place or one space, what is meant to be joyous one minute can turn dangerous the next. As people crowd up against each other, individuals start to feel crushed, and panic can set in. If the crowd starts to move or sway, feet can become unstable, and should one happen to fall amid the crowd, the danger for harm can become very real unless someone reaches down and sets that person back on his feet. That is exactly what God did for David.

In Psalm 18:16–27, David recounts how God fully delivered him from the hands of Saul. The waters surrounding David were deep ("many," v. 16), his enemies were "strong," and they "hated" him (v. 17). If David had to fight alone against them, they would have been "too strong" for him (v. 17). His enemies were also too fast for him. They intercepted him and stood in his path, ready to destroy him (v. 18). During this time, God kept David from falling. What a testimony to the truth that God will sustain and hold up His children until He delivers them.

God did eventually deliver David and set him on a broad, wide place where he had room to turn, to move, to breathe, and to thrive. He delivered David from the unbearable circumstances pressing in on him. He reached down, pulled David up, and set him on his feet, leaving him unencumbered and at peace. God heard and God delivered. David's deliverance was especially sweet because it came when the difficulties were the greatest and flowed from the fact the God loved and "delighted in" him (v. 19).

God delights in you, my sister. You may feel like you are being crushed from every side and you cannot see a way out. Perhaps you feel as if your feet are about to stumble. Or maybe, at this very moment, you are staring straight into the face of the enemy, and you do not know which way to turn. As His daughter, the Lord will support you and sustain you in the midst of it all. In due time, you, too, will taste the sweet fruit of deliverance when God lifts you up and sets you on a broad place.

Terri Stovall

Prayer: *Thank God for the fact that He delights in you. Confess to the Lord your weakness in the midst of difficulties and the fact that you cannot face these days apart from Him. Ask God to help you keep your eyes on Him who is your Sustainer. And when His deliverance comes, thank Him for all that He has done.*

Personal Reflection: ....

....

....

....

....

....

God Rekindles

Psalm 18:28–34

"For you will light my lamp;
The LORD my God will enlighten my darkness.
For by You I can run against a troop,
By my God I can leap over a wall." (vv. 28–29)

The success of a long-distance runner rests in the runner's training, especially her ability to get in long-mileage runs at least every other week. When those mileage runs reach distances of thirteen, fifteen, twenty miles and longer, many runners must start or end their runs in the dark. One of the dangers of running in the dark is stumbling and falling on unseen hazards. This danger has inspired numerous products that attach to shoes, hats, and clothing to light the path just ahead of a runner. Many runners have been sidelined with injuries resulting merely from a fall. A woman once asked a physician for the secret to living long life. His answer was simple: "Don't fall."

In Psalm 18, David has just come through one of the most difficult times of his life. He had been pursued relentlessly by Saul and other enemies. He was overwhelmed, afraid, and distressed. Then God delivered him and placed him back on solid ground. But, like many who serve in ministry, some of the most difficult times can leave one feeling burned out, melancholy, and discouraged, craving any light to show them the way and to inspire the confidence to move forward. They need their lamps rekindled so that they do not fall in the darkness.

David was faithful and righteous, and God rekindled and revived David's lamp, bringing comfort to his soul. When David believed he might die, God lifted him up and rekindled his lamp. God heard David, God delivered David, and now God rekindled David.

In Psalm 18:16, David felt as if he were drowning, but in verse 29, he possesses superhuman strength, with the ability to leap walls and single-handedly run against full troops.

As believers, we are running a marathon. To run it well, we must run in such a way that God's light enlightens our paths. You may have just come through a very trying time of service, ministry, or life circumstance, leaving you tired. Maybe you are laboring under many discouragements or feeling like you are walking in dark places. Sing these verses that David penned as an encouragement to you that God will be a light to you. Trust the Lord to rekindle what the enemy attempts to extinguish.

Terri Stovall

Prayer: *Ask the Lord to be a light to your path so that you will know where to walk. If your soul needs revival, confess that to God and ask Him to rekindle your strength. Thank Him for enabling you once again to perform confidently whatever task He has set before you.*

Personal Reflection: ....

....

....

....

....

God Provides

Psalm 18:35–50

"You have also given me the shield of Your Salvation;
Your right hand has held me up,
Your gentleness has made me great.
You enlarged my path under me,
So my feet did not slip." (vv. 35–36)

When I moved into my first apartment as a college graduate, I was on my own four hundred miles away from home. I bought my first piece of furniture—a desk, with "some assembly required" (basically a package of five hundred pieces and twenty-five hundred screws, nuts, and bolts). All I had was a Phillips-head screwdriver. Unfortunately for me, all of the screws required a different type of screwdriver and a hammer. I was determined to put this desk together so I ended up using a butter knife for a screwdriver and a rock for a hammer. I did get the desk put together, but it was so wobbly I was afraid to set anything on it until I could acquire the right tools to assemble it correctly.

David concludes Psalm 18 by looking back, with a thankful heart, upon all the Lord provided for his deliverance, victory, and success. There is a time to look back to see the hand of the Lord and His provision.

When we are going through trials and difficulties, we may not be able to see how we got through those times. Looking back, though, David could see that God had provided exactly what he needed when he needed it. God had "heard" (v. 6), "delivered" (v. 17), rekindled (v. 28), and provided (vv. 35–36):

- God gave David a "shield of . . . salvation," which protected him from the death stings of the enemy (v. 35);
- God gave David a strong "hand" that held him up when he felt as if he was drowning in deep waters (v. 35);

- God gave David "gentleness" that allowed him to be one of the greatest examples of godly leadership in the Scriptures (v. 35);
- God gave David a broad "path" to set his feet upon, which allowed him to stand firm and not to stumble (v. 36).

God provides for His children exactly what they need for the tasks at hand. God does not give butter knives when we need screwdrivers, nor does He give us rocks when we need hammers to stand firm against the evil one.

Be encouraged that God hears your cries. Be confident that God will deliver you in His time. Be comforted that God will rekindle a fresh spirit within you. Be thankful that God provides all you need exactly when you need it.

Terri Stovall

Prayer: *Think back over the times during which God provided for you. List the ways that He made sure you had exactly what you needed when you needed it, and then thank Him for being your ultimate provider.*

Personal Reflection: ....

....

....

....

....

The Sanctifying Scripture

Psalm 19:1–14

"The law of the LORD is perfect, converting the soul;
The testimony of the LORD is sure, making wise the simple;
The statutes of the LORD are right, rejoicing the heart;
The commandment of the LORD is pure, enlightening the eyes;
The fear of the LORD is clean, enduring forever;
The judgments of the LORD are true and righteous altogether.
More to be desired are they than gold,
Yea, than much fine gold;
Sweeter also than honey and the honeycomb.
Moreover by them Your servant is warned,
And in keeping them there is great reward." (vv. 7–11)

In John 17, Jesus prayed what is known as the "High Priestly Prayer." As Christ prayed over His disciples He said, "Sanctify them by Your truth. Your word is truth" (v. 17). The success of a follower of Christ is solely dependent on one thing—her intimacy with God's Word. Psalm 19 demonstrates why the life of a believer must be bound to the Word of truth.

- **The perfect law of the Lord converts our souls (v. 7).** Without God's Word, we would not know the Word made flesh, Jesus Christ, or experience the salvation through His death on the cross and resurrection from the dead.
- **The testimony of the Lord is sure, making wise the simple (v. 7).** In a world full of uncertainty, one thing remains steadfast—God's Word, which convicts us and teaches us wisdom.

- The commands of the Lord are right and pure (v. 8). Because of the purity and veracity of God's Word, you can have joy, understanding, and hope for the future, since His Word is truth for all time.
- God's Word is more desirable than honey (v. 10). The more time we spend with an open Bible, heart humbled and ready to hear what the Lord says, the more He instills a desire for Him.
- By God's Word we are warned and rewarded (v. 11). Because the Lord is a loving Father, He gives us boundaries in His Word. God lays out the consequences for sin—death and hell. However, the Lord is gracious to show us the rewards in following Him.

Perhaps you have been neglecting the Word of God in your walk with Jesus. You may be frustrated and feel as if your relationship has become dry and withered. Do not let the devil burden you with guilt. Confess your sin and open God's Word. Get a good Bible reading plan, and schedule time in your day to be spent with the Lord. Actively pursue the Lord in His Word, and you will be refreshed.

Lauren Johnson

Prayer: *Pray that you will be sanctified by God's Word. Ask the Lord to place in your heart a deep desire and passion for His Word. Ask the Lord to help you obey His precepts.*

Personal Reflection: ....

....

....

....

Radical Dependence

Psalm 20:1–9

*"Some trust in chariots, and some in horses;
But we will remember the name of the LORD our God." (v. 7)*

The great theologian and reformer, Martin Luther, is said to have exhausted himself depending on his good works to earn his salvation. He so wanted to earn his way to heaven that he sold much of what he had, lived in a sparse little room, and did chores for the other priests in order to have right standing before the Lord. Luther continued in vain to quell the uncertainty in his soul by fasting and praying. Finally, the Lord spoke clearly to Luther as he read Romans 1:17—"For in it [the gospel of Christ] the righteousness of God is revealed from faith to faith; as it is written, 'The just shall live by faith.'" In that moment, Martin Luther felt peace and joy. He had finally rested in Christ and not himself. Just as Luther learned the danger of misplaced trust, so, too, the Israelites understood that everything from salvation to victory in battle meant dependence on the Lord.

Psalm 20 is a picture of radical dependence. The people of Israel realized that both David and the nation's heart trajectory toward the things of the Lord determined their success. Their enemies, the Philistines, relied on their blacksmithing skills and horses to win battles. However, the Israelites' hope did not rest in the schemes or talents of men but in the Lord their God (v. 7). This psalm serves as a prayer template for depending on the one "called Faithful and True" (Rev. 19:11).

- **Depend on the Lord for salvation (Ps. 20:1).** We cannot save ourselves. Our righteousness is "like filthy rags" before the Lord (Is. 64:6). Salvation is God's work, and our job is simply to have faith in Him (see Eph. 2:8–9).

- Depend on the Lord for help and strength (Ps. 20:2). Everyone needs God's wisdom and strength to live from day to day. Your strength is limited but God's is infinite.
- Pray for a right heart (vv. 3–5). As you depend on the Lord, He creates in you a desire to obey Him—a will in line with His own. An attitude of the heart that says, "Lord, what do You want in this situation?" is a radical expression of obedience and dependence.

Praying for your life to align with the Lord's, resting in His watchcare, is not for you alone. You can be a blessing by using this psalm to pray for those whom you love or even for your enemies. If the nation of Israel believed David needed reassurance of the Lord's presence, how much more should we lift up those in leadership and people we know?

Lauren Johnson

Prayer: *Ask God to give you grace today. Ask the Lord for wisdom and guidance in all of your decisions. Confess your independence. Tell the Lord you need Him. Pray for your family and friends to depend on the Lord.*

Personal Reflection: ....

....

....

....

....

He Is Strong

Psalm 21:1–13

"Be exalted, O LORD, in Your own strength!
We will sing and praise Your power." (v. 13)

The sound of many little feet racing on the tile floor to be first into the kitchen caught my attention. "Mom, look at my muscles!" confidently called my oldest, flexing his burgeoning biceps as hard as he was able. His two younger brothers quickly followed suit, with the two-year-old proudly grunting and displaying his manliness along with his older heroes. Squeezing the bicep of each, I replied, "You are all so strong! Look at those muscles!" Grinning and giggling, they ran to pursue feats of strength in the backyard. The earnest desire of my young sons to become strong men merits my encouragement and praise. As their mother, I would be neglectful not to notice and honor their strength. If that is the case, how much more neglectful are we when we fail to notice the strongest One of all?

The Lord God deserves praise for His strength. Our God is *El Shaddai*, God Almighty. In His strength the Lord created the heavens and the earth. He chose a people for Himself and led them out of slavery. He raised up judges, prophets, and kings. He came as a baby to be "God with us" (Matt. 1:23). He performed signs and wonders. He died, was buried, and rose again on the third day. He conquered sin, death, and hell. He saves and reconciles sinners to Himself. He builds His kingdom. His Word never returns void. He will return again one day. When we are weak, He is strong.

No one is more worthy of our praise than the Lord Almighty. For every victory you gain in life, He is the One who won it. For every overcoming that is yet to happen, the Lord will ultimately triumph. How much more so the victories of His church? When you gather with other believers on Sunday and sing praise and hymns as the body of Christ, you are affirming and exalting the King of

kings, who alone is strong. The Lord's kingdom grows through the work of His bride, the Church, because of the strength of His Spirit.

However, in the midst of life's pain, distractions, and loss, the Lord's strength can be forgotten. When you forget who the Lord is and do not trust that He is strong enough to help you and take care of your problems, your life can become a pity party. The remedy for any good old-fashioned pity party, however, is praise. When you are hurting, open up the Psalms and recall all that God did for His people. Believe that He can do that for you. When you feel rejected or confused by life's circumstances, open up the New Testament and see all that Jesus has done for you. There is always something for which to praise Him, something to be recalled about His vast strength.

Lauren Johnson

Prayer: *Thank the Lord for His strength. Admit you are weak and need Him to move in your life. Thank Him for the victories He has won for you.*

Personal Reflection: ....

....

....

....

....

....

The God Who Hears

Psalm 22:1–21

*"They cried to You, and were delivered;
They trusted in You, and were not ashamed." (v. 5)*

The silence in my home was suddenly pierced by the frantic cry of my frightened son, "Mama? Are you here?" My husband and I could hear his cries grow louder and the pounding of his feet grew nearer as he ran through the house searching for us. We called to him from the garage where we were exercising, but he could not hear us. At last he breathlessly and tearfully flung open the door of the garage to find us: "Oh! I thought you had left us because I couldn't hear you!" My husband and I hugged him, reassuring him that we would never leave him. We were there, even if he did not hear us.

There are spiritual moments in life when we feel like a scared child who does not hear an immediate response from his parents. The psalmist felt afraid when he cried, "O My God, I cry in the daytime, but You do not hear; And in the night season, and am not silent" (v. 2). Maybe you have prayed for your husband's salvation for years, and he still has not given his heart to the Lord. Perhaps you are in the middle of a major decision and feel overwhelmed because you have not received a clear answer from the Lord about what to do. You may be helplessly watching a loved one in physical pain with no relief in sight and wonder if God sees his hurt. Your precious child may be running from the Lord and you wonder if God will ever answer your prayers to draw your child back into a right relationship with the Him. Life can make you feel left in the dark, all alone, frightened, and crying: "Lord, are you there? Do you hear me?"

Precious one, your prayers are not wasted. Your tears are captured in God's bottle (Ps. 56:8), and He hears every word you pray. Your Deliverer is coming. Just as the Lord heard the pleas for a child from the barren and hurting Hannah, the Lord hears you (see 1 Sam. 1:19–20). In the midst of the perceived

silence of God in your life, do not lose faith. The Lord is working His plan in your life and changing you.

Remember the character of the Lord in times of struggle. "If we are faithless, He remains faithful; He cannot deny Himself" (2 Tim. 2:13). God is faithful, and He cannot be anything but faithful in your life. God is not deaf; He hears you. Because the Lord is holy and true, you can trust Him to come to your aid. Jesus is with you in the heartache, pain, and sorrow. Be still. Keep praying. Keep listening. Keep waiting. Keep trusting. Your King will answer.

Lauren Johnson

Prayer: *Ask the Lord to remember you. Is there a matter you have been bringing before the Lord but without His response? Give it all to Him. Persevere in your prayer.*

Personal Reflection: ....

....

....

....

....

....

....

A Story to Tell

Psalm 22:22–31

"A posterity shall serve Him.
It will be recounted of the Lord to the next generation,
They will come and declare His righteousness to a people who will be born,
That He has done this." (vv. 30–31)

Gasping for air, with hands and feet nailed to a rugged cross, Jesus groaned: "My God, My God, why have You forsaken Me?" (v. 1; see Matt. 27:46). Psalm 22 is a messianic psalm, pointing to the suffering that Christ would endure on our behalf. While the first twenty-one verses of Psalm 22 describe the agony of the cross, the latter half of the psalm proclaims His victory. What Satan meant for Christ's defeat and the end of humanity's hope was crushed by the blood of our perfect Savior on the cross as Jesus paid the ultimate price for reconciliation. Three days later, an empty tomb and a risen King meant victory over Satan's schemes, sin, death, and hell. Christ's death and resurrection give us a story to share—the Story, the Gospel, the Good News.

If you are a believer in Christ, then you are the posterity serving Him of whom Psalm 22:30 speaks. The task of recounting belongs to us, but what a joyous job! We have been given forgiveness of sin. Christ exchanged the filth of our sin for His righteousness so that we might be in right standing before the Father. Jesus has set us free. Our assignment is to tell the captives, those enslaved to sin, about the freedom found in Jesus Christ. No man, woman, boy, or girl can earn salvation. Jesus paid the price for sin on the cross. All of the praise goes to Him because "He has done this" (v. 31).

There is no higher or greater calling than to declare Jesus' righteousness to people. From the earliest days of the church, Christians have suffered and died for the cause of Christ. Stephen was stoned while preaching Jesus (Acts 7:54–60). Paul was beaten and suffered greatly while spreading the gospel

(2 Cor. 11:25–28). Missionaries from Adoniram Judson to Lottie Moon have traveled across oceans and continents to share the love of Christ with the generations. Even today, Christians with the name of Jesus on their lips are put to death. Jesus is worthy of it all.

Whether or not you are called to the mission field, you have been given the commission to go and tell your neighbors near and far what Christ has done to secure your salvation (see Matt. 28:18–20). Perhaps you are a stay-at-home mom, then you can tell your children about Jesus and show them what He looks like daily. If you are a teacher, pray for the children in your class to know King Jesus, the greatest Teacher ever to walk the face of the earth. Tell the cashier at the grocery store that Jesus loves her and has a plan for her life. Just love Jesus enough to tell people about Him!

Lauren Johnson

Prayer: *Pray for lost friends and family members. Ask the Lord to give you boldness and opportunities to share the Gospel story. Pray for missionaries who are sharing Jesus at home and abroad.*

Personal Reflection: ....

....

....

....

....

The Good Shepherd

Psalm 23:1–3

"He makes me to lie down in green pastures;
He leads me beside the still waters.
He restores my soul;
He leads me in the paths of righteousness
For His name's sake." (vv. 2–3)

Sheep-shearing time had arrived in West Texas, and my family and I had been invited to a ranch to observe. The sound of bleating sheep greeted us. Ranch hands were busy at work catching sheep and shearing them—exhausting, physical labor. We were recruited to help gather a group of sheep for shearing in another pen. The process involved yelling and gesturing with our arms to get the sheep to go in the right direction. Each sheep was counted, and its wool was put in a bag matching its tag number. The real-life experience gave me a new appreciation for the Shepherd of my soul.

In the book of Genesis, Jacob, a shepherd by trade, is the first to refer to the Lord as "the Shepherd" (see Gen. 47:1–4; 49:24). The psalmist David, also a shepherd, sees the Lord as his spiritual Shepherd. David would have been intimately familiar with shepherding. He would know the concern and love of a shepherd for his sheep. David probably recalled the many times he had guided his sheep to lush pastures, to calm waters, and to safe paths. The Lord had led David the same tender, caring way David had led his own sheep. The Good Shepherd leads and cares for us the same way (see John 10:11–14).

Our Shepherd knows what we need to keep journeying on our pilgrimage. That He makes us lie down in green pastures shows that the Lord leads us to places of rest as well as abundant provision. The Word of God is the most fertile pasture. As we feed on His Word, our souls are given the nutrients needed to thrive. The Good Shepherd also leads us to still waters, which allow sheep and

thirsty children to drink safely until full. Jesus, as the Living Water, leads us to refreshing waters of life (see John 4:14).

Shepherds know the paths for their sheep to safely reach places of refreshment and refuge. When you drift off the path of righteousness, the Good Shepherd is there with His rod and staff to bring you back on the pathway. Although we may resent the pull of the Shepherd's staff and the pain of His rod, Jesus disciplines us as a shepherd to bring us back into right relationship with Him. The Shepherd's steps are faithful, and we can follow them in confidence.

How are you doing, little sheep? You have a Good Shepherd. Follow wherever He leads.

Lauren Johnson

Prayer: *Thank the Lord for how lovingly He shepherds and watches over your life. Admit your stubbornness and ask the Lord to help you follow well.*

Personal Reflection: ....

....

....

....

....

....

A Heap of Goodness and Mercy

Psalm 23:4–6

"Surely goodness and mercy shall follow me
All the days of my life;
And I will dwell in the house of the LORD
Forever." (v. 6)

Rebecca's grin lit up the room as she shared with me the latest good thing God had done in her family's life. Rebecca and her sister Catherine had been grieving the recent loss of their mother. While both ladies walked with the Lord, the difficulty of losing a parent had taken its toll, and sometimes they wondered if God could restore joy in their lives. Catherine was not only reeling from the death of her mother but also battling the disappointment of infertility. She and her husband Jeff had been hoping to have children for several years to no avail. All of that combined to make Rebecca's news more precious and the clear hand of the Lord in their lives more than evident. Not only were Catherine and Jeff adopting, but also they were getting two sweet sisters, mirroring the relationship of Catherine and Rebecca. In response to the mighty blessings of God on her sister in becoming a mother and upon herself in becoming an aunt, Rebecca said: "God just keeps heaping on the goodness!" Their story perfectly demonstrates the truth found in Psalm 23:6.

The goodness of God is often clouded by the distractions of the day. We mistakenly view Him who gave His only Son as stingy. This psalm clearly sets forth the goodness of God. The Lord's goodness pursues us. The goodness of our Lord did not stop at Calvary. Not only does He extend salvation to us, but He also heaps and pours out upon us "every spiritual blessing" and does "exceedingly abundantly above all that we ask or think" (Eph. 1:3; 3:20).

Perhaps you would not describe your current situation in life as "good." Nevertheless, your circumstances do not negate the goodness of God. God's

character defines goodness. Shadrach, Meshach, and Abednego professed faith in God before being thrown into the fiery furnace. The Lord was indeed able to save them, but if He had not, they still would not bow down to any other gods (see Dan. 3:1–25). God blesses you when you cling to Him because He is good.

Mercy or lovingkindness (Hb. *chesed*) is a blessing. His steadfast love and covenantal loyalty are unfailing, unwavering, and ultimately fulfilled in Christ. You are faithfully loved by a good God. His love extends from the cross, through forgiveness, and includes a relationship with Him. His blessings are beyond measure and ultimately eternal.

As you follow the Lord, be assured that His goodness and mercy are not far behind. Whatever you may be experiencing at the moment is temporary. The Lord is good and is walking with you. He faithfully loves you.

Lauren Johnson

Prayer: *Thank the Lord for His goodness and mercy toward you. Think specifically about how God has shown you His goodness and praise Him for it. Ask the Lord to help you serve Him faithfully just as He has been faithful to you.*

Personal Reflection: ....

....

....

....

....

Ascending the Hill

Psalm 24:1–10

"Who may ascend into the hill of the Lord?
Or who may stand in His holy place?
He who has clean hands and a pure heart,
Who has not lifted up his soul to an idol,
Nor sworn deceitfully." (vv. 3–4)

Ascending "the hill of the Lord" referred to traveling to Jerusalem to worship the Lord, especially for feasts and sacrifices. This ascension psalm expresses the praise of God as Creator (vv. 1–2), asks probing questions (vv. 3–6), and portrays messianic hope in terms of the King's entrance into Jerusalem (vv. 7–10; cp. Zeph. 3:14–17). This psalm asks a question that is still relevant today. This question is not just for Sundays but for everyday. How do I prepare to worship, to meet with God face-to-face?

- **Clean hands and a pure heart (Ps. 24:4).** Do your actions and motives honor God? The psalmist explains that those with "clean hands and a pure heart" may ascend the hill of the Lord. Have you lost your temper with your children or husband lately? Do you hold a grudge against someone? What do you need to confess to have clean hands and a pure heart before the Lord?
- **Having no other idols (or gods, v. 4).** To whom do you lift the thoughts of your heart? Are you placing your needs only at the feet of your husband or a trusted friend? Then he or she has become an idol. How do you spend your time, money, and greatest effort? Your priorities reveal your gods.
- **Honesty before the Lord and others (v. 4).** Too many say "yes" too quickly and are then unable to follow through with commitments

because of overbooking ourselves. We disappoint others and ourselves. We pretend that we are fine and everything is perfect, unwilling to be vulnerable and admit our great need for the Lord to make us more like Him. When you are truthful in your heart and with others, you are ready to worship the Lord.

When our hearts are prepared to worship, the Lord blesses. When you seek after the Lord, worry is replaced with worship. "But seek first the kingdom of God and His righteousness, and all these things shall be added to you" (Matt. 6:33). To know Him more should be the cry of our hearts. Be heart-ready to worship every day, and watch the Lord who is mighty in battle fight for you (Ps. 24:8).

Lauren Johnson

Prayer: *Be still before the Lord, searching your heart for any sin. Ask the Lord to forgive you. Be honest in your need for him. Tell the Lord you desire to know Him above all else.*

Personal Reflection: ....

....

....

....

....

Asking for Help

Psalm 25:1–7

"Show me Your ways, O LORD;
Teach me Your paths.
Lead me in Your truth and teach me,
For You are the God of my salvation;
On You I wait all the day." (vv. 4–5)

In our self-sufficient culture, asking for help can be very challenging. Just like a toddler is prone to do, my own heart often cries out, "I'll do it myself!" Only after I fail do I reach out to others for help. This selfish desire is rooted in a high opinion of myself and my ability. I am struck by the psalmist's bold trust, not in himself, but in the Lord: "To You, O LORD, I lift up my soul," and "I trust in You" (vv. 1–2). I want to make a faith-filled response of trust and a conscious decision to turn to God first. When I turn immediately to God, I can respond to His guidance.

In verses 4 and 5, the psalmist begins to petition the Lord for help and direction. He first admits that even his ways and his paths belong to the Lord. Oftentimes, we want to choose the correct path for ourselves. But, because the Lord is the God of our salvation, He has already created us and molded us for the paths He has for us. Our decision-making is not so much about making the right choice as it is walking in the path God has created for us. Of course, this requires daily walking with the Lord and studying His Word for us.

First the psalmist established his trust; then he acknowledged the paths of the Lord. Finally, he asked God for direction in going forward: "Lead me" and "Teach me" (v. 5). Asking for help is not a last resort for the psalmist; it is primary. He knows his own limitations and sees the unlimited wisdom of God. He pleads for guidance by God's truth. His Word is the only thing that sustains those who follow Him.

The psalmist's humility and teachable heart enable him to move forward. After asking for direction, he makes a conscious decision to wait for the Lord. God's timing is not usually our timing. We must make the conscious decision to wait for Him. Following after the Lord's path means waiting patiently for Him to guide us.

Melanie Lenow

Prayer: *Ask the heavenly Father to forgive your prideful disobedience and seek His direction in your life. Declare your trust in the Lord and seek to know His Truth. Thank Him for your salvation and accept His instruction.*

Personal Reflection: ....

....

....

....

....

....

Being "In the Know"

Psalm 25:8–14

"The secret of the LORD is with those who fear Him,
And He will show them His covenant." (v. 14)

Everyone wants to be "in the know." We study the weather to know exactly when the next storm will hit. We study the news to see what our leaders are saying or doing. We spend endless hours on social media to know what our friends are thinking. We like to be the one with the information. Sadly, believers are most ignorant about the things of God.

The psalmist tells us how to be "in the know" about the things of God (v. 14). We might not understand everything, but God never intended to keep His counsel a secret from us. He wants to reveal to us His covenant and His ways. They are all open for our understanding. So why are we sometimes lacking so much in knowledge? The key to understanding is the fear of the Lord, which includes three things: knowing His Word, believing His Word, and doing His Word.

When our oldest daughter was a baby, I was sometimes overwrought with anxiety. I functioned fine on a daily basis, but irrational fears would overcome me even though I was knowledgeable about common dangers for a baby. One day, the Lord gave me this verse: "For God has not given us a spirit of fear, but of power and of love and of a sound mind" (2 Tim. 1:7). I needed to grow in my fear of the Lord to fight anxiety. I had to act on the fact that He gave me a sound mind. I had to trust that God enabled me to love my daughter. I had to believe that the fear I was feeling was not given to me by the Lord and trust Him. God revealed to me His secret counsel because I grew in my fear of the Lord.

As we seek to learn about what is going on around us in the world, let us first desire to seek after the things of God. While I might not always know the

latest news or the latest trends, I want to be wise in the secrets of God. Only then can I understand and interpret things around me accurately.

Melanie Lenow

Prayer: *Thank the Lord for loving you so much that He wants you to know His counsel. Seek His forgiveness when you follow worldly knowledge and lack godly wisdom. Fear Him as you trust Him, believe in Him, and follow His Word more.*

Personal Reflection: ....

....

....

....

....

....

....

You Are My Guard

Psalm 25:16–22

"Let integrity and uprightness preserve me,
For I wait for You." (v. 21)

When Paul was in prison, he had cruel, Roman guards. They watched over him with intensity because they would be held accountable with their own lives. They were fierce, cruel, and merciless. However, on multiple occasions in Acts, Paul and others were singing hymns and praying. As the guards watched, Paul acknowledged and reached out to the God who was ultimately watching over him.

At the end of Psalm 25, David is overcome with the afflictions of the world around him. He is distressed, suffering, and hated by his enemies. He feels alone and vulnerable. Just like Paul's cruel guards, the only people on earth looking out for David meant him harm. David calls out to His God. He declares his trust in God, praises Him for salvation, and asks Him for forgiveness. Finally, at the end, David is left with one request: "Guard me and deliver me." The psalmist takes refuge in the only one that can truly protect him. In verse 21, integrity and righteousness are personified to watch over David. He could only see evil and affliction of others, but he appealed to his righteous God to watch over him.

The weight of the world can be overwhelming to us. There is so much evil around us, and it is hard not to feel oppressed. We see our leaders as controlling the events of the world. The stresses of our own relationships dictate our actions. Our emotions are unguarded, and our souls are vulnerable. Heed Paul's charge: "Set your mind on things above, not on things on the earth" (Col. 3:2). The psalmist sets his eyes on the integrity and righteousness that are direct attributes of God. He chose to believe God's promises instead of man's threats. Then, he waited in expectant trust for God to protect him. When we set our eyes

on things above, we take our eyes off temporal fears and focus on the eternal protection of God.

Melanie Lenow

Prayer: *Stand on the promise of God's protection. Choose to acknowledge daily His integrity and goodness, which guard you. Remember that the evil of this world will not last forever. The Lord is more powerful than your enemies. Wait for His victory.*

Personal Reflection: ....

....

....

....

....

....

....

....

Declaring Our Righteousness

Psalm 26:1–12

"For Your lovingkindness is before my eyes,
And I have walked in Your truth." (v. 3)

"I didn't do it!" That was the response of my son when I asked him about an expensive yet broken toy. My son immediately began his defense. "I didn't even go in the play room! I've been playing with my own toys! I am careful!" All those statements were true, but it was not beyond reasonable judgment to think he was capable of breaking the toy, but he wanted me to know that this time he made better choices.

Throughout Psalm 26, the psalmist similarly proclaims his own righteousness. He asks the Lord to vindicate or judge him to prove he had lived with integrity. He lists the ways he had purposefully avoided the company of sinners. Maybe you and I wonder why David felt the need to explain his innocence. He may have known his own heart and capabilities. As with my son, the psalmist knew that he was capable of the mistakes of the past.

David went from being a man worthy of condemnation to a man standing firm on his innocence. The catalyst for this change lies in his shift toward the things of God. Instead of sitting around with worthless people, David chose to sit at the Lord's altar. In contrast to associating with hypocrites, he raises his voice in thanksgiving to God. Instead of having his hands in evil bribes, the psalmist chooses to wash his hands in innocence. At the end of the chapter, David declares how he is able to do it all. He explains the source of his righteousness: "My foot stands in an even place" (i.e., on level ground, v. 12). He does not claim responsibility for the level ground but claims that level ground allows him to live with integrity.

As believers, we have access to that same level ground. We can firmly plant our feet on a solid foundation. We can see our own righteousness, but we know

we are not righteous in and of ourselves. We are only righteous because of God who loves us and places His own righteousness upon us. When we have a right view of ourselves, we know we are capable of sin. Therefore we are even more thankful for our firm foundation in Christ. That thankfulness grows in our hearts and bursts forth as everlasting praise to the One who is truly righteous.

Melanie Lenow

Prayer: *Thank the Lord for showering you with His grace and mercy. Thank Him for taking you as a wretched sinner and transforming you into a person of integrity and good character. Recognize that only through Him can you make good choices for life. Apart from God, you are nothing. Praise Him for His goodness and favor. Praise Him to the world so that they might see His goodness in your life.*

Personal Reflection: ....

....

....

....

....

....

....

The Lesson of the Dogwoods

Psalm 27:1–3

"The LORD is my light and my salvation;
Whom shall I fear?
The LORD is the strength of my life;
Of whom shall I be afraid?" (v. 1)

One of my favorite spring traditions, growing up in the Deep South, was to go camping with my grandparents. Almost immediately after Christmas, I would begin counting the days until it finally warmed up enough for our trip. We would drive several hours south to camp at the Natchez State Park campgrounds. I loved going in the spring because the dogwoods were in bloom. We would arrive to discover a forest covered in small, white blossoms woven into the dark green pine trees. In the wild, dogwoods always grow alongside much larger trees like pines and oaks. They thrive in partial shade, but the larger trees also help protect them from harsh weather conditions. It is possible to grow dogwoods alone for landscaping, but they thrive best in the wild under the protection of the forests around them.

Psalm 27:1 paints a picture in the same light as dogwoods. The Lord is the strength of our lives. Whom should we fear? Of what should we be afraid? We are like the dogwood planted firmly beside the large pine tree. We flourish because of the grand protection of our Father in heaven. When we grow firmly planted beside Him, we need not fear the dangers of the world. We are not meant to fight these enemies by ourselves, for we grow beside and underneath God's overarching protection. We do not have to fear Satan's darts or the darkness of the world. God's perfect protection shades us just enough. God allows enough light to come through so that we will be guided but not blinded. He only allows through its branches what He desires us to experience. The psalmist goes on to proclaim that he will not fear evildoers, foes, or enemies. His heart

will not be afraid even if war breaks out. How can he be so fearless? He knows whose protection he is under.

Dogwoods can be grown independent and on their own. However, without protection they are then much more fragile and easily damaged. The strongest dogwoods thrive under the branches of a tree that is greater in size. In the very same way, you cannot fight the battles of life on your own. You might look beautiful, but you will be fragile and easily broken. On the other hand, you will flourish and grow when tucked under the protection of God, standing firm in the promise of His salvation.

Melanie Lenow

Prayer: *Thank God for His loving protection in your life and acknowledge that everything comes through the branches of His love. Stand firm beside the root of His salvation. Seek His forgiveness when you become afraid due to a lack of faith, and ask Him to help you trust Him more.*

Personal Reflection: ....

....

....

....

....

....

One Wish

Psalm 27:4–6

"One thing I have desired of the LORD,
That will I seek:
That I may dwell in the house of the LORD
All the days of my life,
To behold the beauty of the LORD,
And to inquire in His temple.
For in the time of trouble
He shall hide me in His pavilion;
In the secret place of His tabernacle
He shall hide me;
He shall set me high upon a rock." (vv. 4–5)

If you could ask the Lord for one thing, what would it be? Would you ask for protection? Or do you want to be rewarded and exalted? Do you want to be happy and have a life of ease? David asks for one thing, but not for any of the above requests. His one request is to "dwell in the house of the LORD all the days" of his life, gazing on "the beauty of the LORD" and "seeking Him in His temple" (v. 4). While David may have wanted to stay in God's temple forever, never to leave and enter the rest of the world, I believe his request was slightly different.

Dwelling in the house of the Lord, gazing on His beauty, and seeking Him are not actions that must take place only in the temple. These actions describe more accurately a constant fellowship with God. They resemble a daily relationship of knowing God personally. Daily, we dwell with Him through prayer and renewal of our minds. We can gaze on His beauty by studying Scripture or by looking at His amazing creation. We can seek Him in His temple by practicing the discipline of corporate worship with fellow believers. David proclaimed that more than anything else, he wanted an intimate relationship with God.

When we have daily fellowship with God and we pursue this type of a relationship, our other desires fall into place. God protects David by concealing him in His shelter and hides him under the cover of His tent (v. 5). God not only protects but also rewards or exalts us in the presence of our enemies. David's head was lifted high, symbolizing triumph over his enemies (v. 6). Finally, a result of daily fellowship with God is a happiness that only comes from Him. Shouting for joy, singing praises, and making music to the Lord will all characterize the joyful lives of those who love God.

You might seek protection or exaltation on your own, or you might even attempt happiness. But any of these goals apart from God are worthless and shortsighted. Jesus commanded: "Seek first the kingdom of God and His righteousness, and all these things will be added to you" (Matt. 6:33). All the other things of this world that we seek will dim in comparison to seeking first the daily fellowship and personal relationship with God.

Melanie Lenow

Prayer: *Purpose in your heart to seek daily after the Lord. Desire your fellowship with Him to be sweet and holy. Seek forgiveness of your sins. Thank the Lord for providing a way for you to have a relationship with Him. Thank Him for loving you and granting you innumerable blessings.*

Personal Reflection: ....

....

....

....

The Fear of Loneliness

Psalm 27:7–10

"Do not hide Your face from me;
Do not turn Your servant away in anger;
You have been my help;
Do not leave me nor forsake me,
O God of my salvation." (v. 9)

You will find in the top 10 of any list of fears women face the fear of loneliness, which is reflected in many forms. Some women fear the end of an important relationship. Some fear being left all alone to provide for themselves. Some fear that their friends will not like them anymore or their husbands will leave. The fear of being abandoned and alone leads many women to act out in desperation. Either they overcompensate by pursuing their own independence or they cower to the pressure of attempting to please everyone.

However, the fear of loneliness is not just specific to women. The psalmist is struggling with the same battle (vv. 7–10). First, he is bold, but by the end fear has creeped in. He begs God: "Do not hide Your face from me; Do not turn Your servant away in anger; . . . Do not leave me nor forsake me . . ." (v. 9). He begins to panic that God will leave him. I understand this panic well, and I bet you do too. All of us have had a time in our lives where we have been overcome by fear of loneliness or abandonment.

What are we to do in those situations? We should follow the lead of David and speak truth to ourselves. Even if "my father and my mother forsake me, Then the LORD will take care of me" (v. 10). Earthly relationships break down, sin runs rampant in lives that are not committed to Christ, and sometimes the temptation to leave prevails. Even the closest relationships between children and parents or husbands and wives are at the risk of dissolving if given over to continual sin. However, you can stand firm with the psalmist and proclaim

that your relationship with God is not the same as in human relationships. The Lord will never leave or abandon us. In the Old Testament, God makes covenants with Noah, Abraham, Joshua, Samuel, Isaiah, and Jeremiah never to leave them. He also communicates through the prophets to speak these words to all the people of Israel.

Jesus reminds His disciples of His presence as He commands them to take the gospel to the whole world: "I am with you always, even to the end of the age" (Matt. 28:20). In Hebrews 13:5, the writer encourages his readers by reminding them that "He himself has said, 'I will never leave you nor forsake you.'"

The fear of loneliness is not uncommon. However, when the fear begins to bubble up in your soul, take the same direction as the psalmist and proclaim truth to your soul. The overwhelming truth is that God will never leave or abandon you. God is right there beside you to care for you as only He can.

Melanie Lenow

Prayer: *Thank your heavenly Father for His promise to never leave you and for His desire to have a personal relationship with you. Remember that His Word is the Truth that never changes and will always speak to your uncertain soul.*

Personal Reflection:

All's Well That Ends Well

Psalm 27:11–14

"I would have lost heart, unless I had believed
That I would see the goodness of the LORD
In the land of the living.
Wait on the LORD;
Be of good courage,
And He shall strengthen your heart;
Wait, I say, on the LORD!" (vv. 13–14)

People often say, "All's well that ends well," when arriving at the planned destination even when the journey is a little bumpy. In theory, the happy ending justifies the struggle to get there. While the saying is not always true, I do believe it describes well the journey described in Psalm 27.

At the beginning of the chapter, David confidently declares his faith in God as his stronghold. He embraces the struggles before him, knowing that God will protect him from his enemies. Do you ever start a similar season of life? You are strong in your faith and confident in your Lord, ready to face the enemy in any trial that comes your way. Then, just like David, your strength runs dry or you become hurt by the debris of life. Your life turns out to be something different than you expected. David faltered as well and found himself in the pit of fear of loneliness and abandonment.

Then, David makes a choice. He chooses to believe God more than he is moved by the circumstances around him. He speaks God's truth to himself. He embraces the challenges that the Lord has given him and trusts God with the results. He emphatically speaks out about trusting God, certain that he "would see the goodness of the LORD in the land of the living. Wait on the LORD. Be of good courage . . . Wait . . . on the LORD!" (vv. 13–14).

If you have started out soaring but have fallen somewhere along the way, your story is not over yet. Follow David's lead and proclaim your faith in God's promises. By simply trusting the Lord's good and perfect plan for your life, you are acting out your faith and moving forward in a positive way. If you follow Christ as your Savior, I am certain that you will see the Lord's goodness one day in the land of the living. When you end a season of growth by firmly standing on God's promises and declaring that you will wait on Him to move again, you have ended well. Then the whole trial is worth it.

Melanie Lenow

Prayer: *Ask the Father to hold you strong when you have no strength. Lift your eyes to Him when you are discouraged. Thank Him for promising never to leave you. Trust Him and His goodness, and wait on Him to move in your life.*

Personal Reflection: ....

....

....

....

....

....

Between a Bed of Nails

Psalm 28:1–9

"The LORD is my strength and my shield;
My heart trusted in Him, and I am helped;
Therefore my heart greatly rejoices,
And with my song I will praise Him." (v. 7)

Women want to know that they have someone to trust who will walk alongside them, fight for them, and win their battles. In this verse, David knows that while he has enemies surrounding him the Lord has heard his cry. The Lord is his strength and shield! David has a helper!

When one of my daughters was four, "The Power Team" came to our church. This group of very strong men used their feats of strength to share their faith in Christ. Her pastor daddy was asked to be a part of the program. His part required him first to lie on a bed of nails. Then another board full of nails was placed on his chest. And a hundred-pound block of ice on top of that. One of the members of the team would then take a sledgehammer and hit hard to burst the block of ice resting on the chest of the pastor, her daddy.

As the team began to set up the feat, my husband lay down atop the bed of nails, and the second bed of nails was placed on top of his chest. Finally the ice was placed upon him. My sweet little girl stood quickly to her little feet, barely able to see over the pew. She turned to me and asked, "They gonna hurt my daddy?" Her lips quivered. "Don't let them hurt my daddy." I scooped her up and whispered, "It's going to be all right sweetheart. Your daddy is a strong man."

The team member raised his sledgehammer high into the air, and it came down crushing the ice. There was a split-second pause as the crowd waited for the reaction from the pastor. Suddenly he rolled off the nails, jumped to his feet, and gave the fist pump of victory to the crowd! The people roared with excitement!

When the night ended, the crowd was swirling around the pastor; and our daughter squeezed her way to him and grabbed her daddy's hand. As they left the sanctuary, my daughter walked confidently beside her daddy, head turned up and eyes sparkling.

The Creator of this universe is waiting for us to declare that He is our strength and our shield! He will deliver us. We can walk in His strength, knowing He is the shield that will protect us.

Diane Nix

Prayer: *Thank the Lord for delivering and protecting you! Declare that He is your strength and shield. Trust Him with your whole heart and praise His name. He is always with you during the hardest times of your life!*

Personal Reflection:

Glory and Holiness

Psalm 29:1–11

"Give unto the Lord the glory due to His name;
Worship the Lord in the beauty of holiness." (v. 2)

As a young girl, I desperately needed to know that there was something bigger than I in the universe. I dreamed of far-off places. There was just one problem; I lived on a West Texas farm surrounded by cornfields. The nearest small grocery store was a forty-five-minute drive, and most of my younger life was spent working and playing in my own world.

One of my favorite places to dream was the roof of my family home, especially when the cornfields had matured to the tasseling stage. As far as the eye could see, it looked like a huge yellow carpet. I imagined that a great hand was running back and forth over the land, causing the carpet to ripple. While I felt very small, I was aware that at any moment that great hand could scoop me up and pull me close.

Those farm days are long behind me. I have been blessed to travel the world and to imagine that great hand of the Lord as He carved out the Grand Canyon or took His finger and lifted the highest peaks. I have hiked in a Canadian forest and discovered the beauty of His creation in a small running brook, and I have spent days in the heat of the desert land of western Africa.

When you are surrounded with the beauty of His creation, it is easier to give God glory and worship Him. However, the "rubber meets the road" when you are a woman trying to make it through the day, wondering if anyone notices that you are the one pulling the load. Giving God glory when life seems unfair and worshiping His holiness amidst pain are truly the greatest challenges of the Christian life.

The root meaning of the Hebrew word *glory* is to "be heavy or weighty," often in the sense of being "honored." The word *holiness* is at its very essence

a "being set apart." Holiness is God's nature. You and I are to live our lives in such a manner that we acknowledge the "weightiness" (glory) of who God is. As we walk through this life, day in and day out, season to season, we are to live as being called out and set apart, bowing to worship and acknowledging that nothing passes His eye. We need only to acknowledge *Him* in all things. He loves us and is deeply concerned with every single detail of our lives.

Diane Nix

Prayer: *Glorify your Lord by honoring His name! He is God, and you are not. Seek His help in your daily life. Bow and worship Him for the beauty of His holiness.*

Personal Reflection: ....

....

....

....

....

....

....

Where's the Joy?

Psalm 30:1–12

*"For His anger is but for a moment,
His favor is for life;
Weeping may endure for a night,
But joy comes in the morning." (v. 5)*

The three-way call started off: "What have you done?" I did not hesitate. I told them everything and the two other friends listened. They gave godly counsel. They heard my plan of how to remedy the situation and helped me work through the painful process of repentance. I wept. I wept as I never had before.

I felt shame. I felt guilt. I felt God's anger because I knew better. I knew what I had done was wrong. I had been on the other side of this kind of sin, and the sting of allowing myself to fall prey to the same sin was very painful. I knew that God's anger was righteous and just. I knew that my sin was against Him and Him alone. I am grateful that those moments are not forever moments.

The problem came when I rejected the grace given me. I beat myself up constantly. I let the great enemy lie to me and whisper untruths about my usefulness. I lived grieving that I had failed in my walk. I secretly held on to this perceived condemnation for a very long time. Until one day I heard a question that stopped me in my tracks: "Where's the joy?"

God is first and foremost our perfect heavenly Father. The word *Abba* (Aramaic) expresses a very intimate and inseparable relationship between Christ and the Father and between believers (children) and God (Father). If you have accepted Christ, then You are His daughter. You have a perfect Father who will not stay angry at you when you admit your wrong. He does not withhold favor from you when you are truly sorry for what you have done. He is perfect and complete in His forgiveness.

When you and I are made aware of our sinfulness or if we get caught in a particular sin, we can stop. Just push "pause" and let the Holy Spirit do His work. God's anger is for a moment while His favor is for a lifetime. He does not punish you and then stay angry. He is the perfect Father. When you and I recognize His anger because of our sin and follow these steps, we can live in joy and with the favor of our *Abba*!

Repentance and forgiveness are steps to receive favor and joy! Recall what you have done and confess it. Remember and say what your Father says about your actions. Repent and turn away from doing it again. Resolve to walk in His grace and mercy every day.

Diane Nix

Prayer: *Ask the Lord to help you pause and remember if you are living under condemnation. Seek His favor in your life, and rest in the joy of your heavenly Father.*

Personal Reflection: ....

....

....

....

....

....

I'm Not in Control

Psalm 31:1–18

"My times are in Your hand;
Deliver me from the hand of my enemies,
And from those who persecute me." (v. 15)

When I was six months into a high-risk pregnancy, I would go to bed and fall asleep only to wake up making plans. Our enemies were surrounding us. There were lies spoken about our character and no clear source as to who had started the rumors. I cried out to the Lord to deliver us and help us. I recalled His goodness and reminded Him of our faithfulness.

Later I lay there in my pregnant state, making plans. If we were fired, we could not move because of the pregnancy. How would we pay rent? How would we pay for the delivery and care of this newborn? "Stop. Breathe. Sigh. Deep breaths. Slow down. Go to sleep." I would then lie there praying and thanking God for the pregnancy. I praised Him for all that He had done for us. Slowly the warring thoughts would start again. I was physically and emotionally exhausted.

One morning in my devotional time, as I read Psalm 31, I felt as if I was reading my own story. I had a reminder that morning: My life was in God's hands. The best that I could do was to praise Him for His protection, pray for His direction, and make living for Him a priority. I could not take away what was said about us. I could not control another person's tongue. I could not control the thoughts of others. I could only do what I knew God wanted me to do. I surrendered to a perfect heavenly Father, who loved me and saw my life from the beginning to the end.

A family motto arose from this time in our lives: "No matter what others do or do not do, we will work hard to do what God says is right and bring glory

to His name." We have not always been successful with our motto, but it has served as a guide for our family.

We are not in control. We waste spiritual, emotional, and physical energy trying to fix what only God can repair. Do what you need to do before the Lord (1 John 1:9). Leave the results to Him. Speak less. Pray more. God loves you, and He will use everything in your life for His glory and your good (Rom. 8:28). You can trust Him with this promise!

Diane Nix

Prayer: *Surrender your control to God, trusting Him to protect you and guide you. Keep your focus on Him when you cannot control anything or anyone in your life. Trust the Lord because your life is in His hands!*

Personal Reflection: ....

....

....

....

....

....

....

On the Shelf

Psalm 31:19–24

"For I said in my haste,
'I am cut off from before Your eyes';
Nevertheless, You heard the voice of my supplications
When I cried out to You." (v. 22)

I felt as if my husband and I had been placed on a dusty shelf. I knew for certain that God had seen where we were and decided that, because we had not performed perfectly, He could not use us anymore. Circumstances were screaming that we had nothing to offer but failure, and the world surrounding us screamed it as well. Compared to the world's definition of success, we were not just failures; we were miserable failures.

As deep depression settled over me, I made a quick decision to emotionally retreat. Most women learn to hide hurt feelings very well. We hide what is going on deep within while going about life as if nothing is wrong. I got busy. Activity kept my mind from going to my emotional reality. On the shelf. Marked "unusable." I learned to hide my disappointment with my heavenly Father. But truth be told, I did not understand Him at all.

I kept reading my Bible. I kept praying. Then, slowly, one by one, God began to send across my path women who would share their stories with me and ask for my advice. I would hear myself telling them parts of my story and the lessons learned through the reading of the Bible and prayer. I would speak of His faithfulness and testify of His goodness during my most difficult days. I heard myself, and I believed. Now truth be told, there were times as I was sharing when the very words I spoke from my lips were like a healing ointment to my own soul.

One day, as I was praying, I realized that I was not on the shelf marked "unusable." I was on the shelf waiting to process, heal, and learn lessons from

the difficult days of life. At the same time, my husband, having had some of the same feelings, was fasting and praying. One morning in his prayer time, he heard the Father speak: "You are motivated by success. The first part of your life was marked by success; the last part of your life will be marked by significance."

Do you hear this? When on a shelf, our lives are not to be wasted, but every moment we are surrendered to the Lord is used! The world's measure of success is never the same as our heavenly Father's. Your life is stamped with significance because you belong to Him.

Diane Nix

Prayer: *Cry out to the Lord and seek His help. Be faithful to pursue Him. Persevere with courage every day, knowing with great certainty that you will waste nothing when surrendered to Him.*

Personal Reflection: ....

....

....

....

....

....

Are You the Only Woman?

Psalm 32:1–11

"Blessed is he whose transgression is forgiven;
Whose sin is covered.
Blessed is the man to whom the LORD does not impute iniquity,
And in whose spirit there is no deceit." (vv. 1–2)

I could not look him in the eye because I stood seething with anger. "I understand you have a right to be angry, but what I do not understand is the intensity and level of your anger," he helplessly stated. At that moment, something rang true deep inside. My anger was not just for that moment. I was angry because I expected to hear a half-truth.

Exposure could come at any moment. I felt unbearable shame and guilt. Because of these emotions, I was harboring anger and was ready to unleash on my husband in order to justify my own choice to withhold information from him the year before. Both while we were engaged and newly married, my husband had asked what he believed to be a normal question. Unknown to him, that question sent me to depths of guilt and shame because of previous sin. I felt sure that this sin would be a disqualification for our marriage so I had responded with a half-truth.

The half-truth now plagued me. It was the tormentor's tool, wearing me out. I constantly replayed messages from the enemy in my head. It was as if I had handed our greatest foe a hammer with which to beat me at any moment of the slightest marital disagreement. My husband's statement that day drove me to seek out a counselor for the first time in my life.

I remember shaking as I sat down in his office. Then, like a cork had been popped off a bottle, I spewed out my story. When I finished, the counselor asked, "Do you really believe that you are the only woman who has ever committed this type of sin?" I stared at him in astonishment. "Well, I guess not," I stammered.

We spoke briefly about the love of the Father and His willingness to forgive us of our sin if we only let Him, and then the counselor prayed with me. That night, I nervously told my husband the ugly truth. His reaction—grace and mercy. He held me as I cried tears of repentance, and he prayed healing over me.

The psalmist declared in these verses that the one in outright rebellion is forgiven and restored. Blessed is the one whose accidental missteps and moral failures are covered as if they never happened. Pardoned are the ones who confess their sins and agree with the Lord about their failures. The Lord does not require any more payment for the sins already forgiven. He paid the penalty for our sins on the cross.

Diane Nix

Prayer: *Ask the Lord to remind you that His mercies are new every morning. Seek His forgiveness and cleansing. Allow Him to reveal to you where you have sinned and walk freely in His forgiveness all the days of your life!*

Personal Reflection: ....

....

....

....

....

....

In His Goodness

Psalm 33:1–9

"For the word of the LORD is right,
And all His work is done in truth.
He loves righteousness and justice;
The earth is full of the goodness of the LORD." (vv. 4–5)

What sweet assurance in a world where truth is increasingly more relative: "The word of the LORD is right, and all His work is done in truth" (v. 4). It is common to hear someone's argument against truth begin with these words: "Well, that may be true for you, but it is not true for me." While in college, I had a dear agnostic friend. We had many conversations about truth. His favorite argument against the truth of the Bible was the infamous example of a wheel in which each spoke represents a belief, all leading to ultimate truth, even if the journeys to that truth are vastly different. He would ask me if I could at least agree with that supposition. I always came back to the fact that I had experienced Jesus, the One who claimed that He Himself was the one "way, the truth, and the life" (John 14:6). I had seen His goodness, and I could not believe Him to be true and also accept other worldviews as viable.

People are quick to trade truth for something lesser because it may not initially feel right or good. God's truth is reliable:

- There is only one way to enter into the eternal presence of God.
- We are to lay down our lives as a living sacrifice.
- All life is viable and valuable.
- God has a perfect design for the family as a man and a woman in covenant marriage.
- We were created to work.

- We are to forgive as we have been forgiven.
- We are to count it all joy when we face trials of many kinds.

Sometimes these true words of the Lord seem harsh and unloving. But, the earth is full of His goodness (Ps. 33:5).

In God's goodness, He sent His only Son that we might have life, eternal and abundant (John 3:16; 10:10). In His goodness, He allows us to know His good, pleasing, and perfect will (Rom. 12:1–2). In His goodness, God calls us and equips us to have the same attitude as that of Christ Jesus (Phil. 2:1–5). In His goodness, all are created equal, from conception to the last breath (Gal. 3:26–29). In His goodness, a man leaves his mother and his father and cleaves to his wife (Gen. 2:24). In His goodness, we receive an eternal inheritance as a reward (Col. 3:23–24). In His goodness, forgiveness is ours, both to give and to receive (Eph. 4:32). And, in His goodness, we can be mature and complete, lacking nothing (James 1:2–4). May we trust fully in His goodness!

Monica Patrick

Prayer: *In a world where evil seems rampant and the hearts of men are so very far from God, look to that which is right and true. Find great comfort and joy in the goodness of your Father God.*

Personal Reflection: ....

....

....

....

God's Plans Are Always Good

Psalm 33:10–15

"The LORD brings the counsel of the nations to nothing;
He makes the plans of the peoples of no effect.
The counsel of the LORD stands forever,
The plans of His heart to all generations.
Blessed is the nation whose God is the LORD,
The people He has chosen as His own inheritance." (vv. 10–12)

As a high school senior, I had grand plans. I was going to attend a university far from home, majoring in some form of communications. I would be married between my sophomore and junior years, and after graduation I would work for a couple of years as a journalist or in theater. Then we would begin our family, consisting of four children—two girls and two boys. The Lord had very different plans. He had kingdom purposes in mind, not the dreams of an idealistic young woman. In reality, I attended a state college that was 46 miles from home, majoring in English Education; and I was not married until I was thirty-four! My nearsighted plans were of no effect in light of God's counsel.

These plans I had as a girl were not on the same scale as the counsel of nations. But, while God has plans that involve nations, He also has plans that involve individuals. His heart is very specifically for me and you. While sometimes He brings our personal plans to nothing, His plans are always good.

"Blessed is the nation whose God is the LORD" (v. 12). I think we could say, "Blessed is the woman whose God is the Lord—the woman whom He has chosen as His own inheritance." The plans God had for me were so much greater than anything I could have imagined, sweet opportunities to grow in Him and be involved in His kingdom work. He took me to Nicaragua to minister to young people who now serve Christ around the world as missionaries, teachers, and industry leaders. He took me to Utah to help plant a church in a land rich in

religion but poor in its knowledge of salvation through Christ alone. He took me to a secular job in Houston to engage professionals in the gospel and to meet the man who would become my husband. My husband is a man who loves Jesus, hears and obeys Him, and serves me and our children (all four of them) sacrificially. He is a man of vision and passion and great courage. At eighteen, I could not have dreamed of someone of my husband's caliber.

Sweet sister, trust fully in the plans that the Lord has for you. When your small plans do not come to pass, do not despair but look ahead in great anticipation toward the plans God has for you who are chosen to be His own inheritance. He who chose us is faithful.

Monica Patrick

Prayer: *Realize that your simple plans are of no substance in light of God's plans for you. Trust Him wholly and receive His unending love for you; wait patiently for Him.*

Personal Reflection: ....

....

....

....

....

....

If I Will Trust in You

Psalm 33:16–22

*"Our soul waits for the L*ORD*;*
He is our help and our shield.
For our heart shall rejoice in Him,
Because we have trusted in His holy name.
*Let Your mercy, O L*ORD*, be upon us,*
Just as we hope in You" (vv. 20–22).

"It's not good." "Spread to the bones of the pelvis and spine. . . ." "Stage 4 breast cancer." Oh, Father God, no, it cannot be. Please come, Lord Jesus, in my life, in my body; my hope is in You alone. I was diagnosed with incurable stage 4 breast cancer at age forty-one. The initial cancer diagnosis, prior to discovering it had metastasized, was not without hope, but this, news of this potentially terminal illness, seemed hopeless.

My husband and I had four children, ages six, four, three, and seven months at the time of my diagnosis, and thoughts of their not being able to remember their mama plagued me. At times, as I cried out to the Lord, there were simply no words, and I know that the Holy Spirit was interceding on behalf of my groaning. As I clung to all I knew to be true, trusting that Jesus, not cancer, numbered my days, despair began to give way to hope.

As I began treatments, my husband and I waited on the Lord. We waited to see how treatments would affect my body and if I would be strong enough to endure them while still caring for our children. The Lord was our help and in His mercy my body was strong, even stronger it seemed than before the diagnosis. We waited on results from scans to see how the cancer was responding to treatments, and there was great rejoicing to hear that the cancer was no longer visible in my body and the bones that had been destroyed were re-growing. God demonstrated His great mercy to us. Today, we continue to wait, from scan to

scan, to see if the cancer has returned, trusting still that God is the one who numbers my days.

Perhaps you are waiting on the Lord—for a loved one who has strayed far from the Father, or for physical, emotional, or spiritual healing? Are you waiting for the gift of a spouse or the blessing of a child or the restoration of a relationship? Whatever it may be, God's great mercy is upon you. You can and must choose to trust Him. Recount the times He has proven faithful.

Today my children are nine, eight, six, and four. They will not only have memories of their mama, but they also have a story of healing and hope, which they may not have had without my battle with cancer. Recently as we rejoiced in what God has done in the last year, my daughter shared her gratitude that God had healed Mommy of cancer. As I type, I am weeping. My hope is in You, Lord.

Monica Patrick

Prayer: *In those moments when you are unsure or afraid, trust in the Lord. He is your help and shield, your certain hope in times of uncertainty.*

Personal Reflection: ....

....

....

....

....

Joined Together in Praise

Psalm 34:1–7

"I will bless the Lᴏʀᴅ at all times;
His praise shall continually be in my mouth.
My soul shall make its boast in the Lord;
The humble shall hear of it and be glad.
Oh, magnify the Lᴏʀᴅ with me,
And let us exalt His name together." (vv. 1–3)

These verses are a reminder to "bless the Lord at all times" and "exalt His name together," but what seems a simple task can be a battle. Often our first inclination is complaint rather than praise. When we gather together, many times we find fault rather than blessing. Hearts that are not set on the goodness of our God overflow with despair rather than gladness.

Some mornings in our home we wake to a case of "the grumbles." Someone was awakened before she was ready. Not all of the kids can fit on mommy's lap for a cozy moment. The cereal is soggy. The toast is burnt. Mommy's coffee gets cold before she gets a single sip. A glass of milk is spilled not once, but twice. Someone else gets the best place on the couch when we are reading books together. Sigh. Sometimes we remember to stop and sing together, "Count Your Blessings," taking turns sharing those blessings for which we are thankful—a comfortable bed and a warm house, clean clothes, cereal instead of eggs, the sun shining through our windows, Jesus and His death on the cross—each recognizing the goodness of our God. In those moments of praise and of counting our blessings together, our hearts are changed from "grumbles" to gladness.

One of the greatest gifts of the body of Christ comes as we edify one another. There is no better way to do so than to encourage others by coming together to exalt the name of the Lord. I have a sweet friend who serves as such an encouragement to me in those times when praise is not the thing that is in

my heart or on my tongue. She is quick to interrupt when I start down the slippery slope of discontent or fear or judgment and simply says, "Let's pray." As we lift my concerns, my hurts, or my sin to the Lord, it almost always moves into a time of exalting His name together. Then I am filled with gladness. My outlook is changed. I am more likely to invite others into the simple, yet profound, act of magnifying the Lord with me.

May we covenant to come together with hearts prepared to exalt the name of the Lord. He is greatly to be praised. May we magnify Him together, that the humble may hear and be glad. As followers of Jesus, our unified posture of praise will serve as a testimony of His goodness to the world. Rather than allowing our differences or our disappointments to define and divide us, may we join together to praise and lift high the name of Jesus, boasting in Him alone.

Monica Patrick

Prayer: *Join your heart together with others in praise to the Lord. Let the world hear your boasting and be glad.*

Personal Reflection: ....

....

....

....

....

Taste the Lord's Goodness

Psalm 34:8–18

"Oh, taste and see that the LORD is good;
Blessed is the man who trusts in Him!" (v. 8)

Sometimes my kids miss out on a tiny bit of deliciousness because they refuse to taste and see that it is good. For example, the other day I purchased some sopapillas—warm, cinnamon-and sugar-coated, honey-drenched sopapillas. I had to beg them to taste these pastries. They feared the unknown. Of course, once they had tasted them, I had to share because, as I had promised, they were amazing. Isn't it that way with God sometimes? He says, "Trust me. This is going to be good." But we hesitate, not convinced that we can trust Him completely.

How ridiculous! Even as I type, I recognize the absurdity of the obvious. Of course, all that God has for us is good. He is tried and tested and true, but there are still times we find ourselves hesitant to taste and see His goodness:

- When God says, "Step out in faith and take that job. I know it is far from all you know, and the pay is less, and you are going alone, but trust Me."
- When He says, "Reach out and welcome that lonely one into your life. Be vulnerable, loving, and kind. I know you fear rejection. I know you fear having to give more of yourself than you feel you can give, but trust Me."
- When He says, "I hear you. Even though that dream you have dreamed for years remains unfulfilled, I hear you. Trust Me."

We have to choose whether or not we move toward God in faith—so that we can taste that which He has placed before us and see that He is good—or stay in the place we know and believe to be safe. Oh, ladies, what a travesty when we miss out on the abundant blessings of the Lord because of our unwillingness to trust Him.

The Bible is replete with stories of women who stepped forward in faith and tasted the goodness of the Lord. Sarah welcomed Isaac, a beloved son, years past her time of bearing children. Esther courageously approached her king on behalf of her people and found redemption for an entire nation. Mary, the mother of Jesus, was visited by an angel, receiving in faith the word he had for her and becoming the earthly mother of the One who would eventually take her sins to the cross and the sins of the entire world. Mary, the sister of Martha, faced the scorn of those closest to her that she might sit at the feet of her Savior and receive "that good part" (Luke 10:42).

Sweet sister, what is it that the Father is asking you to trust Him with today? Trust Him. Taste and see that the Lord is good.

Monica Patrick

Prayer: *Make a commitment to taste and see that God is good. He is faithful in all things. Open your heart to the blessings God has for you.*

Personal Reflection: ....

....

....

....

....

Redeeming Our Afflictions

Psalm 34:19–22

"Many are the afflictions of the righteous,
But the LORD delivers him out of them all. . . .
The Lord redeems the soul of His servants,
And none of those who trust in Him shall be condemned." (vv. 19, 22)

One of our sons has dyslexia. It has been hard watching him struggle to learn to read. We suspected something was wrong when he was younger. In some ways we knew it was dyslexia or other learning problem, but we hoped things would eventually click. They did not. As his younger brother began to thrive as a reader, he grew increasingly frustrated. We had him evaluated and received a formal diagnosis. With that information, we moved forward, explaining to our son how God had designed him to learn differently and adjusted his schooling accordingly. While reading continues to be challenging for him, he loves a good story and longs to be able to read them for himself. So, he presses on, and he is overcoming.

There are moments when we would desperately like for it to be different for him. We want reading to be effortless for him as it has been for his sister and his younger brother. We want him to be able to pick up a book and not just to look at the pictures but to read the words with ease. However, in the economy of God, that is simply not to be. So we trust God to redeem this affliction, and He is working in our son. God is developing in our son diligence and quiet humility that will serve him well. He is learning to trust God's perfect plans above his own because he has strengths and weaknesses that are his alone. We remind him that God wants to use each of them, even this struggle to read, to further His kingdom.

Our son's dyslexia is not a condemnation. Yes, it is a hardship and an affliction; but God *is* redeeming the struggle. Sisters, do not try to avoid the

114

adversity that will come in your own life or in the lives of those whom you hold dear. God does not allow hardship to come without purpose and without plans to redeem it. Romans 8:28 is not simply a platitude; it is truth: God works "all things . . . together for good to those who love [Him], to those who are the called according to His purpose."

When Paul asked God, three times, to remove his "thorn in the flesh," the Lord responded in love, "Paul, I have this. My grace is enough." (see 2 Cor. 12:7–10). In the life of our sweet boy, we know that God's grace is enough. So, ladies, whether your afflictions come in the form of dyslexia or cancer, heartbreak or loss, or any other trial that may come, you must decide to trust in God and His goodness. As you trust in God, there will be no condemnation.

Monica Patrick

Prayer: *God's ways are not your ways, but His ways are always for your good. Trust in God fully.*

Personal Reflection: ....

....

....

....

....

....

Trusting in Our Sure Salvation

Psalm 35:1–18

"Plead my cause, O Lord, with those who strive with me;
Fight against those who fight against me.
Take hold of shield and buckler,
And stand up for my help.
Also draw out the spear,
And stop those who pursue me.
Say to my soul,
'I am your salvation.'" (vv. 1–3)

As I have prayerfully sought God in preparation for writing this devotional, the kids and I have read the passage several times. Our middle son wanted to know who was fighting against us in these verses. Before I could respond, he said, "Oh, I know! It's Satan. He's the one who fights against us." From the mouths of babes. Our battle is indeed not "against flesh and blood, but against principalities, against powers, against the rulers of the darkness of this age, against spiritual hosts of wickedness in the heavenly places" (Eph. 6:12). The battle is not only real but also intense. However, this fact we know: "He who is in you [believers] is greater than he who is in the world" (1 John 4:4). The Lord *is* your salvation, dear one.

I love Bible stories of how God rescued those whom He loved and received great glory in the midst of the rescue. The story of David, who wrote this psalm, is a good example. Of course, this story is much beloved in our home with three boys. David conquered lions, bears, and giants. He was a faithful friend and a formidable foe. He was loyal, for the most part, and God rescued him and saved him; for ultimately, One from David's line would bring about the eternal salvation for all who will believe in Him. Do not doubt for one moment that Satan, knowing the promises of God, was not intensely determined to destroy David.

Yet, David called out, and God pleaded his cause. He was David's salvation just as He is ours.

Our battles may not include physical foes coming against us. There may be no need for spear or shield, but we are in constant, desperate need of the help of the Lord. Do you agree? For without Him, there is no salvation from hopelessness and fear; no salvation from selfishness, pride, and disappointment; no salvation from sin and its relentless striving to keep us far from communion with the Lord. Satan longs to keep us from truly experiencing God. He is "like a roaring lion, seeking whom he may devour" (1 Pet. 5:8). He wants to rob us of the abundant life that abiding in Christ brings. He wants the glory that only God deserves. To be sure, our Father will "plead [our] cause." He is our salvation.

Monica Patrick

Prayer: *Do you know that God alone is your salvation? The battle often feels too intense, but trust Him to plead your cause and bring salvation.*

Personal Reflection: ....

....

....

....

....

....

Blessed Assurance

Psalm 35:19–28

*"And my tongue shall speak of Your righteousness
And of Your praise all the day long." (v. 28)*

Our family went hiking this week. It is January, but here in Texas the weather has been mild this winter, so we went hiking. I'll be honest. We don't usually go hiking without Daddy. I am sorely outnumbered with four kiddos nine and under, but the weather was right. The kids were itching to be on the move, and frankly, I needed to get out of the house. So, we packed a lunch and headed out. What a beautiful day it was! The heavens declared the glory of the Lord and all creation sang His praises.

As we hiked through the leaf-bare trees, on the constant lookout for wildlife, God did not disappoint. We saw the grandest great blue heron I have ever seen, spreading his massive wings to take flight from the river. After he flew from the water, the heron landed in the marsh across the way. We paused behind some tall grasses bending in the breeze to see if we could spy him. He was so very still, yet the distinct blue-gray of his feathers and his height helped us spot him among the muted colors of the winter marsh. We stood in awe of God's creativity.

As we continued our hike, we saw a few American coots. They are black with distinct white bills. They were lovely creatures floating on the river. Flying overhead were flocks of geese, not extremely large flocks, but very noisy. We had such fun listening to them call to one another and watching them fly with precision in their majestic V-formation. We kept an eye out for deer, alligators, and buffalo, to no avail. The animals we did see, however, prompted us to speak the "praise [of our God] all the day long."

My sweet family gathered bright green moss and spotted different types of lichen. We found fossils in the rocks along the trail and climbed trees and

ran down hills. We collected sticks and enough rocks to fill our pockets. It was a lovely day filled with the praise of our God for the diversity of His creation.

I have always loved the chorus of "Blessed Assurance" by Fanny Crosby: "This is my story, this is my song. Praising my Savior all the day long." May that truly be our story! A story of voices lifted in praise to our Father is the greatest story of all. Our days are not always filled with the happy giggles of children and the honking of geese and the sound of the trees rustling in the breeze. However, our days are always filled with the goodness of God, and He is always worthy of our praise, all the day long.

Monica Patrick

Prayer: *Praise the Lord, for He alone is worthy of your song of praise. Let your tongue declare the glory of God and the beauty of His creation.*

Personal Reflection: ....

....

....

....

....

....

The Faithful, Steadfast Love of the Lord

Psalm 36:1–6

"Your mercy, O LORD, is in the heavens;
Your faithfulness reaches to the clouds.
Your righteousness is like the great mountains;
Your judgments are a great deep;
O LORD, You preserve man and beast." (vv. 5–6)

For years, in January my husband and I took an anniversary cruise to some tropical destination. One reason I loved this annual trip, aside from the most important alone-time with my husband, was the wonderful contrast of the sunny, balmy days with the cold, dreary days back home. That's the way we are with many things. We appreciate them more when we can recognize the contrast.

In Psalm 36:5–6, beautiful words remind us of the nature of God. We, as human beings, cannot measure how far to the heavens or how far to the clouds. Similarly, we cannot measure the vastness of God's love; it is immeasurable. We are reminded that just as the mountains are immovable, His righteousness is immovable. The psalmist uses word pictures to help us grasp the boundless, steadfast character of God.

Yet, much like my appreciation for the tropical weather was heightened when contrasted with the cold weather back home, we can more fully appreciate these characteristics of God when they are put in contrast. The preceding four verses describe those who are not God but rather creatures created by God. In Psalm 36:1–4, we find a list of the blatant sins of those opposed to God. These "wicked" men and women have "no fear of God," speak deceitfully, and act foolishly—all the while convinced that their sins will not be discovered.

Before you and I react with outrage over such "workers of iniquity" (v. 12), be reminded of Paul's words, "And such were some of you" (1 Cor. 6:11). Let's face

it, even on this side of salvation, at times we still are prone to speak deceitfully, act foolishly, and try hypocritically to cover our sins. Our sinfulness demonstrates our great need for the steadfast love of the Lord and His unmerited favor.

As we ponder the contrast between God and us, let us have a proper view of who God is and who we are, a people in need of salvation. Let us be grateful for the Lord's unlimited faithful love. As He preserves us, He meets every need. He is faithful in keeping His promises, sending a Savior to cover our sins. Today, let us be reminded of our great need for a merciful, just God. Let us meditate on the height and depth of God's love for us—love that is firm and unshakable.

Denise O'Donoghue

Prayer: *Praise the Lord for His steadfast love, faithfulness, righteousness, and justice. Seek His forgiveness when you defy Him. Try to have spiritual eyes to recognize your ever-present need for Him. Thank the Lord for loving you.*

Personal Reflection: ....

....

....

....

....

....

The Shadow of His Wings

Psalm 36:7–12

*"How precious is Your lovingkindness, O God!
Therefore the children of men put their trust
under the shadow of Your wings." (v. 7)*

Bird feeders are located in my back yard. When I slow down enough to enjoy sitting on my deck, seeing all the types of birds that come to feed gives me great pleasure. However, I have never really seen a bird hiding in the shadow of its mother's wings. Since that is the picture David gives us in today's verse, I decided to do a little research. I found wonderful images of mother birds with their offspring nestled under their wings. All baby birds need their mother's protection; but for some, such as chickens and turkeys, it is critical for their survival. Since they nest on the ground or on low-hanging branches of trees, they are protected with the wings of their mothers. Without this protection, the offspring would be vulnerable to predators and likely would not survive.

This imagery of a baby bird nestling up under his mother's wing is used often in Scripture to depict the relationship of God to His people. In Psalm 17:8, David asks God to hide him in the shadow of His wings for protection from the wicked who are after him. In Psalm 57:1, David speaks of taking refuge in the shadow of God's wings as he hides from King Saul in a cave. In Psalm 63:7, David is singing under God's wings as he remembers how God has been his helper and has upheld him with His right hand. In Ruth 2:8–12, Boaz commends Ruth as she left her father, mother, and homeland to take refuge under the shadow of the wings of the God of Israel. She left all behind and confidently put her trust in the God of her mother-in-law, Naomi.

Baby birds assuredly burrow under the wings of their mother because they recognize that she sustains them by feeding them and caring for them constantly. They can trust her. David reminds us in the verses we read yesterday

and today why we can confidently seek shelter or protection under the shadow of God's wings. We run to Him because of His faithful, steadfast love. His love is not ever going to change; it is firmly fixed on us, His children. We can put all our trust in Him, and, as David tells us, this assurance is precious and valuable. I would add that it is critical for our survival.

While we may not be in danger of being gobbled up by a predator, the world in which we live is broken. As you meditate on this verse today, are you, like David, depending on God's shelter and protection from the distressing things of this world? Are you nestled there, confidently singing of the wonderful ways He has been your refuge and help? If not, I urge you to spend today pondering His steadfast, immovable love for you.

Denise O'Donoghue

Prayer: *Approach the Lord for His help today. Seek refuge in His great love. Rest under the protective shadow of His wings.*

Personal Reflection: ....

....

....

....

....

....

It's Not Fair

Psalm 37:1–6

"Commit your way to the LORD,
Trust also in Him,
And He shall bring it to pass." (v. 5)

This psalm was written to address a problem that is as prevalent today as it was when David penned these verses—the apparent prosperity of wrongdoers. Consider a few modern-day examples:

- My neighbor just got the new car I want but cannot afford; I've heard them brag about cheating on their income taxes.
- My husband and I desperately want a baby; my single coworker just joked to me about having her third abortion.
- My heart's desire is to be married; all the single guys seem to go for the girls who are happy to sleep around.

If we are not careful, we are in danger of becoming frustrated, angry, bitter, distracted, or envious of the prosperity of those who do not follow the Lord. Our hearts become anxious. We want to cry out: "It's not fair! Everything seems to go right for those wrongdoers while God ignores me." Just like our original parents, Adam and Eve, when we fall into this sort of thinking, the enemy has us right where he wants us—questioning God's goodness. Not only that, our responses are often sinful: anger, bitterness, envy, etc.

Fortunately, David gives clear instructions about what we are to do when we see evildoers or wrongdoers prosper. First, we learn from Psalm 37:1 that we are not to fret (be worried or anxious): "Do not fret because of evildoers, nor be envious of the workers of iniquity." Jesus reiterates this in His Sermon on the Mount: "Do not worry about your life" (Matt. 6:25).

Second, our focal verse says, "Commit your way to the Lord." The word "commit" (Hb. *galal*) carries the idea of rolling a burden off yourself onto someone else. This description is helpful because it gives us the picture of taking our feelings of unjust treatment to the Lord. Peter reiterates this approach of "casting all your care upon Him, for He cares for you" (1 Pet. 5:7).

The focal verse also says that we are to trust the Lord. He will act according to His timetable. David addresses the short-lived nature of the evildoers: "For they will soon be cut down like the grass and wither as the green herb" (Ps. 37:2).

The apparent prosperity of the wicked will be temporary. Therefore, when we feel as if life is unfair for us, we need to refocus and look to God. Appropriate actions include these:

- Refrain from being anxious or worried.
- Roll the burden onto the Lord.
- Trust Him to act justly according to His perfect timing.

Denise O'Donoghue

Prayer: *Is it easy for you to get caught up in what you perceive to be great injustices around you, especially when you see that those who don't follow God prosper? Keep your focus, and trust solely on God, not on the prosperity of others.*

Personal Reflection: ....

....

....

....

Be Still

Psalm 37:7–22

"Rest in the LORD, and wait patiently for Him;
Do not fret because of him who prospers in his way,
Because of the man who brings wicked schemes to pass." (v. 7)

Be still. How many of us really know what that means today? Whenever I ask people, "How are you?" or "How are things going?" the word *busy* seems nearly always to be included in their response. I think it is precisely because of the busyness of our world today that we feel we must always be doing something. Sitting idly and doing nothing seems foreign.

Psalm 37:7 continues the theme we studied yesterday. What are we to do when we see those not following God prospering? We are to do three key things. Ultimately, we are to roll that burden over to the Lord and trust Him to take the proper action. Now what? Psalm 37:7 tells us that we are to be still before the Lord and wait patiently.

Since we have already established the fact that very few of us know how to be still, what do we do while we wait patiently? Let me offer a few suggestions. As we ourselves become still or quiet before the Lord, let us:

- Reflect on the mercy that God has bestowed on us through the sacrifice of His Son Jesus (Rom. 5:6–10).
- Relish His great love for us. No matter what our circumstances, nothing can separate us from His great love (Rom. 8:35–39).
- Remember our relationship to Him. He is our loving Father, and we are His children. He has already promised justice for us (Luke 18:7–8a).
- Rest reassured in knowing that His will for us, including His timing, is always best for us (Rom. 8:28–29).

- Realize His promise that one day we will no longer endure injustices (Rev. 21:4).
- Renew our minds through the reading of His Word (Rom. 12:2). Our worldly instincts would have us feel sorry for ourselves or seek our own ways of righting the situation. Instead, we need to allow our thinking to be transformed to the point that we embrace God's will in our circumstances.
- Refocus our attention by interceding for others (1 Tim. 2:1–4). Pray for those in authority, pray for those who are lost and in need of a Savior, pray for those who are sick and hurting.
- Rejoice, giving thanks for all of the blessings God has bestowed upon us (1 Thess. 5:16–18).

Of course, simply doing these things as we are still and waiting patiently on the Lord will not change our circumstances. Such actions, however, will settle our minds and strengthen our testimonies of our great God to a watching world.

Denise O'Donoghue

Prayer: *God is sovereign, and He knows we need to be still. Although your nature is not to wait patiently, especially when living in such a wicked and unfair world, give God glory and honor by fully trusting Him to act, bringing about His perfect justice in His perfect timing.*

Personal Reflection: ....

....

....

127

Hold My Hand

Psalm 37:23–40

"The steps of a good man are ordered by the LORD,
And He delights in his way.
Though he fall, he shall not be utterly cast down;
For the LORD upholds him with His hand." (vv. 23–24)

To fall down is embarrassing and often brings physical hurt. Recently, during a big ice and snow storm, my husband wanted to go to the hardware store to buy salt and sand for the driveway, and he asked me to go along. I did my part by doing everything I knew to do to prevent falling when I went outside. I put on the right boots, carefully considered each place I was going to put my foot down, and walked slowly. Not only that, my husband was by my side and had a firm grip on my right arm. Even with all of these precautions, I still could have fallen. However, I know that if I had slipped, my husband would have scooped me up in a second and placed me back on my feet.

Today's verse tells us that the Lord establishes our steps. What is our destination? As believers, we can envision our "destination" as becoming increasingly like Jesus. He has established our steps and helps us arrive at our destination by giving us directions through His Word and by filling us with His Holy Spirit. Our part is to love Him, spend time with Him in Bible study and prayer, worship in community with fellow believers, and love others.

Even with all the safeguards mentioned above, we can still fall into sin as we journey to our destination. Some of those sins are discussed in earlier verses of Psalm 37. For example, we can be easily provoked when the wicked prosper, giving way to wrong attitudes of envy (v. 1), worry (v. 7), and anger (v. 8). Colossians 3 adds malice, slander, filthy language, and more to the list of sinful responses.

The psalmist does have good news! Even if we do fall into sin, we will not stay down because the Lord is holding our hands. Furthermore, Jesus is our advocate and propitiation if we who have placed our trust in Him do sin (1 John 2:1–2). These sins of envy, worry, anger, and the like cannot have control over us because of His wonderful grace (Rom. 6:14).

Today, let's be filled with comfort and joy in the realization that even though we may stumble and fall in our journey to be like Christ, the Lord is ever faithful to put our feet back on solid ground because He holds our hands and lifts us up.

Denise O'Donoghue

Prayer: *Thank the Lord that He has established your steps. Thank Him for giving you all you need to become like Him. Thank Him for the comfort of knowing that even if you slip and fall today, He is holding your hand and will put your feet back on solid ground.*

Personal Reflection: ....

....

....

....

....

....

Why Do the Saints Suffer?

Psalm 38:1–22

"LORD, all my desire is before You;
And my sighing is not hidden from You.
My heart pants, my strength fails me;
As for the light of my eyes, it also has gone from me." (vv. 9–10)

Those who followed Jesus when He walked the earth were quick to assume that any sickness was a result of sin (see John 9:1–2). However, Jesus taught that there were other reasons for sickness and disease (see John 9:3). In this day and age, we are very reluctant to believe any sickness or suffering is a result of sin, especially our own. Perhaps it is because we really have no answer for the question of why followers of Jesus get sick, suffer, and die.

The truth of the matter is that some suffering is the direct result of specific sins. Psalm 38 describes a great list of maladies (vv. 2–8, 10–14, 17, 19–20) as well as the open confession of his sin (vv. 1, 18). The psalmist knows that his condition is directly tied to his sin. Psalm 38 includes descriptions of his suffering: a wretched state of health, guilt over past sin, the account of abandonment by friends and family, the threat from enemies—all of which culminate in inner pain and turmoil. These words are not written to help us diagnose the sufferings of others but to give an example of our response in our own situations.

When you have sinned, you should follow the instruction of David, the writer of this psalm. You should not try to hide the sin, but acknowledge it (vv. 3–4) and confess it before the Lord (v. 18). Repent or you may experience inner turmoil from guilt and shame and a "burden" that is "too heavy" to bear (v. 4). You can cry out in your sufferings. Then you should remember that there is nothing that is hidden from the Lord.

In our focal verses, the psalmist admits that God knows his situation quite well. God knows that he is sick, his family and friends have abandoned him,

and his enemies seek to destroy him. The awareness that God knows all things drives the psalmist to seek God and cry out to Him. In verse 15, he declares his hope in God and his belief that God will hear and answer his prayer. Finally, he declares the Lord to be his Savior as he earnestly pleads for God to hurry to help him (v. 22).

In summary, the actions of the psalmist teach believers how to respond in times of suffering brought on by sin: confess sin, cry out to the Lord, remember the Lord knows full well the situation, and place hope in God for His forgiveness and salvation.

Denise O'Donoghue

Prayer: *Desire the Lord more than sin or self. Renew your commitment to repent quickly when you sin and always put your hope in God.*

Personal Reflection: ....

....

....

....

....

....

It's a Choice

Psalm 39:1–13

"I said, 'I will guard my ways,
Lest I sin with my tongue;
I will restrain my mouth with a muzzle,
While the wicked are before me.'" (v. 1)

Have you ever spoken angry words when someone insulted you? Have you ever attempted justifying words for what came from your mouth? We want to put the blame for our actions on someone who has provoked us. In reality, whatever comes from your mouth comes only through your choice. You either choose to speak sinfully or to guard your mouth faithfully.

The author of this psalm understood this principle and took full responsibility for his words. Apparently, those to whom he refers as "the wicked" often placed him in a position of choosing what would come from his mouth in response. Not only did he take responsibility, but he resolved that any provocation would not end in sinful speech.

Lest any of you have trouble figuring out what might constitute sin with your tongue, let's consult Scripture for insight. The tongue can be used to:

- flatter (Ps. 5:9);
- slander (Ps. 15:3);
- speak deceitfully or lie (Pss. 34:13; 50:19; 78:36; 109:2; Prov. 6:17; Jer. 9:5);
- speak bitter words (Ps. 64:3); and
- boast (Ps. 12:3).

"I like your new hairstyle" is not the sort of complimentary flattery addressed here. Instead, it is flattery with an ulterior motive—a hidden agenda. Slanderous words are spoken as insult or in attempt to defame someone's

character. Deceitful speech may be half-truths or words carefully crafted to imply something without actually saying it. Lying is, well just that, lying. A better choice is to speak only truth motivated by love (Eph. 4:15).

Bitter words are often words spoken from an unforgiving heart, aimed at hurting or retaliating against the person to whom they are spoken. The apostle Paul admonishes that we put away all bitterness (v. 31). He continues that the right choice is to be kind and compassionate, forgiving one another because we have received forgiveness in Christ Jesus (v. 32).

Do not be tempted to boast in your appearance, wisdom, power, or riches. All of these things point to you and give the appearance that you have these things by your own merit. However, we are told that if we boast, it should be in Christ alone (1 Cor. 1:31). Therefore, the right choice is to declare that all we have is because of the grace and mercy of Jesus and is not of our own doing.

I doubt that the psalmist David actually put a muzzle on his mouth to keep from sinning with his tongue, but he did guard his tongue carefully. You can do the same with the choices you make when you are tempted to sin with your mouth. Remember, there is always a choice.

Denise O'Donoghue

Prayer: *Decide to please the Lord with the words from your mouth. Close your devotional time with a prayer of commitment.*

Personal Reflection: ....

....

....

....

It Is My Pleasure

Psalm 40:1–17

"Then I said, 'Behold, I come;
In the scroll of the book it is written of me.
I delight to do Your will, O my God,
And Your law is within my heart.'" (vv. 7–8)

I quickly ordered my food in response to the welcoming voice on the other end of the drive-through intercom. After she efficiently read back my order to check its accuracy, I thanked her. To my surprise, she said: "My pleasure!" I was taken aback for those words are rarely heard in this context. Later, I learned that this particular restaurant regularly trains all their employees to respond to every customer in like fashion. It also pierced me. I thought about my responses to the Lord when He reveals His will to me. Do I tell Him that it is indeed my pleasure, my joy to obey Him?

In this psalm, David recalled the wonderful works of God and his desire to let everyone know what God had done for him. How do you respond to the grace, mercy, and power God has shown to you? David recognized that just performing religious duties—making sacrifices and giving offerings—was not enough. God wanted more—David's whole heart.

The New Testament tells believers to "present your bodies a living sacrifice, holy, acceptable to God" (Rom. 12:1). David willingly presented himself to the Lord, recognizing that God had appointed him to serve as king over Israel. He declared that indeed his greatest delight and joy was to obey God, to do what He commanded, and to do so from the heart!

Even more grandly, these words point to the messianic Son of David, the King over all kings, the Lord Jesus Christ. Indeed, all that is written in "the scroll of the book" reveals this King, a point driven home to two discouraged disciples leaving Jerusalem for Emmaus after the crucifixion (Luke 24:13–32).

All the Scriptures, all the Law and the Prophets, testify of Jesus (John 5:39). Jesus also insisted that His "food"—His satisfaction and delight—were "to do the will of Him who sent Me" (John 4:34). He obeyed every word of God, every direction of God; to do so was His true joy, and in obedience He endured death on a cross!

So often, I am tempted to do just enough to get by in my relationship with Christ as I dutifully check the list of my own legalistic expectations. I read my Bible; I pray; I go to church—check, check, check! But, what a difference comes when I am flooded with complete satisfaction in Christ, and He calls me to follow Him. I cannot wait to hear Him speak through His Word or through prayer; I love being with the believers of the church; and I cannot wait to obey what the Lord asks of me. It truly is "my pleasure."

Janet M. Wicker

Prayer: *Present yourself anew to the Lord. Tell Him it is your pleasure, your delight, to do whatever He asks of you. Arise, then, and obey from your heart with His joy!*

Personal Reflection: ....

....

....

....

....

135

When a Friend Betrays You

Psalm 41:1–11

"Even my own familiar friend in whom I trusted,
Who ate my bread,
Has lifted up his heel against me." (v. 9)

My parents used to say: "Don't kick a dog when it's down." They were telling me that when someone you love, trust, and enjoy as a friend is suffering and defenseless, it is not the time to treat her with added hurt or contempt. Instead, she deserves your love and compassion. But, that is not what happened to David in this psalm. In earlier verses we learn that he is "in time of trouble," "on his bed of illness . . . on his sickbed." He even says that his enemies are eagerly waiting for him to die, and they visit him only to find ways to slander him. But the most hurtful blow to David comes not from these evil opponents but from a friend.

Although the friend is not mentioned by name, we know it was someone with whom David had a close relationship. He trusted this friend and had invited him to his table to share a meal. Some have proposed that it was Ahithophel, the king's confidant and counselor, who joined his rebellious son Absalom in a treacherous conspiracy to dethrone David (2 Sam. 15–17).

This phrase "has lifted up his heel against me" describes literally the lifting up of a foot in order to kick someone. It is the picture of a hurtful wound, one most of us have experienced in our lives. Someone you trusted turned against you—someone you had trusted with your deepest thoughts and affections "kicked you when you were down." The betrayal has left a sharp pain in your heart even now as you recall what happened.

Our High Priest Jesus understands because His trusted companion Judas betrayed Him (John 13:18). Yet, the wounding by a "familiar friend" was the fulfillment of God's redemptive plan. The imprisoned Paul understood, writing in

his last letter about a situation when "no one stood with me, but all forsook me" (2 Tim. 4:9–18). Paul followed the Lord's example and asked that this sin not be held against them. More than ever, in this time of betrayal and abandonment, he knew that the Lord stood with him and gave him the strength to continue to preach the gospel.

To experience the opposition of Satan and his legion is one thing, but it is another to experience the betrayal of a friend. In that moment, may we forgive as Christ forgave us. May we also never forget that our Lord stands with us and will not abandon us. He is a "friend who sticks closer than a brother" (Prov. 18:24).

Janet M. Wicker

Prayer: *Be honest before God about a time of betrayal that still feels like a "kick in the gut." Release forgiveness toward the one who hurt you so deeply, and rejoice that you are not alone or abandoned in Christ.*

Personal Reflection: ....

....

....

....

....

....

Tell Yourself the Truth

Psalm 42:1–5, 11

"Why are you cast down, O my soul?
And why are you disquieted within me?
Hope in God, for I shall yet praise Him
For the help of His countenance....
Why are you cast down, O my soul?
And why are you disquieted within me?
Hope in God;
For I shall yet praise Him,
The help of my countenance and my God." (vv. 5, 11)

I have to admit it; I talk to myself. I warn myself about driving too fast or rebuke myself for having a wrong attitude. I have even argued with myself over an issue. But, I am in good company as I read the words of this amazing psalm, and you are, too! The psalmist is speaking to his own soul, his true inner self, asking questions and even giving words of counsel to himself.

The words come from the heart of someone deeply distressed and depressed. He is desperate for God and is crying constantly while others mock his faith in God. He remembers happier days of joy and praise but now wonders if God has forgotten him. Notice the questions he asks: "True Self, why are you in such despair that you are laid low? Why are you in such inner turmoil?"

Years ago, I looked honestly at myself and asked the same questions. You see, my husband and I wanted to have a child, but I could not conceive. Doctors tried several treatments, but nothing seemed to work. Five years later, we learned that I was finally pregnant. I rejoiced in "the house of God" as we testified of God's faithfulness to answer our prayers.

In the beginning of the second trimester, the doctor arranged an ultrasound imaging session to "see" our little miracle. I will never forget what

happened next. After pointing out a few things and then growing silent, he turned off the screen and said, "I am so sorry but this pregnancy is over. Your baby has stopped developing." A wail unlike anything I had known erupted from deep within me, and I began to sob uncontrollably. This heartbreaking news began my season of despair. Not only was I crying constantly, but I felt that I was a complete failure, and I had lost hope. I did not want to leave home; and if I did, I avoided all eye contact.

On Sunday morning, while alone and recovering from necessary surgical procedures, I finally opened my Bible and read these words that penetrated my sad and even angry heart. "Hope in God, for I shall yet praise Him." The words jumped off the page and I saw the truth: Instead of believing Satan's lies that God had abandoned me, I knew I must now wait for God in confident trust that He is in control and praise Him in faith in the midst of it all. Little by little, words of worship began to spill out of my mouth. I knew God's face was turned to His distressed daughter! The bondage of depression was being broken and hope returned!

Janet M. Wicker

Prayer: *Is it time to give your soul a "pep talk" of truth? Ask yourself these hard questions. Then, choose to praise God in the midst of it all. Thank Him for His past works. Keep the lines of communication with the Father open as He turns toward you to renew your hope.*

Personal Reflection: ....

....

....

Daytime Mercies and Nighttime Songs

Psalm 42:6–10

"The LORD will command His lovingkindness in the daytime,
And in the night His song shall be with me—
A prayer to the God of my life." (v. 8)

The words on the sign planted near the front door of my friend's home said: "WARNING! Protected by Home Security System, 24-Hour Surveillance." I was intrigued and asked, "Oh, I see that you have a security system; what kind is it?" To my surprise, she laughed and said: "Oh, I don't really have one. That fake sign is just to make burglars think I do and back away from my home!" That is when I learned you can buy for your house fake signs or stickers saying you have protection when you really do not. Some "experts" think it deters thieves who just want to make a quick entry and escape, but they also warn that this false statement can be risky. They remind you that the smart burglars can recognize a "con" and break into your home anyway.

I have always battled fear; and since my husband sometimes had to leave me home alone with the children, I wanted a real security system with that added feature of twenty-four-hour, round-the-clock surveillance. I was so thankful when he employed a local, reputable alarm company to come to our house to do the job! I could lay my head down at night knowing they were "watching" and guarding my house from possible intrusions.

This psalm reminds me that my God is greater than any security system devised by man. He watches over me day and night wherever I am! When waves of depression wash over me with fear, grief, or anguish, I remember that the great I Am will command His lovingkindness and merciful redemption to come to me during the day. And, when it is night, He will give me a prayer song to sing.

Paul and Silas had every reason to be depressed! They had faithfully preached the gospel in Philippi but were falsely accused, beaten with rods, and thrown into the depths of prison with their feet fastened to stocks. However, at midnight the entire prison heard them singing His song and prayer to their great God. The Lord sent an earthquake, and everyone's chains fell away. As a result, many were saved and the prisoners even received an apology from the magistrates who had jailed them (Acts 16).

My mother understood this truth, for the nights were hardest when she battled cancer. Sometimes, she thumbed through an old hymnbook to remember familiar words of faith until the day would dawn bringing more clarity. Do not believe the lie that you are all alone and that God does not love you. Fix your heart on His love and sing His song in your night!

Janet M. Wicker

Prayer: *Confess your fears, your questions, and your hurt to the Father. Ask Him to give you faith to trust His mercy. Open your mouth to sing your prayer to Him right now.*

Personal Reflection: ....

....

....

....

....

Cast Down or Lifted Up?

Psalm 43:1–5

"Why are you cast down, O my soul?
And why are you disquieted within me?
Hope in God;
For I shall yet praise Him,
The help of my countenance and my God." (v. 5)

Do you love the funny emojis you can choose to attach to your text messages? They are bright yellow faces with eyes and a mouth, but they express all kinds of obvious emotions. I can choose from more than eighty of them on my phone alone! It is true that our faces reflect all kinds of feelings. The Bible calls it the "countenance" and speaks of prideful, angry, sad, troubled, cheerful, joyful, and glorious countenances.

Depression, such as mentioned here, can have several causes, but many doctors think they can be seen in three major categories: difficult and trying experiences, your way of thinking and responding to challenges, and possible physical deficiencies. The person who is depressed feels abandoned, has no hope for future change, and sees almost everything through a negative lens. Such emotion causes a person's face to be darkened, and the eyes look away from contact with another person and usually focus downward. The face is "cast down" or "fallen." You have seen it before and probably experienced this feeling yourself.

I will never forget the precious young mother I met in Juneau, Alaska, while serving in a mission church there. Overwhelmed by her complicated situation, she was in obvious despair. She still came to our fellowship but would avoid eye-contact and conversation. On this particular day, the pastor chose a song for worship entitled, "Because He Lives," by Bill and Gloria Gaither. As we began to sing, I could see her from my perch on the organ bench. Tears flooded

her cheeks as she sang. It was as if no one else was in the room as she looked heavenward and a literal brightness flooded her face. She told us later that she had come to church asking God to speak to her, or she was going to end her life. The message of this song of praise reminded her of the truth of God's love and light, and hope was reborn.

Here, God is called "the help of my countenance," for He can change the darkness that clouds our faces. When in deep distress, David also praised God as the "One who lifts up my head" (Ps. 3:3). When He works within us, everyone can see the difference on our faces. His light, joy, and hope are reflected on our countenances. You who are "cast down," look to Jesus!

Janet M. Wicker

Prayer: *Ask God to shine His light into your heart to show you the truth about His love and grace. Trust Him with your situation, and turn it completely over to Him. Then, turn your eyes to behold Jesus and look fully into His beautiful face!*

Personal Reflection: ....

....

....

....

....

....

Victory through the Favor of God

Psalm 44:1–16

"For they did not gain possession of the land by their own sword,
Nor did their own arm save them;
But it was Your right hand, Your arm, and the light of Your countenance,
Because You favored them." (v. 3)

In October 1962, when I was just ten years old, we all became aware of a serious threat off the coast of Florida in a tiny country called Cuba. Our enemy Russia was constructing missile launching sites just ninety miles from our Florida coast. A confrontation between the United States and Russia brought us to the brink of possible nuclear war. In our little public school in coastal Georgia, we had bomb drills just like our usual fire drills. When the siren sounded, students were supposed to dive under their desks and sit very still in a crouched position with hands held over our heads. This technique was nicknamed the "duck and cover" maneuver.

The large newspaper in Jacksonville, Florida, carried a picture and instructions for constructing an underground bomb shelter complete with homemade air filtering systems. My uncle built one and filled it with homemade preserves, canned vegetables, and water supplies. I will never forget how it felt to descend into the cramped, dark, and dank shelter, wondering what the world would look like if we actually were bombed by nuclear weapons. To tell you the truth, I know now that neither of those preparations would have saved us from a nuclear attack.

The psalmist is recounting how God had given Israel possession of the land that He had promised to them. God also reminds the people that it had nothing to do with their military power or their abundant provisions, for they had neither. Instead, His strength and power, as symbolized by the right hand and arm, and His blessing and favor had accomplished the great victories they

had experienced. In Psalm 20:7, David recognized the people's dependence on the Lord: "Some trust in chariots, and some in horses; but we will remember the name of the LORD our God."

One of the most significant mileposts in my Christian life came when I realized I absolutely could not live the Christian life on my own. I had tried and tried only to fail time and again. I felt defeated and overwhelmed. I learned that I was never expected to do it myself. Instead, God's life was infused into my life by His Spirit, and His strength overwhelmed my weakness to perform whatever He asked of me. Are you trying to live in your own strength? Are you performing the "duck and cover" against Satan and finding yourself defeated when he attacks? God has shown favor toward you in His Son Jesus. Avail yourself today of His strength and power!

Janet M. Wicker

Prayer: *Thank God that He has not left you without help. Confess your weakness and inadequacy for the task of following Him. Recognize His strength is perfected in your weakness, and live in the victory He has already won for you!*

Personal Reflection: ....

....

....

....

....

Desperate Times Call for Desperate Praying

Psalm 44:19–26

"Why do You hide Your face,
And forget our affliction and our oppression?
For our soul is bowed down to the dust;
Our body clings to the ground.
Arise for our help,
And redeem us for Your mercies' sake." (vv. 24–26)

A few days ago, an attractive woman literally ran to me after we had closed the Bible study. It was her first time to attend our women's study, but she choked out the words: "Please, I need help. I am desperate. I can't do it. Nothing works." I embraced her, and asked her to tell me what was wrong. She quickly told me that she had been addicted to alcohol since she was sixteen years old. Though she was a believer and had been in and out of rehabilitation programs, she was still overcome by this addiction. She asked: "Doesn't God know? I am desperate and I think I will die if I am not delivered from this pain. I need His help. Please, won't you help me? I've been crying all night through the study."

I looked at the young woman helping me that evening and asked her to find some mighty prayer warriors and bring them to us. She returned with two other believing women of God, and we gathered around the distraught lady to pray, laying our hands upon her. We cried out in desperation to our God and pleaded with Him to "Arise for our help, and redeem us for Your mercies' sake" (v. 26). After a time of fervent confession and petition, we arose from that place. She left with peace, and I pray that she knew His victory as well.

You may think that God has turned His face away from you and your pain, agony, and defeat. The enemy certainly wants you to feel that He has forgotten you or even fallen to sleep. The psalmist describes such a time when he felt

completely helpless and possibly close to death. He desperately cried out to the merciful and compassionate God to move into action to help and redeem him.

Hannah was desperate to have a child and fell on her knees in tears to pour out her heart to the Lord. Her prayers were so full of emotion and intensity that the insensitive priest, Eli, accused her of being drunk. But, she told him she had come to cry out to God with her heart's desire to have a son (1 Sam. 1). When you are desperate—at the end of your resources and of yourself—cry out in earnest prayer to God. He will arise to take over and help you. He will arise to show great compassion and mercy. He did that for Hannah, and she gave birth to a son, Samuel, which means literally "God hears." Yes, indeed He does!

Janet M. Wicker

Prayer: *Believe that God is attentive to your deepest needs and has not forgotten you in your suffering. Pour out your heart to Him in honest desperation. Believe that He will arise to meet your need, to help you, and to show you His abundant mercy.*

Personal Reflection: ....

....

....

....

....

....

A Noble Theme

Psalm 45:1–9

"My heart is overflowing with a good theme;
I recite my composition concerning the King;
My tongue is the pen of a ready writer." (v. 1)

I first discovered this verse in high school. I needed to write a theme paper and was not feeling too confident about my ability to do so. The words were jumbled in my mind and nothing I could think of sounded right. As I opened my Bible for my devotion time that day, I happened to read this verse: "My heart is overflowing with a good theme; I recite my composition concerning the King; my tongue is the pen of a ready writer" (v. 1). God knew what I needed to get me through my writer's block. My faith in God grew. I can still remember that day over four decades later. At the time, I thought I would be finished with writing for others when I finished school, but my writing was just beginning. The same God who encouraged my high school writing is at work in my life today.

As my understanding of the Bible has grown, I have come to understand the context of this verse much more clearly. This psalm is a love song for royalty. The psalmist wrote of God's power and the inspiration His words provide. Writing flows from the heart. As we fill our minds with the Word of God and meditate on His truth, we can write and speak with greater clarity and purpose. Our source is higher than our human minds. Even though most of us are not part of royal families, we are adopted by God, the King of kings, and our words must reflect this new relationship.

Communicating with others is like a picture constantly being painted and repainted. We work hard to find just the right shade of words to meet the need in the moment. We must ask God to help us communicate better in everyday situations. Whether speaking or writing, we want our communication to reflect our King. When you send a greeting card to a friend, welcome your husband

home at the end of a work day, send your children off to school, speak kind words to a friend in crisis, or handle a tough situation at work—you must allow God to shape what you communicate to others.

Trust God to give you the right words in the right moment. Fill your mind and heart with His truth, so you are ready to share what is needed. Work on your writing and speaking skills, believing God will inspire you with a good and noble theme.

Ann Iorg

Prayer: *Saturate yourself with God's Word to gain wisdom as you write and speak His truth in a clear and loving way. Guard your heart from bitter words, and remember that gratitude cures attitude.*

Personal Reflection: ....

....

....

....

....

....

....

The Beauty of Trust

Psalm 45:10–17

"Listen, O daughter,
Consider and incline your ear;
Forget your own people also, and your father's house;
So the King will greatly desire your beauty;
Because He is your Lord, worship Him." (vv. 10–11)

This psalm was written in the context of describing a royal wedding. The spiritual application, however, is easy to make. When a couple marries, they join a new family; the new union created has never before existed. This transition is often difficult for the new couple and their extended families. A wholehearted commitment to each other enables the young couple to bond together in trust and love. When they bond with each other securely, a beautiful new relationship emerges. If either person is unable to make a healthy separation from the birth family, problems arise in relating to their extended families.

The word *forget* in these verses may seem too strong, but God wants us to understand the importance of healthy separation. While we maintain our love for our family of origin, the priority for newlyweds is building their own new family. In a spiritual sense, we must let go of our former lives and commit ourselves wholeheartedly to God when we start our relationship with Him. As long as we cling to our old relationships and way of life, we cannot bond securely in our new spiritual union with God.

Understanding the next part of the verse requires looking to the New Testament for some clarification. Similar terminology is found in Peter's writings: "For . . . in former times, the holy women who trusted in God also adorned themselves, being submissive to their own husbands, as Sarah obeyed Abraham, calling him lord" (1 Pet. 3:5–6a). You may have struggled with this verse, but consider that Peter is overstating a concept to make the point. The

150

word *lord* is not capitalized and is a reference to the leader. If you are married, you need to respect your husband's leadership. Wives want to show love, which is a wife's *need*, but God wants a wife to show respect for her husband, which is *his need*. As we learn to respect our husbands, we learn even greater respect to the Lord of lords. The beauty God desires is found in "the hidden person of the heart"; like the "holy women who trusted in God," we can put our hope in God, and adorn ourselves with "the incorruptible beauty of a gentle and quiet spirit" (v. 4).

God is our King. The beauty God desires is inward, not outward. Spiritual beauty is a wholehearted trust in God's love for us. We worship Him in response to a secure relationship to a loving King.

Ann Iorg

Prayer: *Thank God for being a loving King. Let go of your old way of life, forgetting the past and claiming a new future with Him. Learn to trust in your secure relationship with the King of kings so you can reflect the inward beauty God desires.*

Personal Reflection: ....

....

....

....

....

Help in Times of Trouble

Psalm 46:1–7

"God is our refuge and strength,
A very present help in trouble.
Therefore we will not fear,
Even though the earth be removed,
And though the mountains be carried into the midst of the sea;
Though its waters roar and be troubled,
Though the mountains shake with its swelling. Selah" *(vv. 1–3)*

Living in the western United States has given me a new appreciation for these verses. I have been through two mild earthquakes; and although neither was very serious, our furniture moved and our house shook. I have also lived near the ocean for more than twenty years and enjoy going to the beach in both summer and winter. The waves are calm on some days and dangerous on others. Signs warn of "sneaker waves," which come in randomly and sweep people off their feet. One of them knocked me down, showing me the ocean's power to overwhelm anyone at any time. My love for the beach means that we have also vacationed near the ocean. In the Hawaii Volcanoes National Park, a live volcano constantly dumps lava into the sea and creates rising steam plumes. A fascinating sight to see—but from a safe distance!

These experiences have been great reminders of God's protection described in these verses. Earthquakes, lava, and ocean waves can be terrifying when we are exposed to their full force. However, God is even more powerful! Trust in God as a calming refuge—even when the earth is moving and waves are crashing. My first earthquake happened early in the morning. I woke up and asked my husband, "What's that?" He replied, "An earthquake." I rolled over and went back to sleep! My trust in God and also my sleepy head, allowed me to go back to sleep peacefully, knowing God would take care of me.

My confidence in God was not so strong as a younger woman. All kinds of fears plagued me. Because my father died suddenly of a heart attack when I was a child, it has taken me a long time to learn to put aside the imaginary "what ifs" and trust God. First John 4:18—"There is no fear in love; but perfect love casts out fear . . ."—has been an anchor helping me cling to God in the midst of my fears. I have learned that I do not have a fear problem; I have a trust problem. If I really believe the all-powerful, all-knowing God of the universe loves me, how could I possibly be afraid? When our world is shaking and storming, God is our strength. He does not prevent every difficulty, but He sees us through them. God is always there when we need Him.

Ann Iorg

Prayer: *Learn to trust in God's power and His love for you, especially when you are facing difficulties in life. Remember that God is always there for you and will carry you through whatever comes your way.*

Personal Reflection: ....

....

....

....

....

....

God Is God

Psalm 46:8–11

"Be still, and know that I am God;
I will be exalted among the nations,
I will be exalted in the earth!" (v. 10)

Children often ask perplexing questions. One inquisitive preschool daughter of a seminary professor asked her mother, "Where did God come from?" The mother was not sure how to answer such a weighty question, so she decided to default to her theologian-husband. She said, "Your dad will be home in a few minutes. Let's ask him." When the father came home, he pondered the question for a moment and replied, "Well, if we knew where God came from, He wouldn't be God."

God has no beginning and no end, a claim that cannot be made for anyone else. His purposes will ultimately be fulfilled—without exception. Knowing these truths is comforting. We can stop struggling with our circumstances, our inner turmoil, and with others. God is God, and His purposes will be accomplished.

So much in this world is outside of our control—the weather, natural disasters, health issues, and some relationships. Without the peace of knowing God and trusting that His purposes will be fulfilled, how can anyone sleep at night? People foolishly try to escape the turmoil lack of faith in God creates by self-medicating with drugs, alcohol, and other placebos. Still, people struggle in perpetual frustration since nothing substitutes for faith in God to fulfill His purposes.

Various translations use different words in this verse, but the message remains the same—"stop your fighting" (csb); "cease striving" (nasb); and "be still" (nkjv, esv). When Satan sneaks thoughts of doubt and discouragement into our minds, we have a recourse—"casting down arguments and every high

thing that exalts itself against the knowledge of God, bringing every thought into captivity to the obedience of Christ" (2 Cor. 10:5). We refuse to dwell on or act on those negative ideas. Imagine taking evil thoughts prisoner, tossing them into a locked cell, and throwing away the key! That's the image this verse communicates about overcoming destructive thoughts by meditating on God's truth. Memorizing and quoting Scripture over and over when troublesome thoughts enter your mind is the best way to gain control over every doubt about what God wants you to think and do.

God is God whether we trust Him or not. He will ultimately be exalted, whether we exalt Him or not. We might as well stop struggling and share the victory He assures. We can rest in His powerful love and get through each day in peace—no matter what happens or what disturbing thoughts may try to confuse us. God is God, and you are not!

Ann Iorg

Prayer: *Thank God for being God. Thank Him for giving you the power to overcome wrong thinking. Thank God for promising that He will be exalted in the nations and on the earth. Believe in Him, and trust His power.*

Personal Reflection: ....

....

....

....

....

King Over All

Psalm 47:1–2

"For the Lord Most High is awesome;
He is a great King over all the earth." (v. 2)

Most women love a good fairy tale—a damsel in distress gets rescued by a prince who becomes a king. The dreamy palace is always beautiful and elegant. The prince becomes a wise and benevolent king with his loving queen by his side. A good soundtrack helps!

Somewhere inside all of us is a desire to relate to an all-wise, all-knowing leader—a perfect king. We want to know that there is someone greater than we are, who has the power to make things right, and who has the privileges we can only fantasize about enjoying. Examples of earthly kings are often disappointing. They are only a shadow of the perfect king whom we envision. We long for someone better.

Imagining a perfect king is appealing to us because of our great need for God. God is the great King. He is wise and powerful. He can make things right again. He enjoys all the privileges we desire, and best of all He really loves us! Our King is awe-inspiring, to be feared, and everything we dream a King should be. Our King is ruler over all the earth, even the universe. There is nothing outside of His control.

Since our God has these attributes, why are we discouraged? Why do we struggle to believe in Him? In our world, it does not always look like God is in control. There are so many problems like health issues, relational breakdowns, and financial woes. Faith comes in at this point. We have the truth of God's Word, which speaks about both the greatness and goodness of God. We have to decide if we believe what we see around us or what we read in the Bible.

God allows us to experience this strange dilemma. He wants people to genuinely love Him. He has little desire to relate to those who are only interested

in following Him for what they may get from the relationship. God allows our struggles to see where we stand. Do we really love Him and trust Him as our King? Or, do we just come to Him for what we can get from Him in the moment?

Our response to this verse is crucial. God is King—whether things look like they are going well or not. God is King over all the earth even when people do not acknowledge His authority. We serve a real King, better than those we imagine in our fairy tales. He is an awesome ruler over all the earth.

Ann Iorg

Prayer: *Praise God as a real King. Honor Him as the King, not a king. Thank Him for giving you the privilege of being in His kingdom. Honor Him in good times and bad, in every way, every day.*

Personal Reflection: ....

....

....

....

....

....

....

Our Inheritance

Psalm 47:3–9

"He will choose our inheritance for us,
The excellence of Jacob whom He loves. Selah" *(v. 4)*

Everyone appreciates getting an inheritance—something you receive just because someone loves you. An inheritance reflects the wise stewardship and generosity of the giver. An inheritance should promote gratitude since the receiver did not earn the gift.

In the movie *The Ultimate Gift*, a grandfather passes away and leaves an inheritance to his children and grandson. In a surprising turn of events, rather than leaving the grandson money, he makes the young man learn valuable lessons in order to receive his share. He learns to work, to give, to be grateful, to forgive, and a few other important values. Because he has to learn those things before he receives the inheritance, the grandson is able to use what he receives in a purposeful way. The movie powerfully demonstrates that money can be harmful unless you have the character to use it for good.

This story reminds me of God's inheritance for us. He works hard to build our character before He gives us all He desires. We have from God not only the ultimate gift of our Savior, but we have gifts that keep on giving.

First, we have the gift of **salvation**. We are lost in our sins and Jesus died on the cross to take the punishment for the wrongs we have committed. Jesus paid the price, then gave us a fresh start on a new life. Second, we have the gift of **sanctification**. Jesus convicts of sins and offers the power to change through the Holy Spirit. We are not locked into who we were, but we are free to reach our full potential in Christ. Third, we have the gift of **sharing in God's work**. God gives us the privilege of helping others through sharing our faith and helping people grow. Finally, we have the gift of **glorification**. Someday, we will be

perfect in heaven with our Father. We will experience no more sin, no more sorrow, and no more pain. Our weaknesses will not limit us any longer.

While we are on earth, we are tempted to look at our circumstances, our homes, and our bank accounts to determine how much God loves us. But like the grandfather in the movie, God is using circumstances to build our character so we can use our inheritance wisely instead of foolishly wasting it. He wants to give us so much, but will we receive His gifts and use them wisely? That is the challenge of making the most of the eternal inheritance we have been given.

Ann Iorg

Prayer: *Thank God for His ultimate gift, not one you deserved, but one given because of His grace and love. Appreciate all God has done, is doing, and will do for you. Ask Him to help you use what He has given for His honor and glory.*

Personal Reflection: ....

....

....

....

....

....

Wisdom's Perspective

Psalm 49:1–4

"My mouth shall speak wisdom,
And the meditation of my heart shall give understanding." (v. 3)

Everyone wants to be wise, understanding life's complexities for both ourselves and others. God alone possesses and gives wisdom to people: "If any of you lacks wisdom, let him ask of God, who gives to all liberally and without reproach, and it will be given to him" (James 1:5). In this psalm, the writer contrasts human wealth and self-sufficiency with the reality of our mortality. We have a hard time looking past what we see in the present. When we see others who are rich, we may feel like we have been short-changed by God. However, the psalmist understood that what we have on earth is temporary. All the money in the world cannot save our souls. In the end, eternity is what matters.

This world is just a passing moment in time. The writer understood this reality because he had a biblical worldview. His relationship with God, deepened by constant reading, memorizing, and meditating on God's Word, helped him grasp the truth. He was not fooled by appearances. When you have gazed into a clear mirror, you are not fooled by a distorted image reflected by one of lesser quality.

How do we gain the perspective of God's wisdom? Wisdom comes as you read God's Word consistently; your thinking is reframed. There are some over-arching concepts in Scripture that help you understand more detailed passages. First, God is the all-powerful creator and controller of the universe. Second, God is relational. He created us for a relationship with Him, so we cannot please Him without listening and talking to Him. He also created us to relate well to other people. God wants us to care about others like He cares about them: "Jesus said to him, 'You shall love the Lord your God with all your heart, with all your soul, and with all your mind.' This is the first and great commandment.

And the second is like it: 'You shall love your neighbor as yourself'" (Matt. 22:37–39). Third, God is eternal. His timelessness gives Him a perspective we lack because of our mortality.

God was willing to suffer in the short-term so His long-term goal can be satisfied. Jesus' sacrificial death on the cross is the ultimate example of this principle. God waited for the right time to send Jesus, who died for us. Now, all who believe can have eternal life with God. God is patient and sacrifices for the greater good. When we are struggling with life being unfair or frustrated that things are not going as we desire, wisely remember God's powerful, relational, and eternal perspective. Then adopt His perspective as your own.

Ann Iorg

Prayer: *Thank God for His wisdom and perspective as you live your life. Remember what God said in His Word. You will have wisdom and understanding by obeying His Word.*

Personal Reflection: ....

....

....

....

....

....

What Money Cannot Buy

Psalm 49:5–20

*"Those who trust in their wealth
And boast in the multitude of their riches,
None of them can by any means redeem his brother,
Nor give to God a ransom for him—
For the redemption of their souls is costly." (vv. 6–8a)*

Our family lived for twelve years near San Francisco in one of the wealthiest counties in California. Because the area had very few Christians, it was easy to get a picture of wealth without wisdom. People were obsessed with their homes, cars, and dogs, but they neglected their family's relational needs. They bought premium organic foods to stay healthy but simultaneously ruined their health with alcohol and drugs. They pursued all kinds of recreational activities and traveled the world searching for happy experiences.

All their wealth could not buy what they needed most, and their lifestyle choices revealed they were searching for salvation and the abundant life it brings. Jesus paid for our salvation and all we have to do is receive it as a gift. It cannot be bought. Pride stops many people from relating to God because they do not want to admit their need for salvation, which they cannot earn or buy on their own. They foolishly trust in riches and try to insulate themselves from their pain with what money provides.

Christians wisely recognize that God has given us money to use appropriately. We need wisdom to manage our resources. By a global standard, most American Christians are wealthy even if they feel poor compared to others in their communities. We are challenged to be wise stewards of what God has entrusted to us, not fools who use it destructively.

When economic downturns come, they remind us to trust God and continue to be good stewards. No matter our circumstances, we must give

generously, remembering that God owns all He has shared with us. While no one person can give enough to meet all human need, all of us are responsible to give generously to help others.

Avoid being rich fools wasting money on temporal matters. Instead, be wise stewards investing what God has given you in things that are eternal. When you give to mission projects reaching other people with the gospel, you are giving to something that will last. When you provide for your family and give extra to those in need, you are wisely using God's resources. Give generously to meet human needs and share the gospel. You may never be as wealthy as some people in your community, but you can invest wisely for eternity. You can store up eternal rewards with your earthly investments.

Ann Iorg

Prayer: *Thank God for giving you resources. Seek His help to have an eternal perspective on wealth. Pray for wisdom, and give in ways that fit into His kingdom plan. Do not trust in riches but wisely use the resources that God gives you to advance His purposes.*

Personal Reflection: ....

....

....

....

....

Why Do We Give Offerings to God?

Psalm 50:1–23

*"Offer to God thanksgiving,
And pay your vows to the Most High." (v. 14)*

Have you ever thought about why we give offerings to God? Why do we tithe? Why do we give to God? You might say: "We tithe because Scripture tells us to do so" or "Sometimes we give to God because there is a need." For example, your church may be expanding and need financial support to carry out an extension project; all utility bills of the church must be paid off; or all the mission projects need money. Yes, these are legitimate reasons. However, sometimes we forget the most important reason to offer a sacrifice to God—thanksgiving.

Psalm 50:9–13 corrects a misunderstanding about offering a sacrifice to God and about God Himself. In verse 7, the Lord calls the attention of Israel: "O Israel . . . I will testify against you; I am God, your God!" What kind of God is the God of Israel? Verse 8 continues, "I will not rebuke you for your sacrifices or your burnt offerings, which are continually before Me."

The practice of offering sacrifices is not wrong. God does not prohibit it; otherwise, the whole sacrificial system in Israel would have been canceled at that time. What makes a sacrifice wrong is when the motive and purpose of the person offering the sacrifice based on a wrong understanding of God. Verses 9–11 show that the Lord does not *need* animal sacrifices because all the animals are His. He also does not eat or drink the sacrifices (vv. 12–13). The God of Israel is not like other gods who claim to live upon sacrifices and grant favors to their worshipers based on the sacrifices. The God of Israel does not need human beings to feed Him. The motive and purpose for offering sacrifices to God is not to satisfy God's needs. God is self-sufficient and owns the whole universe. In his commentary on Psalm 50:9, John Calvin said, "Man can never benefit God by any of his services."

What is the point of offering sacrifices to God? Rather than benefiting God with our services, God benefits us with His actions. As an expression of thanksgiving for what God has done for us, we offer Him our money, time, energy, service, and devotion. After God answers our prayers, we pay our vows to Him with a heart of thanksgiving.

Offerings are only the concrete expression of our thanksgiving and praise to Him. We give not because God needs but because God has given to us. What has God done for you that prompts your thanksgiving offerings to Him? Just think of Jesus, who has suffered for you, died for you, and been resurrected for you. Does He deserve our whole-life thanksgiving sacrifice?

Hongyi Yang

Prayer: *Pray that God will fill your heart with thanksgiving and that you can find creative ways to offer your thanksgiving sacrifice to Him.*

Personal Reflection: ....

....

....

....

....

....

I Am a Christian. What Should I Do If I Sin?

Psalm 51:1–11

"Create in me a clean heart, O God,
And renew a steadfast spirit within me.
Do not cast me away from Your presence,
And do not take Your Holy Spirit from me." (vv. 10–11)

Before I became a Christian, I seldom felt that I did anything wrong. When I did something wrong, I would not admit it or think it had something to do with God. At the moment of my conversion, sixteen years ago, I suddenly felt that I had done many things wrong and realized I sinned against the One who created me. I asked God to have mercy on me and to forgive all my sins. Then, I experienced an inexpressible peace that I had never tasted before. Until one day when I thought I had lost it!

Soon I understood why I had lost this peace—because I sinned against God. Yes, I found that I had sinned even after becoming a Christian. I felt that my sin affected my relationship with Him. I was not able to concentrate on reading the Bible. God seemed to be far away from me. The indescribable peace that I had recently obtained was gone. What should I do? I knew something had gone wrong between me and Him. I also knew that it was because of me not Him. I did what David did here—not in exactly the same words, but with similar meaning, I asked the Lord: "Create in me a clean heart, O God, and renew a steadfast spirit within me. Do not cast me away from Your presence, and do not take Your Holy Spirit from me" (vv. 10–11). I sought God's forgiveness and the peace came back immediately!

Psalm 51 is known as David's prayer of repentance. After Nathan the prophet confronted David about his adultery with Bathsheba and the murder of her husband Uriah, David realized that he had greatly sinned against the Lord. He prayed this famous prayer, with which Christians of all generations can

identify. David knew that only God can "create a clean heart" and only God can "renew a steadfast spirit." He asked God to cleanse him from his sins (vv. 7–9) and to restore him and his relationship with God (vv. 10–12). A Christian must confess and repent after she sins. Christians will still sin in this present life on earth. The only way to deal with this problem is genuine repentance before the Lord, who will surely cleanse and restore us. The apostle John affirmed: "If we confess our sins, He is faithful and just to forgive us our sins and to cleanse us from all unrighteousness" (1 John 1:9–10).

Hongyi Yang

Prayer: *Examine your heart and life to see if there are any sins hindering your fellowship and communion with the Lord. If so, pray this prayer of repentance and ask Him to forgive you and restore you. You will surely experience the peace of God!*

Personal Reflection: ....

....

....

....

....

....

Regaining Joy

Psalm 51:12–19

"Restore to me the joy of Your salvation,
And uphold me by Your generous Spirit.
Then I will teach transgressors Your ways,
And sinners shall be converted to You." (vv. 12–13)

After asking God to cleanse him from his sins (vv. 7–9), David prayed that God would restore him—creating a clean heart in him, renewing a steadfast spirit in him, and restoring to him the joy of salvation (vv. 10–12). Sin steals our joy. Temporarily, sin may bring a sense of pleasure and happiness. However, sin eventually leads to distress, depression, and despair. David knew the effects of sin. He vividly described them in another psalm: "When I kept silent, my bones grew old through my groaning all the day long. For day and night Your hand was heavy upon me; My vitality was turned into the drought of summer" (Ps. 32:3–4). There is no joy in a sinful and unrepentant life.

Although believers will not lose their salvation after they sin, they may lose their joy. Have you ever lost your joy, whether briefly or for a long time? Do you know the reason(s)? There may be many reasons, and each case is different. However, one possible reason is an unresolved sin in your life. The only way to regain your joy is to repent and ask God's mercy, just as David does in Psalm 51. He knew that only God could restore to him the joy of salvation. He also knew that only God, through His Spirit, could uphold him and keep him from falling again (v. 12b). We need God's grace and power not only to cleanse and restore us but also to sustain us for righteous living.

Then David committed himself to teach transgressors the ways of God so that they would turn to Him. A person who is saved and has experienced God's forgiving grace will not and should not keep it to himself. You cannot help expressing the amazing salvation from God and sharing with others the

goodness of God, just like the Samaritan woman, who joyfully told her testimony, even without hiding her shameful past, to everyone she met.

Once you are forgiven by God and have received the grace of salvation, you have the qualifications to be a witness for the Lord. You do not need to be a Bible teacher, a seminary professor, or a professional minister in order to teach transgressors God's ways and help them return to God. Your life experience of learning God's ways, experiencing His forgiving grace, and knowing His power of restoration give you the authority to teach those who rebel against God and persuade them to take the same way as you did to return to God.

Hongyi Yang

Prayer: *Spend time with the Lord. Ask yourself if you have the joy of salvation. If not, ask yourself when you lost it and why. Deal with the issue that has robbed you of joy before the Lord. If you are joy-filled, thank God for His grace and pray that He will give you opportunities to witness for Him.*

Personal Reflection: ....

....

....

....

....

....

Trust in the Lord and Praise Him Forever

Psalm 52:1–9

"I will praise You forever,
Because You have done it;
And in the presence of Your saints
I will wait on Your name, for it is good." (v. 9)

People who think that they can achieve their purposes and obtain what they want through evil means and deceitfulness are always with us. They climb up social ladders by trampling on others. They gain wealth through lies and deception. They build their reputations upon boastful words and achieve success through schemes to destroy others. They slander people and report information with a purpose of harming others. How do you respond to these people? If you find that they are doing you harm, how do you deal with it, especially if you are afraid of them?

In Psalm 52, David answers these questions. He himself had experienced difficulties caused by people who wanted to harm him. The composition of this psalm is associated with an incident in which Doeg the Edomite betrayed David by informing King Saul of David's location. Saul summoned and then killed the priests who had helped David when he had fled from Saul (1 Sam. 21:1–9; 22:6–22).

This psalm has three parts. The first part describes the character of a "mighty man," probably Doeg the informer (Ps. 52:1–4). He boasts in evil, speaks lies, devises destruction, and loves evil more than good. Interestingly, the description of his wickedness mainly focuses on his words. He is a person who brings others destruction primarily through his words.

The second part of this psalm notes: In the end, God will intervene and destroy such a person (vv. 5–7). He will become a laughingstock and a bad example. The third part shows that the one who trusts in the Lord will be "like a green

olive tree in the house of God," and he will praise the Lord forever (vv. 8–9). In verse 9, the psalmist gives thanks to and praises the Lord because the Lord has brought judgment upon these wicked people and has protected him. Even though God has not acted yet, David will "wait on" His name with confidence, "for it is good." The main theme is clear: Those who appear strong through wickedness and deception will be destroyed by God, but those who trust in the mercy of God will live and praise the Lord forever.

David gives counsel for dealing with people who are conspiring evil to harm us. Such a person may achieve his goal temporarily, but in the end he will be judged by God. We just need to trust God and wait for His deliverance and vindication. After He intervenes, we give thanks to God and praise Him not just for a while but forever.

Hongyi Yang

Prayer: *Have you ever been shaken when you find certain people intending to do harm to you in wicked ways? Fix your eyes upon God and ask Him to give you faith and confidence in His justice and love for you. Without His permission, nothing will happen.*

Personal Reflection: ....

....

....

....

....

God Is My Helper

Psalm 54:1–7

"Behold, God is my helper;
The Lord is with those who uphold my life." (v. 4)

During this time in his life, David was in the midst of much distress. Saul, king of Israel and David's father-in-law, was trying to kill him. David became a fugitive and hid wherever he could. Doeg the Edomite betrayed him by informing Saul about David's visit to Nob. Now another group of people, whom David called "strangers," also rose up against him (v. 3). Have you ever been in situations like these, when some people mistreat and persecute you and others help them to achieve their evil purposes for you?

Most of us have had similar experiences. Maybe your boss does not like you and deliberately gives you trouble. Your colleagues cooperate with him to trap you. Or your fellow-workers falsely accuse you and your supervisor believes them. Perhaps your in-laws do not accept you and you are excluded from your spouse's family. Even in the church, supposedly characterized by love and justice, some people may abuse you and others afflict you with slander and false accusations. Nearly everyone has been wronged, misunderstood, mistreated, or even falsely accused and persecuted. Like David, we can let such situations drive us to our ultimate asylum with the One who not only is able but who also will protect us.

"Save me, O God, by Your name," David cries at the very beginning of this psalm (v. 1). His urgent plea is for protection. He knows that only God can and will deliver him from such an extreme circumstance (v. 4b). God will punish his enemies and destroy them (v. 5). Then the psalmist will voluntarily offer sacrifices to God and praise His name (v. 6).

When you are in situations like those David encountered, remember that "God is my helper; the Lord is with those who uphold my life" (v. 4). Notice

that instead of "The Lord is with me," David says, "The Lord is with those who uphold my life." This picture of God shows Him among David's friends and caring for David through them.

Some believe that this expression in Hebrew is the same as "The Lord is my only upholder." In either sense, God is the One who preserves his life. God may miraculously deliver you by Himself or through other people. In both cases, the Lord ultimately is the One who protects and delivers you from all trouble. We all have sufferings in the world, whether physical, relational, financial, or circumstantial. Remember and trust what the same God says in the New Testament: "In the world you will have tribulation; but be of good cheer, I have overcome the world" (John 16:33b).

Hongyi Yang

Prayer: *Reflect on how God delivered you out of troubles in the past. Give thanks to Him for what He has done and for the friends whom He has brought to uphold you. Entrust all your current troubles to Him and wait in confidence for His deliverance once again.*

Personal Reflection: ....

....

....

....

....

Flee to the Lord!

Psalm 55:1–11

"So I said, 'Oh, that I had wings like a dove!
I would fly away and be at rest.'" (v. 6)

For a period of time in my life, I was thinking like David. I desired to escape from circumstance in which daily I was questioned, humiliated, despised, ignored, and excluded. Short moments of being absent from these circumstances were rare breaths of fresh air for me. As I read this psalm, I can understand and identify with David's feelings.

This psalm is a prayer, a very emotional prayer. At the beginning, David pleaded with God to be attentive to his supplications (v. 2a). Instead of asking God for something, he poured out his heart before God and expressed how he felt at that moment: "I am restless in my complaint, and moan noisily. . . . My heart is severely pained within me, And the terrors of death have fallen upon me. Fearfulness and trembling have come upon me, And horror has overwhelmed me" (vv. 2b–5). He was anxious, distressed, terrified, and desperate; and David communicated his emotions honestly before the Lord (vv. 2–8).

"So I said, 'Oh, that I had wings like a dove! I would fly away and be at rest" (v. 6). Escape! This desire filled his heart and was probably the only option for him. Unrealistically David imagined himself as a dove escaping from his situation while, in reality, he fled to the Lord in prayer. We know the rest of the story found in the psalm. The psalmist regained strength, hope, and faith in the Lord. At the end of the psalm, he declared, "I will trust in You" (v. 23c). His trust in this almighty and just God dispelled his fear, anxiety, and desperation.

What is your way of escape from unpleasant circumstances, anxiety, fear, and desperation? Do you watch a funny movie when you feel depressed so that you can laugh and temporarily forget your problem? Do you go shopping or eat to calm your fears? Do you take anxiety pills or talk with your friends? Do

you try to work it out through your own devices without acknowledging the Lord? Any of these may be helpful to some extent or for the moment. However, through years of struggling, I have gradually understood that the best and most effective way to handle my struggles is to pour out my heart before the Lord, as David did. Sometimes, it is too painful even to formulate words in my mind, but God understands my heart. Even being silent before Him brings comfort, strength, and hope. The source of strength to which you run when you are in distress makes a difference. Ultimately, nothing or no one can give you comfort and hope except the true and living God.

Hongyi Yang

Prayer: *If you are anxious, fearful, or depressed now, go to the Lord and tell Him your feelings and emotions with words or in silence. Flee to the Lord. He will never disappoint you.*

Personal Reflection: ....

....

....

....

....

....

What a Friend We Have in Jesus

Psalm 55:12–21

"For it is not an enemy who reproaches me;
Then I could bear it.
Nor is it one who hates me who has exalted himself against me;
Then I could hide from him.
But it was you, a man my equal,
My companion and my acquaintance." (vv. 12–13)

Psalm 55:12–13 cites one more reason for David's deep distress—the treachery of a close friend. This friend was described as his "companion" and "acquaintance," one whom David knew well. This friend shared spiritual intimacy with David in worshiping the Lord: "We took sweet counsel together, and walked to the house of God in the throng" (v. 14). The betrayal of such a close friend, mixed with the fear of his enemies, was almost more than David could bear: "My heart is severely pained within me" (v. 4).

The afflictions coming from your enemy are expected because an enemy seeks to destroy. However, the reproach from a friend is shocking because a friend is loved and trusted. We can hide from the attacks of our enemies because we are on guard against them. However, a friend's betrayal is hard to escape because it catches us off guard. We expect that some nonbelievers may slander, mock, and hurt us since they do not know the Lord or how to treat their fellow human beings with love. They may hate us because they hate Jesus. However, sometimes our fellow believers, rather than nonbelievers, hurt us the most. This hurt is unexpected and hard to accept. Those who can break our hearts the most are sometimes closest to us, such as a husband, child, friend, or coworker.

I do not know why God lets some of us experience deep personal hurt caused by one of our intimate friends. Joseph was betrayed by his own blood

brothers. David was reproached by his unnamed companion. Jeremiah was mistreated by his own people. Jesus Himself was betrayed by one of His twelve disciples—Judas Iscariot. Jesus is a friend who will never reproach or betray you. Having tasted the sufferings in the world, Jesus is the One who can comfort you and give you strength to overcome all you suffer in the world.

The lyrics of the hymn "What a Friend We Have in Jesus" magnify this theme: "Do thy friends despise, forsake thee? Take it to the Lord in prayer!" David eventually overcame his distress because he "took it to the Lord in prayer." Through prayer, he became confident that the Lord would deliver him. He sang, "As for me, I will call upon God, and the Lord shall save me" (v. 16).

Hongyi Yang

Prayer: *Thank God for the faithful friends that He has brought into your life. They are wonderful gifts from Him. If you have been betrayed by a close friend, reflect on Jesus, who also experienced the same pain of betrayal. He knows what you have gone through or are going through and will heal you at a proper time.*

Personal Reflection: ....

....

....

....

....

Let God Take Charge of Your Burden

Psalm 55:22–23

*"Cast your burden on the LORD,
And He shall sustain you;
He shall never permit the righteous to be moved." (v. 22)*

Some nights I have trouble falling asleep. I close my eyes and give all my effort, but I remain awake and my brain stays active. I toss and turn on my bed and do not feel sleepy at all. Sometimes I think that I probably have drunk too much tea or coffee, or my allergies may prevent me from sleeping, or perhaps the room temperature is too high. However, the truth of the matter is that in many cases, I am too anxious to have a restful sleep. I did not sleep at all the night before my dissertation defense. I could not fall asleep the night before I led a Bible study for the first time. I did not sleep for two nights in a row when I took the national college entrance examination. Fears, worries, and anxiety prevented me from having a good night's sleep. I carried my burden all the way to bed.

David carried a different burden in Psalm 55. His enemies were persecuting him and seeking his life. He was terrified and desperate (vv. 1–8). Even worse, he had just learned that one of his close friends had betrayed him (vv. 12–14). Verses 20–21 may be a portrait of this person: "He has put forth his hands against those who were at peace with him; He has broken his covenant. The words of his mouth were smoother than butter, but war was in his heart; His words were softer than oil, yet they were drawn swords." David's burden was unbearable. Where could he unload his burden? With whom could he share his burden?

David cried out: "Cast your burden on the Lord, and He shall sustain you; He shall never permit the righteous to be moved" (v. 22). He did not say, "Share your burden with the Lord" but, "Cast your burden on the Lord." You do not just share some of your burden with the Lord; instead you "cast," "give," or "throw" them on Him. The Hebrew word *burden* here has the connotation of "gift" or

"what is given." All our burdens actually are "given" by God. He allows what happens to us and He knows what we can bear. Every burden we carry has been measured by God. He will not let you be completely crushed. Instead, He will sustain you: "Therefore humble yourselves under the mighty hand of God, that He may exalt you in due time, casting all your care upon Him, for He cares for you" (1 Pet. 5:6–7).

Hongyi Yang

Prayer: *What burden are you carrying now? Go to the Lord and entrust your cares, worries, and burdens to Him and let Him take charge.*

Personal Reflection: ....

....

....

....

....

....

....

Tears in a Bottle

Psalm 56:1–13

"You number my wanderings;
Put my tears into Your bottle;
Are they not in Your book?" (v. 8)

Have you ever felt like you were walking around with a target on your back? David felt like that when he was being chased by Saul. In an hour of deep despair and fear, David fled. Running away and taking refuge in cities such as Nob and Gath, David was confronted with several hurdles. From eating the consecrated bread in the tabernacle (1 Sam. 21:1–6) to acting like he was insane (1 Sam. 21:10–15), David certainly got creative when thinking of ways to protect himself from his tormentors.

In Psalm 56:1–4, David cried out for mercy and deliverance from death at the hands of his enemies. Consumed with fear but strengthened by faith, David affirmed that through God alone he was given the power to praise and trust Him. David reminded the Lord of the sufferings he had endured while in exile and then suggested that these sufferings automatically qualified him to have his prayers answered and his enemies defeated (vv. 8–9). Do you remind God of the heartache through which you have walked, as if He is not omniscient? God knew about David's wanderings and numbered them (Ps. 121:8). Over the years, archaeologists have unearthed small tear bottles in which mourners collected their actual tears before depositing the bottle at the graveside of a loved one. The point is simply that God is aware of what we feel and how we suffer. His records are accurate.

The statements of faith and praise in this psalm provide assurance that human beings and circumstances cannot overcome those who place their trust in God alone. This hope is rooted in God's justice and mercy. The psalmist's

tears of lament are so precious to God that He collects and preserves them. Be assured that you are precious to God, too.

Are you facing seemingly impossible circumstances or fearful situations? Do you believe that God hears your cries to Him and that He cares for you? In the midst of fear, those who trust in God can recall these wonderful words of the psalmist and be confident of God's deep love.

Jessica Pigg

Prayer: *Fear of Saul temporarily clouded David's faith in the Lord. When battling both seen and unseen enemies, you may easily take your eyes off God and place them on temporal things. Are you fixing your eyes on God or man? Pray that you fear the Lord more than you fear man. Join the psalmist David who said: "This I know, because God is for me" (v. 9).*

Personal Reflection: ....

....

....

....

....

....

The Perfect Refuge

Psalm 57:1–11

"Be merciful to me, O God, be merciful to me!
For my soul trusts in You;
And in the shadow of Your wings I will make my refuge,
Until these calamities have passed by." (v. 1)

Do you have a place of escape—a sacred place in which you find refuge? Let me guess; it is probably not a cave. After his deliverance recorded in Psalm 56, David fled for protection in a cave. Psalm 57 introduces the phrase "Do Not Destroy" in the title, which prescribes the tune to which the psalm was to be sung. The heading or title of this psalm refers either to David's escape from Saul into the cave of Adullam (1 Sam. 22:1–2) or to David's refusal to take Saul's life in a cave in the wilderness (1 Sam. 24:1–7).

The opening words of Psalm 57 are identical with those of Psalm 56 ("Be merciful to me, O God"). David depended on the grace of God to see him through the many trials he encountered. David's cries of worship and prayer for help turned the cave into a sacred place where he could hide and take refuge under the "shadow of God's wings." The image of hiding under the protective spread of the divine wings is used several times in the book of Psalms (17:8; 36:7; 63:7). Despite circumstances, David would take refuge in the shadow of God's wings until the storms had passed.

Rather than focusing on the treacherous attack of the wicked (Ps. 56), the psalmist here brings to the foreground a confident sense of God as the place of "refuge" in time of trouble. The term *refuge* is defined as a condition of being safe or sheltered from pursuit, danger, or trouble. David knew all too well what it was like to be on the run and in the crosshairs of his enemy. However, he had taken refuge in the Lord many times in the past, and he knew the Lord was

faithful to deliver him until his calamities passed. The term *calamities* refers to a destructive storm that could engulf an individual.

Finding refuge in God does not mean the psalmist will escape any remnant of suffering. That refuge is in the midst of trouble and provides an enduring confidence even in the face of all evidence to the contrary (Ps. 57:4). Despite having begun as a lament (vv. 1–4), this poem ends on a confident note with words of thanksgiving and praise (vv. 6–11).

As you read through these psalms, you can appreciate the honesty David brought to the Lord when experiencing loss. He cried out, asked questions, and at times expressed anger. Yet, he was always transparent and confident he would find peace in the "God Most High" (Hb. *'Elohim 'elyon*, v. 2). Do you rest in the confidence of God? Do you find refuge in Him or in worldly things?

Jessica Pigg

Prayer: *Ask God to focus your eyes on His sovereign protection and not the storms that attempt to engulf you. Seek the prefect refuge, and He will give you perfect rest.*

Personal Reflection: ....

....

....

....

....

Rescued

Psalm 59:1–17

"I will wait for You, O You his Strength;
For God is my defense." (v. 9)

In June 1995, Scott O'Grady's plane was shot down over enemy territory. He remained focused on the fact that his rescue package would eventually come, even though he could hear the approaching steps of his enemy. After almost a week, O'Grady's faith that he would soon be rescued was rewarded when he heard two CH-53 Sea Stallions with 51 U.S. Marines from the 3rd Battalion approaching. Just as O'Grady had faith that his rescue would eventually come, so, too, did the psalmist watch for his coming rescue.

Psalm 59 continues the string of laments going back to Psalm 54. Despite the attacks of the enemy coming from all directions, the psalmist remains confident because God is a refuge and fortress in times of trouble (59:16). The title suggests that this prayer is connected to the season in David's life when Saul sent men to kill him. David prayed for deliverance from the enemies who sought his life for no good reason (v. 3). Describing the vicious threats and attacks of his enemies, David said that they "growl like a dog" (vv. 6, 14). There are many ways the "dogs" of our world continue to plague us. They still snarl in the background, nip at our heels, threatening to undo us.

What keeps us from dissolving into fear and despair? What hope do we have? Psalm 59 offers us the picture of a God who laughs at His enemies (v. 8). Even with the vicious snarling and snapping of all the "dogs" of our world, God remains faithful and in complete control.

After an initial invocation of God and plea for deliverance, the psalm is divided into two stanzas, each of which concludes with a similar refrain (vv. 9, 17). Just like O'Grady watched for his coming rescue, the psalmist responded to the enemy's attacks by watching diligently for the coming of God's strength and

deliverance (v. 9). God's strength had already occurred and had become a cause for praise, and the psalmist moved to acknowledge that God was the source of his own strength (v. 17). God not only had the power that delivered but also provided the psalmist with strength to endure faithfully in the face of the enemy onslaught. This demonstration of faith is the very definition of standing within the protective refuge of God.

The term "defense" (Hb. *misgav*, "lofty place or rock affording shelter and protection; refuge"; vv. 9, 17) is an image not only portraying the security and protection David found in God. This is true not only for the psalmist, but also for believers as well. When our eyes are waiting and watching for God to come and lift us up to a height that the enemy cannot touch, our eyes no longer focus and dwell on our circumstances. What dogs are nipping at your heels? In what ways and aspects of your life do you need to wait for the Lord?

Jessica Pigg

Prayer: *With thanksgiving, pray and praise God for being the blessed hope and glory that will one day appear to rescue you from this world (Titus 2:13).*

Personal Reflection: ....

....

....

....

....

Prayer for Restoration

Psalm 60:1–12

"Give us help from trouble,
For the help of man is useless.
Through God we will do valiantly,
For it is He who shall tread down our enemies." (vv. 11–12)

As a pastor's wife, I have the unique privilege of seeing restoration occur in a variety of ways. Just over the past years, I have seen a marriage that was affected by unfaithfulness and abandonment restored after countless hours of prayer and counseling, as well as a family united and restored after the return of a prodigal child. I am sure that you, too, have seen the beautiful picture of restoration played out right before your eyes or in your local church. The term *restoration* is an act of being restored back to the former or original condition. Psalm 60 (like Pss. 44 and 108) is a national lament and plea for deliverance following a painful defeat by a foreign enemy. The defeat is viewed as divine rejection and punishment, and within this psalm there is an urgent prayer for the *restored* favor of God.

Psalm 60 expresses distress and grief over Edom's successful attack on the southern part of Judah while David and most of his army were fighting in the north. The poem's initial tone is one of defeat rather than victory. During this time, military defeat was viewed as a sign of God's rejection or displeasure upon a nation (v. 1). Such defeat seemed as devastating as an earthquake (v. 2), affecting the people so that they experienced confusion (v. 3), wondering why God had failed to come to their rescue. However, those who fear the Lord have confidence in His power (v. 4).

In verse 11, the psalmist calls upon God directly to aid His people against their enemies and acknowledges that human power is ultimately to no avail. David recognized that the help of man was "useless" in the difficult

circumstances in which David and his men found themselves. Despite beginning as a lament, this psalm ends on a triumphant note of victory. The psalmist faithfully clings to hope in God and ultimately defeated the Edomites or Syrians (v. 12; 2 Sam. 8; 1 Chr. 18:3, 12). David expressed confidence that God would defeat the enemies of His people (Ps. 60:11–12). This confident assurance must be read as a hopeful profession of faith, standing as it does in such close proximity to the preceding pictures of divine abandonment and human powerlessness.

Israel has no hope unless God is willing to act in her behalf. The earlier commitment of God to divide the land for the sake of His people remains the hope that God still has plans to maintain His covenant promises (vv. 6–8). Therefore, the psalm is able to conclude with a triumphant shout: "Through God we will do valiantly, For it is He who shall tread down our enemies." In what ways do you need God to act in your behalf?

Jessica Pigg

Prayer: *Praise God for restoring you in times when you have been defeated by sin. Trust Him to help you in the future when you face trouble.*

Personal Reflection:

Kiss the Waves

Psalm 61:1–2

"Hear my cry, O God;
Attend to my prayer.
From the end of the earth I will cry to You,
When my heart is overwhelmed;
Lead me to the rock that is higher than I." (vv. 1–2)

A pastor once said, "I have learned to kiss the wave that throws me against the Rock of Ages." What does it look like to "kiss the waves"? Visualize yourself praising God in the midst of the storm, remembering how He delivered you in the past and trusting Him to deliver you today. Learning to "kiss the waves" is a gift of God's grace because it throws you wholly into His faithful arms.

As in many of the psalms, notably the psalms of lament, the poet sought the safety of God's presence in difficult times. As in so many of the pleas for deliverance, the psalmist begins by calling God to listen to his predicament ("Hear my cry"). The cry is an urgent request for God to "attend" to David immediately. The phrase "from the end of the earth" is used several times within the Psalter and Old Testament to refer to the most remote and isolated areas of the world (v. 2). In this passage, the phrase has been interpreted in several different ways. First, it has suggested David's experiencing exile from his home or his being near death (v. 2). Second, the phrase also depicts David's alienation and spiritual distance from the Lord. In any case, he continued to pray, earnestly petitioning God to hear and attend to his cry.

Isolated and distant from support and familiarity, the psalmist's heart becomes "overwhelmed" (v. 2). Doesn't that happen to us, too? When we take our eyes off God, our strength and rock, we begin to feel overwhelmed. The image of the Lord as "rock" is a familiar one in David's writings (Pss. 18:2, 31, 46; 62:2, 6, 7). In this verse, the refuge that David is seeking is envisioned as a

remote and rugged cliff in the wilderness. The word *rock* used here normally describes a rocky outcropping that could provide natural defenses to those on the run from their enemies. David longed to be guided to a "rock that is higher," likely a reference to God Himself (Ps. 18:2). One can almost picture the psalmist frantically reaching upward along the rock and seeking the down-stretched hand of God to pull him to safety.

Jessica Pigg

Prayer: *Ask the Lord to teach you what it means to "kiss the waves," which throw us against Him. The storms that come will not last forever, but He will. Finally, read and pray to God (Pss. 18:2; 61:1–2).*

Personal Reflection: ....

....

....

....

....

....

....

At Home in the House of God

Psalm 61:3–4

"For You have been a shelter for me,
A strong tower from the enemy.
I will abide in Your tabernacle forever;
I will trust in the shelter of Your wings. Selah" (vv. 3–4)

Her name is Norma Oliver, but I have the privilege of calling her Gram because I am the thirteenth of her seventeen grandchildren. She is the quintessential grandmother who cooks amazing meals, makes you laugh until you cry, loves and supports, and always has a candy stash. For me growing up, her home was always the place where I wanted to sit and dwell for hours, a safe shelter from all that was happening outside its walls.

As the psalmist reflected on past experiences of deliverance and protection, he continued to hope that God would again be his "shelter" and "strong tower from the enemy" (v. 3). Time after time, God had sheltered the psalmist from his enemies, and God would remain his shelter and strong tower. Like Psalm 61:3, Proverbs 18:10 describes Yahweh as a "strong tower" that provides safety to "the righteous," who run to Him for protection. During the time of David, such towers were often included within the defense strategy of a city and acted as the final secure place, if the city walls were breached. Just as the towers provide safety, Yahweh is the strong tower, high and inaccessible to your enemies.

In Psalm 61:4, the psalmist switches metaphors to envision an even more secure life abiding "forever" in the "tabernacle" of God. The verb "abide" (Hb. *gur*) means to live as a resident alien or guest. To abide in God's "tabernacle forever" is unmistakably reminiscent of Psalm 23:6. However, the verb "dwell" (Hb. *yashav*) in that verse stresses permanently settling in a place. Although the psalmist desires the absolute security of the divinely exalted "rock" (61:2),

he will settle for the more tentative status of a sojourner in God's "tabernacle" (v. 4). David knew he would be secure forever in the "shelter" or protection of God's "wings" (cp. Pss. 17:8; 27:5; 31:20; 32:7; 60:4; 91:1; 119:114). In whatever circumstance or location David found himself, he would continue to seek security and refuge in the presence of the Lord.

Do you seek refuge in the presence of the Lord? Is His tabernacle a place where you want to "abide" or "dwell" forever? Let's be women who seek to be present with the Lord each day, sitting still long enough to hear His voice, praying and praising His name, and truly abiding in Him as we walk through the trials this world throws our way.

Jessica Pigg

Prayer: *Take a moment to sit and abide in the presence of God. Allow your prayer time to reflect on God as being your perfect shelter and place of absolute rest from the stress of life and sin.*

Personal Reflection: ....

....

....

....

....

....

I Do Solemnly Declare . . .

Psalm 61:5–8

"For You, O God, have heard my vows;
You have given me the heritage of those who fear Your name." (v. 5)

You may remember your wedding day when you stood in a white dress in front of your friends, family, and loved ones to say your vows. After you and your groom repeated those vows to each other, did you both just leave them at the altar? Or, did you carry those vows with you, remembering and cherishing them? Much like our relationship with Christ, marriage vows are not just a wedding ritual, they are commitments that must be renewed day after day, year after year.

In Psalm 61:5, the "vows" to which David refers are those made as part of his prayer for deliverance during a time of distress in which he promised to praise God's name. The psalmist's vow to praise God's name in the midst of such tension and isolation reveals his commitment and devotion in his relationship with God. This is not some secret promise made to himself but a commitment he has made openly before an almighty God. This mention of "vows" is also repeated in the final verse (v. 8). The vows made by the psalmist were not promises made just once; rather, they indicate a covenant that required daily renewal and fulfillment ("That I may daily perform my vows"). To leave commitment at the wedding altar is almost invariably to condemn the relationship to failure from the start. Therefore, if we would truly desire to find protection under the wings of God, we must bind ourselves to Him in longing and desire and build a relationship of lasting commitment.

Those who "fear" or reverence God's name enjoy His "heritage" (Hb. *yerushah*, "possession, inheritance"), a term identifying with both the promised land and the benefits of life in the covenant with the Lord. This "heritage" is one that sustains those who "fear" God even when they find themselves crying to God from "the ends of the earth" (v. 2). So, what does it mean to fear

God? Fear of God is not trembling with terror like a traitor awaiting the king's judgment. Instead, it is the appropriate awareness that you are absolutely and completely dependent on God for everything. As a woman who fears the Lord, you are to be constantly aware that you are in the presence of the holy, just, all-powerful God of the universe. This awareness means that you devote yourself to Him and His ways, completely pursuing Him above all things and deliberately committing your life to glorify Him.

Jessica Pigg

Prayer: *Share with God the vows you have made to Him, and commit afresh to follow those vows in worship and fear before Him.*

Personal Reflection: ....

....

....

....

....

....

....

Our Refuge

Psalm 62:1–12

"Trust in Him at all times, you people;
Pour out your heart before Him;
God is a refuge for us. Selah" (v. 8)

Anxiety and fear mark our society. Fear arises from the sensationalized daily news to international events: natural disasters, wars, as well as our uncertain, debt-ridden world economy. Our sense of well-being is constantly being assaulted. As women, we also bear the concern for our families—the health and welfare of each family member as well as concerns for their future. But is this how the Christian is supposed to live?

Our focal verse commands us to trust the Lord "at all times." Trust is faith in action. If we really believe (which is faith), we will trust the Lord. Then we will walk in peace. We experience this peace when we choose not to be anxious but to turn our anxious thoughts into prayer requests (Phil. 4:6–7). We are to lift these requests to the Lord as we "pour out our hearts before Him."

The Spirit of God has the ability to lift us above the circumstances of our lives as we turn to the Lord so we can begin to view them from an eternal vantage point. This perspective helps us reject the intrusive thoughts of anxiety and worry, which often bombard our minds. Take "every thought into captivity to the obedience of Christ" (2 Cor. 10:5). Thus, instead of worrying, we turn those anxious thoughts into prayer requests. Cast "all your care upon Him, for He cares for you" (1 Pet. 5:7). As we pray, then we can claim and receive His peace, which will literally build a protective fortress around our hearts and minds (Phil. 4:7).

Do you desire the peace of God? Then stop worrying! It is a choice or an act of your will. At first, tremendous effort and concentration may be necessary to declare war on those anxious thoughts. But, as you continually turn them

194

into prayer requests, you will find that doing so becomes a spiritually healthy habit. You will learn to recognize those anxious thoughts as diabolical intrusions and refuse to allow them into your mind. Instead, you will let them drive you to prayer. Then in His presence, you will find "fullness of joy" and pleasures forevermore" (Ps. 62:11)! Remember, Jesus alone is trustworthy. Place all your trust in Him, for "God is our refuge" (46:1).

Donna Gaines

Prayer: *Ask the Lord to help you obey His command to "trust in Him at all times." Obey His command to "be anxious for nothing" but to pray about everything (Phil. 4:6). As you trust the Lord instead of worrying, you will be able to live in His peace. I encourage you to pray the Word of God. As you pray His Word, you are replacing the lies of worry and anxiety with the power of His truth.*

Personal Reflection: ....

....

....

....

....

195

Thirst for Him

Psalm 63:1–5

"O God, You are my God;
Early will I seek You;
My soul thirsts for You;
My flesh longs for You
In a dry and thirsty land
Where there is no water.
So I have looked for You in the sanctuary,
To see Your power and Your glory." (vv. 1–2)

When our third child was an infant, I became very dissatisfied with my lack of intimacy with the Lord. I began to pray daily that I would thirst for Him like a deer pants for the water brook (Ps. 42:1). Much like the psalmist, I was experiencing a dry, desolate time in my spiritual life, and the drought left me longing for Him! After about six months of praying that prayer, I realized one day that I could not get enough of His Word. God was instructing me and had ignited a hunger for Him that only He could satisfy.

I had committed to meet with the Lord every morning. I prepared a place at the end of our couch. My Bible and journal were on the end table, prepared for my meeting with the Lord. I began systematically reading through the Bible. The more I read and comprehended, the more I wanted to know. I left my Bible open during the day and would long for moments that I could sit down, picking up where I had left off. God was answering my prayer!

I encourage you to ask the Lord to grant you this hunger and thirst for Him. Do not settle for religion, but long to experience a living relationship with Jesus Christ. This intimacy with Him will ruin everything else for you! You will not be able to get as excited over temporal things as you did in the past because

a new, deeper, and more extravagant love will have captured your heart and imagination!

But I must warn you, there are no shortcuts. This journey is a long road of obedience that leads to triumph, joy, and victory in the spiritual realm. You must depend upon the power of the Holy Spirit to enable you to choose Jesus—to choose obedience. His strength will enable you. This obedience requires that you and I deny our flesh, take up our cross daily, and follow Him (Luke 9:23). Obedience to His Word leads to satisfaction and fulfillment in this life and anticipation for real life in His presence one day.

Donna Gaines

Prayer: *Begin your prayer time by offering yourself as a living sacrifice to the Lord. Pray Romans 12:1 to Him. As you offer yourself to God as Master, denying your flesh, you are able to gaze upon Him and experience His glory. It is only as you submit your will to His that you please Him and are able to commune with Him and obey Him.*

Personal Reflection: ....

....

....

....

....

....

Safety in the Shadow

Psalm 63:6–11

"When I remember You on my bed,
I meditate on You in the night watches.
Because You have been my help,
Therefore in the shadow of Your wings I will rejoice." (vv. 6–7)

What a beautiful picture this psalm paints! Can you envision yourself in the shadow of His wings? I am reminded of our little grandson Charlie, who just learned to walk. Because he and his family live out of state, we communicate by FaceTime and videos sent through text. My husband and I get so excited when we receive one.

In a recent video, little Charlie went from holding his mom or dad's hand to venturing out walking on his own. Even as he walked, his parents were never far away. They hovered over him like a mother bird, ready to swoop him up for the rescue if needed.

The psalmist declares that he will follow close to the Lord. We can only follow the Lord closely when we are obeying Him. When we obey, we know that His right hand will uphold us. We are assured of His protection. Like Charlie, we may be wobbly and unsure of our steps, but the Lord will watch over us.

My daughter and son-in-law's protection of little Charlie as parents reminds me of what Jesus said: "If you then, being evil, know how to give good gifts to your children: how much more will your Father who is in heaven give good things to those who ask him?" (Matt. 7:11). As parents we want what is best for our children. We go to great lengths to provide for them and to protect them. If necessary, we will work two jobs and stay up all night with them when they are sick. If we being evil do this, how much more will our heavenly Father do for us?

Our Father God is good, and He only does good. Believe His Word and stand on His character. Even when your feet wobble and you think you may not be able to stand, follow close, clinging to Him. God is your helper; and because He is, you can rejoice in the shadow of His presence. Sing for joy and watch as He upholds you.

Donna Gaines

Prayer: *One of the most effective ways to pray is to pray God's Word. Personalize the text as you lift your requests before His throne. Pray something like this: "Father, when I lie on my bed, I want my thoughts to be of You. Help me to meditate upon You and Your Word. Should I wake in the night, let my first thoughts be of You. I thank You that You are my Helper, and I rejoice in the shadow of Your wings. Help me to follow close to You and may Your right hand hold me."*

Personal Reflection: ....

....

....

....

....

....

Protect My Life

Psalm 64:1–10

"Hear my voice, O God, in my meditation;
Preserve my life from fear of the enemy." (v. 1)

What do you fear? What keeps you awake at night and puts a knot in your stomach? Do you fear someone? Do you have a real or perceived enemy? In this psalm, David, who had many enemies, is asking the Lord to protect him not only from his enemies but also from the "fear of the enemy." Fear brings its own kind of torment. David's enemies were after his life, and their bitter words were piercingly sharp. He describes their schemes as he pours his heart out before the Lord.

You and I also have a very real enemy who plays on our emotions and feeds our fears. Satan assaults the truth of God and can manipulate our feelings. That is why we cannot "feel" our way into a new way of acting. Instead, we must think (according to God's Word) and use our actions to move into a new God-anointed way of feeling. If we will choose to act according to God's Word, eventually our feelings will line up.

Paul reminds us: "For God has not given us a spirit of fear, but of power and of love and of a sound mind" (2 Tim. 1:7). If God has not given us fear, then who is the source of fear? Satan is the great intimidator. We stand against his schemes with the Word of God. Claim the power, love, and sound mind that are yours in Christ.

Remember, dear one, feelings are not truth. You may need to repeat that statement several times. Feelings are not truth! God's Word is truth. Begin today to replace the lies of fear and discouragement with the truth and hope found in God's Word. God is faithful, and you can depend upon His character.

David trusted that the Lord would deal with his enemies. You can depend on His protection as well. David knew that ultimately others would fear the

Lord because of God's intervention. He closed Psalm 64 with these words of hope: "The righteous shall be glad in the LORD, and trust in Him. And all the upright in heart shall glory." Choose today to find glory in the Lord and to thank Him for how He will defend you.

Donna Gaines

Prayer: *As you read through the Psalms, personalize their words and pray them back to the Lord. God desires to reveal Himself to you through His Word. His Word is living and has the power to displace your fear and instill within you hope. Using the Word as your guide, pray in the pattern of the psalmist: "Father, I know that You will take care of my enemies. You will deal with those who rebel and use their bitter words as arrows against me. I know that one day all men will fear You and declare Your works."*

Personal Reflection: ....

....

....

....

....

....

....

....

His Goodness Our Abundance

Psalm 65:1–13

*"You crown the year with Your goodness,
And Your paths drip with abundance." (v. 11)*

Our year was crowned after Christmas when all our children and grandchildren joined us in our home to end the old year and begin the new year. With four married children and ten grandchildren, we were blessed with abundance! Our hearts and our home overflowed. Nothing is more thrilling than having all our children home at once. Watching the cousins play together fills me with joy that is almost indescribable.

All good gifts come from our gracious and benevolent God. One of my favorite Old Testament characters is Moses. God spoke to him like a friend. Moses experienced a miraculous forty days and nights on the mountain with the Lord. God gave Him the law and the instructions for the tabernacle. He was so impacted by the manifest presence of the Lord that His face shone with a brilliance that caused him to veil it. But, at the end of those forty days, the people sinned grievously.

After the great sin of the people with the golden calf, Moses interceded and pled with the Lord not to remove His presence from the Israelites. God's presence was the only thing that set them apart from the other nations around them. The Lord assured Moses that He would not remove His presence but would continue to go with them.

Moses then boldly asked for an even greater experience of God's revelation and said, "Please, show me Your glory" (Ex. 33:18). God replied by saying, "I will make all My goodness pass before you, and I will proclaim the name of the Lord before you" (v. 19). God's goodness displays His glory. His goodness is revealed in His name.

202

The Bible is clear: "Every good and perfect gift is from above, and comes down from the Father of lights, with whom there is no variation or shadow of turning" (James 1:17). Are you walking with Him in intimacy? If you are, then you will experience His goodness. God is good. No variation or shadow is in Him; He is only light. You can trust Him completely.

Choose to praise the Lord with David for His awesome deeds, His strength, power, and faithful provision. Ask the Lord to help you experience the intimacy with Him that David and Moses enjoyed. You will experience no greater goodness than His presence.

Donna Gaines

Prayer: *Pray this psalm back to the Lord: "Heavenly Father, I know that You are the one who visits the earth and waters it. You greatly enrich it. You provide us with food and with all we need. Please crown my year with Your goodness and allow the paths You have chosen for me to drip with abundance. I will shout and sing with the hills and rejoice in Your plentiful provision" (paraphrase of vv. 9–13).*

Personal Reflection: ....

....

....

....

....

Refined as Silver

Psalm 66:1–15

"For You, O God, have tested us;
You have refined us as silver is refined." (v. 10)

I experienced a very dark time in my life after a move to a new city. A struggle was going on in our church, and my mother-in-law had suffered a stroke and needed to be moved to a skilled-care nursing facility. I remember visiting nursing homes, trying to make this decision in the midst of concern over our daughters' adjustment to the move and of trying to encourage my husband. After my third or fourth nursing home, I pulled over on the side of the road, looked up at the sky, and yelled, "Lord, really . . . in the midst of all the pain and difficulty, I have to visit nursing homes?"

This time was a period of refining in my life as everything stable had been shaken, and I had to live out what I professed to believe. Psalm 66 begins by extolling God's goodness to Israel. The psalmist praises Him for His works and encourages all the people to let their voices of praise be heard. God had miraculously delivered the Israelites from the Egyptians and brought them through the sea to dry ground (v. 6).

The Lord also refined His people who were constantly going astray. We often read about the Israelites and wonder at their unbelief. But, are we really much different? We who live on this side of the cross, who have the revelation of Jesus, should, of all people, be willing to place our whole faith in Christ. But, we often allow doubt and unbelief to crowd out what we know is true.

Our good God only allows the fire of refining to remove the sin or dross in our lives in order that it might be exposed, confessed, and forgiven. Sin separates and ultimately destroys. Because God loves us, He refines us.

"The refining pot is for silver and the furnace for gold, but the LORD tests of hearts" (Prov. 17:3). God's refines so that we might have pure, undivided hearts

because the "pure in heart . . . shall see God" (Matt. 5:8). God is always at work conforming us to the image of Jesus (Rom. 8:29).

God allows trials in our lives to bring our dross—such as sinful attitudes, unforgiveness, bitterness, or selfishness—to the surface so that it can be removed. Someone has said that the refiner keeps placing the silver in the fire and removing the dross until he can see his reflection. God's goal is like that of the refiner. He desires to see His reflection in us.

Donna Gaines

Prayer: *Ask the Lord to reveal any unconfessed sin in your life. The only way to walk blamelessly with the Lord is to confess and turn away from all revealed sin. Then, bless the Lord for hearing your prayer and granting His mercy.*

Personal Reflection: ....

....

....

....

....

....

His Faithful Love

Psalm 66:16–20

"Blessed be God,
Who has not turned away my prayer,
Nor His mercy from me!" (v. 20)

Have you ever blown it? Have you ever wanted a second chance? Maybe you stuck your foot in your mouth. Or maybe you conveniently lied, avoiding telling the truth in an attempt to manipulate a situation. Perhaps you gossiped about a friend or betrayed a confidence.

On the other hand, maybe you are the one who has been betrayed, and your anger and unforgiveness have turned into bitterness. Perhaps you are estranged from a family member. Or possibly, in order to cope with the stress in your life, you have turned to drugs or alcohol. Are you looking for fulfillment of legitimate needs but trying to fulfill them in illegitimate ways—ways that God prohibits in Scripture?

Would you like to start over? If so, I have wonderful news for you. God will help you begin again. I am so grateful that our God is not just the God of a "*second* chance," but of "*another* chance." When you study the Bible, you will begin to see the consistency of God's character. God is a God of redemption, restoration, forgiveness, and salvation. He has revealed His heart through His Son Jesus Christ. While on earth, Jesus always looked into people's hearts and saw their potential—the person God had created them to be—and called forth that person. He met every individual at the point of his or her need.

Christ did that for Peter after he denied Him three times. I cannot even imagine the grief and guilt Peter must have felt when Christ turned to look at him after his third denial and the crowing of the rooster. The Bible says that "Peter went out and wept bitterly" (Luke 22:62). I am sure he thought he had

206

completely blown it and would never be able to experience intimacy with Christ as he had once known.

However, Jesus restored him in John 21 and then chose Peter to preach at Pentecost where three thousand people came to Christ. The Lord still does that today. This psalm begins by calling God's people to worship and remembrance of what He had done for Israel. Then the psalmist talks about God personally (Ps. 66:13). The Lord had not turned away his prayer. If you come to the Lord in honesty and humility, He will not turn you away. He will grant you His mercy.

Donna Gaines

Prayer: *If you have blown it or if you are made aware of a sin that needs to be confessed, stop right now and ask the Lord to forgive you. He has promised that if you will confess your sins, He will forgive you and cleanse you from all unrighteousness (1 John 1:9). He is faithful to His Word, and His desire is for you to experience His faithful love in all of its fullness and joy.*

Personal Reflection: ....

....

....

....

....

....

207

Living in Joy

Psalm 68:1–3

*"But let the righteous be glad;
Let them rejoice before God;
Yes, let them rejoice exceedingly." (v. 3)*

The repetition of words in Scripture should pique our ears like the ears of a deer when it is startled by rustling leaves. Hearing Scripture should beckon our attention. In this verse, "shall" is repeated three times followed by action verbs. This short helping verb is hinged to the reader's attitude and determination to rest in the Lord rather than present circumstances. Let me be clear, I realize that is a sentence easier written than performed. A determined choice must be made. To rest in times of trial is completely against the sinful nature (or at least it is against mine).

Here, the Lord reminds His children to be glad and joyful even in a world full of sin, destruction, and heartache. Such joy is only possible when you view this life, and all it contains, with the biblical perspective of knowing a secure eternity with the Lord. Yes, the death of loved ones, disease, war, persecution, and severe heartache come; but, as God's children, we alone have hope in a hopeless world. This life may seem overwhelming, but it is just a breath compared to our eternity with Christ.

As a mom with five children, I repeat myself all day. I know I sound like a broken record, but at times I have to be an audible reminder to the young minds God has entrusted to me and my husband. My prayer is that as they mature, they will need my reminders less frequently as the thoughts and behaviors we have strived to shape in them become as natural as breathing and walking. That is our hope!

God is repeating Himself in this verse and reminding you to be glad, resting your heart in His joy today. Exult yourself in God; live today in joy as a

testimony to others of the peace and security God bestows on His children. Take a few moments and meditate on all the Lord has given you through both your salvation and eternal inheritance. If you have time, write down all the eternal blessings that you receive through Christ. They will greatly surpass all difficult circumstances you may face in this world. I love the famous words of Thomas Watson a seventeenth-century Puritan pastor: "In prayer, we act like men; in praise, we act like angels."

Karen Allen

Prayer: *Thank your heavenly Father, who knows you completely. Trust Him to know your fears, your concerns, and your present and future challenges. Ask the Holy Spirit to refresh your joy when circumstances of this world pull you down into despair. Thank Him for the manifold blessings you receive through Him both here and in eternity. Allow Him to fill you with His joy and allow His light in you to be a testimony of Him to those you encounter today.*

Personal Reflection: ....

....

....

....

....

....

Our Great Defender

Psalm 68:4–18

*"A father of the fatherless, a defender of widows,
Is God in His holy habitation." (v. 5)*

What are some nouns you would choose to describe yourself? I could choose: daughter, sister, wife, mother, teacher, baker, runner, baseball lover, and craft-addict. You can tell a little about me from my choice of words. These are words I choose to describe myself, probably not what my children would choose for me.

The Bible has been described as a "Him-book" (homonym for hymn book) because we can learn so much of God and His character through His Word. In this passage David celebrates the faithfulness of God in moving the people of Israel from Egypt to Canaan under the leadership of Moses. Upon the inspiration of the Holy Spirit, David chose two words to describe the Lord: Father and Defender. What is even more encouraging is the two groups mentioned in this verse—orphans and widows. The mention of these two groups reflects the Lord's care for the weak and the abandoned. God's character is revealed in His determination to uplift the downtrodden and comfort the lonely. Widows and orphans are those without a defender and provider. When families are bereaved of their leader, God takes care of them and fills that void in their lives.

This characteristic of God is the opposite of earthly rulers and kings. Mortal leaders surround themselves with people of influence, resources, and power. They associate with those who can build them up, enhance their position and strengthen their power. This wisdom is of man. Thankfully, this is not the nature of our Lord. Throughout Scripture God cares for the miserable and surrounds Himself with the lowly. Though God is high and exalted in glory, He still cares for those in lowly positions. God is not impressed by greatness, as we think of it, but rather He chooses the weak and lowly things of this world as vehicles for His great works so that the glory for what is accomplished goes to

210

Him alone. If you think of yourself as being poor, weak, or unimportant, do not consider that as a handicap or disadvantage but instead as an opportunity for God to show His transforming power in you (see 1 Cor. 1:26–31).

Karen Allen

Prayer: *Thank the Lord for loving you and adopting you. What a privilege to be called His child and to be able to petition Him as your father! Thank Christ for atoning for your sin on the cross and for His amazing grace in your life. Open your eyes to see people as God sees them, and ask Him to give you a heart of compassion for those without a defender and provider. In a world needing God's love, seek to demonstrate His love to others. Look for an opportunity to share His love with someone hurting and needing the transforming gospel today.*

Personal Reflection: ....

....

....

....

....

....

Count Your Blessings

Psalm 68:19–27

"Blessed be the LORD,
Who daily loads us with benefits,
The God of our salvation! Selah." (v. 19)

As a mom with five growing children, I must set rules for our kitchen pantry. I am convinced that our two sons would eat all day if allowed. They love to return home from school on the days when I have gone grocery shopping. Typically, when picking up my children on the day of my midweek store run, as the vehicle door opens I am greeted with: "Did you go to the store today?" If I do not set parameters on what can be consumed at specific times, then I would make trips to the grocery store each day . . . and sometimes I do make daily trips.

Our nature is to exhaust our resources without thinking about the future. Whether it be money, time, food, diet points, cell phone minutes, we consume today without thought for tomorrow. The Lord, being our Creator, knows our nature. He knows that we need Him and all His benefits daily. I am so thankful that I cannot ever exhaust the goodness of God in my life. I desperately need His love, mercy, grace, and forgiveness in my life on a continual basis.

Consider the mental image this verse paints with the verb *loads*. In my mind, I see it as a barrel packed full of all the benefits from the Lord. Each benefit is wrapped up for the right moment in my life. For example, when my child is disobedient, I can unwrap wisdom and patience. When I am stressed, I can dwell on God's faithfulness in my life. When I am hurting, I find peace in knowing that the Lord is my protector. He continually blesses you and me daily with the benefits we need to live a life honoring Christ in this world. We never have an excuse not to honor Him. He has given us everything we need for godliness in a godless culture daily.

Another aspect to note in this verse is that David wrote it for God's people to experience in present time. It points our hearts to praise God for being the same for us in the present as He has been for others in the past. A reflection on the past causes us to look ahead in time to what God will yet do. We can recount all the benefits the Lord has preserved for His people in the past with a certain, hopeful, and confident spirit, knowing that He will also sustain us with those same daily benefits. We may not know what trials and difficult times are in our future, but we can face them with the assurance that we will be gifted by God with everything we need in a way that points others to Christ. God has not only given us eternal life, but He continues to bestow on us daily everything we need to live this life for His glory. What an amazing God!

Karen Allen

Prayer: *Thank the Lord for His abundant goodness in your life and for daily pouring out His goodness. Confess your need for Him and for His daily benefits in your life. Thank Him for empowering you to live each day through His Holy Spirit.*

Personal Reflection: ....

....

....

....

....

Our Awesome God

Psalm 68:28–35

*"O God, You are more awesome than Your holy places.
The God of Israel is He who gives strength and power to His people.
Blessed be God!" (v. 35)*

Awesome is a word commonly used, especially by adolescents, but carrying two greatly differing meanings. The most commonly used definition is the meaning "great or extremely good." Each birthday I hear my kids exclaim that their gifts are "awesome" . . . again. However, that is different in this passage. David is crying out to God, declaring that He is "awesome," meaning that He is "extremely impressive, inspiring great admiration, apprehension, or fear." What a vast chasm between the two understandings of the same word!

David refers to the Lord as "the God of Israel." Israel was God's chosen covenant people, and He was their God. Israelites were not known for their physical or emotional strength. In fact, they were known as a weak people. However, God gave the Israelites strength and power because He knew they needed it. God chose this small, inferior group of people to display His majestic strength and power on the earth so that there could be no confusion of their source of strength. The God of Israel was an awesome God.

Since God is our Creator, He knows what each of us needs, and His timing is always perfect. The God of Israel is the same loving Father we have access to through Jesus Christ today. God wants us to acknowledge our weaknesses and petition Him for strength and power to face our tasks. Some days you may have an attitude similar to the stiff-necked Israelites, feeling you have everything within your control. However, before long a battle comes your way, and you cry out for help. God wants His children to want Him. You do not have to face your day alone, but you have access to amazing strength and power because you have

access to an awesome God! Knowing you have a God enabling you to live life as a display of His glory should remove all fear and anxiety.

Take encouragement and comfort from the words of the apostle Paul: "'My grace is sufficient for you, for My strength is made perfect in weakness.' Therefore most gladly I will rather boast in my infirmities, that the power of Christ may rest upon me. Therefore I take pleasure in infirmities, in reproaches, in needs, in persecutions, in distresses, for Christ's sake. For when I am weak, then I am strong" (2 Cor. 12:9–10). See your difficulties and trials as opportunities to allow your awesome God to enable you with His strength and power as a testimony to others.

Karen Allen

Prayer: *Be grateful that God has formed you and knows you, your weaknesses, and your fears. Ask Him to give you strength and power to face whatever comes your way today. Thank Him for your salvation through Jesus Christ and for the strength and power He bestows on you. Let others see His power in your life today.*

Personal Reflection:

A Mighty Fortress

Psalm 71:1–24

"Be my strong refuge,
To which I may resort continually;
You have given the commandment to save me,
For You are my rock and my fortress." (v. 3)

Recently I have been teaching my younger children how to diagram sentences. I may be one of the few people on the planet who finds this fun. My children are not as strange as I am, and they completely loathe this task in our grammar studies. However, I find it both useful and enlightening to diagram this verse. Note or circle the five personal pronouns in the passage.

How encouraging! Not only is our God a strong refuge for those who seek Him, but He is also my strong refuge. David wrote this psalm to each believer, stressing that God cares for all His people, and He alone can care for each one individually. David knew the personal care of God. He could pen passages of God's protection and care because he experienced it throughout his life. Many Bible scholars believe that this psalm was written when David was driven from his throne by his son Absalom. In any case, our God is the same God David worshiped and still provides the same refuge for His children today.

In Scripture, the phrase "strong refuge" refers to a place of safety or peace in the midst of danger. Oh, dear friend, why would you ever want to leave such a wonderful place? Notice the present tense of this verse. God is your Savior in the past (salvation), and He is also saving you every day (from sin through His ongoing sanctification). Do not miss the important adverb in the first clause—"continually." We can never tire or petition our God too much. We can repeatedly rely upon Him and His care. Bible commentator John Gill wrote: "The Lord is as a wall of fire around His people, a munition of rocks, His salvation is as wall and bulwarks, and His power as a garrison in which they are kept."

Many saints before us have taken refuge in the Lord and were never disappointed. The great Reformer Martin Luther penned some thirty-six hymns but is best known for his beloved "A Mighty Fortress Is Our God." This hymn has comforted many souls, as saints have lifted their voices to his carefully chosen words. When my husband and I were married, I walked down the aisle to Luther's beloved hymn as both a testimony and prayer. Take a moment now and reflect on the sweet refuge God has given you in heaven and also here on this earth.

Karen Allen

Prayer: *Thank the Lord for your salvation in Jesus Christ and for His continual protection over your life. Express gratitude for how He cares for you personally and provides you a place of protection. May God's peace come over your life today as you trust in Him and in the care He provides for His children.*

Personal Reflection: ....

....

....

....

....

....

Come Ye Sinner, Poor and Needy

Psalm 72:1–4

*"He will bring justice to the poor of the people;
He will save the children of the needy,
And will break in pieces the oppressor." (v. 4)*

The first time I encountered Christ's words in the Sermon on the Mount, I was struck that the Lord would desire us to be "poor in spirit" (Matt. 5:3). Our culture despises the afflicted, downtrodden, and needy. However, throughout the pages of the Old Testament the Lord has repeatedly demonstrated His care for the humble and poor. Moreover, the New Testament is filled with examples of Christ's special interest and care for the needy. Our mighty God is completely impartial in judging our earthly resources. If we were never broken over our sinfulness, we would not even see our need for Christ. If all the riches of the world were ours, would we still yearn for the Lord?

The apostle Paul penned these words as a reminder of Christ's love and of our attitudes toward one another: "For you know the grace of our Lord Jesus Christ, that though He was rich, yet for your sakes He became poor, that you through His poverty might become rich" (2 Cor. 8:9). Charles Spurgeon encourages us: "Happy are God's poor and needy ones; they are safe under the wing of the Prince of Peace, for He will save them from all their enemies." May you find happiness in the loving arms of the Lord regardless of your resources or needs.

Not only does the Lord save you from the penalty of sin through salvation, but He also saves you from the power of sin by the work of His Spirit. Our oppressor, Satan, continues to work in the hearts of men. While we are promised eternal security with Christ in heaven, our lives on this earth are often filled with partiality, oppression, and persecution. Believers should not be surprised when they do not experience love here. Rather they should consider themselves "sojourners and pilgrims" on this earth, traveling to their

eternal home (1 Pet. 2:11). Our ultimate hope is in Christ's return, when He will destroy Satan and all of the deceiver's manifestations on this land. Christ will not return in the lowly and humble manner by which He came in Bethlehem. He will come to crush Satan and execute justice.

Joseph Hart wrote the beautiful hymn "Come Ye Sinners" in 1749. This hymn contains rich truths of God's care for those who come to him weak, broken, and needy: "Jesus ready stands to save you, full of pity, love and power." Dwelling on these truths has comforted many saints before you, and I pray you find comfort in these truths as well.

Karen Allen

Prayer: *Thank your gracious Father for His Word and the incredible truths He has given you. Thank Him for loving the unlovable, poor, and needy. Approach Him with your needs and cast all your cares on your heavenly Father now.*

Personal Reflection: ....

....

....

....

....

....

....

Laying Down Crowns

Psalm 72:5–20

"Yes, all kings shall fall down before Him;
All nations shall serve Him." (v. 11)

Tuesdays and Thursdays are long days in our home. These days I homeschool our five children. I love it, but it is exhausting. One of our favorite subjects is history. Learning the drama behind some of the kings has been fascinating, and it always keeps my children's attention. They never tire of hearing stories about Alexander the Great, King Arthur, Charlemagne, and William the Conqueror. Their eyes open with excitement to hear of the conquests and downfalls of these kings.

Our youngest son was especially intrigued with King Tutankhamun. He was fascinated to learn Tut became Pharaoh when he was his age, only nine years old. His death and burial chamber, filled with over five thousand treasures, birthed great conversations and questions. Clearly, this king did not know or understand Christian death and eternal life. However, this episode sparked great discussion with my children regarding kings and their limited power on this earth. It always gives me great encouragement to remind their young minds that there is only one King who ultimately rules over all—Jesus!

This verse states that earthly kings possess only limited power. Regardless of their power, kingdom, or sphere of influence, not all humanity will pay reverence—however mighty the kings may be. Moreover, in Scripture the entire world will be brought under the subjection of the authority of Christ. Although men may rule over us, God is still in control: "The king's heart is in the hand of the LORD, like the rivers of water; He turns it wherever He wishes" (Prov. 21:1).

Our world seems to be in a downward spiral. The media fills our homes with tragic news and stories of utter chaos. Remember that we know the end of the story. The victor is Jesus, who promises victory over evil, and *all* nations

will bow before Christ. Our desire should be to see the gospel spread to the uttermost parts of the earth so people, tribes, and nations can know and serve the Lord. Take comfort from the apostle Paul: "At the name of Jesus every knee should bow, of those in heaven, and of those on earth, and of those under the earth, and that every tongue should confess that Jesus Christ is Lord, to the glory of God the Father" (Phil. 2:10–11).

Karen Allen

Prayer: *Thank the Lord that He is in complete control of this world. Praise the Lord for His sovereign control in this universe, and allow His peace to come over the troubles that dominate your heart today. Seek opportunities to share His Good News with others.*

Personal Reflection: ....

....

....

....

....

....

....

My Eternal Portion

Psalm 73:1–28

"My flesh and my heart fail;
But God is the strength of my heart and my portion forever." (v. 26)

Thinking of death never tops one's list of favorite subjects. We live each day according to our schedules, knowing death will eventually come but desiring it to be in the far distant future. However, being reminded of your mortality can bring balance and clarity to your lives. In this passage, the combination of flesh and heart conveys the whole person—the physical body and the soul. What a comfort it is to know when all the powers of the mind and body are eventually exhausted, the Lord will provide our eternal strength and joy.

"Strength of my heart" is a beautiful way of stating "that on which my heart relies." From Scripture and self-awareness, we learn our hearts can be wicked and deceive us (Jer. 17:9). The heart cannot love what the mind does not know. Without the knowledge of God and a relationship with Christ, our hearts will rely on what we can gain: wealth, fame, power, influence, friends, physical appearance, or material possessions. Nevertheless, the situation for those without Christ is hopeless, as nothing they can accumulate in this world will meet the needs and comfort God alone provides in the end.

Not only does God anchor our hearts, but He is also our eternal portion. *Portion* is a word pregnant with meaning. In the modern context, portion is used with diet plans, but in the Old Testament it refers to sharing a meal, sacrifice, or inheritance. To remember that although the ungodly may flourish here, their prosperity is temporal. Our inheritance is eternal, reserved for us in heaven. Each time the word *portion* is used within this text, the believer is reminded that whatever may happen in this world, she has a possession that transcends all trial, difficulty, and tragedy.

Every day this world offers increasing violence and pain, which makes it far too easy to be discouraged with the circumstances we face daily. However, our hearts are reminded that God is our strength and portion. If we have Him, we need nothing else. Our flesh and hearts will eventually fail, but we have an eternal hope and portion waiting for us in heaven with our Savior.

Karen Allen

Prayer: *Thank the Lord for being your Savior and for the eternal hope you have through Jesus Christ. Remember daily that you have God as your strength and portion forever. Fix your hope in Him and not temporal pleasures on this earth. Develop a love for God's Word so that your mind will continue to learn of Him and, thus, love Him more. Thank Him for this sweet promise, that although your heart and flesh will indeed fail someday, He is the strength of your heart and your portion forever.*

Personal Reflection: ....

....

....

....

....

....

What I Know for Sure

Psalm 74:1–23

"The day is Yours, the night also is Yours;
You have prepared the light and the sun.
You have set all the borders of the earth;
You have made summer and winter." (vv. 16–17)

A well-known television and public personality often ended her broadcast and magazine articles with this question: "What do I know for sure?" As God's covenant people, we need to ask the same question and be certain that we have the right answer.

This psalm is one of several that lament the destruction of Jerusalem and the temple. The reader feels the agony of the author in the first verse: "O God, why have You cast us off forever?" Perhaps you have keenly felt that way yourself: Why has God allowed these sorrows? Does He see my suffering? Nestled in the second half of the psalm, verses 16–17 reassure us of God's divine power and faithfulness.

Genesis 1 records the acts of creation—light dividing the darkness, the separation of land and water, the establishment of the seasons. Since the day of creation, God's world has operated according to His decrees. His ownership cannot be disputed. He is the God of nature and time (see Gen. 1:14–18; Job 38:12).

The psalmist specifically notes the division of day and night as well as the establishment of seasons. Yes, God has the power to create, but He also has the power continually to preserve. Matthew Henry, in his commentary on this passage, puts it beautifully: "It is He that opens the eyelids of the morning light and draws the curtains of the evening shadow."

What do these verses teach us about God? How do they reassure us when we, like the psalmist, are grieved and do not sense God's presence? Just as God's loving care over His creation is constant, we remember His steadfast love for

His covenant people is trustworthy. His love is sure, and it is eternal. If He is faithful to the order of creation, how much more faithful will He be to His very own children?

Note how the psalm progresses from personal doubts and questions to the acknowledgment and praise of God for His faithfulness to His creation and people. When we see the sun by day and the moon by night, when we feel balmy breezes or shiver in a chilly wind, we are reminded of God's steadfast love and care over His creation and His people.

The beloved hymn, "Great Is Thy Faithfulness" expresses the steadfast love of God so clearly. The second stanza encourages the believer to join with all nature in praising our faithful God who not only prepared the day and night but ordered the seasons and the light.

Susie Hawkins

Prayer: *Ask your Father in heaven to open your eyes and heart to grasp His faithfulness and steadfast love. Remember today that He not only created you, but also He preserved you by His love.*

Personal Reflection: ....

....

....

....

....

The Final Word

Psalm 75:1–10

"For exaltation comes neither from the east
Nor from the west nor from the south.
But God is the Judge:
He puts down one,
And exalts another." (vv. 6–7)

Like most Americans, we watch a lot of sporting events in our house. We have our favorite teams and watch their games faithfully, agonizing over defeats and celebrating every victory. In all sports, there is one factor that never changes—the final calls by the umpire or referee, who is the ultimate judge for a play. When a call with which we disagree is made, we yell at the television in frustration and anger. When a call is made to our team's advantage, we marvel at the wisdom and skill of the referee. Like the call or not, the referee is the ultimate judge in the game, and his rulings stand. This is true whether you are watching an NFL game or first graders falling over themselves in their attempt to play basketball. In sports, the referee/umpire has the final word.

The verses above describe God's role in this world as the ultimate Judge. He holds all power, authority, and control over the affairs of mankind. The author of this psalm notes that exaltation does not come from many sources (v. 6). Perhaps he had certain kingdoms or nations in mind when he specified that power does not come from the east, west, or south. God's perfect judgment is universal and not limited to certain geographical places. The word *exaltation* carries several nuances, such as one who is "set on high or lifted up" or one who has the ultimate authority. But that kind of power should be understood within the context of God's will, His divine judgment, and His appointments.

This author then explains how God judges: He "puts down one, and exalts another" (v. 7). Councils, electorates, or political regimes may choose

a ruler, but that ruler has been determined by God Himself. God is behind the scenes in the rise and fall of nations, which should be a great assurance to believers.

While most of us will never be rulers or kings, this principle is relevant to us as well. If we receive God's favor on our lives or ministries in any way, we must remember that it is not because of our own brilliance or extraordinary abilities. God raises up and puts down leaders. His decision is always right (see Ps. 50:6; 1 Sam. 2:7–8; Dan. 2:21–22). God does what He pleases and is pleased with what He does.

Susie Hawkins

Prayer: *Thank your heavenly Father for His judgments, which are perfect and righteous. Stay firmly anchored in the truth that God and God alone is judge over all. See His hand in everything and trust Him with all your heart.*

Personal Reflection: ....

....

....

....

....

....

Can You Hear Me Now?

Psalm 77:1–20

"I cried out to God with my voice—
To God with my voice;
And He gave ear to me." (v. 1)

One of the businesses I frequent is owned and operated by a woman whose family immigrated from South Vietnam after the Vietnam war. She is Buddhist and next to her cash register is a corner shelf, which always contains a lit candle, bits of food, and a small Buddha statue. I ask her questions about her faith, and she is always eager to share her customs and traditions with me. Recently we had a conversation about prayer, and I left her that day freshly aware of the unique nature of prayer in Christianity. Our prayers are not to an impersonal god, angel, or spirit. We have no need to wonder if we will make it to heaven, to know the state of our *karma*, or pray to ancestors to put in a good word for us. Our God is alive, He is real, and we can be confident that He hears the prayers of His children.

This short verse expresses such a profound truth. The psalmist was in great distress and cried out to God in desperation. This word *cry* in Hebrew expresses "crying out, especially for aid." "Then they *cried* out to the Lord and He delivered them out of their distresses" (Ps. 107:6, emphasis added). This crying is not just weeping; it indicates tears with anguish, deep sorrow, or helplessness. Not only did the psalmist cry out in his spirit but also with his voice. One thing is certain about the psalmists—they did not mince any words in their prayers. They were emotional, brutally honest, and apparently very loud! In Hebraic linguistics, repetition of a word or phrase is used for a reason, indicating an intensity and emphasis to the statement. The author wants the reader to understand clearly his fervency and pleas for God to intervene in his circumstances.

God hears our prayers, though every prayer is not answered as we wish. God is not some sort of heavenly vending machine. We do not have an official

prayer formula that ensures our desired answers. Better than that, we have a heavenly Father, a personal God who knows us, loves us, and hears the cry of our hearts.

Perhaps this verse is part of your story. All of us have experienced times of grief and distress, cried out to God, feeling abandoned and alone. Yet be assured of His listening ear and His presence with those who are His. May the psalmist's testimony be yours as well.

Susie Hawkins

Prayer: *Embrace a fresh understanding of God's presence in your life. Thank God for the assurance that He knows your heart and hears your prayers.*

Personal Reflection: ....

....

....

....

....

....

....

Fickle or Faithful?

Psalm 78:1–72

"For their heart was not steadfast with Him,
Nor were they faithful in His covenant.
But He, being full of compassion, forgave their iniquity . . ." (vv. 37–38a)

Psalm 78 is one of most dramatic narratives in the Old Testament—the story of the wilderness wandering of the Israelites. They were led by fire and a cloud, ate manna ("angels' food," v. 25), and drank water that gushed from a rock. Who could imagine such things?

At that time, God's covenant people were in a state of chaos, having narrowly escaped Pharoah's armies and suddenly facing survival in the desert. These two verses summarize the essence of this psalm: Man is fickle, but God is forgiving. The psalmist forcefully makes his case against the Israelites by specifically pointing out God's provisions and charging them with abysmal failure to obey Him. For example:

- God "divided" the Red Sea and made a way of crossing (v. 13).
- "He led them with the cloud" by day and fire by night (v. 14).
- He provided abundant water (v. 16), sent them bread from heaven (v. 24), and delivered meat into their camp (v. 27).

What was the response of the Israelites to these supernatural provisions? They rebelled against God (v. 19); they "did not trust" Him (v. 22); they "did not believe" (vv. 22, 32); they "lied to Him" (v. 36); they "provoked" and "grieved Him" (v. 40). Their offenses did not happen once but repeatedly (v. 41). Three times the psalmist points out the reason for their wicked behavior: They did not remember the works of the Lord (vv. 7, 11, 42).

How could the Israelites see such stunning miracles firsthand and not remember them? We do the same thing because our hearts are naturally unstable. We are really not that different from the Israelites!

According to Scripture, recounting the ways God has met our needs in the past is not merely sentimental—it is actually biblical. By remembering God's intervention on our behalf, his preservation and blessings, our faith is strengthened and our spirit energized. Remembering works both ways. God remembered that His people were "flesh, a breath that passes away and does not come again" (v. 39). Again and again He had compassion on His people and forgave them.

The take-away lesson from this passage is that when we stop and remember what God has done for us, it changes us. When is the last time you took some time to remember the ways God has blessed you in the past seasons of your life? If you do, you will find your faith strengthened and your heart firmly established in God's ways.

Susie Hawkins

Prayer: *Ask the Lord to forgive you for the many times you have failed Him because of your weak faith. Recall the many times God has shown you His grace and mercy. Thank Him for His faithful love.*

Personal Reflection: ....

....

....

....

The Shepherd and His Sheep

Psalm 79:1–13

"So we, Your people and sheep of Your pasture,
Will give You thanks forever;
We will show forth Your praise to all generations." (v. 13)

One of the most interesting things to see on a trip to Israel are the flocks of sheep that still roam the hills in the Galilee and around Bethlehem. In the midst of a twenty-first-century culture, the ubiquitous sheep and the shepherds with their staffs are a dramatic contrast with modern life and a constant reminder of their biblical imagery. Sheep are ever present in the biblical story, appearing early in Scripture (Gen. 4:2) and used as a common metaphor for God's people. Ancient Semitic cultures were agrarian, which explains the plethora of biblical images and stories regarding crops, harvest, and farm animals. In the New Testament as well as various passages in the Old Testament, Jesus is called "the Lamb of God," connecting the sheep sacrifice with Jesus' sacrificial death (Is. 53:6–7).

A few of the most beloved passages on shepherds and sheep are found in Psalm 23, Psalm 100, and John 10, each reassuring the believer of God's protective love and care. This imagery of God as Shepherd is a very descriptive metaphor for God and His people. For example, in John 10:1–18, Jesus refers to Himself as "the good Shepherd" and lists some of the qualities of such:

- He owns the sheep, thus entering through the door (v. 3).
- He knows them, calls them by name (v. 3).
- He leads them and goes before them (vv. 3–4).
- The sheep know His voice (vv. 4–5).

Believers are comforted to picture Jesus as their shepherd in a near perfect description of divine love. But why are we compared to sheep and not pigs or

another animal? I would much rather be pictured as a sheep than a pig. Clearly there are a number of similarities between sheep and God's people. We may be like sheep in these ways:

- Sheep tend to wander away from the safety of the flock.
- They respond (hopefully) to their shepherd's voice, and not another's.
- They need to be led; they are unable to find their way.
- They are vulnerable to attacks from powerful forces.

God is "the Shepherd and Overseer of your souls" (1 Pet. 2:25), and in His pasture there is security and joy. What is your response to this wonderful truth? You must cultivate thankfulness for all God has done for you. Gratitude should be the most common characteristic of God's people. Added to an attitude of gratitude is the responsibility and privilege or declaring God's goodness and mercies to the generations that follow us. You must be intentional about this and never miss the opportunities that come your way. Proclaim boldly with me: He is our Shepherd. We are His flock. Forever we will follow Him.

Susie Hawkins

Prayer: *Express thankfulness to God for His loving care. Pray that you will be faithful to share the blessings He has so generously given you.*

Personal Reflection: ....

....

....

....

233

Hear Our Prayer!

Psalm 80:1–7

"Give ear, O Shepherd of Israel,
You who lead Joseph like a flock;
You who dwell between the cherubim, shine forth!" (v. 1)

"Susan Kay, what is this?"
"Susan Kay, look at me!"
"Susan Kay, get in here right now!"

As a child, I knew that if my parents called me by my full name, I was in trouble (and deserved to be). Their tone of voice, as well as their use of my full name, guaranteed that I would soon have to face the consequences for my actions. When I heard my full name used, I knew "the rest of the story."

The same emotional energy is felt in the opening prayer of this psalm. The author is not just politely addressing God but adding powerful descriptors, as if he is reminding God of His identity. The psalmist's theological understanding of God's nature is demonstrated by his choice of words. God is the "Shepherd of Israel," gently leading His people "like a flock"; yet His holy presence in heaven affirms His power and sovereignty. This psalm was written in the context of the Babylonian captivity of the Israelites. They despaired over the destruction of the temple and the devastation of Jerusalem. But more than that, the Israelites grieved over the state of their nation, referred to as "a vine" (vv. 8–16). Their losses were more than they could bear, and they cried passionately for God's intervention.

In this psalm, "Joseph" is an archetype for the Israelites. Usually the biblical writers use Jacob in that way, but here they chose to use Joseph. Why would the author do that? Perhaps they believed that what was happening to

the Israelites was reminiscent of Joseph's story. Dearly loved by his father, he had flourished in his younger days before he was sold into slavery and ended up in a foreign land completely alone. The Israelites, like Joseph, had been taken captive against their wills. They, as Joseph had been, were in a "prison" with no means of escape. The story of Joseph culminates with the restoration of his family; the psalmist fervently prayed for a similar outcome for his people.

What a contrast between the picture of God leading His people and His dwelling between the cherubim in heaven. God enters our dimension of time and space while reigning in heaven. The imagery of the cherubim was a familiar one for the Israelites, who were pictured in Scripture as constantly surrounding God's throne in worship and praise for His holiness.

The final phrase, "shine forth," encourages the reader to remember the *Shekinah* glory of God that radiates from His throne. This brilliant light indicates God's presence and favor, exactly what the psalmist is seeking—i.e., the blessing of God on His people. Oh that I would pray with such passion and theological understanding!

Susie Hawkins

Prayer: *Thank the Lord for His promises. Ask Him to strengthen your faith and resolve today to believe His Word and remember that His presence is ever with you.*

Personal Reflection: ....

....

....

....

At the End of the Rope

Psalm 80:1–13

"Before Ephraim, Benjamin and Manasseh,
Stir up Your strength,
And come and save us!" (v. 2)

Occasionally people who feel frustrated and helpless say, "I'm at the end of my rope!" This idiom means that they have reached the limits of their endurance. The mental picture is one of holding on tightly to a rope for support, while losing one's grip and slipping to the very end. This image seems to be an apt description of how the psalmist is feeling in this short verse.

Verse 1 mentions Joseph. Verse 2, then, logically mentions Ephraim and Manasseh, Joseph's two sons, as well as his brother Benjamin here. Joseph and Benjamin had the same mother (Rachel), and their tribes were naturally grouped together (Num. 2:18–24). In Psalm 80:2, the names of God's children are noted, personalizing their relationship in the mind of the reader. The psalmist begs God to rescue them from their enemies and save their nation.

The verb "stir up" (Hb. *'ur*) means "to rouse, excite, or awaken." The urgency and almost panic in the author's voice is heard. He is bewildered at God's seeming apathy or disregard for the plight of His people. In several psalms, the writer begs God to wake up (e.g., "Rise up," Ps. 7:6; "Awake!" Ps. 44:23). Although the psalmists did not actually believe that God was sleeping, the imagery conveys their frustration with God's choice not to intervene in desperate circumstances. God does not sleep. However, there are times when, just like the psalmist, we *feel* as if He is sleeping or distant because we seem to get no response to our prayers.

This prayer brings to mind a New Testament scenario in Luke 8:22–24. Jesus was sleeping in the boat in the midst of a dreadful storm while His disciples cried out to Him: "Master, Master, we are perishing!" (v. 24). The unspoken question in these instances is clear: Does God not care what is happening to us? Why doesn't

He do something? The psalmist does not doubt God's power to defeat Israel's enemies. The question is really much more agonizing: Why won't He help me?

All Christians have struggled with this question at one time or another. If you have not, then just wait. You will. It is all part of the life journey. The only answer to this question on this side of heaven is: God is sovereign and will act in a way that works for good in His kingdom. You may not be particularly comforted, especially if you are in a crisis, like the psalmist. Nevertheless, this biblical pattern will teach you to trust quietly in God and wait for Him to act. At first, the response is a discipline, but eventually it will lead to joy.

Are you at the end of your rope? If so, remember that God is there with you.

Susie Hawkins

Prayer: *Ask the Lord to help you to quieten your spirit. Keep your eyes fixed on Him and hold your faith firmly. Thank the Lord for His saving power.*

Personal Reflection: ....

....

....

....

....

....

Shine on Us

Psalm 80:14–19

"Restore us, O LORD God of hosts;
Cause Your face to shine,
And we shall be saved!" (v. 19)

"This is a nightmare," said my friend, standing in what had been her kitchen. She had undertaken the ambitious project of restoring her older home to its original structure. Walls were torn out, dirt and dust covered everything, and we had to climb over piles of bricks, wood, and debris as we walked around. She had dreamed of restoring her lovely old home by removing the modern structures and materials, and recovering its original beauty. Her overwhelming challenge was twofold: first, removing the old; second, restoring by adding the new. While bringing back the gracious style of her dream home was her desire, we both agreed that building another house would have been much easier.

This psalm was likely written during the time of the Assyrian or Babylonian exile when the Israelites were captured and carried away to foreign lands. The psalmist prays first for God to restore His people, to bring them back to their roots and a strong faith in Yahweh, the one and only God. Interestingly, the biblical use of "restore" implies not only a return to the original condition but also an improvement (Is. 61:7; Jer. 30:17; Joel 2:25–26). Likely the psalmist was remembering the "glory days" of Israel under her early kings—Saul, David, and Solomon. The beauty of the temple, together with the prosperity and justice that characterized that time (2 Sam. 8:15), was a distant and painful memory. The spiritual restoration of God's people was the cry of the psalmist's heart. But, that restoration would be complete only through the genuine repentance of the Israelites for their grievous sins and gross disobedience.

The phrase "cause your face to shine" is an Hebraic expression asking God for His favor and blessing. This phrase is an echo of the Aaronic blessing, the priestly prayer of the Old Testament (Num. 6:24–26). When God's face is referenced, it means the holy joy of His presence is remembered. The reverse is also true, as the psalmists occasionally beseech God not to turn away or hide His face from them, meaning to abandon them or ignore their prayers (Pss. 27:9; 69:17; 102:2).

Restoration, blessing, and favor will be followed by God's salvation or the rescue of His people. Like the Israelites, our hearts can become cold and rebellious. And like the Israelites, our hearts can be spiritually restored. Infinitely greater than the satisfaction of enjoying the beauty of a restored home, our hearts are content and filled with joy when God has done His work of restoration in our lives.

Susie Hawkins

Prayer: *Pray for the Lord to restore you by forgiving your sin and giving you a fresh joy in Him. Ask Him to shine His face upon you, that His gracious favor would be upon you and your family.*

Personal Reflection: ....

....

....

....

....

Living Full and Obedient

Psalm 81:1–12

"But My people would not heed My voice,
And Israel would have none of Me.
So I gave them over to their own stubborn heart,
To walk in their own counsels." (vv. 11–12)

Growing up as the youngest of four children, I learned a *lot* from my brothers' mistakes. I did make my fair share of willfully disobedient choices, of course! But I also learned what not to do when it came to negotiations with the "parental units." One act of my eldest brother *never* yielded positive results—plugging his ears so he would not hear the commands of my mother or father. He reasoned: "If I don't hear them, then I can't listen to or obey them." His logic was misconstrued and disillusioned.

When I read Psalm 81—which describes Israel is not heeding, not obeying, and ultimately as hating the Lord (vv. 11, 15)—I cannot help but mentally picture Israel as my brother. My parents were no more my brother's enemy than God was the enemy of Israel. But how often did Israel see God as the enemy? Although Yahweh was the one who had set them free (v. 6), rescued them in their distress (v. 7), and brought them out of Egypt (v. 10), He wanted to do much *more* for them. He wanted them to open their mouths so He would fill them (v. 10). Sadly, His people "would not heed" His voice" (v. 11).

Sobering passages like this one remind me of the depths to which my own stubbornness has the potential to plummet (Jer. 17:9). How often do we see God as the enemy? He may not approve our grand plans for life and bring that perfect husband, job, or child into our lives. Maybe He allows tragedy to strike or does *not* save you from financial ruin or marital despair. You may be left picking up the pieces and wondering where God is.

In actuality, stubbornness is the enemy. Stubbornness can be the death of the good that God wants to bring into our lives. When God is calling you to ministry or asking you to befriend a particular woman in your church or asking you to give more than you feel comfortable to give, He is asking you to "open your mouth wide" so He can "fill it." God does not want you to have a chasm of emptiness in your life; He wants to fill your life with good things (Ps. 84:11). Do not limit all that God would do because you have got your fingers in your proverbial ears. Trust Him; He is not the enemy. Listen. Learn. Live *full*!

Sarah Bubar

Prayer: *Ask the Lord to search your heart and see if there is any stubbornness in you. Surrender fully to Him in response to His love and forgiveness. Follow the Lord and not your own plans, and seek to know the difference.*

Personal Reflection: ....

....

....

....

....

....

God-Sized Regret

Psalm 81:13–16

*"Oh, that My people would listen to Me,
That Israel would walk in My ways!" (v. 13)*

"Oh, that [Hb. *lu*, "if only"] My people would listen to Me" is quite possibly the saddest phrase our Father ever uses in relation to His people, the children of Israel. The lament is steeped with regret for what is to come and what will never be. The phrase "if only" suggests that dreams are shattered and plans are now changed, signifying a chain reaction. While human hindsight may be 20/20, God's vision is always perfect. He sees what was, what is, and what will be. But He also sees what *could* be.

Yahweh describes what *could* have been in the lives of His precious people, revealing that He had every intention of quickly vanquishing every enemy (v. 14). Yahweh, wanted to fill to overflowing the lives of His people: "Open your mouth wide, and I will fill it" (v. 10) He wanted to satisfy them "with honey from the rock" (v. 16). The desire of God is clear: He wants to unload His blessings onto His children, "exceedingly abundantly above all we ask or think" (Eph. 3:20).

While God is limitless and immeasurable, one thing does limit what God can do for us—our disobedience. Our lack of submission does not limit His control or sovereignty, and it has absolutely no bearing on His love for us. But our choices *can* and *do* affect what God chooses to bring into our lives and what He chooses to hold back. This was true in the lives of the people of Israel, and it is true in my life.

These words are sobering and demand self-reflection: "The haters of the LORD would pretend submission to Him" (Ps. 81:15). You mean I can *look like* I am being submissive to God without *actually* being submissive to God, and that becomes not just hypocrisy, but *hatred*?! I never want to submit to Him merely

out of a sense of duty or a desire for human approval. I want to be authentic, not artificial. I never want God to say, "Oh, Sarah, if only you had listened to Me and followed My voice in your life. I had all these blessings waiting for you. I wanted to fill your life, but you would not obey."

Take time right now for introspection. Do you have some regrets you need to confess to the Lord? Are you faking your submission to the Lord, or do you really seek to heed His voice? Are you an artificial or authentic Christian? Does your obedience originate from a heart's desire to bring honor to God alone?

Sarah Bubar

Prayer: *Humble yourself before your Heavenly Father. Ask Him to help you walk in full submission to Him and His Word. Confess anything false or artificial about the way you are living, and be authentic as His light shines through you.*

Personal Reflection: ....

....

....

....

....

Nowhere Else I'd Rather Be

Psalm 84:1–10

*"For a day in Your courts is better than a thousand.
I would rather be a doorkeeper in the house of my God
Than dwell in the tents of wickedness." (v. 10)*

In my first class, on my first day of seminary back in 2008, I met Diane. We instantly became friends and then roommates—the best of friends. Fast forward eight years—past the the graduations (hers and mine), her wedding day, her move to Colombia where she and her husband are missionaries, my move to Florida, the births of her two adorable children—and we are *still* the best of friends.

In 2016, I learned that she and her family had a six-hour layover on the east coast of Florida while en route to Texas from Colombia. I immediately purchased a round-trip ticket to that airport in order to spend those six hours with her, meeting her daughter who was born overseas, and reconnecting with my best friend. It made no difference to us that we had to visit in an airport restaurant—a somewhat uncomfortable venue. After not seeing each other for four years, we just wanted to spend the time together. When you are close to someone and have that type of relationship, where you are and what you are doing do not matter as long as you can be in each other's presence.

The psalmist had similar thoughts about the Lord's presence: "My heart and my flesh cry out for the living God" (v. 2). When he looked at creation and saw how every sparrow had its home, the psalmist remembered that his true home was in the presence of his King (v. 3). His true heart's happiness was found in the presence of God. He would rather be in a cramped doorway at the house of God than comfortably sitting in the tent of those who opposed his God (v. 10). Soul fellowship has less to do with the location and more to do with the

company. No matter how comfortable a tent might be for dwelling, his soul could find true comfort only in the presence of God.

What is the intimacy level of your relationship with Christ? When given the choice, would you rather spend time with the Lord or another hour watching television? Do you reserve Sunday mornings for worship? If your church only met very early in the morning, would you still go? What sacrifices do you make to spend more time with your King? Can you, like the psalmist, truly say, "Better is a day in your courts than a thousand anywhere else"?

Sarah Bubar

Prayer: *Approach the throne of Yahweh your King and thank Him for being accessible to you. Thank Him for making a way for you to have unhindered fellowship with Him. Take full advantage of His favor. Hunger and thirst for God's presence in an insatiable way so that you can truly echo these words of the psalmist.*

Personal Reflection:

245

Be Happy

Psalm 84:11–12

"O LORD of hosts,
Blessed is the man who trusts in You!" (v. 12)

A simplistic and holistic truth resonates in this psalm: "Blessed is the man who trusts" in the Lord (v. 12). *Blessed* can also be translated *happy*, reminding me of the hymn, "Trust and Obey": There is no other way to be happy (or blessed) in Jesus but to trust and obey.

When I was growing up, my father ran a teen summer camp in the Adirondack Mountains of upstate New York. Every Sunday morning during breakfast, campers would break from their usual tradition of scarfing down their food, and we would have a worship time around the mess hall tables. Every week hundreds of teenagers lifted their voices in worship, singing hymns to the Lord. While the experience was unimpressive at the time, thirty years later I have nothing but gratitude for those Sunday mornings. Singing hymns put us in the mind-set of worship and opened our hearts for the Word that was about to be shared. Because of this memory, I love the old hymns of the faith.

John Sammis, who wrote the lyrics to the hymn "Trust and Obey," and the sons of Korah, who penned Psalm 84 thousands of years before him, both knew this universal fact: True happiness lies in absolute trust of the Lord and unrelenting obedience to Him. Even though generations, cultures, and histories separated these musicians, the consistency of how God works remains steadfast. He seeks our good (Rom. 8:28) and does not withhold His blessing from us when we "walk uprightly" with Him (Ps. 84:11). When we, in full surrender, trust Him without wavering, our hearts are never more content. Calamity may strike an obedient follower of God, but even in the midst of that storm, God promises peace and even joy (James 1:2–3).

What about you? Do you trust in the Lord? When you look at your life can you say that you truly set your hope and confidence completely on Him? Are you walking "uprightly"—obeying, pleasing, and relying on the Lord? Scripture is clear: When you are trusting God, then you are "blessed." Are there areas of your life in which you may be missing out on the "good" and the blessedness God wants to give you because you are not trusting Him?

Sarah Bubar

Prayer: *Thank the Lord for being such a good and all-knowing God. Seek His help to learn to truly trust Him not just in your mind but in your heart as well. Take courage to look at your fears and remind yourself that God is your sun and shield! He alone is worthy of your trust!*

Personal Reflection: ....

....

....

....

....

....

The Favor of God

Psalm 85:1–13

"LORD, You have been favorable to Your land;
You have brought back the captivity of Jacob.
You have forgiven the iniquity of Your people;
You have covered all their sin. Selah" (vv. 1–2)

The favor of God seems like such an ephemeral and intangible endeavor. So often we float through life wanting to be happy and have peace. We desire an easy, guilt-free, and prosperous life. If it is difficult or marred with heartache, we must be doing something wrong. This thought could not be further from the truth. To get back into favor with God, we must grovel.

In this psalm, the sons of Korah rehearsed the history of God's work in relation to His people and spelled out their future hope in how God will continue to work in their lives. The verb phrase "have been favorable" (Hb. *ratsah*, "be delighted or pleased with") describes God's grace toward His people. The same word underscores why God's people were able to have victory over their enemies: "For they did not gain possession of the land by their own sword, nor did their own arm save them; but it was Your right hand, Your arm, and the light of Your countenance, because You favored [Hb. *ratsah*] them" (Ps. 44:3). The victory experienced by Israel was based solely on God's favor—not because their army annihilated their foes or because their strong arm drove out their enemies. No! God Himself did those things, and He did so because of His "mercy" (85:7, 10).

God is amazingly consistent in how He relates to His children. If you have accepted Christ as Savior, you possess the favor of God, not because you have done anything to earn it or be worthy of it (Rom. 3:23) but simply because God, in *His* faithful love, imputed unto you the righteousness of His precious Son (2 Cor. 5:21)—you have been made righteous through Christ.

Watchman Nee, in his book *The Normal Christian Life,* considers asking God for things He has already given absurd, likening it to asking to get into a room that you are already in.* Those who have willingly received, in Christ, forgiveness for their sins have the favor of God. Praise the Lord!

In the beautiful grace of the gospel, what I have earned (guilt, death, eternal condemnation, and separation from God) has been replaced, through God's grace in Christ, with what I do not deserve (freedom, life, peace, and eternity to walk in fellowship with a holy God). Salvation is truly awe-inspiring.

Sarah Bubar

Prayer: *Thank the Lord for His salvation and the favor enjoyed by those who belong to Him. Ask the Lord to help you never take for granted His favor nor to cheapen it by trying to earn the free gift of grace.*

Personal Reflection: ....

....

....

....

....

*Watchman Nee, *The Normal Christian Life* (Carol Stream, IL: Tyndale House, 1977), 57.

Do You Have a "God Complex"?

Psalm 86:1–7

*"For You, LORD, are good, and ready to forgive,
And abundant in mercy to all those who call upon You." (v. 5)*

In twenty-first-century America, it is very easy for women to get a "God complex." The myriad of feministic influences convince us that we can do anything or be anything, that gender is no barrier. If we imagine it, we can do it. If we try hard enough and push hard enough, we can shatter that glass ceiling whether in the corporate world, at home in the domestic world, or in the religious world. We imagine ourselves as gods in our own worlds!

And yet reading passages like Psalm 86 never makes it more obvious that we are unlike God. David remembers who he is, who his God is, and the vast differences between him and God. The passage focuses first on David as a person—"poor and needy" (v. 1). He is aware that he needs God's protection (v. 2) and God's grace (v. 3). He knows that joy is not found in life; but in turning to God (v. 4). Verse 5 takes a pivotal turn to extol the true character of God.

- **Good.** The nature of God is to be good, warm, caring, affectionate, considerate, and helpful. We see this truth consistently portrayed from His patient leading of the Israelites in the wilderness (Ex. 13) to His ministry of healing (in the Gospels)—even when people did not show their appreciation (Luke 17).
- **Ready to forgive.** The word used to describe God's forgiveness is anticipatory. God knows our sinful nature, yet because of His nature, He is forgiving us!
- **Abundant in mercy.** The word "mercy" (Hb. *chesed*) denotes "covenantal loyalty"; love or lovingkindness that is unwavering, constant, committed forever. People who display this type of love are the truest

of friends. They are steadfast in their opinion of you and your value. Their decisions regarding you are always for your betterment. This type of love is possessed by God in abundance.

Sarah Bubar

Prayer: *Take a moment to have an honest conversation with the Lord. Tell Him ways in which you see your need of Him. List them before Him and make your needs a matter of prayer. Then ask the Lord to make you aware of times you do not think you need Him, areas of your life that you think you can handle on your own. List those as well, and confess them before God.*

Personal Reflection: ....

....

....

....

....

....

....

I'm Not Good Enough to Be God

Psalm 86:8–10

"For You are great, and do wondrous things;
You alone are God." (v. 10)

To forget who God is when you have lost sight of who you are is inevitable. God chose to remind me of this particular lesson in a rather creative manner. I broke my tibia—a large crack down, not across my tibia bone—as I was climbing into a speedboat.

Because I could put absolutely *zero* weight on this bone if I wanted it to heal, and because I knew trying to use crutches for eight weeks was going to result in my using my leg more than my doctor allowed, I complied with being in a wheelchair for two months. Getting around to do normal tasks was so difficult! I live on the second floor of an elevator-free building. Life quickly became impossible! I had to depend on people for everything: driving, cleaning, going home at the end of a full day of work, returning the next morning, picking up things I dropped on the floor. I learned many things in those eight weeks, like a deep appreciation for my friends and family. I learned to depend on them and to ask for help.

I also learned rather quickly that I was a needy person; even more specifically, I needed God. This verse influenced my life. While for those eight weeks my neediness was on display, obvious to all, in reality my neediness had always been there—broken leg or not. I just did not want to see it. I wanted to be capable of pulling myself up by my own bootstraps and achieving success in life, ministry, relationships, finances, everything. In reality, however, I am incredibly unsuccessful in those endeavors when I try to do them apart from God's work in my life. Jesus said, ". . . without Me you can do nothing" (John 15:5). He also said, "I do nothing of Myself" (John 8:28). If Jesus Christ, Savior of the world, did nothing without his Father's consent, why do I think I can keep God on the sidelines of my life as if He is my own personal cheerleader or coach? No! He alone is *God*! He is coach, cheerleader, offense, *and* defense! He is every player! He calls every play. *He is God.*

I am not enough to be God. I am only enough to be me. But that is all the expectation God has of me—for all of me to be dependent on all of Him.

Sarah Bubar

Prayer: *Thank the Lord for this humble reminder that apart from Him you are nothing. Seek His help to keep this mind-set throughout this day, this week, this life. Get out of His way and cheer God on as He works in your life.*

Personal Reflection: ....

....

....

....

....

....

....

Unite My Heart

Psalm 86:11–17

"Teach me Your way, O Lᴏʀᴅ;
I will walk in Your truth;
Unite my heart to fear Your name." (v. 11)

I absolutely love working on a team! Unity is paramount for the success of a project—first within the leadership and then within the body as a whole. Unity is needed in sports teams, in war tactics, and in a home. Why? Because when it comes to working as a team, unity affects everything. Without unity, there is disunity, which leads to distrust, and finally to dysfunction. When you have disunity, you have more than one leader vying for power over the whole. When you have disunity, tensions rise, emotions flare, and you lose sight of your real enemy. Disunity is like cancer to your team, rotting away productivity and success.

Disunity can also appear within oneself. Part of you wants to go this way while the other part of you wants to go the other. The heart says, "Yes!" but the brain says, "No!" Paul talks about this dichotomy throughout his writings (see Rom. 7:19–23; Gal. 5:16–17). The apostle Paul understood his moral weakness as a human being as well as sin's strength in his life. He did not always follow the Lord, and he did not always resist sin's power and control. We are no different than Paul in our inward struggle. God alone can unify our flesh to walk in the Spirit.

The psalmist was well aware of this battle between the mind and the heart, between the Spirit and the flesh. One of my college professors said, "Sin is the intruder in your life! Don't let yourself be victimized by it!" The psalmist longs for the truth-filled and trustworthy instruction of Yahweh God to quiet his flesh and awaken his Spirit, unifying the whole man to walk in obedience before the Lord. The psalmist pleads with God to unite his heart with the truth as his mind

takes in the Word of God. Having this time with the Lord is important to feed your Spirit and unify your heart and mind. Keep at it!

Sarah Bubar

Prayer: *Ask the Lord to give you a hunger and thirst for His Word so you may see His character on every page. Experience God's presence afresh every morning and pray like the psalmist each day.*

Personal Reflection: ....

....

....

....

....

....

....

The Song of Your Life

Psalm 89:1–10

"I will sing of the mercies of the LORD forever;
With my mouth will I make known
Your faithfulness to all generations. (v. 1)

Our family loves music. We love to sing, play, dance, and listen to music. My husband is a worship pastor, so one of the perks of his particular calling is the exposure our four children have to many different kinds of music. Naomi, our five-year-old, particularly loves to sing! And she has a strong, confident voice that can always be heard. If she is happy, she sings, "I Love Jesus. He made goldfish and the trees and the sky and my toys," or if she is said, "Jesus loves me even when I'm sad. He knows my heart."

With our lives, our family also "sings" in the ways we respond to the realities of life. We can sing of joy over God's faithfulness or sorrow over the disappointments of life. The writer of Psalm 89 made a decision to worship God despite the heartache His people experienced at that time. Jerusalem had been destroyed and the temple torn down. David's line of kingship seemed to be threatened with extinction, but the psalmist chose to remember God's faithfulness and lovingkindness.

Each of us has days, and sometimes seasons, of disappointment and heartache. What song does your soul sing when those times come? Twice the author says, "I will . . . ," revealing that we have a choice to make. Will I choose to worship God or give in to worry, doubt, fear, and anger? Worship, joy, faith, and belief all begin with the decision that says, "I will." The choice does not always come easily, but over time it can become the default disposition of our hearts (Rom. 12:2).

How is this choice possible? Remember what you know to be true about God! The psalmist remembered the mercies of God to the people of Israel. God

had acted with lovingkindness toward them over and over, and He does so today. As we remember how God has been faithful in the past, our faith and resolve are strengthened to face the challenges of today and the uncertainty of all our tomorrow.

The author sang a song of instruction (Hb. *maskil*). I have four sets of little eyes watching me every day. Others are watching you, and you are teaching something by how you react to life's realities. You and I have the great privilege of teaching the songs of God's faithfulness and mercy to future generations. What song is your life singing today? May your melodies soar beyond your mood as you choose to worship.

Kristin Yeldell

Prayer: *Take an honest assessment of your own heart, examining your true reactions and heart's disposition toward challenges. If there is worry, fear, anger, bitterness, or unforgiveness there, confess that to the Lord. Thank God for all the ways He has shown His mercy to you, and ask Him to help you make the choice to worship Him. Close your prayer by committing to God, "I will sing of the mercies of the Lord forever."*

Personal Reflection: ....

....

....

....

....

The Ultimate Promise Keeper

Psalm 89:11–52

*"My covenant I will not break
Nor alter the word that has gone out of My lips." (v. 34)*

I will never forget May 13, 2005. That day changed all the rest of my other days. Eric and I stood before a gathering of friends and family in Louisville, Kentucky, and committed our vows to one another and to God: "To love and to cherish, for richer or poorer, for better for worse, in sickness and in health, till death do us part." We could not have known then what the following years would bring. Multiple moves, ministry highs and lows, the loss of a baby and the births of four others, health challenges, personal struggles, rich friendships and others that brought heartache—none could be anticipated. Yet in all that has happened, the covenant commitment we made on that sunny Kentucky day, by the grace of God, has not changed.

In marriage and in life, we learn faithfulness to each other because we have a God who is deeply faithful and committed to us. He is the ultimate "Promise Keeper." Psalm 89 paints a picture of a defenseless people with a "broken down" wall and a stronghold that has been destroyed, a people who are weakened by the exploitation of their enemies, as soldiers without swords and youths who have grown old (vv. 40–45). All of these things left the people questioning the validity of God's covenant and the truthfulness of His promises to them.

Can you identify with the description of Israel? Do you feel weak, defenseless, and defeated? Maybe you have found yourself in a marriage or work situation that did not turn out as you expected it. God did not omit the struggling of His people. God is not shaken by your honest words of hurt. But we cannot wallow in the hurt. God instills confidence and security as we remember two important truths from this verse.

God keeps His promises and His Words are true. Israel had many moments of questioning. Their circumstances said that God had forgotten them and turned His back on them. What are your current circumstances telling you about God? God had not forgotten His people, and He will not forget you. "For all the promises of God in Him are Yes, and in Him Amen, to the glory of God through us" (2 Cor. 1:20).

As it has been often said, "I don't know what the future holds, but I know Who holds my future." Trust your days to the ultimate Promise Keeper. You will not regret it.

Kristin Yeldell

Prayer: *Rejoice today that God keeps His promises! Pray through specific words of promise that speak to a situation you are currently facing. Thank God that His words are true and that He will make good on what He has said He will do.*

Personal Reflection: ....

....

....

....

....

....

Trusting the Eternal God

Psalm 90:1–6

"Before the mountains were brought forth,
Or ever You had formed the earth and the world,
Even from everlasting to everlasting, You are God." (v. 2)

A lot of things happen that cause us to question our time on earth. Bad news from a doctor, being fired from a job, the dissolving of a relationship, or the death of a dear friend or family member raise uncertainties about all our tomorrows, leaving us feeling insecure and fearful.

God is the Creator of time, and He is eternal. He is not limited by time or its constraints because He existed before the world was even spoken into existence: "Even from everlasting to everlasting. You are God."

The psalm, attributed to "Moses the man of God" and the only psalm associated with him, was written as the older generation of Israelites who had left Egypt were dying off in the wilderness (Num. 14). The psalm praises the eternal nature of God against the backdrop of the realities of the brevity of human life. God's judgment was coming against the people of Israel because of their unbelief. God had delivered them from captivity in Egypt and promised them He would deliver them into Canaan. As they looked around, they were afraid and filled with unbelief. The fear and unbelief tempted them to act in disobedience to God's commands.

God is eternal, but we most definitely are not! Our time on this earth is limited to the days He has appointed for us. Will those days be filled with obedience motivated by belief in God's commands or unbelief that fuels our disobedience?

Moses was a man who had a unique relationship with this eternal God. The Lord knew Him "face to face" (Deut. 34:10–12). They shared a close and intimate relationship. He was most at home in the love of the Lord. Yet this

intimacy was not casual or flippant but filled with awe over God as the eternal Creator.

The Israelites were faced with the monumental task of entering the land of Canaan, which seemed to be inhabited by giants. Are you facing a giant today? Is there a task God has called you to do that looks like an impassable mountain in front of you? Remember: God is the one who created the mountains, and He existed before they ever were. Believe that God will equip you to accomplish what He has called you to do!

Kristin Yeldell

Prayer: *What is your current attitude toward time and eternity? Recognizing that God is eternal and that He has a plan to use you to advance His kingdom during your time on earth, ask Him to help you walk in obedience and belief today!*

Personal Reflection: ....

....

....

....

....

The Master Teacher of Time

Psalm 90:7–12

*"So teach us to number our days,
That we may gain a heart of wisdom." (v. 12)*

None of us ever feels that we have enough time and money. "Where did the time go? I just don't have enough hours in the day." Many days I feel overwhelmed with all I need to accomplish and under-equipped actually to complete the tasks. Time and money are similar as both require good stewardship.

The psalmist (identified here as Moses) voices this prayer to God in light of the frailty and brevity of man's experience here on earth: "In the morning they [children of men] are like grass which grows up . . . In the evening it is cut down and withers" (v. 5b–6). He makes a simple request: "So teach us. . . ." The acknowledgment of the writer's need for a teacher signals something very important as we consider our use of time. You must know your limitations. Personal weaknesses must be identified. How many hours of sleep do you need to operate at your best? Are you eating a healthy, balanced diet? Are you an extrovert who is refueled by being around people or an introvert who needs more time alone? Knowing your physical limitation will help you to order your time so that you may be effective in serving Christ.

God has created you to advance His kingdom her on earth, and there are callings that He has on your life alone. What unique purpose does He have for you? Are there "distractors" that are keeping you from living out God's priorities? Social media can be a wonderful thing, but it can also be a major time-waster! If my family sees the top of my head (because I'm staring at the screen of my phone) more than they see the whites of my eyes, something is out of order. God has given us His priorities. The first is to "love the LORD your God with all your heart, with all your soul, and with all your mind." The second is to "love your neighbor as yourself" (Matt. 22:37–39).

These commands should direct how you plan your day. Jesus willingly put on the limitations of human flesh. He knew His purpose— "to seek and to save that which was lost" (Luke 19:10). Jesus also knew the importance of regularly being alone with the Father (e.g., Mark 1:35). If Jesus needed time with the Father, what kind of praise must there be in our hearts to think that we can get through a day without Him?

Wisdom comes from the Master Teacher. Remember: *Private time* with God in prayer and the Word clarifies God's *purpose* for you and sets the priorities for your day. Time is short, so teach us Lord!

Kristin Yeldell

Prayer: *Confess the areas of your life where you are wasting time. Ask God to clarify His purpose for you today, and to help you see any seeming "interruptions" as opportunities to further advance His Kingdom. Commit your time to Him.*

Personal Reflection: ....

....

....

....

....

The Beauty of the Lord

Psalm 90:13–17

"And let the beauty of the Lord our God be upon us,
And establish the work of our hands for us;
Yes, establish the work of our hands." (v. 17)

I recently saw an obnoxious bumper sticker in our South Florida town: "I live where you vacation." Having grown up in South Florida, I have become very used to the bright blue skies, palm trees, clear water, white sands of the beach, and the breathtaking sunsets. One would think we spent most of our days at the beach with all this loveliness around us! With four young children, I have to confess that my eyes are often counting heads, making sure we have all of our bags and all of our people. By nature, I am not a good "noticer" of my surroundings. I am a worker, a doer! Life can be hurried and rushed, leaving little opportunity to observe the loveliness around me. It can be difficult to break from the daily tasks to enjoy the beauty of this place we call "home."

One would think that to appreciate beauty, work would have to be put aside. This prayer of Moses says otherwise! The "beauty of the Lord" and "work," though at first glance seeming to compete with one another, actually are inseparably united.

What is the beauty of the Lord? He is holy, completely set-apart, lovely in all His character. Martin Luther has called this beauty the "deluge of grace."* The beauty of His grace and holiness shine on us and illumine all we do in our service to Him.

Work and service done apart from the enabling power of the Holy Spirit are devoid of power and light and true beauty. Moses recognized the great need each of us has for the Lord to shine on us His grace and holiness. In contrast then, everything done apart from Him is gray and devoid of true life. Have you found yourself operating independently from the Lord? Do you care for

your family, serve your church, and attempt the daily tasks of life on your own strength? "The work of our hands" described by Moses will be established and enduring only when the light of Christ shines on us.

I want to do better about observing the creation God has surrounding me. But more than that, I want to set my heart on gazing at the beauty of the Lord in the person of Jesus Christ. As I begin each day looking at Him in the pages of His Word, the light of His truth and His character shines on my heart and fills me for the tasks ahead. Look to Jesus and go in the light of His Spirit. "Yes, establish the work of our hands" for the glory of God and the advancement of His kingdom.

Kristin Yeldell

Prayer: *Ask God to help you slow down to see the beauty of the Lord. Commit all of your plans for the day to Him, asking that He would fill you with Himself and shine on all you do.*

Personal Reflection: ....

....

....

....

*Charles H. Spurgeon, The Treasury of David: Volume 2 (Peabody: MA: Hendrickson Publishers, 1988), 85.

Welcome Home

Psalm 91:1–16

"Because you have made the LORD, who is my refuge,
Even the Most High, your dwelling place." (v. 9)

When I was in college, my visits home were rare because of the many miles that separated the two. My college in Jackson, Tennessee, was 984 miles from my "home" in Naples, Florida. While college was exciting and filled with new friendships, experiences, and lessons, there was nothing like going "home." Walking into my parents' house, I felt an immediate sense of welcome, rest, and relief. Even twenty years later, I still feel this way when I walk through the double-doors of that familiar place.

Your experience of home may not be the same as mine. For you, home may bring up feelings of betrayal, hurt, and anger. In these verses, the psalmist speaks not of a physical dwelling but of God as our "refuge" (v. 2) and "dwelling place" (v. 9).

Where do you go when you are uncertain or anxious, angry or hurt, needing direction for a decision to be made? You could run to many places with these emotions—to food, to shopping, or to other people. The word *refuge* is a military term and indicates strength or protection. Seeing God as our refuge implies that there will be a battle. On this earth, forces of evil will seek to defeat all that is good. Do not be surprised when the challenges of battle come. When they arise, is God your refuge?

Believers are called to be at home in Christ. He alone is truly the safe place, where He welcomes us with loving and open arms. I can see my mom standing at the door with arms wide open for a welcoming hug. In a similar way, Christ extends His welcome to us. His arms are wide open, and He says, "Welcome home!" (Rom. 14:3; 15:7).

Are you "at home" in Christ today? Have you made that first decision to turn to Christ in repentance and receive His offer of forgiveness and salvation? No true rest is found apart from a saving relationship with Jesus Christ.

If you are saved but still find your heart restless and anxious, consider what other people or things you may be seeking instead of Him. Take a moment to list those and commit them to the Lord.

The psalmist notes that we have a choice to make: "Because you have made. . . ." Have you made the Lord your "dwelling place"? Your heart will be restless with any other "dwelling" apart from Him. As you choose to make Christ your refuge, you will find rest and protection from the battles of life. You may not be immune to its effects, but you can be protected by your Refuge. Welcome home, friends.

Kristin Yeldell

Prayer: *Run to the Lord today! Thank Jesus for making a way for you to enter into His presence (Heb. 10:19–22). Pour out your heart to Him and find rest for your soul.*

Personal Reflection: ....

....

....

....

....

Flourish in the Lord

Psalm 92:1–15

"The righteous shall flourish like a palm tree,
He shall grow like a cedar in Lebanon.
Those who are planted in the house of the LORD
Shall flourish in the courts of our God.
They shall still bear fruit in old age;
They shall be fresh and flourishing,
To declare that the LORD is upright;
He is my rock, and there is no unrighteousness in Him." (vv. 12–15)

Having lived in the plains of Texas, I was not unfamiliar with bad weather, though I had no idea what to expect from a hurricane! A few short months after moving to Florida, Hurricane Andrew ripped through South Florida and left a path of destruction. Homes and businesses were ripped apart, and power lines were downed. The one thing consistently left standing—palm trees! Though some sustained damage, many of the trees withstood winds up to 145 miles per hour. While debris scattered the streets and foundations of homes were left bare, the palms stood strong and erect, only missing some of their branches.

The picture of the palm tree given in Scripture is one of permanence, strength, and stability. Those who are righteous are like a palm tree. Christ alone gives us His righteousness as a grace-gift and covers us with that righteousness before God. When the storms of life beat against the godly person, the winds cannot take her down. Storms may include illness and death, relational hurt and betrayals, financial challenges, and uncertainties. The righteous may bend in the wind, but they will not fall over. The psalmist gives us a clear picture of how to be strong like a palm tree.

As a follower of Christ, we are called to be deeply **rooted in intimate relationship with God**, abiding in Christ, and experiencing full fellowship with Him on a

continued basis. Relationships grow through time spent with the Lord in prayer and in reading His Word. Our roots grow deep, and we are strengthened. Charles Spurgeon has said: "Once planted in the Lord, we shall never be rooted up, but in His courts we shall take root downward, and bring forth fruit upward to His glory forever."[*]

The blessed result of abiding in Christ is **fruitful service** that lasts. The psalm states that even in old age fruit is born. What encouragement that should bring us! As seasoned saints live their days in faithful relationship to the Lord, their lives are a testimony of God's grace and faithfulness. The storms of life may come, but their deep-rootedness in Christ causes the fruit to spring upward and out for His glory. Effectiveness for God's kingdom does not diminish but increases with age.

There is not only mention of growth but of **flourishing in grace**. We can go through storms and not just survive, but thrive! When Christians suffer well, a beautiful testimony to God's good faithfulness comes.

Are you facing a storm? Plant your roots down deep in Christ. Abide and rest in Him, trusting that He is your Rock and cannot be moved! May your roots go deep in the immovable God, and your flourishing fruit will testify to the greatness of His Name.

Kristin Yeldell

Prayer: *Go to Christ as your Rock and your firm foundation. Ask Him to strengthen you by His Word and bring fruit even in difficult seasons. Thank Him for His faithfulness to you in all things.*

Personal Reflection: ....

....

*Charles H. Spurgeon, *The Treasury of David: Volume 2* (Peabody, MA: Hendrickson Publishers, 1988), 120.

The Blessings of God's Word

Psalm 94:1–15

"Blessed is the man whom You instruct, O Lᴏʀᴅ,
And teach out of Your law." (v. 12)

The psalmist in this chapter faced difficult circumstances (vv. 1–7). He acknowledged God as the ultimate refuge for the righteous, despite his current circumstances. Why does God allow us to encounter difficulties? God sees, hears, and knows all of the trials we will face in our lives (vv. 8–11). God wants to use difficult circumstances to mature our faith, increase our reliance upon Him, and deepen our understanding of His Word. He wants to use the details of our lives for our good and for His glory, even if we do not currently understand exactly how or why (Rom. 8:28). We need to trust in God and turn to His Word, especially during trying times.

God's Word presents the path to a blessed life. "Blessed is the man whom You instruct, O Lᴏʀᴅ, and teach out of Your law" (Ps. 94:12). Blessedness flows from receiving God's instruction. To receive His instruction, we must spend time in personal Bible study. How faithful are you to dig into the truth of God's Word—not listening to others share about what they have learned from God's Word or even reading about what others have learned or reading a devotional book such as this one. Instead, in-depth Bible study is an intentional verse-by-verse, book-by-book examination of God's Word.

Have you made a commitment in your life to study the Bible systematically? We receive instruction from God through His Word, and ultimately we receive the blessing of the Lord. This kind of Bible study requires hard work but results in great reward. Scripture will not return void but will accomplish all that God desires (Is. 55:11). Choose to follow the path that leads to a blessed and fruitful life.

God desires a relationship with you. He also desires that you be conformed to the image of His Son (Rom. 8:29). As you continually behold the character of God and strive to conform to His image, you will mature in your Christian walk. We need to look into the perfect law of liberty and continue in it (James 1:25). This entails intently studying the Word of God and continually striving to apply it to your life. Will you seek to faithfully study the Bible? The path to a blessed life hinges on knowing, meditating on, and applying the instruction of the Lord. I pray you will develop a deeper love for God and His Word and that you will be conformed to His image. Then you will live a blessed life all for your good and ultimately for God's glory.

Joy Martin White

Prayer: *Ask God to give you a passion to know Him better through an in-depth study of His Word. Commit to spending time studying, meditating upon, and applying God's Word to your life.*

Personal Reflection: ....

....

....

....

....

....

Find Your Comfort in Christ

Psalm 94:16–23

"In the multitude of my anxieties within me,
Your comforts delight my soul." (v. 19)

For the most part, I have not had a life-long struggle with anxiety. I am normally not overly emotional. Typically I allow things to roll off my back as I move on with life. But my life has changed. Recently, I experienced a crushing blow. I unexpectedly lost a twenty-seven-year-old loved one, who to my knowledge never made a decision for Christ. My spirit sank and my soul bears a heavy burden as I mourn this personal loss. I have spent weeks living in grief and regret. Then I sit down and read, "In the multitude of my anxieties" and feel God's graciousness wrap around me. God knows that life in this fallen world sends never-ending waves of anxieties. In fact, Jesus guarantees His disciples: "In the world you will have tribulation" (John 16:33). In this life, trials and tribulations will come. Yet we are to "count it all joy" (James 1:2). But how do we do that?

First, understand that when you have a problem, God has a purpose. God uses difficult circumstances in a variety of ways:

- To turn us to Him and deepen our relationship with Him.
- To mold and make us into the women He wants us to be.

Sometimes you may experience a painful trial that later will provide a platform for ministry to others facing the same trial. Dear sister, please know that when you have a problem, God really does have a purpose—and it is all for your good and His glory.

Second, know that when you have a problem, God provides peace. In the midst of the most difficult circumstances, you can have peace in Christ, for He has "overcome the world" (John 16:33).

Third, understand that when you have a problem, God has a plan. The psalmist writes: "In the multitude of my anxieties . . . , Your comforts delight my soul" (Ps. 94:19). In his commentary on Psalms, Charles Spurgeon writes that these comforts flow from our communion with God. We can take comfort in His attributes, in His promises, and in His gracious presence. God Himself is the ultimate answer for dealing with your difficulties. God's comfort can pull you from the depths of depression and out of the alley ways of anxiety. When delighting in God, earthly circumstances no longer overwhelm and demand full focus. Instead, you should be focused on Christ. He, through His pain, conquered yours.

Joy Martin White

Prayer: *Seek to cast your cares upon Christ, and seek comfort in His character. Pray that God will use the difficult things you face for your good and His glory.*

Personal Reflection: ....

....

....

....

....

....

....

In the Hands of the King

Psalm 95:1–11

"Oh come, let us worship and bow down;
Let us kneel before the LORD our Maker." (v. 6)

I vividly remember the first time I ever held my adopted daughter Rachel on Wednesday, January 26, 2005. Sitting on a green leather couch in a beach house, I first held my five-week-old baby, who weighed 5 lbs. and 8 ounces. I could not believe this beautiful tiny baby girl was forever mine. My husband and I had the responsibility to shepherd her heart and her life toward God. I soon became a helicopter parent, trying to control everything. But entering the teen years, it becomes more apparent that I am not ultimately in control.

Have you ever felt the burden of trying to control everything? A focus on Psalm 96 reveals that the Creator God controls all. Our call is to worship, while resting in the hands of our Maker.

Recognizing God as our Creator makes life a stewardship and not an ownership. Children, relationships, ministries, possessions, and talents—they all belong to Him. This perspective affects the way we rear our children, manage our homes, and minister to others, using our influence to serve well, as an act of worship for God's glory.

Recognizing God as our Creator makes life valuable. As the people of His pasture and the sheep of His hand (v. 7); God created us as His image-bearers, giving life value and worth (Gen. 1:27). Therefore, our identity comes not in our appearance or in our work, but in the fact that God created us in His image. Our looks, our fading youth, our talents, and our desires do not define us. Rather our satisfaction and identity are found in Christ alone.

God is our Maker. He loves us and knows us intimately, to the tune of knowing every single hair on our heads (Luke 12:7). Before this God we are called to "worship and bow down; let us kneel before the LORD our Maker" (Ps. 95:6).

When you feel like you are losing control, please realize that God holds everything in His hands. God is faithful. You can trust Him. You can even trust Him with the lives of your precious children. You must turn everything over to God, to worship and bow down to your mighty Maker, whose capable hands control all.

Joy Martin White

Prayer: *Praise God for being the mighty Maker of the heavens and the earth. Relinquish control of your life to His all-powerful hands. Thank God for being faithful and trustworthy.*

Personal Reflection: ....

....

....

....

....

....

....

The Good News of Salvation

Psalm 96:1–13

"Sing to the LORD, bless His name;
Proclaim the good news of His salvation from day to day.
Declare His glory among the nations,
His wonders among all peoples." (vv. 2–3)

Throughout Scripture, the Bible commands obedience in many ways. Some instructions are gladly embraced, such as gathering together to worship, fellowshipping with others, and loving our families. But this passage presents a command many women overlook: "Proclaim the good news of His salvation from day to day." When did you last share your faith? I don't mean posting a Bible verse on Facebook or Instagram. I mean when is the last time you sat down with a person and shared the good news of the gospel with her? Maybe you do not fully understand the gospel yet or what you need to be sharing with others. Let me clarify the good news of His salvation.

The Bible clearly teaches that every person who has ever lived, with the exception of Jesus, has sinned or done something wrong (Rom. 3:23). The consequence for our sin is death and hell, which means eternal separation from God, who is holy and perfect. The good news is that God loves us so much that He provided a way for us to go to heaven and spend eternity with Him. "For God so loved the world that He gave His only begotten Son, that whoever believes in Him should not perish but have everlasting life" (John 3:16). Jesus Christ came to earth as a man born of a virgin, lived a perfect life, died a painful death on the cross, and rose from the dead three days later to provide the only way to salvation. In response, we are called to confess our sins (1 John 1:9), repent of our sins (Acts 3:19), and place our faith in what Jesus did for us on the cross (Gal. 2:16). Then, by grace and through faith, we are saved from our sin (Eph. 2:8–9). This message is the good news of salvation!

You may already have a relationship with Christ—you have confessed, repented, and trusted Christ alone for your salvation. So how does this passage apply to you? God calls you to proclaim the good news of salvation and declare God's glory among the nations. God desires that all come to repentance (2 Pet. 3:9), yet they cannot receive this good news unless they hear (Rom. 10:17). Are you actively seeking to share the good news of the gospel with others? If not, why? Examine your heart and life and seek to be obedient to the Scriptures. We are all called to share the good news, the glory of Christ, and His wonders among all peoples, so let's do it!

Joy Martin White

Prayer: *Ask God to give you a burden for the nations. Pray specifically for people in your life who do not know Christ. Then pray that God would provide you with divine appointments to share the good news of salvation with them.*

Personal Reflection: ....

....

....

....

....

....

Love What God Loves and Hate What God Hates

Psalm 97:1–12

"You who love the LORD, hate evil!" (v. 10a)

As Christians, we often recoil at harsh words like *hate*. But evil is a condition worthy of an emotion as strong as hate. Evil distorts and destroys the good purposes of God; therefore, we rightly hate evil.

Our modern-day society likes to paint a picture of a loving God, and God is love (1 John 4:16). However, the world fails to recognize God's holiness (Is. 6:3). God's holiness provides a stark contrast to evil: "Woe to those who call evil good, and good evil" (Is. 5:20). These words accurately depict a society that fails to recognize God's holiness. Both love and holiness are character traits of God, and we need to embrace both in equal measure. If we love God, who is holy, we should hate all that is unholy.

There are many kinds of evil to be hated. For example:

- Evil that is in our own lives; our own personal sin. We should never embrace our sin but turn from it in broken repentance, to God who will not only forgive our sins but will also remove them from us "as far as the east is from the west" (Ps. 103:12).
- Evil that destroys the lives of others, such as drug addiction, pornography, abortion, slavery, child abuse, and homosexuality.
- Evil in this fallen world, such as children starving in Africa, the atrocities being done by terrorists in the Middle East, the persecution of Christians throughout the world, and corrupt governments that keep their citizens in poverty.
- Evils such as sickness and diseases like cancer, dementia, and heart disease. Anyone who has lost loved ones to these diseases knows that they are easy to hate.

From Genesis to Revelation, the Bible is clear that God hates evil. He hates sin and anything that steals His glory or causes His saints to stumble. Evangelist Billy Graham once remarked that God hates sin even more than a father hates a rattlesnake that is threatening the life of his child. This image pictures how much we should hate evil and sin! "Abhor what is evil. Cling to what is good" (Rom. 12:9). Our calling as believers is to hate what God hates and to love what God loves. As you grow in your love for God and love for the things that God loves, you will grow in your hatred of evil.

On days when your soul hurts over wickedness, take heart in the glory and majesty of our holy God who will one day dry every tear and make all things new (Rev. 21:4). God is the ultimate victor over all sin and evil, and He has given us victory through the blood of our Lord Jesus Christ!

Joy Martin White

Prayer: *Spend time in prayer, praying through the list of things you should hate. Let this list trigger many prayer needs that exist in your life and in our world. Thank God for the victory in Christ.*

Personal Reflection: ....

....

....

....

....

"God-Who-Forgives"

Psalm 99:1–9

"You answered them, O LORD our God;
You were to them God-Who-Forgives,
Though You took vengeance on their deeds." (v. 8)

Moses, Aaron, and Samuel all knew God, sought to serve Him with their lives, and interceded for others. Yet like us, they had deeds or actions that were not honoring to God, and they experienced the consequences for their sins.

Moses, who led the Israelites out of Egyptian captivity, was frustrated with the grumbling and complaining Israelites. Instead of speaking to the rock as God commanded, he lost his temper and struck the rock twice to bring forth water (Num. 20:7–11). Moses was forgiven, but there were consequences for his sin. Moses was allowed to look into the promised land from Mount Nebo, but he was not allowed to enter (29:12–15).

Aaron, the high priest, was left in charge of the Israelites while Moses went up on Mount Sinai to receive the Ten Commandments. While Moses was gone, Aaron fashioned an idol in the form of a golden calf (Ex. 32:1–4). He was forgiven, but there were consequences for his sin. Approximately three thousand men died (v. 28), and the people were plagued because of their sin (v. 35).

Samuel, who was the last great judge, failed in his role as father: "But his sons did not walk in his ways; they turned aside after dishonest gain, took bribes, and perverted justice" (1 Sam. 8:3). Consequently, they were not fit to judge Israel, so the people demanded a king. This rejection of God, who ultimately ruled over them (v. 7), was a grievous sin. Samuel was forgiven, but there were consequences for his sin.

Likewise, when you and I sin, there are consequences, even though they may not always be immediately apparent. God takes sin seriously. An old saying points out that "sin will always take you farther than you want to go, keep

you longer than you want to stay, and cost you more than you want to pay." When you are making decisions, keep this in mind! Seek to obey Christ in your thoughts, words, and deeds.

God is holy (Ps. 99:3, 5, 9). *Holy* means to be set apart, separate, without sin. God alone is holy, totally free from all wickedness and sinfulness. God's holiness demands justice. He sent Jesus to pay the penalty for our sins so that we could have forgiveness. He truly is "God-Who-Forgives."

Your response to being forgiven of your sin—by God's grace and through your faith—should be abundant gratitude (Eph. 2:8–9). This gratefulness should result in a life well lived for God. Though you will still sin, you can rest and rejoice in the fact that God is "God-Who-Forgives," and He can make all things new (2 Cor. 5:17).

Joy Martin White

Prayer: *Spend some time in prayer, confessing your specific sins to God. Then pray, reflecting on the character of God and thanking Him for the fact that He is "God-Who-Forgives."*

Personal Reflection: ....

....

....

....

....

Be Less

Psalm 100:1–5

"Know that the LORD, He is God;
It is He who has made us, and not we ourselves;
We are His people and the sheep of His pasture." (v. 3)

All of the kids in our Bible study class called our teacher "Aunt" Fanny, even though we were not related by blood. She challenged us not only to study but also to memorize Scripture. Many verses I know by heart today are the direct result of her life example, powerful influence, and gentle encouragement. Long ago, I learned Psalm 100. As an adult, I even wrote music for accompaniment to its words.

I like to read this particular psalm "upside down." Begin reading with verse 5 to discover the "who" and the "why" of the psalm. Then, sentence by sentence, read all the way back to verse 1. Once you know whom we worship and why, your response to Him will unfold like a beautiful flower.

God is *full* of goodness, mercy, and truth. We are to bless His name as we live our lives. As we allow Him to fill us with Himself, we learn how to "be less" ourselves. We bless God when we are willing to "be less."

Our key verse reminds us that we are to know, recognize, and acknowledge that the Lord is God and that the Lord "made us" (v. 3). "Made" suggests furnishing, fulfilling, and finishing. God provides all that is needed so that we can empty ourselves and allow Him to fill us with Himself and His purpose for our lives.

The psalmist proclaims that we are God's people. Knowing that we are part of the flock of God makes it easier to admit that we are "the sheep of His pasture." Individual sheep travel in a flock, which corporately follows a dedicated shepherd. Sheep find nourishment in the pasture of their shepherd.

Being a sheep in the flock of God provides its own daily dose of humility. Sheep are willing to be led and faithful to follow. Sheep were also potential candidates for sacrifice as a vital element of worship. Their innocence, coupled with the shedding of their blood, was a perfect picture of the Lamb of God, Jesus, who would be slain to take away the sins of the human flock of God.

Many Bible characters, especially in the Old Testament, were shepherds: Abraham, Isaac, Jacob and his sons, Rachel, Moses, David, and others. Their lives in the fields included that moment when they realized that even the shepherds of sheep are the sheep of God.

Becky Brown

Prayer: *Thank the Father for being your Shepherd, for setting a clear path for you to follow, for providing for your needs all along the way.*

Personal Reflection: ....

....

....

....

....

....

283

Heart Conditioning

Psalm 101:1–8

"I will walk within my house with a perfect heart.
I will set nothing wicked before my eyes;
I hate the work of those who fall away;
It shall not cling to me.
A perverse heart shall depart from me;
I will not know wickedness." (vv. 2b–4)

Frequently, character is described as "who you are when you are all by yourself with no one watching." The error in this train of thought is that you are never truly alone. God is always with you, fully aware of every detail of your life. He knows your thoughts before you think them and your words before you speak them. God knows the condition of your heart.

Psalm 101 is attributed to David—the shepherd boy who was the son of Jesse from the tribe of Judah, the songwriter, the giant-slayer, the servant of King Saul, the friend of Jonathan, and the king of Israel in Jerusalem. A reading of all eight verses of this psalm reveals the heart's desire of this anointed king of the people of God. Traditionally, earthly kings and rulers report to those who promoted or elected them to be rulers. David was responsible to God. David desired to please God with his life as a man and with his reign as king.

Samuel described David as a man after God's own heart, chosen by God to be king (1 Sam. 13:14). In Psalm 101, David speaks of two hearts—the "perfect heart" (v. 2) and the "perverse heart" (v. 4). The perfect heart possessed personal integrity and moral excellence, which pleased God. The perverse heart was characterized by crookedness and falsehood; it twisted and turned away from the desires and plans of the holy God. David desired to walk in a pure relationship with God, making daily decisions in alignment with the plans of God for him personally and for the nation of Israel collectively.

Only Jesus, a direct descendant of King David, would live a life of sinless perfection. David, like the rest of humanity, is known for his failures as well as his successes. His adulterous relationship with Bathsheba and his arrangement for the murder of her husband Uriah stand in stark contrast to David's desire to please God with his life actions. When David was alone, he was confronted with his failure to follow after God's own heart. His desire to make things right with God produced some amazing psalms of repentance and confession, leading to his experiencing forgiveness. David had a kneeling heart of worship. A worshiper will seek after God, even from the deepest cavern of failure.

Becky Brown

Prayer: *Confess to your Father your failures. Remember that He is greater than your failures. His forgiveness follows your confession and repentance. Commit to set nothing wicked before your eyes. Seek to become a woman after His own heart.*

Personal Reflection: ....

....

....

....

....

....

285

Blessing Insurance

Psalm 102:1–28

"This will be written for the generation to come,
That a people yet to be created may praise the LORD." (v. 18)

Although the author of this psalm is not identified, line by line the words of this ancient text reveal a deep, abiding sadness coupled with the complete, peaceful assurance found in trusting God. "Zion" is mentioned as being in ruins with its stones turned to dust and ashes. "Zion" usually refers to the city of Jerusalem. Many have suggested that the city has fallen to an enemy. Such an event occurred approximately five hundred years after the reign of King David. Whatever the tragedy or the time in the history of Israel, God is still not moved from His place of authority or weakened in His power of deliverance.

Our focus verse for today is located near the center of the psalm. Prior to our verse 18, the psalmist cries out to the Lord for deliverance from great personal and national affliction. He is spiritually distressed and physically emaciated, having been personally attacked by enemies and feeling totally helpless and isolated—"like a sparrow alone on the housetop" (v. 7). A tiny sparrow would fit completely inside the hand of a man. The whole time the psalmist was feeling lonely and abandoned, he was being held securely inside the hand of "The Sparrow Maker"!

Peace in the midst of the storms of life is found only in the truth of the transcendence of God, who alone endures through all generations. Our hope is secure only when it is placed in Him. Human beings come and go like seasonal grass that blooms, grows, and withers away. God remains. What a reason to rejoice!

The psalmist also finds rest through the hope of the faith of generations to come and will hear the truth from his own children, live it out, and, with dedication to God, pass it on to the next generations. As a never-married single,

I have realized that I will bear no children of my own. It is very important to me to seek out friends who have children I can love as my own. In the front of my Bible, I have written the names of sixteen children whom I have loved as though they were my own.

I am so grateful that the Word of God is written down and available today. Having this guidebook is such a treasure. Being able to read about our blessed assurance is blessed insurance indeed.

Becky Brown

Prayer: *Thank the Lord that your sadness and feelings of failure and loneliness are swallowed up by His presence and purpose for your life. Presently and eternally, your future is secure in Him.*

Personal Reflection: ....

....

....

....

....

....

....

The "Step-Fast" Love of God

Psalm 103:1–10

*"The Lord is merciful and gracious,
Slow to anger, and abounding in mercy" (v. 8).*

Sometimes, only a song will do! There are days when you are so deeply filled with the reality of the blessings of the Lord that mere spoken words do not seem to be adequate. David obviously felt that way frequently. Many of his Holy Spirit-inspired songs and poems comprise the prayer and worship book named "Psalms." Readers of Scripture are the beneficiaries of the overflow of the heart of this shepherd king and "sweet psalmist of Israel" (2 Sam. 23:1). Several other writers—some unknown to us by name but known to God—contributed to the book of Psalms.

Psalm 103 has always been a personal favorite. These twenty-two verses are filled with reasons to sing and shout for joy to the Lord. This psalm has two "bookend" verses which read: "Bless the Lord, O my soul!" (vv. 1, 22). Over the next few days, we will focus on several attributes of God, including His great mercy and forgiveness, which rest between the bookends.

In the providence of God, the book of Psalms is located near the center of the Bible. God was so good to place the devotional book of worship, praise, and lament in the heart of His Holy Word. Verse 8 assures the reader that the Lord is "merciful" and deeply compassionate—He feels our pain, and knows our needs. The Lord is "gracious." He bends down to meet our needs because of His mercy. The Lord is "slow to anger." Even though He knows all, sees all, and has reason to be angry when we reject Him or fail to obey, God loves us enough to restrain His wrath/anger to give time for the disobedient one to return to Him in willing obedience, love, and service. God is also "abounding in mercy." To *abound* means to be exceedingly full, having plenty to go around.

The second time the word *mercy* appears we must seek a deeper understanding for the full meaning. The word is better translated "lovingkindness." Shades of meaning here include "steadfast love," "unchanging love," or even "unfailing love." My little friend, Maley Grace, was learning about mercy. I explained to her about God's big love that never leaves. She began to dance and sing, "O, give thanks to the Lord for He is good and His step-fast love endures forever." I believe she got it perfectly correct. God "steps fast" on behalf of His children of all ages.

Becky Brown

Prayer: *Does the heavenly Father make you want to sing? Mere words will not do when you think of how wonderful God is to His children.*

Personal Reflection: ....

....

....

....

....

....

....

Compass Points

Psalm 103:11–12

*"As far as the east is from the west,
So far has He removed our transgressions from us." (v. 12)*

The lovingkindness (great mercy) and longsuffering (great patience) of the Lord toward His children are completely undeserved. Why God puts up with our rebellion and rejection and recalcitrance even for one moment is a mystery. God made a way to deal with our sinfulness.

God cannot tolerate sin, while people seem to bask in the glow of it. God is holy and set apart. God is perfect. God is sinless. One senior adult gentleman voiced this prayer: "God, we thank You that You are 'other' than us so You can call us out of who and what we are unto Yourself." In order to come near to God, you must repent (turn away from) and confess (acknowledge) your sins and allow Him to deal with them one by one. Sins are like heavy burdens that weigh you down, pushing you further and further away from God. When you turn to God and admit your failures, an amazing response pours forth from God. God forgives your sins. Then God removes your sins.

In our focal verse, David assures us that these confessed sins are separated from us "as far as the east is from the west" (v. 12). East is the direction of the sunrise. West is the direction of the sunset. No matter where you stand on this globe of earth, east is east and west is west. They never meet. However, on earth, there is a northernmost point and a southernmost point. You can travel north to the Arctic or south to Antarctica, stake your flag, and announce that you have arrived at either of those points, completing your journey.

On our side of Calvary, we can look at the center cross and see the compass points of the map of the love of God in the posture of the body of Jesus. His head with the crown of thorns pointed upward toward His Father in Heaven. His pierced feet dripped blood on the earth below. His arms were stretched out

wide in that east-to-west reach, inviting all to come to His Father through His own willing sacrifice.

Mark Hall of the group Casting Crowns penned the lyrics about the arms of God in the song "East to West." Jesus knows how far the east is from the west—one nail-scarred hand to the other. What compass points for you and me!

Becky Brown

Prayer: *Thank the Father for making a way for your sins to be forgiven, cleansed, lifted, and carried away as far as the east is from the west. Confess your sin today, and receive His forgiveness.*

Personal Reflection: ....

....

....

....

....

....

....

Handled with Care

Psalm 103:13–16

"For He knows our frame;
He remembers that we are dust." (v. 14)

Psalm 103 bursts forth from a singing heart. King David is grateful for all the blessings of God. He encourages readers to "forget not all His benefits," which means that we are to remember all of them (v. 2). The lyrics of an old hymn by Johnson Oatman challenged us to count our many blessings, naming them "one by one." The chorus says that as we count our blessings, we will "see what God has done."

One of our greatest blessings is being known by God, our Creator. He remembers us every moment of our lives. We are never out of His care. "He knows our frame" because He was the One who made us. Psalm 139, also penned by David, declares that God formed your "inward parts" by weaving you together inside the womb of your mother (v. 13). As the frame of your bones came together, God was a witness. Your unformed substance was molded and pressed into shape by His hands like a potter presses and squeezes and shapes clay on the wheel (v. 16). Truly, you and I are "fearfully and wonderfully made" (v. 14).

To be known by God indicates that He is assuredly aware of His creation and continues to observe and care for us. The "Knower" and the "known" are relationally connected by personal experience. What a picture of tender loving care! The "knowing" also involves seeing. No wonder our God is also known as Immanuel, literally "God with us," from before conception (Matt. 1:23).

God not only knows us, but He also "remembers" us, meaning that He can never forget us. David is amazed that the great God of the universe would even be "mindful" of us at all (Ps. 8:4). What exactly does God remember about us? He remembers forming the first man, named Adam, from "the dust of the

ground" (Gen. 2–7). He remembers fashioning Eve from a part of Adam's side. He remembers pronouncing the consequences of Adam's sin: "For out of it [the ground] you were taken; for dust you are, and to dust you shall return" (Gen. 3:19). Every baby born since then has been a chip off the old dirt clod. God remembers that we are fragile and finite at best, while He is infinite and all-powerful. The "Gardener" of Eden, Gethsemane, the garden tomb, and of the tree of life brings forth life in each of His dusty creations.

Becky Brown

Prayer: *Thank God for knowing you and remembering you all along the way. Praise Him for His amazing love for you despite your failures.*

Personal Reflection: ....

....

....

....

....

....

Happily "After Ever"

Psalm 103:17–22

"But the mercy of the Lord is from everlasting to everlasting
On those who fear Him,
And His righteousness to children's children." (v. 17)

Psalm 103 shows that as creations of God we are fragile and finite. We are ash piles of dust, quick-bloom and fade-away flowers, and blades of wild grass. All the while, from the womb to the tomb, we are valued treasures of the One who made and provides for our needs. He shows great mercy and deals with our sins. He brings justice for the oppressed and makes His ways known to those who serve Him. He knows us because He made us and remembers us because He loves us. He marks us out and sets us on our unique paths of service.

You should stand in awe and ponder the unfailing and unchanging steadfast love of God (v. 17). The love of God expressed to us is described as His "mercy" (Hb. *chesed*, "lovingkindness"). This love seeks the joy and fulfillment of the object of love. We are the object of God's love! In the New Testament, the Greek word used for God's love toward us is *agapē*. God stands alone as the Giver of such love and mercy. Jesus followed in the footsteps of His Father, loving us all the way from the cross, through the tomb, to the right hand of the throne of God. Jesus has "coming-back-again" love as well.

Those who fear God are the ones who experience His lovingkindness. To fear God means to stand in awe of who He is and what He has done. Our desire to worship God originates in our willingness to stand in awe of Him and to show Him reverence as we seek to honor Him with our lives.

Generations of people have come and gone since the beginning of the human race. God's mercy extends from everlasting to everlasting so every generation will have the opportunity to experience His careful concern. Past generations were covered. Future generations will have the opportunity to rest in this love. Personally, in this present day, you and I can bask in this unfailing love of God. Do not miss the blessing.

"Everlasting" represents the past and future of time outside of time as we know it. My little friend calls it "the on and on and on when we get to live happily ever after with God." That sums it up succinctly and biblically, I do believe.

Becky Brown

Prayer: *Our Father is so precious to shower His unfailing love on you. Ask the Lord to help you share that love with the world around you.*

Personal Reflection: ....

....

....

....

....

....

....

....

Glorious Majesty of God

Psalm 104:1–35

"You who laid the foundations of the earth,
So that it shall not be moved forever,
You covered it with the deep as with a garment;
The waters stood above the mountains." (vv. 5–6)

The anonymous writer of Psalm 104 encloses truths about God between the same "bookend" phrases David used in Psalm 103: "Bless the LORD, O my soul!" Additionally, Psalm 104 concludes with the postscript, "Praise the LORD!" Sometimes only a song or a poem will do when you desire to offer praise to so great and wonderful a Lord as ours. Words, music, poetry, lyric, art—our Lord is worthy of all this praise and so much more. The Bible tells me so as does the whole of creation. Most often, our worship is best expressed in the wonder and awe of reverent silence.

God is both the Creator and the Sustainer of all things. Job 38 and 39 affirm this truth from the pages of the Old Testament. God asks Job, "Where were you when I laid the foundations of the earth? Tell Me, if you have understanding" (Job 38:4). Job does not respond until the beginning verses of chapter 40. Even then, in full astonishment, he speaks of his own insignificance in light of the power and majesty of God. Colossians 1 affirms this truth from the pages of the New Testament. God created all things through Christ Jesus and for Him. The fact that God is the One who made all things is buttressed by the truth that He also holds all things together (vv. 16–17).

God indeed laid the foundations of the earth. He issued the "stay" command, and the earth complied in obedience to its Maker. If only people would be so obedient to stay or to move at His command! At the spoken word of God, the seas were gathered together so that the dry land would appear (Gen. 1:9–10).

God commanded it, and it was so. God *saw* that it was good. God saw to it that it was good. He still tends to every detail of all He has made.

In concert with Job and this anonymous writer of Psalm 104, I stand in awe of God. Light is His overcoat. Heaven is a tent covering for His campsite. Clouds are His chariot. Winds follow His assigned direction. Mountains and valleys become obstacles and channels for the powerful waters that flow through them to nourish vegetation. Animals look to Him for breath and food. The sun, moon, and stars were placed by His hand. Birds and fish fill the skies and seas. Praise the Lord for His majestic power!

Becky Brown

Prayer: *The Father alone is God. He is Creator, Sustainer, Provider, Earth Maker, Sky Maker, Sea Maker, Earth Filler, Sky Decorator, Sea Restrainer, and Maker of man. And He has sent Jesus, our Redeemer. Thank Him for His faithfulness!*

Personal Reflection: ....

....

....

....

....

....

What Is a Happy Life?

Psalm 106:1–7

"Blessed are those who keep justice,
And he who does righteousness at all times!" (v. 3)

At my high school graduation, I gave a speech titled "Success: Money or Happiness?" Little did I know then how true the words of that speech would become in my life. As an American teenager, I had bought into the idea that economic success equaled happiness in life, so I planned to choose the career path that would allow me to make the most money. As graduation drew near, God began working on me to see that the path of true success for my life would be found in following Him. Making right choices by honoring God would bring the peace and fulfillment that I really desired. Twenty years later I can join with the psalmist in declaring the Lord's mighty acts and proclaiming the praise due Him because my life has been so blessed by following God's path instead of my own (v. 2).

Americans tend to relate happiness to a feeling that comes from having everything go our way, whether it be in finances, relationships, physical health, etc. Our fast-food marketing sums it up for us: We want to have everything our way right away. If that fails to happen, then we are not getting what we deserve out of life. Sometimes God allows us to enjoy economic success, fulfilling relationships, or good physical health. A part of God's common grace to humanity is that he "sends rain on the just and on the unjust" (Matt. 5:45). Personal success is not bad in itself, and we can be grateful for outward blessings when they come. However, they can be fleeting. If we are living to pursue anything other than Jesus Christ, then we will always come up short and unfulfilled. True happiness (or "blessing," as Ps. 103:3 suggests) comes from living a life that pleases God.

Doing the right thing, whether in following God's path for your life, refusing to cheat to get ahead, living a godly life among ungodly people, or giving

298

God the glory for any success you may enjoy, may not be the easy route to take. It may even be extremely difficult at times. Jesus said that life will not always go our way, but He also guarantees that peace can be found in Him (John 16:33). What is a happy life? That is a question our world tries to answer with all kinds of temporal pursuits. From an eternal perspective, a truly happy life is one that makes God-honoring choices today as an investment for tomorrow.

Emily Dean

Prayer: *Thank the Lord for the blessings in your life and for filling your life with peace and joy. Keep Him the center of your life, and make choices today that honor Him even in difficult situations. Know that He will fill your life with blessings.*

Personal Reflection: ....

....

....

....

....

....

....

Taking the Long Route to Make His Power Known

Psalm 106:8–18

*"Nevertheless He saved them for His name's sake,
That He might make His mighty power known." (v. 8)*

I wish I could have been there to witness the parting of the Red Sea. Truthfully I am glad I did not have to experience the hardships of Egypt, but getting to watch the Red Sea separate would have been amazing. It is a shame that there was no cell phone video capability back then. Although I think everyone would have been too distracted taking videos to hurry across ahead of the Egyptians. I can just picture Moses telling all the Hebrews to put their phones away and get moving!

Why did God do such a miraculous event at that point in the budding nation's history? He could have led them on an easier route. However, the more direct path would have resulted in immediate war, and He knew they were not ready (Ex. 13:17). Sometimes what looks like the easy route to take is not so easy after all. When God takes us the long way to get us where He wants us to go, it is always for good reason.

On their way out of Egypt, the Israelites could not see why the long route was better for them. They were afraid and complained to Moses when the Egyptians began coming after them (Ex. 14:12). Why, then, did God save a bunch of whiners who were afraid to face their enemies? "He saved them for His name's sake, that He might make His mighty power known" (Ps. 106:8). Multiple times in Exodus we see that God delivered the Israelites from the hands of Pharaoh so that both the Israelites and the Egyptians would know that Yahweh is the one true God. Not only did God want to reaffirm His name to the Israelites, but also He wanted the Egyptians to know that He is the one true God.

People do not always understand God's path. Like the Israelites, we may feel like we are facing a dead end with our enemies right behind us. Yet unlike

us, God sees what is up ahead. He always has a reason for the direction of our lives. In whatever circumstances we find ourselves, He is at work to make His power known not only to us but also to those around us. As Moses said to the Israelites before they crossed the Red Sea, "Do not be afraid. Stand still, and see the salvation of the LORD, which He will accomplish for you today" (Ex. 14:13).

Emily Dean

Prayer: *Thank the Lord for His great power that is available through the Holy Spirit. Remember today that He is working in your life to make His power known even if you cannot see what direction He is taking you. Because of His great name, give Him glory in all that you do today.*

Personal Reflection: ....

....

....

....

....

....

....

Remember the Lord

Psalm 106:19–33

"They forgot God their Savior,
Who had done great things in Egypt." (v. 21)

How could you possibly forget the Lord's awe-inspiring acts at the Red Sea (v. 22)? It seems like the parting of the Red Sea would be a hard event to forget. Yet, over and over the Lord told the Israelites to remember what He had done and to be careful not to forget about Him (e.g., Deut. 7:17–19). Why give the same reminders again and again? God knows humans are forgetful people. Before Moses even had a chance to get down the mountain with the Ten Commandments, ironically the Israelites had already broken the first and second commands by making a calf to worship (Ps. 106:19).

As easy as it is to point a finger at the Israelites, I have to admit that I am forgetful, too. The Lord does such great things in my life, and yet with each new challenge I tend to get spiritual amnesia. I quickly forget how the Lord has so faithfully seen me through every difficult situation I have encountered. How about you? Do you continually remember everything the Lord has done in your life, or do you tend to forget when new challenges arise?

Although often forgetful, the Israelites eventually practiced a good system the Lord gave them for remembering His goodness through feasts and festivals. The Lord also encouraged memorization of Scripture (e.g., Deut. 6:6–8). We, too, need a system for remembering the Lord's goodness in our lives. Reciting Scripture, journaling, sharing with others how God has worked in your life, singing His praises in worship, and continually thanking Him for what He has done are all ways to encourage remembering the Lord's activity in our lives.

Like the Israelites, we are forgetful people. We see new challenges, and we fail to remember how God has faithfully helped us through previous difficulties. Sometimes it seems like the Lord is teaching you the same lesson over and

over. If you are like me, you still need that same lesson because you have already forgotten it! In our church, we often sing this song that helps me on days I am prone to forget: "We will remember."

May we not forget God our Savior who has done great things for us. Instead, may we be a people who remember. How about you? How can you remember all that the Lord has done for you today?

Emily Dean

Prayer: *Be grateful that the Lord is your God and your Savior. Thank Him for all the great and mighty things that He has done for you. Seek His forgiveness when you forget the greatness of your God. Do not forget about Him, but remember His great works in your life today.*

Personal Reflection: ....

....

....

....

....

....

Avoiding Snares

Psalm 106:34–48

"They served their idols,
Which became a snare to them." (v. 36)

Weeds are a nuisance. I think they are a pain every time I go into my flowerbeds to pull weeds. The trouble with weeds is that they will come right back if you do not pull them up at the roots, and sometimes the roots go deep. Unfortunately they just keep coming, so I keep going back to the flowerbeds to pull them up.

The Lord gave the Israelites specific instructions through Moses about what to do when they conquered other nations in the promised land. He said, "When the LORD your God brings you into the land which you go to possess, and has cast out many nations before you . . . and when the LORD your God delivers them over to you, you shall conquer them and utterly destroy them" (Deut. 7:1–2). Why completely destroy other nations? God said clearly that if the other people groups were left, the Israelites would end up intermarrying with them, and those people would "turn your sons away from following Me, to serve other gods" (v. 4). Unfortunately, that is exactly what happened. The Israelites did not completely destroy the other nations, and they did end up intermarrying among people who worshiped idols. Thus, "They [God's people] served their [the Gentiles'] idols, which became a snare to them" (Ps. 106:36).

Harsh as God's judgment to completely eliminate other nations may seem, these were groups of people who worshiped idols and refused to acknowledge the one true God (Rom. 1:18–21). The Lord drove them out because of their "wickedness" (Deut. 9:5). God was preserving His people to worship Him alone so that other nations could see and know that He is God (Deut. 28:10). God's heart is always to reconcile us to Himself, but there are consequences when we disobey. God knew that if the idolatrous nations were not completely destroyed, they would lead the Israelites astray . . . and they did.

To keep sin from getting into our lives and taking over, sometimes we must root out the temptations. Certainly the Lord does not want us to travel down the path of legalism, but it is good to evaluate what temptations in our lives we need to avoid. We each have "weeds" that pop up everywhere, things that distract us from giving God the glory He deserves.

What things in your life have become snares? Whatever consumes most of your time and attention apart from God has the potential to become an idol if you are not careful. Spend some time examining those weeds of distraction you may need to root out today.

Emily Dean

Prayer: *Thank the Lord for His grace and mercy when you stumble on the weeds in your life. Ask Him to help you today to root out the distractions in your life that keep you from giving God the glory He deserves. Beware of temptations when they come so you can turn and go the other direction.*

Personal Reflection: ....

....

....

....

....

....

Finding Satisfaction

Psalm 107:1–43

*"For He satisfies the longing soul,
And fills the hungry soul with goodness." (v. 9)*

What makes you feel truly satisfied? Satisfaction is a universal feeling sought by all humans. Everyone wants satisfaction, and we all try to figure out how to get it. Popular musicians have even become famous singing about their lack of satisfaction in life. If we are all looking for that feeling, then how do we get it?

When you eat a meal, a fine line exists between feeling satisfied and being overindulgent. If you eat too much, the feeling of satisfaction is replaced with misery. During the holidays, I have been guilty of knowing that feeling all too well! However, if you do not eat enough, you never quite feel satisfied. When you are truly hungry and thirsty, even the smallest amount of food or water can bring great satisfaction.

Being satisfied means neither too much nor too little. The writer of Proverbs 30 understood this idea: "Give me neither poverty nor riches—feed me with the food allotted to me" (v. 8). When asked how to pray, Jesus even encouraged the crowds to pray that God would give them their "daily bread" (Matt. 6:11). He did not say to ask for a month's or even a year's supply. He said to ask for daily bread. At another point in His teaching ministry, Jesus even said that He is "the bread of life" and that anyone who comes to Him will not be hungry again (John 6:35). The people eagerly said they wanted the bread from heaven, but they did not understand what Jesus meant. I suspect they were thinking more along the lines of manna or real food. Yet Jesus was telling them that He is what they really need. He alone could give them the deep soul satisfaction their hearts truly desired.

The same is true for you and me today. Is your heart hungry? Does your soul thirst for meaning? Deep down, do you feel empty without being quite able

to put your finger on the reason why? Jesus is the only one who can truly fill that nagging void you sense inside. God provides not only our physical food but also the spiritual nourishment that we need through Jesus. He satisfies our lives with the spiritual sustenance needed for each day, if we will come to Him in faith. God's provision is always enough because He is enough.

Do you need some real bread today? Just ask Him for your daily bread. Do you need some bread for your soul? Just ask. He has that, too.

Emily Dean

Prayer: *Thank God for satisfying your thirst and filling your life with good things. He is your provider and the true sustenance that you need. Trust Him to provide your daily bread both physically and spiritually. Pray that He would satisfy your heart, mind, soul, and body today.*

Personal Reflection: ....

....

....

....

....

....

Trustworthy Instructions

Psalm 111:1–8

". . . All His precepts are sure." (v. 7)

I am so thankful to have a GPS (Global Positioning System). What did we ever do without satellite technology? Although traditional map reading is fun, these days I rely heavily on satellite-driven navigation. Though it may not always direct me on the route I would choose, I trust my GPS to help me get where I need to go. I believe that it works; so I follow its directions. I know that if I get off course, the system will help guide me back to my desired destination.

When finding a new location, you have to trust your directions. Otherwise, you could end up in another city or lost in the middle of nowhere! The same principle applies to our lives. Did you know that there are instructions for life? God gives us His instructions in His guidebook, the Bible. Through the Scriptures, God provides the wisdom we need "for salvation through faith which is in Christ Jesus" and everything we need to be "complete, equipped for every good work" (2 Tim. 3:15, 17). If we do not trust the instructions God gives us, then we could end up wandering aimlessly with no direction.

Do you really believe that God's directions work? If you do not believe they work, then you will not follow them. Just like an out-of-date map, many people believe God's word is out of date. Fortunately, God debunks that myth. His words "stand fast forever and ever" (Ps. 111:8). Though other things may fade away, His word is eternal and unchanging (Is. 40:8). God's instructions are trustworthy because they do not change and never go out-of-date.

You may find yourself in a place in life where you feel like you have gotten off course. If so, God's Word can guide you back in the right direction. He is willing to lead you on the right path if you are willing to follow Him. All you need to do is trust that His directions are the right way and obey the instructions He

gives. He wants to guide us on this journey of life. The problem is that we are not always willing to follow and obey.

God may not always direct us on the route we would choose, but following His direction for our lives is always the best path to take. Any GPS will eventually wear out or need an update. On occasion, my GPS has failed me because I did not have the latest update. God's Word will never fail you. It does not need an update. Choose to trust His instructions today. Believe they are trustworthy. Follow His wise guidance.

Emily Dean

Prayer: *Thank the Lord for providing you with instructions for life through His Word. Thank Him for giving you all the directions you need to follow Him. Trust His Word completely and obey His commands.*

Personal Reflection: ....

....

....

....

....

Having Good Insight

Psalm 111:9–10

*". . . A good understanding have all those
who do His commandments." (v. 10)*

Would you like to be someone who has good insight? I know I would. Discernment does not come easily to me. I am often the last to grasp something. Yet, I can think of countless times the Lord has given me insight into a situation after spending time reading His Word. How about you? Have you ever been reading Scripture and found a passage that provided you with guidance at that particular time you were dealing with a specific situation?

God gives everyone good insight through His Word. The Proverbs are full of key principles for life. All throughout God's Word are guidelines for how to live a godly life. You do not have to be discouraged if you feel that you are lacking in discernment. Insight can be acquired through studying the Word of God. If you do have keen discernment and easily understand a situation, you may need to remember your first point of reference is always God's Word. Our perceptions or the opinions of others can be flawed for many reasons. While seeking wise counsel from trusted mentors or friends is important, the primary path to good insight is through the study of God's Word.

Through consistent study of God's Word, He will provide the wisdom you need for the circumstances you face. Only turning to God's Word when you have problems will leave you overwhelmed and confused because you may feel like you do not know where to begin. You know that you need insight, but where should you look? By developing a habit of spending time in the Scriptures daily, you will be prepared to receive the insights God wants to show you when you are facing a difficult situation.

The first step to receiving insight from God's Word is to ask Him. As you begin your time of study, ask the Lord to give you insight into what you are

reading. As the Holy Spirit speaks to you through God's Word, you may want to write down what God shows you. Then, the hard part comes in actually doing what God says. In this verse we see that people who have good insight do not just read God's instructions. The verse says that those who have good insight follow His instructions. Following what God tells you to do is the key to having wisdom in each and every situation you encounter. Then as you obey, God will continue to give you more wisdom and insight.

Emily Dean

Prayer: *Be thankful that God has given you good insight through His Word. Take time to consult His Word when you are dealing with different events in life. Do not rely on your own wisdom but seek His wisdom in any and every situation you encounter. Seek to follow the Lord and obey what He tells you to do.*

Personal Reflection: ....

....

....

....

....

....

311

Confidence in the Lord

Psalm 112:1–10

"He will not be afraid of evil tidings;
His heart is steadfast, trusting in the LORD." (v. 7)

When I was a child, I was afraid of everything. Literally. I feared my own shadow in the dark. Even into adulthood, anything and everything had the potential to incite fear in my heart, especially after I had children. I became overwhelmed with fear of the worst that could happen to them. Have you ever struggled with the "what-ifs" of life? You know what I mean—all of those scenarios that can run through your mind outlining the worst possible outcome of a situation. Just talking with other people about bad things happening in the world that my children were entering could provoke a deluge of anxiety until I came upon this verse several years ago.

"He will not be afraid of evil tidings; his heart is steadfast, trusting in the LORD" (v. 7). Wait! What was that I read? Was Scripture addressing my anxiety over the "what-ifs"? Yet, there it was right in front of me: "He is not afraid of bad news" (ESV). Fear is covered quite a lot in the Bible. Over and over as I searched Scripture, I saw the words, "Fear not." Why would God repeat this phrase so many times? Apparently the Israelites needed to hear it. We must need to hear it, too. We humans are fearful people. The good news is that we do not have to stay fearful.

Bad news will come. Jesus said that trouble will happen in this world (John 16:33). Watch the nightly news to know that reality. So what do you do when fears of the "what-ifs" feel like they are going to overwhelm you? Memorizing Psalm 112:7 is a good place to start.

How can your heart be confident even when bad news does come? Choose to trust the Lord. When you choose to trust the Lord, peace will replace the panic rising in your heart. The world can be a scary place. Dwelling on what

may or may not happen will cause you to live out your days in fear and anxiety. Are you glad to know Jesus has a better way for us? I am, too. He told us about the trouble that we would have in the world so that we would know our peace is in Him. He said, "Peace I leave with you, My peace I give to you; not as the world gives do I give to you. Let not your heart be troubled, neither let it be afraid" (John 14:27). Rest in His peace today. Take heart, He has conquered the world (John 16:33)!

Emily Dean

Prayer: *Do not fear bad news. Be confident because He has conquered the world. Choose to put your trust in Him. Ask God to set you free from all the fears and anxieties that keep you from experiencing His peace.*

Personal Reflection: ....

....

....

....

....

....

....

More Than Enough!

Psalm 113:1–9

"He grants the barren woman a home,
Like a joyful mother of children.
Praise the LORD!" (v. 9)

Have you ever desired something that you knew you might never have, yet the desire never seemed to leave? Have you ever found yourself in a place where your heart cried out for something so near and dear to your soul but you had no idea how, what, or when it would be possible? Have you ever felt emptiness in your soul from being in a place that seems barren?

A beautiful reminder is given in Psalm 113:9 of how God can make something that looks impossible into something greater than our imagination. God can take us from complete barrenness and despair to absolute joy and fulfillment. I spent thirty-three years of my life as a single woman. I longed to be married and desired to be a mother. However, I desired to wait on God's timing and for His will to be done. I definitely had days when I felt alone and discontent, wondering if I would ever have the desires of my heart fulfilled.

I am so thankful that God turns our focus off ourselves and onto Him. Daily I submitted my request to Him. God reminded me of the many people whom I could mentor as a spiritual mother. Although I was childless at the time, He had given me a household to influence. As we turn our desires over to God, He grants joy and delight in Him. The result of this answered prayer is worship and praise!

Dear friend and sister, what are the desires of your heart? Do you long for something you think will never be yours? Be reminded today of who God is and His purpose for your life. Although you may feel "barren," God greatly desires to give you influence on many. Our society and culture is in great need of women who will point others to truth and live out biblical womanhood. As you pour out

your heart to Him, God will direct your steps and make what looks like a barren place within your soul into a fruitful place of great meaning as you trust in His plan. "Eye has not seen, nor ear heard, nor have entered into the heart of man the things which God has prepared for those who love Him" (1 Cor. 2:9).

Monica Rose Brennan

Prayer: *Thank the heavenly Father for the plans He has for you. Remember that He is concerned about the desires of your heart. His Word reminds you of who He is and how He is more than enough for you. Trust in the Lord to give you the desires of your heart. Become a woman of influence and find contentment in Him alone. Rejoice as you trust in His plan.*

Personal Reflection: ....

....

....

....

....

....

....

Perishable vs. Imperishable

Psalm 115:1–18

*"Their idols are silver and gold,
The work of men's hands." (v. 4)*

Have you ever grown dissatisfied with God? It is so easy to move your eyes off your Maker and onto temporary pleasures, which you think will fill the longings of your heart. Instead of waiting on God to answer your prayer, have you decided to take matters into your own hands and go your own way?

Discouragement and discontentment easily yield to wrong choices. When you choose your own way, over God's best for your life, you give into a life of idolatry. Idols are simply the "work of men's hands" (v. 4). Anything you place before God in your life is an idol.

> They have mouths, but they do not speak;
> Eyes they have, but they do not see;
> They have ears, but they do not hear;
> Noses they have, but they do not smell;
> They have hands, but they do not handle;
> Feet they have, but they do not walk;
> Nor do they mutter through their throat.
> Those who make them are like them;
> So is everyone who trusts in them" (vv. 5–8).

When I was nineteen years old, I traveled to the country of India on a mission trip with my pastor-father. For the first time, I saw people worshiping gods made with their hands. My heart became so burdened for people who did not know the true, living God! As I began to cry out to the Lord for those needy

people, He reminded me of the many idols to which I often turned instead of turning to Him.

Comfort, stability, and security is often sought in "things" instead of in God. These "things" are perishable and man-made. Jesus said: "I am the way, the truth, and the life. No one comes to the Father, except through Me" (John 14:6). When we place our trust in things more than Christ for identity and security, we deceive ourselves. "And what agreement has the temple of God with idols? For you are the temple of the living God. As God has said: "I will dwell in them and walk among them. I will be their God, and they shall be My people"" (2 Cor. 6:16).

Dear sister and friend, do you know the true God? We can worship and even make with our own hands many false gods and idols. The Bible teaches that only through a personal relationship with Christ as your Savior can you find the true God. Search your heart and ask God to show you if you are worshiping something perishable. God's way is best, and He is the only true God.

Monica Rose Brennan

Prayer: *Recommit to the only true, living God. Turn away from a life of falsehood and walk in trust. Be reminded of who God is and ask Him to use you to point others to the truth that can only be found in Him.*

Personal Reflection:

Always Answered Prayer!

Psalm 116:1–12

"I love the LORD, because He has heard
My voice and my supplications.
Because He has inclined His ear to me,
Therefore I will call upon Him as long as I live." (vv. 1–2)

Do you have a specific prayer request that your soul longs to be answered? Do you wake up with a need in your heart every morning? God always answers prayer (vv. 1–2)! He may not answer in the way you specifically desired or in your timing, but rest assured that God is always at work and answering.

God is drawn to a heart that is desperate for Him (see Ps. 51:17). In Psalm 116, the psalmist is near death and is crying out to God to rescue Him. Are you in desperate need for God's deliverance today? Are you at a place of hopelessness and despair? The psalmist serves as a great example of someone who cried out to God, in the shadow of death. He declares his love for the Lord because He has heard his own faltering voice and supplications.

Many times in my life I have found myself in a low and sorrowful place. My heart has been so heavy that it seemed difficult even to breathe. In those times of utter despair, I have experienced great comfort as I simply poured out my heart before the Lord.

Remember the story of Hannah (1 Sam. 1). Hannah had a broken heart and went to the temple to pour out her request to be a mother before God. Eli, the priest, thought she was drunk. What is so encouraging about Hannah's prayer, to me specifically, is the fact that after she voiced her need before the Lord, she ate and no longer was sad. At that point, she did not know if or how God was going to answer her prayer, but her peace came simply by declaring her request to God.

When was the last time you poured your heart out to God? God hears the cry of your heart. He longs to answer and give you His perfect peace. "You will keep him in perfect peace, whose mind is stayed on You, because he trusts in You" (Is. 26:3). God has a plan for what you are going through and longs for you to make known your love for Him, even when death surrounds you. Will you declare as the psalmist: "I will call upon Him as long as I live" (Ps. 116:2)?

Monica Rose Brennan

Prayer: *Thank the Lord that He is a God who hears and answers prayer. Trust in Him regardless of what you are experiencing. Be reminded of who He is and that He hears your prayers and will answer according to what He knows is the very best for you.*

Personal Reflection:

319

Longing for His Eternal Presence

Psalm 116:13–19

*"Precious in the sight of the LORD
Is the death of His saints." (v. 15)*

Growing up as a pastor's daughter, I attended countless funerals. I could always tell a major difference in the funeral service of someone who had a testimony of Christ living in her versus someone who lived a life apart from Christ. Although there was weeping, there was also rejoicing since you knew your loved one was now in the presence of God and in a much better place. "We are confident, yes, well pleased rather to be absent from the body and to be present with the Lord" (2 Cor. 5:8).

Have you ever felt unloved? Have you ever found yourself in a place of desperation; willing to do anything to feel accepted, special, beautiful, and worthy of affection? As women, we long to be loved and secure. At times, we will go to dangerous lengths to get our heart's desire. God sent His Son so that we would know true love. Jesus desires that everyone would have a personal relationship with Him and accept His free gift of salvation. "For God so loved the world that He gave His only begotten Son that whosoever believes in Him should not perish but have everlasting life" (John 3:16). Once you ask Him to forgive you from your sins and come into your life, He gives you a new identity and a new life in Him.

Several years ago, my 107-year-old great-grandmother, "Lula Craig," whom everyone knew as "Nanny," went to be with the Lord. For the last ten years of her life, whenever I would visit her, she would look into my eyes and say, "Monica, why do you think the Lord will not take me on to heaven? I am ready to go." I would reply that I believed the Lord still had work for her to do and remind her that she was a major encouragement and inspiration to others. Although I cried at her funeral, I found comfort in knowing she was in the

presence of God. Psalm 139:16 declares that God knows the days fashioned for each of us. If you knew what heaven was going to be like, you would do much more rejoicing than weeping at the funerals of saints!

The Lord has prepared a place for you! Do you know for sure that heaven will be your home when you die? Do you have a friend or family member who needs to know Christ? Ask the Lord to give you the words to declare God's truth of salvation to those who desperately need Him. As you are filled daily with His presence, ask Christ to make you ready to see Him face-to-face so He will find your death "precious in His sight!"

Monica Rose Brennan

Prayer: *Thank the Lord for preparing a place for you. As you long for His eternal presence, pray for His words to be a witness to those who do not know Christ.*

Personal Reflection: ....

....

....

....

....

....

321

Faith in an Unchanging God

Psalm 117:1–2

"For His merciful kindness is great toward us,
And the truth of the LORD endures forever.
Praise the LORD!" (v. 2)

Have you ever done something that you knew broke the heart of God? Have you ever doubted God's love and forgiveness for your sin? Be reminded of the character and essence of God and the reality of who God is and what He did on your behalf.

Psalm 117:2 is a verse loaded with truth for meditation and application. God's mercy is so great! Although there are moments when we have blown it and feel like His grace is not enough, the truth is that His grace is enough to cover every sin! God is so stubborn in His love for us, and we are in need of His mercy, which He shows us each and every day. "Merciful kindness" (Hb. *chesed*) or faithful love takes on the meaning of "covenant loyalty." I am so thankful that God does not break covenant with us. He loves us despite ourselves and forgives our past, present, and future sins the very moment we confess Him as Lord and enter into a relationship with Him.

Faith in an unchanging God is possible because His truth "endures forever" (v. 2). Our feelings may change, and people may change, but God and His truth are unchanging. "Jesus Christ is the same yesterday, today, and forever" (Heb. 13:8). When applied correctly, Psalm 117:2 can serve as a prime example of our concern for people who are in need of God's mercy and grace. Because of His mercy toward us, we are to extend that same mercy and grace—regardless! If we are unable to extend mercy to others, then we know nothing of God's grace and forgiveness personally.

"Praise the LORD!" (v. 2) is a response from a heart that has experienced God's mercy, grace, and covenant loyalty. Overflowing worship is the result of someone who has truly tasted and seen that "the LORD is good" (Ps. 34:8).

Have you forgotten how faithful God is in your life? Even when you rebel against God, He is faithful and ready to forgive and extend His hand of grace. Reflect on a time in your life where you have been extended that mercy, and praise God for it today! Is there someone in your life to whom you need to extend that same love? Are you unable to forgive yourself or someone else? Ask the Lord to make known to you if you really belong to Him and have a personal relationship with Him. Forgiveness is only possible when you are in right relationship and fellowship with Christ. He alone covers your sin and the sins of others. Praise the Lord for His character that never changes! Now, that is faith in an unchanging God!

Monica Rose Brennan

Prayer: *Thank the Lord for His faithful love. Remember His truth. Thank Him that His love and mercy endures forever. Extend that same love to others and forgive just as God has forgiven you.*

Personal Reflection: ....

....

....

....

....

From Fearing to Fearless

Psalm 118:1–7

"The LORD is on my side;
I will not fear.
What can man do to me?" (v. 6)

Have you ever felt completely paralyzed with fear over something? Have you ever struggled with anxiety when there were circumstances in your life that you could not control? Have you ever felt crippled by your fear and unable to move forward?

Fear is often difficult to overcome and can keep your heart and mind in bondage for years. Many fears arise in this life: fear of the future, fear of failure, fear of others and their opinions or thoughts about us, fear of the unknown, fear of the past, fear of the present, and fear of the future. Fear comes when there is an absence of trust and faith.

As a little girl I remember being terrified of thunderstorms and running into my parents' bedroom in tears because of the lightning or thunder. My father would gently remind me that God has us in His hands and would protect us. He reminded me that God was the one who sent the storm and that He had a purpose in everything. The truth my father shared with me instilled within my little heart an incredible view of God and His sovereignty. I am thankful that my parents turned my fears into a teachable moment to learn about the greatness of God. There were still times when fear would overtake me and my focus drifted from God to my own challenges.

During my college years, I struggled with fear of making the wrong decisions or making any decision at all. Now my fears center more on what others think of me. Am I doing enough at church, at work, and at home for others to approve? As a wife, I struggle with the fear of not being a suitable helper to my husband. As a mother, I struggle with fears of the unknown for the precious

treasures entrusted to me by the Lord to mold and make into disciples for His glory.

The psalmist was confident that God was greater than anyone else (v. 6). When God is on your side, you have nothing to fear because He is in total control. The psalmist definitely exhibited total surrender to God. Surrender is giving up your will completely and trusting God regardless of your circumstances.

What things are keeping you back from living a life that is fearless? Think about some of the things you fear. Be reminded of who God is—above everyone, everything, and every circumstance. You can move from a place of "fearing to fearless" as you place your trust in Christ and in Christ alone!

Monica Rose Brennam

Prayer: *Be thankful for who God is and that He is in control of each and every storm you face in life. You do not need to be afraid. Trust in Him regardless of your circumstances. Say as the psalmist, "I will not fear" (v. 6).*

Personal Reflection: ....

....

....

....

....

....

Ultimate Security!

Psalm 118:8–18

*"It is better to trust in the LORD
Than to put confidence in princes." (v. 9)*

Have you ever felt insecure and fearful? Have you ever experienced great discouragement because of the misery you felt emotionally?

The psalmist declares his determination to trust in God, in the midst of a place that felt insecure: a place of difficulty (v. 8). "I called on the LORD in distress; the LORD answered me and set me in a broad place" (v. 5). "Distress" (Hb. *metsar*) takes on the meaning of "a narrow and tight place." This place felt difficult and brought emotional stress to say the least! David regained confidence when the Lord provided for him a "broad" place, where his fears turned into freedom as he placed his dependence upon the Lord.

Life can certainly bring its share of unpleasant circumstances and obstacles. The book of James declares that our faith will be tested and that we will experience a variety of trials. We are also exhorted to be joyful in the midst of trials because God is producing in us endurance and contentment (James 1:2–3). Every woman, at times, finds herself in a phase of life or situation that she wishes would end quickly. In the midst of distress, the Lord longs for us to find ultimate security in Him alone, just as the psalmist expressed in this verse (v. 8). In the middle of our most difficult situations, the One who longs for us to find refuge in Him more than any other person, place, or thing is Christ and Christ alone. He is "our refuge and strength, a very present help in trouble" (Ps. 46:1).

Is Christ your refuge and strength? He longs for you to place all your trust in Him! Through the storm, He is gracious to give you strength as you depend on Him above all else for your every need! His way is perfect, and He will never

fail you. "As for God, His way is perfect; the word of the LORD is proven; He is a shield to all who trust in Him" (Ps. 18:30).

Monica Rose Brennan

Prayer: *Have you found your ultimate security in God above all else? Thank Him for His presence. Ask for comfort from Him who hears your cry and works His plan in you. Remember in the midst of difficulty, God works all things together for the good to those who love Him and are called according to His purpose (Rom. 8:28).*

Personal Reflection:

Rejoice Regardless!

Psalm 118:19–29

"This is the day the Lord has made;
We will rejoice and be glad in it." (v. 24)

Have you ever started your day with excitement, and then watched as everything seemed to go wrong? Have you ever had a list of things to accomplish in a day and yet seemed to get nothing done? Expectations are often unfulfilled.

Many mornings I awake with great intentions, and then something happens that definitely puts an end to my productive day! On one such morning, my eighteen-month-old had been up all through the night. Instead of waking up refreshed, I felt like I was about to fall over. I needed sleep, but sleep was an impossibility. I had an entire list of things that must be accomplished. As I felt the day getting worse, I realized that I had not been able to make a cup of coffee, which I desperately needed. In that moment of feeling overwhelmed, I proclaimed out loud, "This is the day the Lord has made; we will rejoice and be glad in it" (v. 24). I said it so loud and with such determination that my little girl overheard me and came running in the room where I was. I then began to sing the children's song I learned as a little girl, "This is the day . . . that the Lord has made. I will rejoice . . . and be glad in it!" Simply voicing this truth reminded me that the day was not about me or my agenda or even my feelings; this day was a gift from the Lord. I began to give the day over to the Lord, asking Him for His direction and wisdom.

Each and every day is a gift from the Lord. Regardless of the circumstances, each day is His. We have the choice of living it for His glory or for our own whims. Joy should be our sacrifice of praise even when we do not feel like it! "For what is your life? It is even a vapor that appears for a little time and then vanishes away" (James 4:14). Rejoice that God is in control over each and every

circumstance that occurs in life, and with His strength you can exhibit joy regardless of what you may be facing.

Do you struggle with rejoicing in the Lord? Be reminded that each day is a gift from Him. He longs for you to worship Him in the good and bad times of life. As you look to Him daily for strength, He will give you the grace you need to live out His plan for your life.

Monica Rose Brennan

Prayer: *Ask the Lord to forgive you for not rejoicing in Him at all times. Seek His grace and strength and be reminded that this is the day that the Lord has made! Rejoice and be glad, regardless of your circumstances.*

Personal Reflection: ....

....

....

....

....

....

Staying on the Path of Purity

Psalm 119:1–9

"How can a young man cleanse his way?
By taking heed according to Your word." (v. 9)

Have you heard the children's song, "O Be Careful, Little Eyes"? The first verse encourages: "O be careful little eyes what you see!" As you may know, the song does not stop with our "little eyes." The writer admonishes us to consider what our ears hear, our hands do, our mouths say, and also has a word for our feet: "O be careful little feet where you go," because our heavenly Father is up above and is looking down in love. He guards and protects our lives.

This catchy tune aimed at children actually contains great wisdom that adults would do well to heed. Our direction will determine our destination. What direction are you headed? The writer of Psalm 119 knew this important truth as well. This psalm is the longest chapter in the Bible, full of wonderful insights about the importance of God's Word. In fact, I make it a habit to read through this psalm several times each year just to remind myself about how God's Word should determine my direction in life. For the next week, we will be looking at several verses within this magnificent chapter.

Before we get too far into our journey, though, consider verse 9. When the psalmist asks how can a young man "cleanse his way," he is asking his readers to consider how a young person can stay on the path of purity. This same idea is found in James 1:27 when James reminds believers to keep themselves unstained from the world. How can this happen? By "taking heed" or guarding your life with God's Word. Picture the Bible as the guardrails of your life, helping you to stay right in the center lane of God's will.

You may be wondering: What about people who have strayed from the path, fallen down in a ditch, and become "stained" by the world? There is good news! Our wonderful God tells us that if we will confess our sins, He is faithful

to forgive us and clean us up (1 John 1:9). Praise God! So, if you find yourself far from where God wants you to be, wandering around in a wilderness of worldliness, ask forgiveness and then get back in the center lane of God's path! If you have already set your feet on God's path, continue to guard your life by learning what God's Word says and then living it out.

Candi Finch

Prayer: *Where are your "little feet" taking you today? Are you on God's path or have you set off on a path of your own design? Spend a few minutes asking God to help you see clearly the direction of your life. Then, ask God to help you to walk on His path today.*

Personal Reflection: ....

....

....

....

....

....

God's Word Is Better Than Jiminy Cricket

Psalm 119:10–16

"Your word I have hidden in my heart,
That I might not sin against You." (v. 11)

In 1940 Walt Disney released the animated children's film *Pinocchio* about a wooden puppet who longs to become a real boy. The Blue Fairy comes along and turns Pinocchio into a living being. In one of the most interesting scenes of the movie, the Blue Fairy makes Jiminy Cricket, a real cricket who likes to follow the rules, Pinocchio's conscience. She says to Jiminy, "I dub you Pinocchio's conscience, lord high keeper of the knowledge of right and wrong, counselor in moments of temptation, and guide along the straight and narrow path." Then she turns to Pinocchio and cautions, "Let your conscience be your guide."

Wouldn't it be great if we each had a "Jiminy Cricket" who would show us right from wrong, counsel us in moments of temptation, and guide us along the straight and narrow path? Well, we do! The Word of God does all of this and more. As we face situations in which we are not sure what to do, the Word of God can show us right from wrong. Scripture will never lead us astray. When we are tempted, the Holy Spirit can use the Word of God to give us strength to resist temptation. However, if we are not reading, learning, and memorizing God's Word, we are not storing up in our hearts and minds truth that can come to our aid when we need it the most.

The psalmist proclaimed that he had hidden God's Word in his heart so that he would not sin against God. The word translated, "I have hidden," means that he treasured and stored up God's Word—essentially, he memorized it. The spiritual discipline of Bible memorization enables us to carry God's Word around with us wherever we go. The psalmist pointed out at least one benefit of Scripture memorization—it helps us to resist temptation when we want to sin. God's Word is also referred to as the "sword of the Spirit" because the Holy

Spirit can bring to mind Scriptures we have memorized to help us fight sin in our lives (see Eph. 6:17). If you were going off to war, you would want to make sure you had adequate ammunition. The Bible acts as ammunition in your daily life. So, it is important to consider just how much ammunition you each have stored up in your heart in order to fight your spiritual battles today.

Candi Finch

Prayer: *If you have never memorized Scripture before or simply have gotten out of the habit, would you consider trying to memorize one verse a week? Spend a few moments asking God to help you develop this new habit. If you are memorizing Scripture regularly, spend a few moments thanking God for the counsel of His Word and for the prompting of the Holy Spirit, and ask Him to help you to let His Word be your guide today.*

Personal Reflection: ....

....

....

....

....

....

Prayer First, Then Study

Psalm 119:17–24

*"Open my eyes, that I may see
Wondrous things from Your law." (v. 18)*

"Ugh! I have read this passage five times, and I still do not understand it!" Have you ever thought something similar? Or, have you ever sat down to spend time alone with God and struggled with a wandering mind? Many years ago when reading Psalm 119, verse 18 hit me like a ton of bricks. I realized that I had a habit of leaving out an important element in my time with God—prayer! The psalmist prayed that the Lord would give him understanding ("open his eyes"), and I realized that many times I simply forget to do that same thing.

Do you remember as a high school student ever struggling to understand an assignment for English? Perhaps it was when you were covering the plays of Shakespeare or diving into *Beowulf* or *The Iliad* or *The Scarlet Letter*. How helpful would it have been actually to be able to talk with the authors of those various works when you stumbled into confusing sections? As believers, we actually can talk to the very author of the Bible and ask Him to give us insight and clarity as we study. We have a direct line to Him through prayer.

The ability to communicate with God—to go into His throne room and present our requests to Him is something far too many Christians take for granted. Pastor Charles Stanley once said, "Remember the shortest distance between a problem and the solution is the distance between our knees and the floor."* I hate to admit how many times I have forgotten that simple truth. I forget that prayer is powerful. During difficulties, many people turn to those whom they trust most to give them advice; it makes sense, then, that when we have difficulty understanding God, we should trust Him enough to ask Him for help.

Before I start studying God's Word each morning, I begin with a simple prayer asking God to help me understand what I am about to read. Or I may just pray Psalm 119:18 back to God. I also struggle at times with my thoughts wandering; so I ask God for help in focusing as I read. Then, like the psalmist, I acknowledge that God's words are wondrous and marvelous, and I ask God to grow my appreciation for His laws each day and that I would have a heart's desire to follow them. And then, I start reading. My simple prayer at the beginning of my quiet time with the Lord has made a world of difference for me in having the right mind-set as I begin studying.

Candi Finch

Prayer: *Consider memorizing Psalm 119:18 and then praying it back to God before you study the Bible each day. Spend a few moments in prayer, thanking God that you can ask for His help when you are stumped in your Bible study.*

Personal Reflection: ....

....

....

....

....

*Charles Stanley, *Charles Stanley's Handbook for Christian Living: Biblical Answers to Life's Tough Questions* (Nashville: Thomas Nelson, 2008), 537.

Have You Eaten Your Wheaties Today?

Psalm 119:25–64

*"My soul melts from heaviness;
Strengthen me according to Your word." (v. 28)*

Have you ever faced a task or a day that seemed impossible, or a road that seemed too daunting? Or, are you just plain worn out, weary, and discouraged? Have you had those days where you want to crawl back into bed, stay in your pajamas, and pray tomorrow will be better? I know I am not the only one who has those "I cannot take it anymore!" kind of days. Some of my married friends with kids have those days where the responsibility of raising kids seems overwhelming. Or, maybe you have been trying to witness to a loved one for many years, and you are just not seeing any results. Or, you are grieving the loss of a beloved friend or family member and struggling with your heartache. I am not sure what you are facing today, but I am willing to guess that you may have had those days where you feel like the task is too tough, the road is too long, or you are just too weary.

If you find yourself having that kind of day (or month or year), may I encourage you with Psalm 119:28? The writer says that his soul is melting from heaviness—what an image! He is weeping with grief, burdened with sorrows, melting like ice does in the Texas summer heat. Yet, watch what he does. First, he is honest about what he is going through—he does not put on a brave face and pretend everything is okay. He is vulnerable, open, and honest with God. We can learn from this example—we can go to God with our deepest hurts and struggles, and He hears us. Second, the psalmist cries out and pleads with God to strengthen him according to His Word. The writer knew what the Word of God could do for him in the midst of his difficulty. The Bible can give us strength to face whatever is ahead of us.

In the 1930s, the breakfast cereal Wheaties became a household name, and famous athletes were used to promote this whole-wheat "breakfast of

champions." At the end of the twentieth century, advertisers began to use the tagline, "Eat your Wheaties today" as a way to remind consumers about the value of their breakfast cereal for good nutrition and strength. For the Christian, the Bible becomes your spiritual Wheaties. A steady diet of God's Word is important so you will have the strength to face whatever life brings.

Candi Finch

Prayer: *Are you facing something tough right now? If so, follow the psalmist's example and go to God, be honest, and then ask Him for help and strength. If you are not struggling right now, spend a few moments praying for those in your life who are facing trials and hardships.*

Personal Reflection: ....

....

....

....

....

....

....

The Master Designer

Psalm 119:65–104

"Your hands have made me and fashioned me;
Give me understanding, that I may learn Your commandments." (v. 73)

Have you ever tried to put store-bought furniture together? Over the years I have purchased several bookcases that had to be assembled at home. Assembling them always took several days because, as I have discovered, I am not especially handy or talented when it comes to these types of projects. During the process, my living room looked like a carpenter's shop had exploded all over it. Tears happened. Frustration boiled over. Patience was severely tested. Band-Aids had to be employed. However, when I look at those bookcases today, I feel a sense of accomplishment.

I discovered a secret through putting those bookcases together: closely following the directions provided by the manufacturer was vital. I have absolutely no knowledge or skills that enable me to be a "master bookcase assembler" or whatever you want to call it. Yet, even though the process stretched me considerably, as long as I did exactly what the directions said, bookcases slowly emerged from the many odd-shaped pieces I was provided. A few times I thought the directions seemed ridiculous; so I went off in my own direction, only to discover that I was the silly one, and my "brilliant" idea only led to shelves that would not fit properly in their designated slots.

You see, someone designed those bookcases. This person then provided meticulous directions on how they were to be assembled. In those moments when I veered from the directions, I was essentially saying in my mind that I thought I knew better than the person who designed the bookcase, who had a plan for how every piece was meant to be used.

As senseless as it was for me to go off on my own path with those bookcases, how much more absurd to say to God that I am going to do my own thing and ignore His directions and design for my life? God is the Master Designer. He made each one of us and fashioned us as Psalm 119:73 proclaims. Like any good designer, God has the blueprints for how we fit together—these blueprints are found in the Bible. Do you ever find yourself wanting to do your own thing and ignoring God's design for you? The end result will be worse than a few ill-fitting bookcase shelves. God fashioned you. He loves you. It just makes sense that we should follow His blueprints for how to live life.

Candi Finch

Prayer: *Spend some time in prayer asking God if there are any areas of your life where you are deviating from His plan and design for you. If He reveals anything, would you confess that to Him and ask Him to forgive you for ignoring His directions? Then, ask Him to give you the strength to follow His blueprints today.*

Personal Reflection: ....

....

....

....

....

....

God's Light and Compass

Psalm 119:105–120

"Your word is a lamp to my feet
And a light to my path." (v. 105)

Have you ever awakened in the middle of the night and needed to leave the safe confines of your comfy bed? No matter what the reason for your nocturnal excursion, if you have ever had to stumble in pitch-black conditions from your bedroom to another room in the house—whether it be the bathroom, a child's room, or some other destination—you know how treacherous that walk can be! Obstacles abound—the shoes left in the middle of the floor by your husband, the bedside table, your dresser, the wall, or maybe even the forgotten toy that lies in wait for your bare feet. Walking in the dark is dangerous!

God knows the dangers and anxiety we can face without a light to guide our path. Unforeseen obstacles and traps await us when we cannot see where to go. His Word is a "lamp to [our] feet and a light to [our] path" (v. 105). As a lamp and light, God's Word provides several important helps for us as we take life's journey.

First of all, just like a light helps give us direction when we are in darkness, God's Word helps show us the way we should go, much as would a compass. As in our discussion of Psalm 119:9, God's Word helps you stay in the center lane of His will—pointing you to true north and helping you to walk on the right path. I love the story of Josiah, the eight-year-old boy who became King of Judah. Josiah's dad and grandfather were really wicked kings; the Bible says that they did evil in the Lord's sight and led others to do the same. However, when Josiah became king, even at such a young age, he allowed God's Word to be his guide: "He did what was right in the sight of the LORD . . . he did not turn aside to the right hand or to the left" (2 Kin. 22:2). In the same way, God's Word can help direct your steps today.

Second, just like a lamp, the Bible **helps us avoid obstacles in our path.** By shining a light in the darkness, the Word of God illuminates our path, helping us to see dangers and preventing us from stumbling. Also, as a light, the Word of God **brings great comfort.** If you have ever been wandering around in utter darkness not sure what is around you, you know the comfort even a small beam of light can bring. The Bible is a beacon in the midst of difficult circumstances. God's Word can give you hope, comfort, and direction. It shows you the way of life!

Candi Finch

Prayer: *Take time in prayer simply thanking God for His Word, how it directs and guides you. What a treasure we have in the Bible!*

Personal Reflection:

341

God's Word Is Better Than Bacon

Psalm 119:121–135

*"I opened my mouth and panted,
For I longed for Your commandments." (v. 131)*

What do you crave? What makes your mouth water and your toes tingle with anticipation? For me, there is almost nothing in this world better than bacon! If I walk into a building and smell it cooking, my mouth begins to water and my mind immediately thinks, "I want some!" Even if I already have a full stomach, I know that the meaty, salty goodness of bacon will hit the spot. I *crave* it!

I do not know what causes you to have that kind of reaction, but I can tell you that a juicy cheeseburger at the end of a long day, an ice-cold Diet Coke when the weather is hot and humid, and a piping hot cup of strong black tea on a rainy day are, as the song goes, "just a few of my favorite things!" As much as I desire and even pant for these gastronomic delights, my prayer is that I would desire God's Word even more.

Too many times I have approached the Word of God like it was some bad-tasting cough medicine or limp leafy spinach (or insert whatever vegetable you do not particularly desire but know is good for you). God's Word is good for you, but it's not just a dry bran muffin. God's Word can delight even the most discerning palate and send your spiritual taste buds soaring. The psalmist declared that "as the deer pants for the water brooks, so pants my soul for You, O God" (Ps. 42:1) and that we should "taste and see that the LORD is good" (34:8). Earlier in Psalm 119, the writer professed, "How sweet are Your words to my taste, sweeter than honey to my mouth!" (v. 103).

These beautiful sentiments should be on the lips of every believer. Yet, far too often, I do not long for God's commandments like I long for bacon. Do you hunger and thirst for the Word of God? I have found that the best way to create an appetite for the things of the Lord is to have a steady diet of the Bible.

Reading the Bible is almost like eating salty potato chips—the more you read or eat the more you want. One other thing I have discovered: If I gorge myself on the things of this world, my appetite for the things of God gradually decreases. I stop hungering for Him because I have deceived myself into believing that worldly things can fulfill me; yet nothing could be farther from the truth. As believers, our spiritual metabolisms were designed to run on godly food—the things of this world will never ultimately satisfy, and in some cases, could even make us sick.

Candi Finch

Prayer: *Ask God to give you a hunger for His Word. Also, pray for discernment to see if you are consuming worldly things that are not good for you.*

Personal Reflection: ....

....

....

....

....

....

....

Does Sin Grieve You?

Psalm 119:136–176

*"Rivers of water run down from my eyes,
Because men do not keep Your law." (v. 136)*

Josephine Butler lived in England from 1828 to 1906. She married George Butler, a clergyman and a teacher, in 1852. They lived in Oxford, then Cheltenham, then Liverpool, and finally in Winchester because George got different teaching or ministerial positions. In 1863, after their six-year-old daughter fell from a banister to her death, Josephine found comfort in her grief by helping others. As she surveyed her city, she saw women who lived their lives as prostitutes and knew that many women entered this lifestyle because of poverty, slavery, or lack of education.

So, Josephine Butler began a campaign against prostitution by reaching out to destitute women. She longed to "rescue fallen women for Jesus." She founded the House of Rest, a home for girls in danger of falling into prostitution and trained these young women to have suitable work skills that would give them a way to support themselves. For the next forty years, she dedicated her life to these women, and her efforts spread all over Europe. She sought to help women who were trafficked across Europe; and, in 1880, she aided in the release of thirty-four British girls from Belgian brothels and helped in the prosecution of the brothel-keepers.

Josephine Butler was a woman who was grieved by sin. Like the psalmist, rivers of water ran down her eyes because people did not keep the commands of God. She sought to be a light in her community to draw people to the Savior. What has always inspired me about Josephine's story is that in the middle of one of the darkest periods of her life, she looked for where God's Word could impact her community and bring healing and wholeness to others. In doing that, she

also found healing in her own life. She called the prostitution and abuse of women what is it—sin.

However, in our world today, I am afraid that far too many believers make light of sin, or worse yet, ignore it, or even refuse to call some things sin that God clearly calls sin. In fact, many of our movies, music, television shows, and other forms of media flaunt sins, and we are entertained instead of sickened by them. Christians are called to be salt and light in the world (Matt. 5:13–16). Just as it did Josephine Butler, sin should grieve us, and we should seek to show people the remedy for sin and the healing that is found in a relationship with Jesus.

Candi Finch

Prayer: *Spend a few moments asking God to help you view sin the way He views sin. Sin causes your separation from God and grieves the heart of your Savior. Ask Him to show you if there is any sin that you are making light of in your own life and pray for the strength to live for Him today.*

Personal Reflection: ....

....

....

....

....

....

Who Do You Go to on Your Bad Days?

Psalm 121:1–2

"I will lift my eyes to the hills—
From whence comes my help?
My help comes from the LORD,
Who made heaven and earth." (vv. 1–2)

When you are having a really bad day, who is the first person you want to see? For me, when I am ugly-crying and needing a little TLC, my first call is either to my twin sister or my mom or dad. I live states away from each of them, but I want to talk to one of them in those moments. Even just their silence on the other end of the phone is comforting as I sob it out because I know they are with me in my grief and that I am not alone. When I was a little kid, I really struggled with nightmares. I would wake up in the middle of the night panicked and crying, and the only thing that would console me would be crawling into the arms of my mom or dad as they rocked me back to sleep.

God is your *Abba* (Arabic), Daddy; He is your Father. The Bible says that He has compassion and an abundance of lovingkindness for His people (Is. 63:7). Did you know that He desires for you to come to Him on your bad days? You can "ugly cry" in His presence; He is with you in your grief. While you cannot physically crawl up into His lap like I could with my parents when I was a little kid, you can go to Him. God wants to be your Helper and your Comforter.

The writer of Psalm 121 knew that help comes from the Lord. The Maker of heaven and earth is your Maker. He knows just what you need in moments of suffering and trial. In fact, Paul knew this truth as well and encouraged the church at Corinth with these words: "Blessed be the God and Father of our Lord Jesus Christ, the Father of mercies and God of *all* comfort, who comforts us in all our tribulation that, we may be able to comfort those who are in any trouble, with the comfort with which we ourselves are comforted by God" (2 Cor. 1:3–4).

Our God is the God of all comfort, and He comforts us so that we can comfort others! What a beautiful domino effect.

So, back to my question, who do you go to on your bad days? Is it possible that you are seeking comfort in the wrong people or places or things instead of going to God for comfort? Do you read His Word and allow it to be a soothing balm to your hurts? Maybe you seek help from another Christian who can comfort you because she has been comforted by God. Can I encourage you to go down these avenues on your bad days? God wants you to come to Him.

Candi Finch

Prayer: *Praise God that He is the God of all comfort!*

Personal Reflection: ....

....

....

....

....

....

....

God Watches Over You

Psalm 121:3–8

"The Lord shall preserve you from all evil;
He shall preserve your soul." (v. 7)

When the psalmist says that God will "preserve" us, what exactly does that mean? The Hebrew word *shamar* (translated "shall preserve") is found six times in Psalm 121: "He who keeps," (vv. 3–4); "keeper," (vv. 5–8). This word denotes guarding and protecting, like a watchman or bodyguard who stays awake at night to guard you and watch out for dangers you may not see.

Verses 3 and 4 picture God as a night guard who is never found sleeping on the job! Isn't that great to know? God does not slumber or sleep; so He is on the job 24 hours a day, 7 days a week, 365 days a year. He does not take vacation days. "The Lord is your shade at your right hand" (v. 5) suggests that God protects your weak side. The word *shade* means protection or defense. The right side was especially vulnerable in battle because the shield guarded the left side but not the right. The psalmist is describing God as a shield where you need Him the most.

In verses 7 and 8, God is said to protect us from all evil, to guard our souls, and to watch over our comings and goings. How does that actually happen? God is not a distant God who cannot be bothered with His creation; He is actively watching out for you from heaven. In addition, He has provided His Word to help protect you, to steer you away from evil and onto the path of wisdom.

However, maybe you have a nagging question creeping in your mind at this point, such as, "Where was God when . . . ?" Where was He when something really bad happened to you or someone you loved? Sister, believe me, He was not absent. Yet, because we live in a sinful world, difficulties can come from many sources—our own sins or the sins of other people, the attacks of the

devil, sickness or natural disasters because we live in a fallen world, and finally, difficulties coming from God Himself.

James 1:2–4 teaches that trials can come because God wants to build endurance in us so we can mature in our faith. Even if you do not understand the source or sources of your difficulties, you can trust that God has not left His post of watching out for you.

Candi Finch

Prayer: *Consider spending a few moments praising God for being your guard and keeper. Or, if you have faced a difficult time and are struggling with "Where was God when . . . ?" would you ask God to help you trust in Him even if you never understand why that difficulty happened?*

Personal Reflection: ....

....

....

....

....

....

....

Why Worship? Three Reasons

Psalm 122:1–5

"I was glad when they said to me,
'Let us go into the house of the Lord.'" (v. 1)

Do you delight to be among the people of God? Do you welcome worshiping on the Lord's Day? This psalm of ascent, written by David, was recited by the people of Israel as they came to worship the Lord in Jerusalem. Like all habits of the Christian life, going to church may not always be what we feel like doing. Also, just as we do with other spiritual disciplines, we can participate in the activity yet still miss the point. This psalm teaches us to choose an attitude of joy about joining other believers to worship the Lord.

Scripture tells us not to neglect "the assembling of ourselves together" (Heb. 10:25). God created us to worship Him. One of the ways we worship Him is by being part of His Body, the Church. In addition to being a command of the Lord, worshiping with other believers at church is a vital part of our own spiritual lives.

Worshiping in the house of the Lord reminds us of our identity in Christ. If you are a Christian, you are a child of God. You are part of God's family and you belong with other believers. Christians living in America have enjoyed the freedom to worship without fear of persecution; yet for millions of our brothers and sisters in Christ, belonging to God's family includes great risk.

Worshiping in the house of the Lord also reminds us that we were never meant to grow spiritually on our own. You need the community of your spiritual family. Even within this short verse, the principle is at work: "I was glad when they said to me, 'Let us go into the house of the Lord'" (Ps. 122:1). That means other people invited David to join them in worshiping the Lord together.

What a reminder that you not only need other believers, but also other believers need you! Your encouragement might be the difference in spurring a

sister in Christ to spiritual growth. In fact, the Holy Spirit has given you spiritual gifts so that you can build up the body of Christ. You were created for community.

Worshiping in the house of the Lord reminds us of what God has done for us and will continue to do. Going to church is a weekly opportunity to recall the death and resurrection of Jesus for the forgiveness of our sins and the certain hope that He is coming again. When we observe a believer's baptism and participate in the Lord's Supper, we remember the spiritual truths represented. This Sunday, allow the Lord to remind you of the identity, community, and blessings that are yours in Christ!

Katie McCoy

Prayer: *Do you want to love the church as the Lord does? Be glad to go to God's house for fellowship with other believers. Remember that you belong to Him, that God created you to need and serve other Christians, and that He has blessed you beyond all measure.*

Personal Reflection: ....

....

....

....

....

....

351

Jerusalem's Peace, Our Blessing

Psalm 122:6–9

"Pray for the peace of Jerusalem:
'May they prosper who love you. . . .'" (v. 6)

If you are a mom, you know how many requests your children can have each day. Often their requests concern their own needs or wants. But what if your children asked you for something that they knew was important to you? How might you respond, not just to their request but also to their concern for you?

Throughout the Bible, God shows His special care for the people of Israel and their capital city of Jerusalem. Beginning with God's promise to give the land of Israel to Abraham's descendants, this city is important to the heart of God (Gen. 12:1–7; 17:7–8). Even though they have rejected their Messiah, God has not abandoned His covenant with Israel. God will continue to be faithful to His chosen people. One day, the people of Israel will recognize their Lord and be saved from their sins (Zech. 12:10; Rom. 11:26–29).

Until that day, a blessing is bestowed on those who seek the good of Israel. When we pray for the peace of Jerusalem, God blesses us! When the Lord made His covenant with Abraham, He promised to bless those who blessed him and curse those who cursed him (Gen. 12:2–3). Just ponder the wonder of such a promise! When we care about Israel like our Father cares, when we share this desire of His heart, we receive a blessing.

Praying for the peace of Jerusalem makes us mindful of the Lord's faithfulness. Our circumstances may tempt us to doubt whether or not the Lord will fulfill His promises. However, just like His covenant with the nation of Israel, God will never forget His Word. We can be confident that He will accomplish His purpose for the nations, for His chosen people, and for His church. No matter what happens in our world, no one can thwart God's plan!

Praying for the peace of Jerusalem makes us mindful of the Lord's coming return. Today, a Muslim shrine called the Dome of the Rock occupies the ancient Temple Mount in Jerusalem, a visible reminder that peace has not yet come to the city. The nation is consistently under threat of terrorist attacks and must constantly defend its borders. These events are not merely geo-political matters; they are not simply about property lines. Rather, conflicts point to the ever-closer return of Christ, Israel's Messiah.

Praying for the peace of Jerusalem makes us mindful of our place in the Lord's redemption. Scripture explains that we have been grafted into the blessing of salvation by God's unfathomable kindness toward us (Rom. 11:17–24)! God always intended to redeem the nations and to use the nation of Israel to accomplish His salvation. We are part of *His* magnificent story that runs through all of human history. May we all be faithful to pray for the peace of Jerusalem!

Katie McCoy

Prayer: *Thank the heavenly Father for His faithfulness to all of His promises. Pray for the peace of Jerusalem. May the name of Jesus be glorified through the Lord's protection of His chosen people!*

Personal Reflection: ....

....

....

....

....

How We Wait

Psalm 123:1–4

"Behold, as the eyes of servants look to the hand of their masters,
As the eyes of a maid to the hand of her mistress,
So our eyes look to the LORD our God,
Until He has mercy on us." (v. 2)

This psalm of ascent, only four verses in length, has a deeply meaningful lesson for us when we are walking through difficult times: As our trials increase, so must our focus on the Lord. Here, the psalmist expresses the suffering of His people. They are filled with disdain for those who are prideful. Yet, when we consider their complaint in the context of the entire psalm, the psalmist seems to be experiencing a trial at the hands of those who are prideful over them. While we may not know the full extent of their circumstances, we know that they were troubled enough to cry out for God's mercy.

Psalm 123:2 teaches us to wait for the Lord to work on our behalf. Instead of striving in our own strength, we are called to endure trials patiently. Consider the imagery used in this verse: We are to wait for God to have mercy on us like servants watch for the will of their masters and like a maid who anticipates the needs of her mistress. While you are watching to see God move for you, watch to see how God will move through you. While you are waiting on God to act, wait on God with your actions.

This verse protects us from becoming self-focused in our struggles. Instead, we are to become more and more God-focused, watching for His will and carrying out His commands. In the great "Hall of Faith" of Hebrews 11, men and woman endured great hardship and persecution and believed that God would be faithful to His Word. Drawing encouragement from their test, believers are told to endure, to run the race, and to focus on Jesus, "the author and finisher of our faith" (Heb. 12:2).

Dear sister, your Shepherd has promised that His mercy will come like the morning. The mountains will crumble into the sea before His covenant of mercy is ever shaken. Now, submit to the work He wants to do in and through you. During this season of waiting, watch for His will to be revealed. Minister to Him like a servant who anticipates the will of her master. Draw near to Him to know what He would have you do. Wait on Him to act. And wait on Him with your actions.

Katie McCoy

Prayer: *The Lord knows your struggles and trials. He sees every difficulty through which you are walking. Wait on His mercy. As you wait for Him to act on your behalf, seek His perfect and holy will. Trust Him and serve Him with your whole life.*

Personal Reflection: ....

....

....

....

....

....

....

Your Creator is Your Help

Psalm 124:1–8

*"Our help is in the name of the Lord,
Who made heaven and earth." (v. 8)*

One of the most simple and powerful prayers you can utter is "Help me, Lord!" Your help is not found in a personal growth program or principles of positive thinking. Your help is found in a Person: Yahweh, the Lord, the God who is (Ex. 3:14). And He is everything that you need.

The psalm recounts how greatly the odds were against God's people. Psalm 124:2–5 describes what would have been certain defeat, had the Lord not intervened on their behalf. Their enemies came against the Israelites like a rising tide, threatening to sweep over their souls and overwhelm them. The Lord refused to give them up to their enemies, and they escaped like a bird released from the snare of a trap.

Surveying this great victory, the psalmist proclaims that their help is in the authoritative, all-powerful name of Yahweh, the Lord who made heaven and earth. The psalmist chose to recall that the Lord created all that is seen and unseen. The first seven verses describe Him as a protector, defender, and deliverer. Yet, verse 8 reminds the reader that He is Creator.

Remembering that our Protector is also the Creator teaches us two important spiritual truths. Holding on to these truths will help you hold on as you wait for God's help. First, because the Lord is Creator of heaven and earth, even your enemies are under His control. Whatever you are up against—fear, conflict, and uncertainty—He remains in control. Ephesians 6:10–18 describes our constant spiritual battle. But be encouraged that God has already given you victory in His name. You are more than a conqueror through Him who loves you (Rom. 8:37). He will never allow you to be swept away by your enemies.

Second, because the Lord is Creator of heaven and earth, He can create your solution out of absolutely nothing! He spoke entire solar systems into existence, and He can deliver you with one word. No matter what your circumstances are right now, He is still the way-maker. He can make a stream in a desert and a straight path through a wilderness. Your Deliverer can still create out of nothing. And He has promised to be your help. Tell that to your fears!

In your spiritual battles, remember who God is. One of the easiest traps is falling into a focus on your struggles instead of your Savior. Remember His promises. Remember His character. And remember that He is your help! If God is for you, who can be against you (Rom. 8:31)?

Katie McCoy

Prayer: *Ask the Lord for His help! He sees every struggle that you are up against. Acknowledge He is the Creator and completely in control of your situation. Thank Him for promising to be your source of help.*

Personal Reflection: ....

....

....

....

....

....

Surrounded by God's Care

Psalm 125:1–5

*"Those who trust in the L*ORD*,*
Are like Mount Zion,
Which cannot be moved, but abides forever.
As the mountains surround Jerusalem,
*So the L*ORD *surrounds His people*
From this time forth and forever." (vv. 1–2)

Geographically, several mountains landmark the city of Jerusalem. They surround the city like high walls, sheltering it against enemies and fortifying it against covert attacks. These mountains include the Mount of Olives, where Jesus gave His farewell Olivet Discourse (Matt. 24:1–25:46); Mount Moriah, where God tested Abraham with the command to sacrifice Isaac and where the temple was built (Gen. 22:2–8; 2 Chr. 3:1); and Mount Zion, where Jesus had the Last Supper with His disciples (Matt. 26:17–30).

Within the city of Jerusalem, Mount Zion is special to the Lord. He loves this mountain more than any other place in His holy city (Ps. 87:2). The security of Mount Zion signified the people's confidence in God's care for them. The Lord has a purpose that cannot be thwarted for the city of Jerusalem (Zech. 14:1–9). Because His purpose for Jerusalem will never be undone, He will defend and protect it for the sake of His name.

This image is used by the psalmist to show how secure we are. God's purpose for you will never be thwarted (Ps. 138:8). He has covenanted Himself to defend and protect you.

The woman who trusts in this covenant-keeping God will be as strong and enduring as this mountain. She will have a tender place in the heart of the Lord, for He always watches over those who hope in Him. She will have immovable

strength, for the Lord will be her personal defense. And she will have unfaltering security, for she will be insulated by the Lord's protection.

You may feel vulnerable, but you are surrounded by the Lord's presence. You may feel pressed on every side by stresses and circumstances, but you are hemmed in by the Lord's presence. You may feel overwhelmed, but you are insulated by the Lord's care. If the Lord is with you, you need not be afraid (Ps. 23:4).

If you are trusting in the character and covenants of the Lord, you are in a place of complete safety. No matter how you are surrounded on the outside or how you feel on the inside, God will not allow one word of His promises toward you to fall. And here is the beautiful truth—the soul-liberating truth—your security is based on His faithfulness to His own word. And He never breaks His Word.

Just as Jerusalem, the precious city of God, is surrounded by strong mountains, you, the precious daughter of God, are surrounded by the present care and protection of the Lord. Look to Him and find all the security your soul needs!

Katie McCoy

Prayer: *Believe that the Lord is protecting you in ways that you do not even see. He is standing guard over your whole life. Thank Him for loving you and for always watching over you. Think deeply about His care for you.*

Personal Reflection: ....

....

....

....

Stop Laboring and Start Trusting

Psalm 127:1–5

"Unless the LORD builds the house,
They labor in vain who build it;
Unless the LORD guards the city,
The watchman stays awake in vain." (v. 1)

Psalm 127 is the only psalm of ascent attributed to King Solomon and is especially significant because Solomon talks about the futility of human effort. The word for *labor* is the same word used throughout Ecclesiastes. Surveying his work, Solomon despairs of his labor and believes it has all been in vain. His writings in Ecclesiastes and in this psalm point to the vanity of working without the Lord's blessing and apart from His purpose.

God created work in the garden of Eden. Work is good. But like all that God created for good, work can become an idol when is elevated it to a level of significance that God never intended. We were created to work. But we were never created for work.

This verse highlights the importance of working God's way. First, we must make sure that our work is in step with God's Word and will for our lives. The nineteenth-century evangelist Dwight L. Moody once said, "Our greatest fear should not be of failure, but of succeeding at something that doesn't really matter." The Lord's ultimate goal for your life is to conform you to the image of Christ (Rom. 8:28–29). His will is that you will grow in the Christian life (1 Thess. 4:3). Are your goals for your life, your family, your career, or your ministry the same as God's goals? If they are not, you will face frustration as you try to build something through your own efforts.

Second, we must make sure that our work is according to God's power rather than our own, which is especially true when it comes to our spiritual growth. Only the Holy Spirit can bring about lasting life-change in us. The apostle Paul rebuked the Christians in Galatia for trying to grow in the faith through human effort rather than through faith in God (Gal. 3:2–3). You may even have godly goals. But when you try to achieve them through self-effort instead of through reliance on the Lord, you labor in vain.

The children of God were never meant to strive. Instead, we were meant to depend up on God's work in us. When we try to build our lives through self-effort, we rob God of receiving glory through us. Sometimes the Lord will allow us to become frustrated with ourselves in order to teach us to depend upon Him instead of our own efforts. What personal goal do you need to surrender to the Lord today?

Katie McCoy

Prayer: *Ask the Lord to show you the areas of your life where you need to depend upon His power. Surrender them to Him now and believe by faith that He can do exceedingly abundantly beyond all that you ask or even dream (Eph. 3:20). Thank Him for caring for you. Give God the glory in all of your life!*

Personal Reflection: ....

....

....

....

....

Created for Rest

Psalm 127:2

"It is vain for you to rise up early,
To sit up late,
To eat the bread of sorrows;
For so He gives His beloved sleep." (v. 2)

You need rest. God created you in such a way that you must have regular sleep. In fact, you cannot function like God intended without adequate rest. Even fitness experts note the physical benefits of rest, including accelerated recovery, more energy, and less stress. Neglecting to get enough rest can also have negative effects on learning and memory, as well as cause serious health crises, including high blood pressure and heart disease. Rest is vital to your physical health.

Practicing patterns of rest helps you remember that God is the one who gives you the ability to do what you need to do. You were never made to do it all. As much as you strive to cross off all the items on your to-do list, you have limits. We all do! Resting reinforces that it does not all depend upon us; it all depends upon God. We are limited, but He is unlimited. Rest is also important for personal creativity; it is nearly impossible to be innovative when you are stressed and chronically tired. Rest is vital to your emotional health.

Rest is important enough to your life that God commanded a day of rest, right after He forbade putting anything before Him, creating an idol, or taking His name in vain (Ex. 20:1–17). When you practice a day of rest, called a Sabbath, your life can be oriented around God. When the Israelites came to the promised land, they not only received God's inheritance, but they also received rest from their enemies (Deut. 25:19). This recognition of Sabbath rest symbolizes our relationship with the Lord and our salvation through faith (Heb. 4:9–10).

Even God rested! After He created everything that is seen and unseen, He rested from all His work (Gen. 2:2). When you practice Sabbath rest, you reflect the image of God. Rest is vital to your spiritual health.

There may be times when you feel as though you do not have enough time to do all that you need to accomplish. You feel burdened, weighed down, and stretched too thin. During these times, you may find setting aside time in the Lord's presence easy to forgo. You forget to talk to Him in prayer and hear from Him through His Word. All the while, He promises to give you rest if you will just come to Him (Matt. 11:28).

Katie McCoy

Prayer: *Dear friend, go to God in prayer today. He knows how weary and worn out you feel. And He wants to give you rest. You can live the abundant life God provides for His children.*

Personal Reflection: ....

....

....

....

....

....

....

The Blessed Life

Psalm 128:1–4

"Blessed is every one who fears the LORD,
Who walks in His ways." (v. 1)

The blessings for the woman who fears the Lord are limitless! One might even say that the fear of the Lord is the key to the blessed life. What is the fear of the Lord? It is a reverential awe of God that creates an awareness of His presence with us and of our personal accountability to Him. The fear of the Lord is expressed in a desire to avoid disappointing Him and in personal patterns of obedience to Him.

The truth is that whatever you fear ultimately has control over you. If you fear what others think of you, you will be controlled by the desire for their approval. If you fear financial lack in the future, you will be controlled by the desire to accumulate money. If you fear being out of control, you can even be controlled by the desire for control! But the fear of the Lord is altogether different! Fearing the Lord leads to freedom. When you fear God, you see Him for who He is, and you are free from the grip of sinful fear.

The woman who fears God need fear nothing else. The Lord watches over the woman who fears Him (Ps. 33:18), personally teaches her the right way to go (25:12), and ensures that she has everything that she needs (34:9). Even more, fear of the Lord is the beginning of all wisdom (111:10). The woman who fears God is also characterized by a spirit of humility, and humility attracts God's special attention (Prov. 22:4; Is. 66:2).

Psalm 128:1 also shows that to fear the Lord means to walk in His ways and to do what pleases Him. As you live your life in reverence to God, He assumes His rightful place in your life. This reverential awe causes you to turn away from sin and to pursue integrity. Fear of the Lord motivated the young Joseph to flee immorality; his awareness of God's presence caused him to run away from

temptation (Gen. 39:7–12). On the other side of the spectrum, those who persist in wickedness have "no fear of God" before their eyes (Ps. 36:1). Cultivating the fear of the Lord protects you from the deceitfulness of sin.

Notice the universal promise of today's verse is: Blessed is "every one" who fears the Lord and walks in His ways! All of these blessings can be yours. Have you been going in the wrong direction? Consider the Lord and His promise to lead those who fear Him. Are you controlled by anxiety? Consider the Lord and His promise to protect those who fear Him. Do you desire the blessing of God on your life? Consider the Lord and His promise to bless those who fear Him. May we be women characterized by the fear of the Lord!

Katie McCoy

Prayer: *Ask the Lord to teach you to fear Him. Make a commitment to live under the blessing of the fear of the Lord and to walk in His ways!*

Personal Reflection: ....

....

....

....

....

....

What Will Outlast You?

Psalm 128:5–6

"The Lord bless you out of Zion,
And may you see the good of Jerusalem
All the days of your life.
Yes, may you see your children's children.
Peace be upon Israel!" (vv. 5–6)

These two verses express the culmination of blessings upon the person who fears the Lord and walks in His ways. The psalmist describes the state of blessedness that comes as a result of how you live your life as it is manifested in your work and family (Ps. 128:1).

To an Israelite, having children was of paramount importance. Bearing a child was directly linked to God's blessing. Whether or not a woman had biological offspring signified whether or not she was in the Lord's favor. The converse was also true; to be infertile was a disgrace. If a woman was unable to conceive and bear a child, her barrenness was considered a reproach from the Lord.

The reason her offspring were so important concerned the object of God's blessing—the promised land. For Hebrew culture, a family measured their blessing and legacy by what they left behind them—their children. If a family had no offspring to inherit their portion of the land, no one would be able to carry on the family name, which would be a disgrace.

When the psalmist describes the blessing of seeing one's grandchildren, he is not just describing long life. Rather, he is describing the inheritance of God's promises. For an Israelite to live long enough to see her grandchildren would be to see the fruit of the personal legacy that she would leave behind. This blessing is reserved for the one who feared the Lord and walked in His ways. She would be honored. She would have a legacy that outlasted the span of her own life.

How can you inherit this happiness? Certainly, children are a blessing and reward from the Lord, and grandchildren are a woman's crown (Ps. 127:3; Prov. 17:6). Yet, perhaps, for the Christian woman, additional sources of joy are her spiritual children.

The woman who evangelizes, nurtures, and disciples others invests in a legacy that will outlast her earthly years. She will live to see the blessing of God on the fruit of her work. Such a woman is wise and demonstrates a godly fear of the Lord (Prov. 11:30). She fulfills her ministry as an ambassador for Christ who makes disciples throughout the earth (Matt. 28:19–20; 2 Cor. 5:20). Every woman—the married with children, the married without children, the single mother, the single woman—can have this legacy. The ripple effects of her life can last for generations. But first, she must fear the Lord and walk in His ways. Are you investing in others who will outlast you?

"Only one life, 'twill soon be past,
Only what's done for Christ will last." ~ C. T. Studd

Katie McCoy

Prayer: *You can leave a lasting legacy by living in the blessings of fearing the Lord and walking in His ways. Invest your life in the things that will matter for generations!*

Personal Reflection: ....

....

....

....

Our Certain Hope

Psalm 129:1–8

"The LORD is righteous;
He has cut in pieces the cords of the wicked." (v. 4)

Jesus accomplished more than we can fathom when He died on the cross and rose again from the dead. For the woman in Christ, His death broke the claim that sin had on her life. Because she has been united to Christ by faith, sin has no more authority over her life than it does on Jesus Himself. The cords of wickedness that enslaved her to sin were cut when she accepted the Savior and His atonement for her sins.

But until we see Jesus face-to-face—either when He brings us to Himself in heaven or returns to us on earth—we who are saved live in what theologians call the "already but not yet." We are *already* saved from the power of sin, but we are *not yet* entirely rid of sin's presence (Rom. 6:1–7; 1 John 2:1), which will happen when Christ returns. We are already heirs of the Father, but we have not yet received all that inheritance (Rom. 8:17; 1 Pet. 1:3–5), which becomes ours when Christ returns. We are *already* citizens of heaven, but we have *not yet* been brought to our true home (Phil. 3:20), which we enter when Christ returns.

The reality of "already but not yet" is not only true in our individual lives but also in the world in which we live. Colossians 2:13–15 tells us that when Jesus died on the cross, He abolished Satan's dominion so thoroughly that Christ put him to open shame. Satan, who is still at work in "the sons of disobedience," has *already* been defeated, but he has *not yet* been banished (Eph. 2:1–3). Hebrew 2:8–9 says that all things have *already* been put in subjection to Christ, but now we do not yet see all things put under Him. Just turn on the evening news and you will be reminded that this world is *not yet* under the

righteous rule of the Lord Jesus. If we only know what we can see, we will be tempted to despair.

Here is where you and I have hope: Because the Lord *is* righteous, we know that He *will* cut into pieces every cord of wickedness in this world. He will work justice for the oppressed. He will make right every wrong (Rev. 19:11). He will cut the cords of the wicked. We have this hope. Until then, we wait for His certain coming; we watch for signs of His return; and we work to do His will.

Jesus Christ, the Righteous One, is coming again! We know where this world is going; we have read the end of the Book. And we know that Jesus wins. May we who have this hope in Him, purify ourselves, just as He is pure (1 John 3:3)!

Katie McCoy

Prayer: *Thank the Lord for cutting the cords of wickedness when He died on the cross. Believe that He is coming again! Live in the certain hope of His return.*

Personal Reflection: ....

....

....

....

....

....

Waiting in a Microwave Culture

Psalm 130:1–8

"I wait for the LORD, my soul waits,
And in His word I do hope.
My soul waits for the Lord
More than those who watch for the morning—
Yes, more than those who watch for the morning." (vv. 5–6)

The concept of waiting is foreign to our society. No longer must we wait for film to develop, coffee to brew, or a movie to rent. Many modern inventions birthed from our desires and demands for speed and efficiency have added to the excitement of living in this fast-paced era. But this progress has not come without cost. For any culture to maintain such a lifestyle of instant gratification, it must inevitably sacrifice, at least on some level, the virtue of patience on the part of the members of its population. Christians must realize that while immediacy is the expectation in our economy, the same may not be said for God's timing.

Psalm 130 is one of the fifteen Songs of Ascents (Pss. 120–134). These lyrics were sung to God in worship by pilgrims traveling to Jerusalem in celebration of the great festivals each year. Since some Bible scholars believe these psalms were sung as the pilgrims ascended the steps of the temple itself, they are identified as Songs of Ascents. While they may not have been written specifically for these pilgrimages, the songs have served as words of worship for Christians on their long journeys. The words of this psalm can encourage Christians today who must often wait on the Lord in their journeys of life and ministry.

Psalm 130 is also one of the seven penitential psalms as the poet who is overwhelmed by his sinfulness cries out to God for forgiveness. In verses 5 and 6, the psalmist declares his resolution to wait for the Lord, patiently and confidently. Following his own personal commitment, the psalmist turns to

the community of Israel to encourage them to wait confidently and expectantly for God to respond (vv. 7–8). The Lord always answers prayer and forgives sin.

Are you in a place of waiting? Do you seem to be the only one in that place, maybe even for some time, believing God at His word and knowing He will intervene? This poem is a reminder that waiting takes as much endurance, or even more so, than doing. God can use this process not only to teach you how to be steadfast, but also how to praise Him while waiting.

Microwaves may have replaced the oven and e-mail surpassed the hand-written letter, but there is no shortcut to replace prayer for communicating with God. His response time may not be immediate, but it will always be right. Learn the discipline of waiting on the Lord in this microwave culture!

Courtney Veasey

Prayer: *Do you ever become impatient with God? Pray with the psalmist for patience as you wait on the Lord and His perfect will.*

Personal Reflection: ....

....

....

....

....

....

To Give the Perfect Gift

Psalm 132:1–18

"I will not give sleep to my eyes
Or slumber to my eyelids,
Until I find a place for the LORD,
A dwelling place for the Mighty One of Jacob." (vv. 4–5)

For gift giving, I often find myself caught up in an elaborate search for just the right item that will convey sincere thoughtfulness to the intended recipient. And by the "right item," I include the gift wrapping, card, and handwritten message as parts of the overall package. Gift cards are simply too generic, only to be used as a last-minute, last-resort option. Depending on the occasion, hours to days to weeks can be spent making gift-giving decisions. And the joy of the recipient at the realization of how well she is truly known and loved becomes the validation making such an effort worthwhile.

In Psalm 132, the psalmist recounts the time when David vowed to the Lord that he would find the perfect location to serve as His dwelling place on the earth. The level of David's commitment to the task is reflected in the hyperbolic language used in his oath, declaring that he would not even allow himself sleep or the luxury of rest until a dwelling place for Yahweh was established. In verses 6–10, David responds to an earlier promise God had made to him. The contents of this promise are recalled (vv. 11–18)—namely, that God would establish David upon the throne of Israel and extend His favor from Zion forever to those of David's lineage who would keep His covenant and testimony. David's urgency to secure the dwelling place of God was not only out of concern for his own sake, but also for future generations of his lineage.

There are days when I realize in sadness that my efforts to please people, and/or to be pleasing to others, have been far greater than what I have given to understanding and pursuing what pleases God. He has given us both

physical and eternal life, and His love for us knows no bounds. Yet so often we are tempted to have God "take a number" behind other people and tasks that we have esteemed as more important. Put the pursuit of your Lord at the forefront of all. Ask what gift He may want to receive from you; then take pains to make it happen. If you take delight in thoughtfulness shown to you, how much more must our Lord do so in whose image you are made?

Courtney Veasey

Prayer: *Recall the promises of His Word and declare those to Him and to yourself anew. For just as with David, the richness of your relationship with God is vital not only for yourself but also for those around you and other generations yet to come.*

Personal Reflection: ....

....

....

....

....

....

373

No Manicure Necessary

Psalm 134:1–3

*"Lift up your hands in the sanctuary,
And bless the Lord." (v. 2)*

Consider how many times in a day you make use of your hands. Unless your hands are restricted physically, these appendages on the end of your arms are used to engage in nearly every human activity. Consider the durability of our Maker's design. Throughout history, humans have used their hands for many different activities. In the ancient era, hands helped to carve out tools and weapons. In the medieval era, hands guided spindles and horses and carried long swords into battle. And in the modern era, hands steer vehicles, program machines, and type on computers. Some activities—like hunting, cooking, and bathing, as well as acts of worship and prayer—have involved the hands of people of every generation. Hands are amazing creations of God!

The Bible teaches that both the human voice and body should be used for worship and praise to God. The poetic prayer-language of the book of Psalms guides believers in ways to approach God. This final Song of Ascents encourages servants of the Lord to lift their hands in His sanctuary, in the holy place, as part of their expression of praise toward God. For Israel, this expression represented an attitude of praise. Hands lifted from the position of a lower place, even the depths of sin and despair at times, to the higher dwelling place of God in heaven demonstrated the confidence of worshipers that the Lord would receive their praise and answer their prayers.

The first two verses of Psalm 134 call worshipers to "bless the Lord" or to praise Him. Verse 3 is a benediction requesting the Lord's blessing on His servants who worship Him. According to the psalmist, worship involves willingness to serve (v. 1) and faithfulness to pray (v. 2). In addition to the singing of music and the teaching of the Word, worship includes the offering of praise

with uplifted hands. What a fitting conclusion to these Songs of Ascents! As the Israelites reached the final destination of their pilgrimage, they worshiped God with whole hearts. Our worship of Him today must also be wholehearted and may include lifting our hands.

Hands are neutral objects, neither good nor bad in and of themselves. God sovereignly gives hands to humans with the freedom to choose how to use them, whether for purposes of goodness or destruction. The psalmist challenges believers today to exercise their freedom in expressions of worship fit for the King they serve. Will you choose to lift your hands to His sanctuary? Jesus is not concerned about the current condition of the fingernails or skin of your hands. His focus is on what outward gestures merely represent—the condition of your heart and your passion for His glory. No manicure is necessary for worship!

Courtney Veasey

Prayer: *Lifting your hands in praise is one way to express your praise. Spend time in prayer expressing your passion for God and your praise for His goodness.*

Personal Reflection: ....

....

....

....

....

DAY 185

La La La!

Psalm 135:1–4

"Praise the LORD, for the LORD is good;
Sing praises to His name, for it is pleasant." (v. 3)

My family might tell you that I came out of the womb singing. I remember writing my earliest song lyrics around the age of four when I put my own words to the tune of a popular commercial jingle. I grew up especially loving bluegrass and country music, thinking for a time that I would make a career writing and singing in those genres. Though I became a Christian as a teenager, the Christian music scene was not of much interest to me. I wanted to write and listen to songs that told stories of people, love, home, and life. To have only God as the primary subject for song writing material would surely make for a limited corpus of lyrics.

When in college, I truly met Christ along my own Damascus road, and this encounter changed not only my career plans but also the direction of my whole life. The country melodies I once cherished and sang for hours on end suddenly lost their appeal. No longer did it make sense to write any lyrics except ones that testified of the Lord. To my surprise I found that scores and scores of material could be written about Him and to Him, only skimming the surface of what could be told about the greatness of such a Savior. Since that time, now over a decade later, praise has continued to be the cadence of my days and the anthem of my life.

The psalmists of Israel learned to give God His due praise more quickly than I. Psalm 135 presents one example where the psalmist repeats an earlier encouragement also echoed later in this text and throughout the psalter: "Praise the LORD," proclaiming Him with an excited voice and even perhaps with the sound of musical instruments.

On what basis is such jubilant praise warranted? The psalmist gives two reasons: the goodness of Yahweh and the delightfulness of His name, which is

to say that Yahweh Himself is delightful. How did He demonstrate His goodness? How was He delightful? The psalm further reveals that the greatness of Yahweh compares to none other (v. 5). Though He is so great and mighty, He has yet chosen Israel as His own possession (v. 4). Continue reading through the lyrics of Psalm 135—do you sense the excitement building?

Will you join in this grateful chorus of praise today? Though you find yourself thousands of years removed from when the psalms were composed, God remains the same, and the well of His goodness and promises of covenant faithfulness have yet to run dry. For that and more let us join the psalmist in proclaiming, "Praise the LORD!"

Courtney Veasey

Prayer: *Think of a praise song you can sing aloud during your prayer time to celebrate the goodness of God. What a privilege to sing praises to the Lord!*

Personal Reflection: ....

....

....

....

....

....

Free to Be God

Psalm 135:5–21

"For I know that the LORD is great,
And our Lord is above all gods.
Whatever the LORD pleases He does,
In heaven and in earth." (vv. 5–6)

Do you ever wonder: If God is fully sovereign, can human beings still have total free will? Yes! God in His creative design sovereignly decided to make you and me free, with abilities to think and create for ourselves. Freedom to choose must not be compromised. Several New Testament examples demonstrate this point. Consider the parable of the Good Samaritan. First, the robbers were not restricted from attacking the traveler on the road. Though they made bad use of their freedom, they were nonetheless allowed the choice. Then, God did not interfere when the priest and Levite passed by the beaten traveler or as the Samaritan stopped to give him aid. God will never force us to do the good we know we ought to do; the choice is ours.

Consider, as well, the interaction among Martha, Mary, and Jesus (Luke 10:38–42). Annoyed with her sister Mary, who opted out of helping prepare and serve dinner to their guests, Martha went to Jesus requesting that He ask Mary to get up and help her. But Jesus, rather, affirmed the choice Mary had made to sit at His feet rather than forcing Mary to help her sister. Mary had a choice.

God is sovereign and has granted you and me free will. These aspects of God are highlighted in Psalm 135:5–6. The psalmist first acknowledges God's supreme nature that no other gods share in His level of greatness (vv. 5–6). Shifting from singular ("I know") to plural ("our Lord") the psalmist recognizes God's greatness in both an individual and corporate sense for the whole Israelite community. He reveals more about God's freedom in that He does

whatever He pleases in any realm (v. 6). And why can Yahweh do as He pleases? Because the heavens clearly belong to Him, as does the earth and all it contains (cp. Ps. 24:1).

At times, believers can feel so in the dark about God's work in their lives. We can be confused by circumstances He has allowed. We can be frustrated when seemingly He is not responding to our requests quickly. Yet in all seasons, we must allow God to be God. He is free to do as He pleases. Unlike us, though, the Lord always chooses to use His freedom for good. Do you trust that God is good, that His ways are right? Consider making today a day in which you trust Him fully.

Courtney Veasey

Prayer: *Surrender your free will to the Lord, and ask for His sovereign guidance in your life. Praise Him for His greatness and trust Him with your life.*

Personal Reflection: ....

....

....

....

....

The Sword and Its Switchblades

Psalm 136:1–9

*"Oh, give thanks to the L*ORD*, for He is good!*
For His mercy endures forever." (v. 1)

Christians often speak of the eternal life granted in Christ, for in Him we do indeed have an eternal inheritance awaiting us in heaven. But how much do we think about the eternal *love* that God has also promised? Eternal life will be ours, but eternal love is ours now and always!

The community of ancient Israel celebrated this reality. Psalm 136 opens with this declarative theme of God's everlasting love and repeats it throughout. If the process of learning involves repetition, then this point of God's ever-present and eternal love was evidently important for the Israelites.

In Ephesians 6:17, the apostle Paul identifies the Word of God as being "the sword of the Spirit." For the New Testament writers in the first century AD, "the word of God" consisted only of the Old Testament. The addition of the New Testament writings to the canon of Scripture has provided believers today with "extended weaponry" as we continue battling against the forces of evil.

Since the Bible is identified as a "sword," I have often referred to smaller units of text or even individual verses as being "switchblades." In fact, I have two jars labeled "switchblades"—one on the vanity table at home and another in my office. Each contains a handful of folded 3 x 5 index cards with various Scriptures written on them. If my clothing for the day has pockets, I typically grab a "switchblade" from the jar, either at home or work, and place it in my pocket. Then, I not only have a Scripture verse with me for reference, but I have Scripture ready to give away for a word of encouragement.

Consider making a "switchblade" container for yourself or as a project to do with others. Books like Psalms and Proverbs are great places to start finding individual Scriptures to write out on the index cards. Verses from these books

of the Bible can usually be isolated without being taken wildly out of context. Psalm 136:1 would be an excellent verse to keep in your pocket! You may also find this practice to be a way of further storing God's Word in your heart or your "vault," as I like to say. The card will remind you over and over again of such truths as today's focal verse: God is good, and His love is everlasting; we should be ever thankful.

Courtney Veasey

Prayer: *Reflect on the truth of Psalm 136:1. Write the verse on an index card to carry as your "switchblade." Be ready for God's Word to encourage you when you need it, or share your "switchblade" of truth with someone else. Thank the Lord for His goodness and mercy!*

Personal Reflection: ....

....

....

....

....

....

....

Search and Rescue

Psalm 136:10–26

"Who remembered us in our lowly state,
For His mercy endures forever;
And rescued us from our enemies,
For His mercy endures forever;
Who gives food to all flesh,
For His mercy endures forever." (vv. 23–25)

Have you ever been in a situation where you were in life-or-death need of outside help for a physical, tangible rescue? Perhaps when you experienced an accident, or got lost without map or compass, or were choking during a meal. I have a memory from childhood of being with my dad at a lake near where we lived and often went fishing. I was around the age of four at this particular time, and I do not recall whether I jumped off the back of the fishing boat myself or simply fell in the water by looking too far over the edge of the boat. Either way, I clearly remember what happened once I was in the water.

Our boat was still close enough to the edge of the lake where the sawgrass, lily pads, and other lake flora and wildlife inhabitants reside. While under the water, I inadvertently got tangled up in the weeds. I remember trying to look through the murky green color to see how close I was to the surface, but I could barely see beyond the blades of sawgrass that crisscrossed over my head. As I began to panic, a large hand suddenly came bursting through the surface of the water, and my dad snatched me up by the back of my T-shirt from the water and debris and placed me back on the boat. Kids in Florida, raised near bodies of water, spontaneously jump in and play. Thankfully for me that day, my dad looked back to realize that my situation was more serious and I was in need of his help.

The Old and New Testaments record accounts of God's people in need of help, even of physical rescue. In Psalm 136:10–22, the psalmist describes what

God had done for His people. Verses 23–25 summarize God's interaction with Israel. In Israel's humiliation resulting from disobedience, God was mindful of them and pulled them up out of the lake, so to speak. Though He had fore-warned them of what their sin would bring (see Is. 2), He yet rescued them. The writer then tells of God's care and the restoration of Israel and the whole world as Creator. And why? Because as the psalmist repeats, "His faithful love endures forever" (CSB).

How do you relate to the journey of the psalmist? Reflect on those times when God tore you from the clutches of an earthly foe. Are you in need of His rescue today? Continue to call on Him in faith, knowing that whether from religious persecution, anxiety and depression, illness, debt, or any other dire circumstance, your Father sees you; and His arm is still mighty to save.

Courtney Veasey

Prayer: *Thank the Lord for searching for you and rescuing you from your sin!*

Personal Reflection:

Put Your Whole Self In

Psalm 138:1–6

"I will worship toward Your holy temple,
And praise Your name
For Your lovingkindness and Your truth;
For You have magnified Your word above all Your name." (v. 2)

"The Hokey Pokey" is a children's rhyming and dance melody written by a British band leader during World War II as a way of cheering soldiers. The song was first officially published in the 1960s, and by the 1970s it was a huge hit at children's birthday parties and skating rinks across America. As a child of the 1980s, I vividly remember trying to get my "right skate in" and back out again without causing a scene!

What does "The Hokey Pokey" have to do with Psalm 138? The ending of the song makes an effective illustration. You may remember that to close out "The Hokey Pokey," each participant is told: "Put your whole self in." Each participant turns her whole body around. The psalmist calls for believers to give their all to the Lord.

The opening verses of Psalm 138 present the content of a pledge made unto Yahweh in worship, a unit that sets the foundation for the testimonial language that follows in the remainder of the psalm. The psalmist declares that he will thank God with all his heart and sing praises to Him, both actions that involve the use of the voice and possibly musical instruments (v. 1). His body is also involved as he pledges to "worship [Hb. *shachah*, "prostrate oneself, demonstrating honor"] toward" Yahweh's temple, to heaven where His court resides (v. 2). To bow completely prostrate before God is to acknowledge not only His superiority but also our human frailty. As the initial posture of worship, the fully prostrated position acknowledged to God that by His grace mankind is both taken from the dust and lifted up. A supplicant would then

assume a kneeling, seated, or squat position for the duration of a longer time in prayer. David seems to cry out from his innermost being as he claims that God answered him and subsequently installed boldness and strength (v. 3). The writer makes clear through this description that worship and confession before God involve one's whole self, from your voice to the depths of your being.

Am I saying that God desires us to imitate the likes of the "Hokey Pokey" before Him in prayer? No, but He might have a good laugh if we did! What He wants is you, all of you, for only Him. What are you waiting for? "Put your whole self in!"

Courtney Veasey

Prayer: *Worship and praise the Lord with your whole heart and soul, your life given totally to Him.*

Personal Reflection:

Confidence for the Future

Psalm 138:7–8

"Though I walk in the midst of trouble, You will revive me;
You will stretch out Your hand
Against the wrath of my enemies,
And Your right hand will save me." (v. 7)

As far back as I remember, I recall my dad saying to my sister and me, "I'm the only man in your whole life who will have always loved you." Promises are made of words, and words mean little if actions are not taken to prove them to be false. This promise from my dad has consistently been reinforced throughout my life as time and again he has demonstrated his love by tangible acts of protection, support, kindness, and discipline. When a father has earned his daughter's trust and she knows without question or exception that he has her back at all times, there is not much that girl might not attempt in seeking to make a difference in this world.

There is a problem in having a loving, trustworthy earthly father. Earthly dads, as great and strong as they may be, are not only restricted as to where they can physically be at any given moment, but sadly, too, they are only available to us for a limited time on this side of heaven. The best news is that whether your dad is like mine—wonderful but finite—or your father could not be described in quite the same way, we all share a perfect Father in heaven. He is just as real, yet even more present and able beyond any father on earth could ever hope to be.

Notice in Psalm 138:7, the realistic understanding about the journey of life. Previously in the psalm, he made reference to an occasion when the Lord had come through for him. Yet, he seems to understand that God's deliverance once does not equal smooth sailing forever. He acknowledges that even as God's own possession, he is not immune to encountering real danger nor enemies

that express real anger. The expectation of future trouble is not lost on the psalmist, but neither is a confidence in the aid of his Father.

Do you need a solid promise from your heavenly Father today? Why not? Give yourself visible access to these words in Psalm 138:7 by writing them out on a sticky note, a canvas, your bathroom mirror, or wherever else you will notice. When you come to a crossroad along your faith journey, as a mentor of mine says, "put your weight down on His trustworthiness." Your Father in heaven has eternally loved you and given you deliverance. Go confidently into your future days, daughter of the King. Your journey is His, and He will see you through to the end.

Courtney Veasey

Prayer: *Share some of your fears with Him and have confidence in your future.*

Personal Reflection: ....

....

....

....

....

....

387

There Is One Who Understands

Psalm 139:1–6

"O LORD, You have searched me and known me.
You know my sitting down and my rising up;
You understand my thought afar off." (vv. 1–2)

To be understood is a daily battle cry of our hearts! Life is difficult to traverse and navigate. More times than can be enumerated, we agonize and pray over a decision or choice only to be criticized later for our choice and the perceived motives behind it. This passage, speaking of God's depth of knowledge and inescapable presence in our lives, brings incredible peace in the midst of confusion and turmoil.

When my girls were very little and given an opportunity to participate in a trip with family, my husband and I did not think it was a good time for them to go for many reasons. However, I knew that decision would not be popular with everyone. I agonized and prayed for wisdom to respond, knowing my motives would likely be questioned. The Lord consistently brought these verses to my mind (vv. 1–2). Although I could have been misunderstood and judged by those around me, I was comforted in knowing that the Lord knew my heart. He knew that I sought His wisdom and counsel and that I desired to please Him. He knew how I agonized over being misunderstood and judged. He was aware of every detail, and He would protect and sustain me.

Living by the truth of God's Word demands that sometimes we make decisions that seem harsh or unyielding. Most of us do not want to come across as dissonant and rigid, while at the same time we are obligated to uphold God's Word. Jesus is the perfect example of always speaking and living truth, while showing love and forgiveness. I find comfort that Jesus knows my heart even when my actions or convictions are misjudged.

These verses have also sobered me on many occasions. I am comforted by His knowledge and also convicted. He is aware of all our thoughts and words before they are uttered (v. 4). Jesus confirms that "there is nothing covered that will not be revealed, and hidden that will not be known" (Matt. 10:26). This psalm has stopped me in my tracks many times, reminding me that I may be able to deceive those around me with words or actions, but God knows my heart. He knows whether I am before an audience of one (Himself) or seeking to impress or please those around me.

This passage brings the comfort and assurance that the only One who sees and knows all has complete understanding. Also, the Lord will judge us according to what He *knows* about our hearts and our actions, not according to what others *see*.

Carmen Howell

Prayer: *Thank the Lord for pursuing you faithfully from your first thought in the morning until your last one at the end of the day. Rest in knowing He understands and convicts you as only He can in those moments when your thoughts and desires wander to selfishness and pride.*

Personal Reflection: ....

....

....

....

....

Trapped

Psalm 139:7–12

"Even there Your hand shall lead me,
And Your right hand shall hold me." (v. 10)

Finding myself trapped is unsettling enough, but trapped and in complete darkness is almost more than I can bear. Have you ever been trapped in an elevator that stopped working? How much worse to have all the lights go out along with the abrupt halt of the elevator? Or maybe you have experienced being trapped in a storm cellar or home in the midst of a hurricane or approaching tornado? Many of us have felt trapped in a relationship with a family member or friend that was darker than dark with no apparent way out. Fear and anxiety creep in very quickly, followed by loneliness and complete hopelessness.

In the verses surrounding David's promise that the Lord will lead and hold him, he elaborates on different pit stops in this life. There are mountain tops, valleys, both exhilarating and exhausting journeys, joys and sorrows, aches and pains, failures and victories. David reminds us that God not only leads but also protects and nurtures us along the way. Think back to the elevator, storm, or relationship experience that came to your mind. Would your perspective have been different if you had with you a trusted friend? In my mind, if I were not going to make it out alive, at least someone would be there to tell everyone I was dead (laugh out loud)! There is something reassuring about not being alone in the midst of a desperate situation.

These verses assure us that we always have a companion—the One who created all, knows all, and controls all things. He sees the full picture and knows more than just the piece of the puzzle facing you right now. Our God and Father sees the beautiful masterpiece that He is bringing together for all eternity. He knows how the blood, sweat, tears, and darkness are going to combine with the beautiful sunshine, rainbows, and colors to shine His light brighter. He not

only will "lead" you every single day as you seek Him, but He will also "hold" you when those questions, fears, and anxieties creep into the journey. How spectacular to have a leader who desires that we follow His path, understands the difficulties and challenges, and holds us all along the way!

So many times, when things around me were completely dark, I have been refreshed to read and know that "the night shines as the day; the darkness and light are both alike to You" (v. 12). My Father, Creator, and Friend is not fearful, anxious, worried, or distraught about my circumstance or relationship. He is in complete control and will work all things "together for good to those who love God" (Rom. 8:28). He alone brings light to the darkness!

Carmen Howell

Prayer: *Whatever your darkness and desperation today, ask God to confirm that your darkness is light to Him. God's light—His presence and provision—will bring true light to your life!*

✒ **Personal Reflection:** ....

....

....

....

....

....

Why Me? Why This?

Psalm 139:13–16

"For You formed my inward parts;
You covered me in my mother's womb.
I will praise You, for I am fearfully and wonderfully made;
Marvelous are Your works,
And that my soul knows very well." (vv. 13–14)

Questions about the origin and purpose of our lives and those around us can be overwhelming. Why am I here and not there? Why do they have it all and I seemingly have nothing? Why do I have more food than I could possibly consume and many starve to death? Why do I struggle with these problems and not with those that so easily bring failure to others? While we will never know the answers to these specific questions this side of heaven, we can be sure that God has a plan and purpose for each of us from the beginning of time.

God's plan is crystal clear in these verses. He has "formed" us from the inside out. Nothing about you or me is accidental—not physical characteristics, mental capacities, strengths, weaknesses, talents, or abilities. I remind myself and my teenage girls of this truth quite often. Images surround us of people who seem to have near perfect bodies and lives. In reality, these images are far from an accurate picture of their lives. However, these verses continually remind me that it really is immaterial what someone else has or looks like because God has "formed me," "skillfully wrought" me, "fashioned" my every day even before any of them existed. Because I have trouble wrapping my head around this truth, I must not whine and complain about my perceived less-than-stellar life (as I sometimes see it). God says that He "saw my substance, being yet unformed. And in Your book they all were written, the days fashioned for me, when as yet there were none of them" (v. 16).

The Lord gave to our family a ministry assignment years ago. We did not understand. We struggled almost daily with the "why" of this assignment. I inevitably came back to this passage over and over. God sees and knows the complete picture, and His ways are always best. This assignment was part of the journey He had prepared for us. Therefore, we walked obediently, joyfully, and faithfully in it until He led us to a new ministry. The assignment was incredibly rewarding in so many ways. I would not trade one day in light of what I learned through it about my Savior.

You may be in a tough place in a relationship, job, or circumstance right now. Remember that God not only "formed" you from the inside out but He also protected ["covered"] you in the womb of your mother before anyone else even knew you existed. Further, He "fashioned" every day of your life. And in case you have any doubts, "marvelous" are His works.

Carmen Howell

Prayer: *Be grateful that regardless of what you look like, feel like, or act like today, you are created and protected by the God who spoke everything into existence and orders every day of your life.*

Personal Reflection: ....

....

....

....

....

Hating Sin Without Sinning

Psalm 139:17–24

"Search me, O God, and know my heart;
Try me, and know my anxieties;
And see if there is any wicked way in me,
And lead me in the way everlasting." (vv. 23–24)

Hating the sin without becoming the sinner can sometimes be a difficult line to walk. David knew this danger and offered a challenge in these verses. In prior verses, David spoke of His hatred for the wicked, those who were fighting the plans and purposes of God at every turn.

You may struggle as I do in hating the sin and loving the sinner. Or maybe your focus on hatred for the sin causes you to miss the opportunities God gives you to bring light to the darkness. I find myself so discouraged about the sin in my life, my family, my church, and this world that I sometimes miss the doors God opens for me to bring light into the darkness. Do you find it easier to moan about sin and its awful consequences than to trust God and get busy serving? My struggle is more with the church than in the world. I excuse the sin in the world much more quickly than the sins of fellow believers.

I have come to the conclusion that I am more critical of those in the church for several reasons—some admirable and some not so admirable. You may have a healthy desire for those claiming the name of Jesus to act in love and righteousness, as the Scripture teaches, instead of selfishness and pride. However, more often than not, I find it easy to critique others because it takes the focus off my sins and shortcomings. David's counsel is clear: Ask the Lord to search your heart and make your heart clean as only He can do: "Examine me, O Lord, and prove me; try my mind and my heart. For Your lovingkindness is before my eyes, and I have walked in Your truth" (Ps. 26:2–3). Honestly, when my focus is on God's work in the lives of others, I lose sight of my own heart and

responsibility before the Lord. How quickly we lose sight of His lovingkindness when our focus shifts from Him to others.

Appropriately, David followed his critique of the wicked with a plea for the Lord to search his own heart. He knew, as I have also learned, that we must quickly move from judgment to mercy and grace, while leaving justice to the righteous One who knows and sees all. God desires for us to see and identify sin in the world around us; but more important, He wants our hearts to be completely His—in every way, in every word, in every action, in every attitude, in every circumstance.

Carmen Howell

Prayer: *Ask the Lord to keep your focus from shifting to your fears, frustrations, and follies. Seek His help to be still before Him, that He may lead you according to His plans and purposes.*

Personal Reflection: ....

....

....

....

....

....

The Victory Is Yours

Psalm 140:1–13

"O GOD the Lord, the strength of my salvation,
You have covered my head in the day of battle." (v. 7)

Battles come in all different shapes and sizes in each of our lives. However, one thing we all have in common in regard to the battlefield—none of us is exempt. We all face battles, at least in part, almost every single day. The psalmist David knew the struggles of this life so well. David was minding his own business taking care of the sheep in the shepherd's field when God called him out to a battle. David knew what it was like to be betrayed, sought after, unjustly accused, and pursued by evil men. He continued to face battles throughout his life as we all do. This psalm is even more reassuring as we consider the source of its words. A word becomes even more meaningful when it comes from one who has lived it!

For those who recognize sin and realize a desperate need that God alone can satisfy, these verses are incredibly encouraging. When we seek Him and the forgiveness that only He can give through His Son Jesus, then we receive the gift of salvation and victory over all the struggles this life throws at us. David reminds us of the strength, hope, and peace we can have in knowing Jesus and experiencing His faithfulness.

Our Sovereign God is the Lord over all things, all people, and all circumstances! He is the benefactor, the strength, and the Sustainer of our salvation. Our present and our future are in His faithful and strong arms. No plan, scheme, or deception will surprise or go unnoticed by Him.

I remember when I have been misrepresented or misunderstood in family or church situations—some intentionally and some inadvertently. Anxiety, fear, and frustration creep in as I seek to discern how to convince people or change things in order to protect my reputation. I have been so blessed by the promise that God will "cover my head." He is the only protection I need; He has

already won! Whether I win in my eyes or the eyes of the world is immaterial; He has won every battle! And while He does not always remove me from the difficulties and pains of the battle, He always protects and provides everything I need to fight through it.

Whatever your conflict or struggle is today, leave it at the feet of Jesus. He is the Protector you will not have to convince or sway because He already knows!

Carmen Howell

Prayer: *Ask the Lord to help you to be confident in the battles you face today. He will sovereignly protect and see you through every single one. Thank Him for the victory!*

Personal Reflection: ....

....

....

....

....

....

....

My Desperation, His Joy!

Psalm 141:1–10

> *"LORD, I cry out to You;*
> *Make haste to me!*
> *Give ear to my voice when I cry out to You.*
> *Let my prayer be set before you as incense,*
> *The lifting up of my hands as the evening sacrifice." (vv. 1–2)*

Every life has points of desperation and urgency. I think of the time I found a snake in the patio furniture on my back porch. Some of you are thinking, "At least it was outside!" However, a snake anywhere near the doors to my house must be slaughtered! I immediately called every man I knew until I found one who would come immediately and dispose of it. The precious man who rescued me from the snake actually liked snakes and picked it up with the intention of keeping it. Since he lived far from me, I allowed it! As I think about how many frantic phone calls I made that day in my fear, I am reminded of some very tough days where I have also frantically and passionately sought the Lord, begging for His intervention and provision.

David certainly knew fear and desperation in his life as he sought intervention from God because of his fears and his own sinful nature. He pled with the Lord to come quickly to him. I, too, have pleaded with the Lord to rescue me from difficult circumstances or relationships. Sometimes I plead with Him to come quickly and rescue me from my own sinful thoughts and motives.

David twice had the opportunity to kill Saul (1 Sam. 24; 26). He had the option of taking the life of the one who was seeking to kill him, but David entrusted himself to God and waited patiently on His timing. Many times, I have wanted to respond in my own way to a person or circumstance but begged the Lord to help me wait on Him and His timing.

In those moments of crying out for help and surrender, such a cry (prayer) is as incense to the Lord. Incense is defined as "the perfume or smoke arising from such a substance when burned." Sweet-smelling incense was burned many times in order to cover the smell of the animals being sacrificed for sins in the temple. Many times I have offered prayers of desperation when I felt I was being destroyed in the "fire" that was burning around me. How incredibly cool that as I cry out to the Lord in need of Him, a sweet aroma of incense rises to Him.

David proclaimed: "The sacrifices of God are a broken spirit, a broken and a contrite heart—These, O God, You will not despise" (Ps. 51:17). Our brokenness in "crying out" and our surrender and humility in "lifting up our hands" are the sacrifices God desires.

Carmen Howell

Prayer: *Be reminded today that God takes pleasure in your cry to Him. Your humility and desperation lead you to "the rock that is higher than I" (Ps. 61:2).*

Personal Reflection: ....

....

....

....

....

....

Complaints to Him Not of Him

Psalm 142:1–7

"I pour out my complaint before Him;
I declare before Him my trouble." (v. 2)

Loneliness and hardship tend to lead to complaints. David found himself alone in a cave fearing for his life. He demonstrates for us the only answer for fear and desperation. He cried out to the Lord (v. 1).

In the cave, David had two options. He could sulk and seek to escape on his own or he could "cry out" to His Creator, Protector, Provider, Father, and Friend. God desires for His children to communicate openly and honestly with Him. He is never disappointed when we voice our complaints and desperation to Him. David "poured out" his heart. *Pouring* is defined as "producing or uttering as a stream or flood; emitting or propelling, especially continuously or rapidly." David was not gently mentioning a few sorrows. His words were flowing freely, abundantly, and without inhibition.

David was not blaming God for his hardship, fear, and desperation. He was simply placing it "before Him." God must already have known David's heart. David was crying out to God so that he could see God's faithfulness and provision, and therefore know His heart! As David freely expressed his complaints and trouble to God, he acknowledged that he was unable to cope. He admitted his desperate need for help! This is what God wants for all of us—total honesty, total surrender, total dependence.

Several difficult seasons of life came to mind as I read this verse. When I experienced more pain and heartache than I ever knew possible and felt more isolated and alone than ever before, I ran to Him. I remember wanting to run far away, yet realized that would solve nothing and ultimately bring no relief. At that moment I began crying out to the Lord. I poured out my every complaint just as David did. I expressed every feeling and desire of my heart to the Lord. I

was not angry at Him but desperate for His intervention in my heart as well as in my circumstances. As I flooded His ears with my pain, He flooded my heart and my mind with His provision and peace. Although my circumstances and situations did not miraculously change in that moment, the Lord provided all that I needed to walk through them. My confession and honesty before Him enabled me to trust His purposes and His plan.

You may be in a very difficult situation or "cave" right now. I encourage you to take every detail to the Lord. Pour out your complaints, questions, fears, and desperations to Him. Recognize that He is not the cause of your pain, but He is aware of it. God is the only one capable of healing, restoring, and giving you the hope for the future. He is able!

Carmen Howell

Prayer: *Have the courage to be honest before God in all things. Pour out my hurts, disappointments, and sorrows to Him, realizing that He is all-sufficient to rescue you from the deepest darkness and loneliness and prosper you through His life and light!*

Personal Reflection: ....

....

....

....

....

401

Petition Leading to Surrender

Psalm 143:1–6

"I remember the days of old;
I meditate on all Your works;
I muse on the work of your hands.
I spread out my hands to You;
My soul longs for You like a thirsty land." (vv. 5–6)

David begins this psalm by pleading with God to hear him—not because David doubted that God knows all things but because our intimacy and fellowship with God grows when we honestly and openly share our hearts with Him. We do not need to tell God what He already knows, but we need to tell God because we are consumed with a need to talk to Him about everything. David recognized his place before the Lord, knowing that although he was sinful, this world did not play fair. Even when he was walking in righteousness, David needed God's intervention or the trials, temptations, and darkness would overwhelm him.

David gives three ways to allow God's Spirit to revive us and transform our darkness to light. First, remove your eyes from the present and "remember" all that God has done in your life and the lives of His saints throughout history. The Scriptures are replete with examples from Joseph, Esther, Ruth, and Paul of how God has brought light from darkness. Recall circumstances and relationships in your life that were very dark but in which God intervened to bring light and provision in ways that seemed impossible to you.

Muse is defined as to "think in silence." We must read and contemplate God's Word. Being quiet is not something easy to do well. In my life and surroundings, as I know in yours, quiet times are very rare. Many times I must get up very early or lay aside another activity, a discipline that is difficult but rewarding.

Second, David alludes here to meditating on God's truth as accompanying the quiet moment. If left to contemplate my plight without the truth of God's

Word I am not led to a better place but instead to a place of confusion, desperation, and fear. In quietly contemplating the present and future in light of God's promises and provision, my heart and mind are restored and encouraged, as yours will be as well.

Finally, David acknowledges his complete surrender and desperate desire for the Lord to fill him. When our hands are spread out in front of us as David depicts here, we are completely vulnerable and ready to receive the Lord's infinite supply of lovingkindness, peace, mercy, grace, wisdom, knowledge, and on and on the list goes. As you remember, meditate, and thirst for God alone, He will refresh you daily as He turns the darkness to light around you.

Carmen Howell

Prayer: *Run, do not walk to the Lord and His Word with your daily desperations, heartaches, and sorrows. Seek the Rock, Creator, Savior, and Redeemer who alone can make any darkness light!*

Personal Reflection: ....

....

....

....

....

....

Hearing by Reading

Psalm 143:7–12

"Cause me to hear Your lovingkindness in the morning,
For in You do I trust;
Cause me to know the way in which I should walk,
For I lift up my soul to You." (v. 8)

David continues his pattern of pleading with the Lord to intervene in his difficult circumstances. He not only sought to be relieved of outward circumstances and situations, but he also asked for the Lord to transform his heart and his thinking through the Spirit's work within him. David recognized that his heart was "deceitful . . . and desperately wicked" (Jer. 17:9). Only God could take care of that problem. He also recognized that he could have perfect circumstances and relationships as the world sees them and still be in the depths of despair. How? Why? We were created by God with a need for Him. Without Him in our lives, there will be a void that nothing else fills.

David prayed, "Cause me to hear your lovingkindness in the morning" (Ps. 143:8). Does the idea of hearing God's lovingkindness seem strange? *Lovingkindness* may be understood as "love showing kindness." When I am longing to see lovingkindness, I think of doing something for someone or someone doing something for me. Yet, David said, "Cause me to *hear*." Don't miss this point! How do we hear from God? He has spoken through His Word. We hear His lovingkindness as we read His Word. There He has already expressed all the lovingkindness He could show. As we read and meditate on His Word, we are reminded of His lovingkindness.

David further asked the Lord, "Cause me to know the way in which I should walk" (v. 8). When we recognize the amazing lovingkindness the Lord has shown to us, we become so grateful that we are ready to respond. We must continue in God's Word to know the way we must walk. Are you catching the pattern? God's

Word is the salve for our deepest sorrows, disappointments, fears, and failures. His Word is also our map for how to walk, speak, act, and live.

Through God's Word and by His Spirit, your soul will be lifted up. Your darkness will turn to light, and your despair will turn to hope. Your loneliness will be met with lovingkindness and joy.

As a mom, there have been days when I was in the depths of despair—needing to give counsel but not even knowing where to start. First, I needed the lovingkindness of the Lord to comfort me, reassuring that when I was totally *not* able, He *is* able. I needed wisdom, knowledge, and peace to know how to proceed. I sought the Lord and His Word, and He answered in every circumstance according to His Word and in His perfect time.

Carmen Howell

Prayer: *Go to God's Word in your despair and "hear" His lovingkindness so you will know the way to walk. Be grateful that when you know His lovingkindness and faithfulness, you will prosper in obedience.*

✒ **Personal Reflection:** ....

....

....

....

....

Our Warrior King

Psalm 144:1–8

"Blessed be the Lord my Rock,
Who trains my hands for war,
And my fingers for battle—
My lovingkindness and my fortress,
My high tower and my deliverer,
My shield and the One in whom I take refuge,
Who subdues my people under me." (vv. 1–2)

Psalm 144 was written by David, Israel's most successful and beloved king. In this passage, he recounts the victory God gave him over his enemies and thanks God for his success. But, this passage is not reserved only for the Israelites; we can also sing this victory song.

Many believers find themselves caught up in a battle with the enemy of our souls, Satan. Scripture compares him to a lion roaming around looking for someone to destroy, and he seems to have his eyes set on you (1 Pet. 5:8). You have been beaten down, belittled, and nearly defeated by the world around you. Some of you are facing the foe of financial defeat, and you need a Deliverer. Others are suffering under the constant strain of a deadly illness, and you need a Shield from the pain. And some are flailing under the weight of an addiction or sin, and you need a Rock to be your foundation.

God has not left you alone, defenseless, and vulnerable. He is present, and He is ready and willing to train you for battle. He will take your feet from the sinking mire of this world and set you upon a high tower. He will be your stronghold and fortress and then warn you when the enemy is coming. Left on your own, you are vulnerable and susceptible to all kinds of attacks. But, with God's strength you can overcome anything. If you let Him, God will be your

refuge, a safe haven from the enemy and his deadly schemes. But, it requires that you "do life" His way.

In a war, victory is only realized when each player does her part. We cannot expect to experience victory over sin and Satan if we are not willing to surrender our lives over to the One who made us. Jesus tells us: "The thief does not come except to steal, and to kill, and to destroy. I have come that they may have life, and that they may have it more abundantly" (John 10:10).

Dear friend, God is for you. He sent His Son Jesus, who died for you. And, He loves you. He wants you to experience victory and freedom on this side of heaven. My prayer is that you would allow God to be your warrior King. Stop fighting alone and begin fighting in the strength of His might.

Amanda Walker

Prayer: *Express thanks to God for being your warrior King. Run to Him for refuge when you are tired of fighting the enemy on your own. Surrender your dreams, goals, and life to Him so God can train your hands and heart for battle.*

Personal Reflection: ....

....

....

....

....

Praying for Strong Children

Psalm 144:9–15

"That our sons may be as plants grown up in their youth;
That our daughters may be as pillars,
Sculptured in palace style." (v. 12)

This verse seems out of place if you do a casual reading. David moves from praising God for granting him victory over his enemies to asking God to make his children strong and prosperous. As a mother, I can relate to David's prayer for his children. The Lord has blessed me with three beautiful children, and I want nothing more than for my daughters and son to be strong in the Lord. Though they are still young, I have spent many sleepless nights begging the Lord to make Himself real to each of them. With that in mind, let's look at David's prayer.

First, David prayed that his sons "may be as plants grown up in their youth." In a month, my son will be a year old. I jokingly tell him that I want him to remain a baby forever. But, in reality, I know he must grow up. If something is not growing, then it is not healthy. In the spiritual realm, the same is true for our children. Our sons are bombarded each day with ideas, pictures, and messages that seek to drag them away from God. As a college pastor's wife, I see the effects of sons who have been left to figure out life on their own. Their growth is stagnant, and they are in desperate need of help. As mothers, we can point them back to the One who gave them life.

Then, David prayed for his daughters. He asked that they would be "as pillars." The term suggests "corner pillars." A corner pillar is one that gives stability and strength to a structure. Our world needs more women to be pillars of strength in their communities, workplace, and especially in their homes. But, we must be careful when defining strength. The world equates womanly strength with sexual freedom, successful careers, gorgeous bodies, and

financial security. However, God describes a strong woman as one who cares for her family, uses her resources to help others, loves her children, respects her husband, and seeks integrity above popularity.

A strong mother will point her daughter to the Lord. She will model how it looks to love the Lord above all else and then live her life according to that conviction. You cannot expect your daughters to be pillars of strength if you are not striving to be a godly, strong woman yourself. After years spent in war, David was finally looking toward the future. You and I are in a war, but we must look toward the future. Pray that your children will be strong.

Amanda Walker

Prayer: *Ask the Lord to make you a woman who models godly strength. Pray that you would show your children how they can be mighty warriors for God by living according to His standard and not the world's standard.*

✎ **Personal Reflection:** ....

....

....

....

....

....

The God of Hope

Psalm 146:1–10

"Happy is he who has the God of Jacob for his help,
*Whose hope is in the L*ORD *his God,*
Who made heaven and earth,
The sea, and all that is in them;
Who keeps truth forever,
Who executes justice for the oppressed,
Who gives food to the hungry.
*The L*ORD *gives freedom to the prisoners." (vv. 5–7)*

Oppressed, hungry, and imprisoned—turn on the news to hear stories of people who face these realities. But there is another form of captivity and oppression that often goes unnoticed. Many people are caught in a prison that they have made for themselves. They have no hope because they placed their hope in man, who is but a breath, and not in God who gives man his breath (v. 4). You may not know truth because you have looked to people of power and influence to interpret or determine truth for you (v. 3). You do not feel helped because you have relied on others instead of God for your help. But, praise be to God, there is help, hope, and freedom!

Luke 4:17–21 records the coming of Jesus into His hometown's synagogue and proclaiming Himself as the One who gives freedom to the captives, sight to the physically and spiritually blind, and liberty to those who are oppressed. If you are a Christ-follower, God did not save you and then leave you alone. He desires to be actively involved in your life. Some of you are held captive by sin. I implore you to run toward God. You will never be happy until you repent— agree that the action is wrong and turn from that sin. Dear one, there is hope and freedom for you, but it is found only at the foot of the cross.

For those oppressed because of past choices, there is help for you. Satan loves to exploit our past mistakes and render us ineffective. However, Jesus promises complete forgiveness and restoration to those who turn from their sins (1 John 1:9). Do not give one more round of ammunition to the enemy. Accept God's forgiveness and walk in freedom.

Some people are oppressed because of another's actions against them. God sees every act of injustice against you, and He promises to respond. You may not see justice or restitution on this side of heaven, but one thing is certain: God will act on your behalf. He will not allow that individual to get away with hurting one of His daughters. You can praise Him because He sees you and will help you. May you trust Him again.

Amanda Walker

Prayer: *If you are held captive by sin, repent and ask God to forgive you and give you freedom. If you are oppressed, pray that God would execute justice on your behalf and then give you hope to praise Him again.*

Personal Reflection:

The God Who Strengthens

Psalm 147:1–20

"For He has strengthened the bars of your gates;
He has blessed your children within you." (v. 13)

Psalm 147 is the second of five "hallelujah" psalms. The psalmist is praising God for bringing the Israelites back from Babylonian captivity and restoring Jerusalem as a place of strength, peace, and prosperity. But, Jerusalem had not always been a place of safety.

Ancient Jerusalem was surrounded by a vast wall with entries and exits only through gates. The gates were made secure by bars that ran across them. When an army attacked, the gates could be shut and then held secure by their reinforced bars. The psalmist is quick to remind the Israelites that God gives strength and security rather than mere physical structures. In times past, Jerusalem had been overrun and the inhabitants hauled off into captivity. The gates had not held strong because there is no power in man-made things.

This lesson is applicable to us as well. Instead of running to God, often we run to tangible ways to keep us and our families safe. We lock our doors, get rid of the TV, use every form of safety measures for our computers, and monitor the friends of our children. However, the enemy is still attacking us. We see our daughters struggling with their identities, our sons struggling with sexual purity, and our marriages struggling to stay vibrant.

Why do believers forget to go to God? We have tried to strengthen our own gates instead of trusting God. Our children need their parents to put God first in their marriage, so they can see how much God loves them (Eph. 5:22–33). Our daughters need to see their mothers accept who they are in Christ instead of belittling their bodies, accomplishments, and positions in life. Instead of emotionally shutting down when difficulty arises, our husbands need us to fight for them and our marriage.

I realize these things can only be accomplished by the power of God's Holy Spirit working within us. That is the point! We can no longer live our lives in our own strength and expect everything to work out. We are weak; but, praise God, He is strong.

What is the result of relying on God to strengthen our gates? He blesses our children. Our children will not be perfect or escape difficulty. But, when difficulty comes, they know God will fight for them. When our children see us putting our trust and strength in God, then they, too, will have confidence in Him. What about you? I want my children to turn to God in times of need instead of turning to an individual.

Amanda Walker

Prayer: *Thank God for how He has protected you in the past. If you have relied on your own strength to fight the enemy, ask God to forgive you. Then turn to Him for help.*

Personal Reflection: ....

....

....

....

....

....

....

....

413

The Importance of Private Praise

Psalm 149:1–9

"Let the saints be joyful in glory;
Let them sing aloud on their beds." (v. 5)

Do you have a regular discipline of praising God? The question is not whether or not you regularly go to church or attend a Bible study. I am asking something deeper than that. I know many women who are involved in almost every aspect of their church's ministry. They teach Bible studies, lead their women's ministry, teach children on Sunday morning, and sing in the praise band or choir. But, they do not have the habit of daily worshiping the Lord, praising Him for who He is and what He has done on their behalf. Sometimes we are tempted to get so involved in doing things *for* God so that we miss time *with* God.

"The LORD takes pleasure in His people" (v. 4). The Lord delights in you and is pleased with you. I understand this best when I consider my three children. They do not have to do or give me anything in order for me to delight in them. They bring me joy just by being present in my life. However, some of my favorite moments come when my girls crawl up in my lap, hand me a book, and then ask me to read to them. I love the feeling of having them snuggled up next to me; and for a moment, time stands still. Ladies, your heavenly Father wants the same from you.

Oftentimes, we have an incorrect understanding of private worship (some call it a quiet time). Some think of a quiet time as a stiff, boring spiritual discipline that must be done in order for God to bless us and continue to be happy with us. If we miss a day, then we better watch out for God's judgment. I would be heartbroken if my daughters viewed me in this manner. We need to spend time with God, just like my girls need me to be present with them.

Yesterday, our inability to do life in our own strength was considered. Your quiet time is your opportunity to snuggle up on the couch with your heavenly

414

Father, converse about the events of the day, praise Him for how He has acted on your behalf, and then ask Him for the help you need to conquer the day ahead. Your time of private worship is not meant to be a check list but to be a daily relationship with your Creator.

So, again, I ask: Do you have a regular discipline of praising God? If not, then I encourage you to make your quiet time a priority. If yes, then share with someone what encouragement He has given you today.

Amanda Walker

Prayer: *If you do not have a hunger for God and His Word, ask Him to kindle within your spirit a desire for Him. Begin now by praising Him for who He is; then thank Him for what He has done for you.*

Personal Reflection: ....

....

....

....

....

....

....

Praise the Lord!

Psalm 150:1–6

"Praise the LORD! Praise God in His sanctuary;
Praise Him in His mighty firmament!
Praise Him for His mighty acts;
Praise Him according to His excellent greatness!
Praise Him with the sound of the trumpet;
Praise Him with the lute and harp!
Praise Him with the timbrel and dance;
Praise Him with stringed instruments and flutes!
Praise Him with loud cymbals;
Praise Him with clashing cymbals!
Let everything that has breath praise the LORD.
Praise the LORD!" (vv. 1–6)

This passage is one of the most exhilarating in Scripture. The reader has difficulty reading this passage with being moved by the awesomeness of God. He alone is worthy of our worship and praise. However, God does not leave His creation to wonder how He desires to be praised. In this short passage, God describes specifically how, where, and why we are to worship Him.

First, consider the place for worship. We are to worship God in His sanctuary. I am sure some of you just had images of a building adorned with gold fixtures, stained-glass windows, and uncomfortable pews. But, I want you to think deeper. First Corinthians 6:19–20 says that those who are Christ-followers are now God's sanctuary. Therefore, we are to worship God with our entire being. While beneficial and certainly encouraging to gather with fellow believers, we no longer must go to a specific location to worship God. Our lives should be a reflection of our worship.

Why are we to praise Him? Ladies, God has done so much for you! If you were to sit down and try to write out all the ways the Lord has blessed you, you would run out of ink. Think back over the past year, month, and week; then praise God for how He has sustained you, helped you, saved you, encouraged you, loved you, and given to you.

This passage also shows how God desires to be praised—with music and with dance. Translation: Our worship of God should be extravagant! The psalmist said to praise God not only with "loud cymbals" but also "clashing cymbals." God is not afraid of our worship. If we can raise our hands and shout at a sporting event for our children, certainly we can shout in praise of our God.

Finally, the psalmist declares who should praise God. "Let everything that has breath praise the LORD" (Ps. 150:6). You and I are included. God delights in the praises of His people. We do a disservice to God and ourselves when we are stingy with our praise and adoration of Him. Do you want to get out of a spiritual rut? Start praising the One who is worthy of all praise!

Amanda Walker

Prayer: *If it has been awhile since you have worshiped the Lord for who He is and what He has done for you, take time to do that now. God, alone, is worthy of all worship and praise!*

Personal Reflection: ....

....

....

....

What Do You Want Most?

Proverbs 1:1–6

*"A wise man will hear and increase learning,
And a man of understanding will attain wise counsel." (v. 5)*

What do you want most out of life? Be honest with yourself. Maybe, at the core of your being you want to be beautiful, successful (whatever that means), or healthy. Perhaps you want most to achieve financial security so you can retire and then really enjoy life. Maybe your heart's desire is to have the acceptance, approval, or applause of others, or of a particular someone; or to live long enough to see your children rise up and call you blessed. Such dreams for living a happy and fulfilled life reflect value systems—sets of priorities that drive your day-to-day decision-making. Is wisdom among your values?

Today, as your devotional journey turns to the book of Proverbs, you encounter in the first seven verses a not-so-obvious invitation to assess your fitness for embarking on a pursuit of wisdom. Let's see if you fit the author's description of those who are ready to pursue the treasures of wisdom gathered in this book.

First, you must already be a wise person (v. 5). In other words, you must have a teachable spirit, knowing that you have a lot to learn *and* are willing to let God's Word conform your thoughts to His thoughts, your perspective to His perspective, and your priorities to His priorities. Second, you must be willing and ready to apply the book's principles for godly living (vv. 2–4, 6). The writer of Proverbs 1:1–6 assumes that you, the reader, want to identify with "the wise man" and "the man of understanding." He also assumes that you want to be able to do the five things noted in verses 2–4 and 6. Reread those verses as questions, considering your answer to each:

- Do you want "to know wisdom and instruction"?
- Do you want "to perceive the words of understanding"?

- Do you want "to receive the instruction of wisdom, justice, judgment, and equity"?
- Do you want "to give prudence to the simple" and "knowledge and discretion" to young people?
- Do you want "to understand" proverbs, enigmas, "the words of the wise and their riddles"?

The writer believes that if your answer to these questions is "yes," then wisdom must be one of your core values—i.e., you prioritize becoming the sort of person who knows how to navigate life successfully and how to teach others this wisdom.

Are you ready for your journey through Proverbs? If wisdom is, indeed, what you want, then accept this book's invitation to listen and learn.

Tamra Hernandez

Prayer: *Claim this promise: "If any of you lacks wisdom, let him ask of God, who gives to all liberally and without reproach, and it will be given to him" (James 1:5).*

Personal Reflection: ....

....

....

....

....

The Master Teacher

Proverbs 1:1–7

"The fear of the LORD is the beginning of knowledge,
But fools despise wisdom and instruction." (v. 7)

Your Bible study group has decided to do an everything-from-scratch Mexican food potluck, and you signed up to bring homemade flour tortillas. Envisioning a perfect pile of warm, mouth-watering, freshly-made tortillas at the beginning of the serving line, you select your recipe, watch an online demonstration video, and quickly conclude, "This will be easy-as-pie!"

Having followed the recipe to the letter, you begin joyfully kneading the dough. Before long, however, your dough is sticky and unmanageable. Adding flour allows you to form the dough into balls, but rolling those into round tortillas does not work so well. The idea of laughing with your friends about these misshapen but otherwise delicious tortillas soon crumbles as you scrape the first one off the griddle.

Making authentic Mexican-style tortillas, like many skills in life, is an art best learned personally—"hands-on"—from someone who has already mastered it and has the patience to coach until you, too, have mastered it. However, to learn any new skill—whether making tortillas, riding a motorcycle, knitting, or playing the flute—also requires you to be teachable. You must respect the master, willingly follow directions, humbly accept correction, and persevere in practice under the master's watchful eye.

Proverbs 1:7 identifies the Master Teacher as "the LORD." He is the God who "made the earth and the heavens" (Gen. 2:4; John 1:3), "made . . . a woman" from Adam's rib (Gen. 2:22), "made a covenant with Abram" (Gen. 15:18), destroyed Sodom and Gomorrah (Gen. 19:24), "was with Joseph" in Egypt (Gen. 39), and "brought . . . [His people] out of . . . bondage" (Ex. 20:2). "The LORD" is the God whose glory filled the temple Solomon built for His

name in Jerusalem (1 Kin. 8:10–11), "the Holy One of Israel" (Is. 17:7; 47:4), the divine Messiah for whom John the Baptist was the herald (John 1:23), and the Spirit by whom Christ's followers are being transformed into His image (2 Cor. 3:16–18; cp. Rom. 8:29)—God the Father, Son, and Holy Spirit (Matt. 28:19).

Knowledge begins with the right relationship with the Lord, and the learner's side of that relationship must be characterized by reverence and obedience rather than defiance and sin. When you "fear" a beloved teacher, mentor, or coach, you are afraid not that they will hurt or abandon you but that your failure to follow their instructions will disappoint them. You submit to their training and correction, convinced that they are committed to your success. Only a fool would do otherwise.

Tamra Hernandez

Prayer: *Invite the Holy Spirit to examine your life to discover whether or not you truly "fear the LORD." Make a new commitment to submit to His training and receive His wisdom.*

Personal Reflection: ....

....

....

....

....

The Father's Instruction

Proverbs 1:8–19

"My son, hear the instruction of your father,
And do not forsake the law of your mother." (v. 8)

According to Proverbs 1:1–7, a "wise" woman is smart enough to be teachable (v. 5), wants "to know wisdom and instruction" (v. 2), wants to "receive the instruction of wisdom" (v. 3), and embraces "the fear of the LORD" as the starting point for a pursuit of wisdom (v. 7). The willingness to walk in obedience to the Lord, thereby growing in wisdom, is clearly set in contrast to the contemptuous attitude of "fools" toward godly living and the discipline required to attain it (v. 7). Notice that in these verses the word "instruction" (Hb. *musar*) is used three times, each in association with "wisdom." *Musar* usually denotes "correction, discipline, or admonition." By closely connecting wisdom and *musar*, the book of Proverbs indicates from the outset that people are not born with wisdom but that they can choose to be trained and disciplined in the application of wisdom.

Who offers such training? Verse 7 asserts the necessity of having the right relationship with the Lord. Choosing to live under God's authority is like taking the necessary first step of enrolling in the "school" of the Master. The Lord Himself will personally train those who surrender their sins to His cleansing and yield their wills to His Spirit.

Verse 8 dives into a series of teachings directly addressing those who commit to being the Lord's disciples (students). The first word of this verse in Hebrew is the imperative "hear" (*shema'*). In Scripture, this verb denotes active listening. The audience is beckoned to do something or to put into practice the message heard. In the book of Psalms, David uses the word in prayer, pleading with the Lord to listen to him: "Hear, O LORD, when I cry with my voice! (Ps. 27:7); "Hear my prayer, O LORD . . ." (Ps. 143:1).

In Proverbs 1:8, the Lord commands the attention and obedience of each of His children with the tender address of a father to his son: "My son, hear the instruction [Hb. *musar*] of your father." Compared with verses 10–19, this is a positive, comprehensive command and an appeal to the child or disciple to obey on the basis of relationship with the father—in ideal terms. Revealing Himself in Scripture as God the Father, He knows better than anyone what your particular experience has been with your father—however wonderful or dysfunctional the relationship, however present or absent he was or is in your life. Proverbs 1:8 projects an ideal relationship between parents and their children, especially those entering young adulthood, in order to illuminate the way God directs the choices of His sons and daughters in Christ. His correction, discipline, and training should continually be given full attention and obedience.

Tamra Hernandez

Prayer: *Are you resisting the Lord's correction or discipline in any area of your life? Hear and obey anew His instruction.*

Personal Reflection: ....

....

....

....

....

423

Voices

Proverbs 1:10–27

*"Turn at my rebuke;
Surely I will pour out my spirit on you;
I will make my words known to you." (v. 23)*

Grammatically speaking, *wisdom* is an abstract noun. To draw a picture of wisdom, for example, would be a tough assignment because it is an idea or concept rather than a "person, place, or thing" that can be experienced in sensory terms (sight, smell, sound, taste, touch). Many proverbs, therefore, illustrate wisdom with examples of people acting wisely and often, for contrast, unwisely.

The message of today's passage (including Prov. 1:28–33 in tomorrow's devotional) is not presented as a concise, memorable proverb. Instead, readers are expected to listen actively both to the teacher's instruction (vv. 10–19) and to the speech given by a personification of wisdom (vv. 20–33). Readers are also expected to apply what they learn from carefully probing connections between these two pieces of the overall message. Let's explore just one connection—discerning whose voice you can trust.

Verses 10–11 present a hypothetical situation requiring wise decision-making: "*If* sinners entice you . . . *If* they say . . ." (vv. 10–14). The first "if" is followed by a comprehensive rule; the second offers an example. This teaching strategy is effective both for parenting and for personal application. For example, as a mother I role-played with my son various scenarios he would likely encounter at school. This activity not only minimized the risk of his being caught unaware and unprepared to resist temptation, but it also provided opportunity for parental guidance that he would remember whenever faced with such situations. As a follower of Christ, I have also determined ahead of time how to respond to various *potential* enticements. In contrast to the hypothetical situation posed

and discussed in verses 10–19, the teacher presents wisdom as real, personal, and vocal (vv. 20–33).

Wisdom "speaks her words," which express the singular voice of God Himself (v. 20). The passage contrasts this one authoritative "voice" with the plural voices of "sinners" urging, "Come with us . . . Let us . . . Let us . . . Let us . . . Cast in your lot among us" (vv. 11–14). Be warned, however, "their feet run to evil." These voices "entice"—they persuade through deception and false promises. Be warned, however, they "lie in wait" and "lurk secretly" to their own harm and shame (vv. 11, 18). Wisdom, in contrast, is out in the open, shouting—not secretly but where everyone can hear, not appealing deceptively to selfish desires but boldly proclaiming the consequences of sin. Furthermore, Wisdom issues one command that reverberates throughout Scripture—"Turn at my rebuke"—and personally guarantees the rewards of obedience.

Tamra Hernandez

Prayer: *Ask the Lord to help you recognize whatever "voices" may be competing with His "voice" of truth (John 18:37). Turn away from the enemy's lies and to God's true Word.*

Personal Reflection: ....

....

....

....

....

Being Willing and Taking Action

Proverbs 1:10–33

*"Because they hated knowledge
And did not choose the fear of the LORD,
They would have none of my counsel
And despised my every rebuke.
Therefore they shall eat the fruit of their own way,
And be filled to the full with their own fancies." (vv. 29–31)*

Adopting the persona of a parent or teacher instructing a young man, the speaker counsels readers on how best to respond to invitations to participate in wrongdoing:

- "Do not consent" (Hb. *'avah*, which conveys a person's inclination or will, v. 10). Stated another way, this advice responds to peer pressure: Be *unwilling* to bend. Determine that you *will not* go along with or agree to be part of sinful plans and activities.
- "Do not walk in the way with them." Better yet, "Keep your foot from their path" (v. 15). If, perhaps, you have entertained the temptation too long (vv. 11–14), take action. Physically separate yourself from the voices of sinners.

The rationale behind this counsel—both to *will* and to *act* decisively when being encouraged to sin—centers on recognizing the enemy's deceptive tactics and realizing that listening to him leads to death.

In verses 20–33, the speaker dramatizes the message through the speech of Wisdom personified. When Wisdom "speaks her words," they convey Yahweh's outcry against "fools [who] hate knowledge" (v. 22). Directly addressing them in the first half of the speech, the Lord reiterates the key command to be heeded

in order to know Him: "Turn at my rebuke" (v. 23), just as Jesus commanded, "Repent" (Mark 1:14–15).

Although Wisdom's speech is delivered publicly, loudly, and prominently, no one is listening—except, hopefully, the reader. The fools have not merely muted the voice of wisdom, however, but they have also reveled in scorn, personally refused to answer the Lord's call, and deliberately ignored the Lord's outstretched hand of help and rescue. In the end, they will get their way—having "freedom" to do whatever they want without interference—only to discover, too late, the terrible consequences: "calamity," "terror," "destruction," "distress and anguish" (Prov. 1:26–27).

Tragically, the fools "would [Hb. *'avah*] have none of . . . [wisdom's] rebuke" (v. 25)—their will was bent on tuning out the truth. Furthermore, they "despised . . . every rebuke" (v. 30) and "did not choose the fear of the LORD" (v. 29). They actively rejected and disdained correction, continually opting to "do their own thing." In the end, they are left with "the fruit of their own way" (v. 31), rotten to the core. But you, reader, can choose (*be willing*) to fear the Lord; you can listen to Him (*act* according to His wisdom); and thereby you can enjoy living "without fear of evil" (v. 33).

Tamra Hernandez

Prayer: *Praise the Lord for making His words known, and submit to His work in you "both to will and to do for His good pleasure" (Phil. 2:13).*

Personal Reflection: ....

....

....

Whoever Listens

Proverbs 1:23–33

"But whoever listens to me will dwell safely,
And will be secure, without fear of evil." (v. 33)

To a Jewish audience familiar with the Torah, verse 33 likely resonates with the Lord's promise to His people after redeeming them from Egypt: "If you walk in My statutes and keep My commandments, and perform them, then I will give you rain in its season . . . you shall eat your bread to the full, and dwell in your land safely" (Lev. 26:3–5). An audience familiar with the Psalms may remember that David's "trust in the LORD" enabled him "both [to] lie down in peace, and sleep," knowing that God alone could make him "dwell in safety" (Ps. 4:5, 8). A Jewish audience familiar with biblical history probably recalls that the reign of Solomon was marked by "peace on every side all around him. And Judah and Israel dwelt safely, each man under his vine and his fig tree" (1 Kin. 4:24–25).

From the beginning of the covenant relationship between Yahweh and the Israelites, whom He rescued from bondage in Egypt, listening to God's wisdom (living obediently under His rule) and "dwelling safely" went hand in hand. An audience that is neither Jewish nor very familiar with the Old Testament might ask at least two critical questions about the verse. First, who qualifies to be described as a person who "listens" to God's wisdom? Second, does God still promise safety and security to such people?

First, listening in Scripture almost invariably denotes obedience. Proverbs 1–2 clearly emphasizes the differences between those who listen to the Lord and those who do not. Proverbs 1:33 concisely characterizes both the appropriate response to God's Word (obedience) and the appropriate source of counsel (God's teaching and correction, personified here as Wisdom). Second, God's promise stands, but He does not guarantee immunity from all physical danger, harm, or fear. However, those who turn from sin to receive salvation in Jesus

Christ (cp. v. 23 and Luke 9:35; Rom. 10:17) are indeed promised eternal security in Him (Eph. 1:13–14).

The writer of Proverbs personified God's truth as Wisdom to help readers understand aspects of the message delivered. Jesus Himself embodies God's truth and has spoken directly (Heb. 1:1–3). His conclusion to the Sermon on the Mount clearly contrasts those who listen to the Lord with those who do not and clearly manifests His divine authority: "Therefore whoever hears these sayings of Mine, and does them, I will liken him to a wise man who built his house on the rock . . . it did not fall . . . But everyone who hears these sayings of Mine, and does not do them, will be like a foolish man who built his house on the sand . . . it fell. And great was its fall" (Matt. 7:24–27).

Tamra Hernandez

Prayer: *Thank the Lord that in Christ your life is eternally safe and secure.*

Personal Reflection: ....

....

....

....

....

Getting to "Point A"

Proverbs 2:1–5

"Then you will understand the fear of the LORD,
And find the knowledge of God." (v. 5)

When you embark on a journey of reading the book of Proverbs from beginning to end, you will profit from frequently consulting 1:7—"The fear of the LORD is the beginning of knowledge, but fools despise wisdom and instruction." Overall, Proverbs is designed to challenge you both to recognize the difference between two approaches to earthly life—the way of wisdom and the way of folly—and to choose the way that leads to eternal life. "Fear of the LORD" is the necessary starting point for pursuing such discernment, and we need help just to get to "Point A." Proverbs 2:1–5 elaborates on how to do that.

In the persona of a father addressing his son, the Lord explains to His child seven necessary conditions for discerning the one starting point for life that does not end in death. As you read, hear the Holy Spirit speaking directly to you.

- **Receive my words** (v. 1). To "receive" involves "taking" as your own or "laying hold of" what is given. You can hear the words of Scripture and even obey its laws and teachings without actually affirming God's rightful reign over your life. Jesus linked rejecting Him as the Son of God with choosing not to receive His words (see John 12:48).
- **Treasure . . .** (Prov. 2:1). Having received God's words, you treat them like treasure, "hiding" them where they cannot be stolen. Psalm 119:11 translates the same verb "have hidden."
- **Incline your ear . . .** (Prov. 2:2). In Proverbs 1:24 the same verb is translated "regarded." In contrast to the "fools" who "hate knowledge" and deliberately turn away from God's outstretched hand, a wise

woman intentionally turns in the direction of God's wisdom and pay close attention to His Word.

- Apply your heart . . . (Prov. 2:2). *Apply* also means "turn" or "incline" (see Ps. 119:36). However, not only are you eagerly listening to what God says but you are also turning your will over to Him.
- Cry out . . . lift up your voice (Prov. 2:3). These verbs take the positive reception and eager application of wisdom to another level. Consider what has prompted you to plead with God or call out to Him in the past. Have you ever begged desperately for "discernment" or "understanding"?
- Seek (v. 4). The verb suggests that you want wisdom badly enough to "look for" it actively and expectantly.
- Search (v. 4). The action of seeking is intensified again to a picture of methodical, thorough, and passionate pursuit of wisdom as the "must-have" of all time.

Is your passion to know and obey God's Word steadily increasing? How determined are you to "understand the fear of the LORD"?

Tamra Hernandez

Prayer: *Ask the Lord to intensify your desire to know Him through His Word.*

Personal Reflection: ....

....

....

....

The One Source of Wisdom

Proverbs 2:6–9

"For the LORD gives wisdom;
From His mouth come knowledge and understanding." (v. 6)

When you receive the Lord's words as your very own, turning in repentance at His rebuke and responding in faith to His invitation to follow Him, you are on your way toward understanding "the fear of the LORD" (Prov. 1:23; 2:5; Luke 9:23). Your "fear" of the Lord is similar to the respect that trumpet player Charly Raymond had for his teacher Carmine Caruso (1904–1987), a saxophone player who became one of the greatest brass teachers. Raymond explains that although he had a degree in performance and a career playing the trumpet in Boston, he reached a point at which he knew he would be unable to continue playing unless the famed "master teacher" could help him. So, he drove to New York City and became a student of Carmine Caruso.

Raymond had heard about this teacher, but that was not enough to correct the trumpet-playing technique that was causing the mouthpiece to cut his lips. No improvement would have come simply from taking lessons if he had refused to abandon his destructive habits. He had to submit to the retraining Caruso prescribed. Likewise, to fear the Lord is to establish the right relationship with Him, in which you trust *Him* to make you the woman He created you to be.

Understanding your fear of the Lord is more like Raymond's ability to reflect on the "discipleship process" of studying under Caruso. Caruso taught Raymond a completely different approach to playing the trumpet. Because he has continued to apply Caruso's instruction, Raymond enjoys a successful career as both musician and trumpet teacher. Proverbs 2:1–5 describes the ever-increasing desire to do life God's way, which culminates in understanding the necessity of continual, lifelong obedience to Christ as your Master Teacher. That understanding enables you both to praise His work and to disciple others.

Verses 6–9 explain why "the fear of the LORD" is the necessary starting point for pursuing a life of wisdom: He is the only source. That does not mean it is in short supply or that He is stingy; you simply cannot get wisdom anywhere else or from anyone else. Ask the Lord for wisdom. He has promised to give generously (James 1:5).

However, Proverbs 2:7–8 identify a specific group of people as beneficiaries of the Lord's storehouse of wisdom. They are "the upright" or righteous ones, "those who walk uprightly," God's "saints." In other words, access to the Lord's wisdom first requires that you have the right relationship with Him (that you "fear" the Lord). Christ's disciples "walk uprightly" only because they have abandoned their own efforts to be righteous and have submitted to His instruction. Are you among them?

Tamra Hernandez

Prayer: *Deliberately stop relying on yourself to fix the problems in your life and ask the Lord to teach you His way.*

Personal Reflection: ....

....

....

....

....

Are You an *Aficionado*?

Proverbs 2:10–12

"When wisdom enters your heart . . ." (v. 10a)

I am decidedly not an *aficionado*, at least not in the way the word was originally used in Spanish. Jean Andrews of the University of Nottingham explains that in Spain, *aficionado* identified those who have "a deep and profound, almost spiritual, love for what is the *art* of bullfighting, not just the sport" and are recognized as such by the "invisible brotherhood of those who have it [bullfighting] in their soul." She further clarifies that being an *aficionado* was "not the same thing as being a fan" or "spectator." As Andrews explains, "You can stand up and shout '*Olé!*' in the stands as much as you like. But if you are an *aficionado*, you have a profound understanding of what it [bullfighting] is, and it can't be taught. It's something you have or you don't have."* I don't have it.

However, Andrews's keen explanation provides insight for understanding verse 10, which opens the section describing protections gained by the fan or seeker of wisdom who becomes an *aficionado*. "Wisdom" refers to the combined knowing and doing of life God's way as a citizen of His kingdom. Under the new covenant in Christ, He writes the law on your heart (Jer. 31:33; Heb. 10:16) and gives you the right to become His child (John 1:12). "And because you are sons, God has sent forth the Spirit of His Son into your hearts" (Gal. 4:6). As Proverbs 2:6–7 points out, "The LORD gives wisdom," but Proverbs 2:1–5 make clear that although He urges the pursuit, He does not force you to take it: "*if* you receive"; "*if* you cry out"; "*If* you seek"; "*Then* you will understand." As wisdom personified says in Proverbs 8:17, "Those who seek me diligently will find me."

Pursuit of wisdom with the intensity described in Proverbs 2:1–5 meets the Lord's faithful and generous response of verses 6–9. Verse 10 sums up the encounter—between the one who hungers and thirsts for righteousness and the One who fills—as the entrance of wisdom into the heart. Wisdom (the personal knowledge of God for which the empty, sin-consumed soul has long starved) gladly accepts the invitation to come in and take charge, and living God's way proves to be "pleasant" and secure.

If you follow Christ, would everyone you know say you are a true *aficionado*—not just a fan of Jesus or a spectator who stands and sings praises with your friends every week? Are you known for having a deep and profound, authentically spiritual love for Jesus that reflects the artistry of His Holy Spirit in your heart? You either have Him or you don't.

Tamra Hernandez

Prayer: *Invite the Holy Spirit to purify your priorities and deepen your commitment to Christ from the inside out.*

Personal Reflection: ....

....

....

....

....

....

*Jean Andrews, "Aficionado," *Words of the World* website, University of Nottingham; film by Brady Haran; http://www.wordsoftheworld.co.uk/videos/aficionado.html.

Safety, Protection, and Deliverance

Proverbs 2:10–22

"So you may walk in the way of goodness,
And keep to the paths of righteousness." (v. 20)

The nation's capital has the highest murder rate in the world. Crime and looting are rampant as the country staggers under economic collapse. Consumer prices recently rose to 800 percent, and that figure is expected to double. People stand in line for hours to buy limited amounts of staple foods and other basic goods at government-regulated prices. The government has kicked out CNN, met unarmed protestors with brute force, and asked the United Nations for help in the face of a severe shortage of basic medical supplies. Insecurity reigns for many Venezuelans as those who govern exemplify decision-making void of wisdom. I suspect that if you asked women in Venezuela to describe what sort of safety, protection, and deliverance they need, they would talk about freedom of speech without fear of being kidnapped, justice for the sons and husbands arrested or killed for protesting, and rescue from the fear of losing the battles for survival.

Proverbs 2:10–22 seems, at first, not to address such circumstances. However, three Hebrew verbs indicate otherwise:

- "Discretion will preserve" (Hb. *shamar*, v. 11) those whose hearts are governed by wisdom. The same verb appears in God's promise to Jacob at Bethel: "I am with you and will *keep* you wherever you go" (Gen. 28:15)—the Lord would keep him safe from harm, watch out for him, and guard his life.
- "Understanding will keep" (Hb. *natsar*, Prov. 2:11)—guard, protect, defend, preserve from danger—those whose hearts are governed by wisdom.

- Basically, "when wisdom enters your heart" (v. 10), the central command center of your life is entrusted to the One who has the power to guarantee its security. Consequently, the Lord is in position to "deliver [Hb. *natsal*] you from the way of evil" (v. 12).

True enough, the promise of safety, protection, and deliverance to those whose hearts are willingly submitted to Christ does not mean freedom from political oppression, reckless governments, or sky-rocketing inflation. Actually, the Lord promises to protect you from something more insidious—"the way of evil."

The people of Venezuela suffer under the decision-making of people "whose ways are crooked" (v. 15), but many of the people themselves "walk in the ways of darkness" (v. 13), too, because Christ does not yet reign in their hearts. Proverbs 2 promises a different kind of security—the ability to see ourselves, the world, its people, and problems from God's perspective. When Christ enters and governs your heart, His Spirit enables you not only to discern and flee from the real dangers of temptation but also to "walk in the way of goodness, and keep [*shamar*] to the paths of righteousness."

Tamra Hernandez

Prayer: *Entrust to the Lord's wisdom the tangible difficulties you are facing today. Ask Him to help you see them from His perspective, recognize the spiritual dangers, and do what is good and right in His eyes.*

Personal Reflection: ....

....

....

The Law and Life

Proverbs 3:1–2

"My son, do not forget my law,
But let your heart keep my commands." (v. 1)

The proverbs in the Bible can be considered ancient "tweets." A proverb is a short, profound saying while a "tweet" is a statement of up to 140 characters posted on social media. Both can communicate a thought in a few well-chosen words, but a proverb states a truth; a tweet expresses an opinion. The proverbs in the Bible are words of wisdom inspired by the Lord God Himself. Each proverb offers godly guidance for everyday life.

An interesting literary tool is used to communicate with the reader in the first twelve verses of Proverbs 3. Odd-numbered verses express explicit mandates, while even-numbered verses note the rewards for obedience. These biblical mandates could be reflected in contemporary parallels. A simple list of dos and don'ts gives godly wisdom and practical advice.

- *Do not* forget God's law; *do* keep His commands (v. 1).
- *Do not* forsake the truth; *do* write truth on your heart (v. 3).
- *Do not* depend on your own understanding; *do* let God direct your paths (v. 5).
- *Do not* seek your own wisdom; do fear the Lord (v. 7).
- *Do not* keep the firstfruits of your labors; *do* honor the Lord with your possessions (v. 9).
- *Do not* despise the chastening of the Lord; *do* love His correction (v. 11).

These verses also illustrate a pattern for presenting God's promises in the Bible. All His promises are true and reliable; some of them are conditional. Conditional promises in the Bible and in life today are reciprocal. Action is

required on the part of both parties. God promises to fulfill a commitment if His children obey His commands. Second Chronicles 7:14 is a conditional "if-then" promise from God to His people: "*If* My people who are called by My name will humble themselves, and pray and seek My face, and turn from their wicked ways, *then* I will hear from heaven, and will forgive their sin and heal their land." God will hear and answer the prayers of His children who seek Him and turn from their sin.

Proverbs 3:1–2 is also a conditional promise: *If* you follow God's law and keep His commands in your heart, *then* your days will be long and your life will be peaceful. That is a precious promise and a powerful proverb! I would like to live a long and peaceful life; so I must keep His Word around me and within me. I must hide His Word in my heart so that I will not sin (Ps. 119:11). This Scripture is an "if-then" promise that I must obey. It is a wise proverb that I must follow. What about you?

Rhonda Kelley

Prayer: *Recommit to keeping God's commands and hiding His Word in your heart. Set some goals for reading five psalms and one proverb each day, then do it.*

Personal Reflection: ....

....

....

....

....

Hide His Word in Your Heart

Proverbs 3:3–4

"Let not mercy and truth forsake you;
Bind them around your neck,
Write them on the tablet of your heart,
And so find favor and high esteem
In the sight of God and man." (vv. 3–4)

Proverbs 3 focuses on the importance of God's commands in the lives of His children. From the Old Testament era until now, the Jewish people have held a high view of Scripture. They often place Scripture on the doorposts of their homes as a reminder to take the Word of God with them wherever they go.

A *mezuzah* is a small container, fashioned today by Jewish jewelers and artisans, that hold verses from the Old Testament. Orthodox Jews continue to wear phylacteries (leather pouches) around their bodies to carry God's Word with them wherever they go. These physical containers have spiritual meaning—an outward display of Scripture should be paired with an inward commitment to truth. God desires for His children to hide His Word in their hearts (v. 3).

I am grateful for the Scripture I memorized as a child. My mother faithfully taught me the Bible and trained me to learn it verse-by-verse. While I may have complained as a child about the difficulty of memorization and the time commitment involved, I now rejoice as I recall those Scriptures hidden in my heart. Now, I try to surround myself in our home and my office with Bible verses on pictures and posters. I wear jewelry with Christian symbols and give gifts with Scripture verses as visible reminders that God's Word must be near to us before it can dwell in us.

Proverbs 3:3 specifically commands God's children to write His words on their hearts. How do you hide His Word in your heart? Have you written His wise teachings indelibly on your heart? Those who follow the Lord must know

His Word and keep it close. Make specific commitments today to prioritize the Bible in your life.

Verse 4 records the promised reward to those who treasure God's Word. Wisdom and guidance are immediate blessings for faithful living. Favor and high esteem in the sight of God and man are other benefits. Financial rewards are not promised for faithfulness. Instead, the results of obedience and righteousness are joy and peace as well as the confidence that God is pleased with you. Unrighteous living inevitably brings personal and spiritual consequences.

This passage moves the focus from formal wisdom to daily devotion. The believer who is committed to God and studies His Word will receive earthly blessings and eternal rewards. So, hide His Word in your heart and live out His Word in your life. Honor and blessing are the rewards for faithfulness and obedience.

Rhonda Kelley

Prayer: *Make a commitment to daily devotion—to study the Bible and hide God's Word in your heart. Let His Word change you from the inside out; then know that He is pleased.*

Personal Reflection: ....

....

....

....

....

Trust with All Your Heart

Proverbs 3:5–10

"Trust in the LORD with all your heart,
And lean not on your own understanding;
In all your ways acknowledge Him,
And He shall direct your paths." (vv. 5–6)

I was about eight years old when Grandmother Harrington shared with me her favorite Scripture verse. She had memorized Proverbs 3:5–6 as a child and loved it all her life. Immediately, that passage penetrated my heart and continues to influence my life today. Each word resonates clearly in my mind and heart daily. I often use the passage to share my personal testimony.

Trust in the Lord. Trust in people is fleeting because they will disappoint you. Trust in things is elusive because they will fade. However, trust in the Lord is reliable and lasting. To "trust" is to be confident in someone or something. As a child I trusted my dad, then he disappointed me because he left the Lord, my mother, and our family. Had my faith been only in my earthly father, I would have faltered. But, my faith was in my heavenly Father who sustained me through the crisis. In time, my dad repented and was restored to the Lord and our family. You must trust in God personally, and He will never disappoint you!

With all your heart. It is easy to give God some of your life and some of your time, but God requires everything! Believers must love and serve the Lord with all their hearts. "All" is the necessary descriptor. He wants and deserves your whole heart!

Lean not on your own understanding. My mother says that "I came out of the womb in charge of the world." I have never lacked confidence. After twenty-five years of education, I earned a Ph.D. The more I learn, the more I realize I do not know. My knowledge is finite and limited while God's knowledge is infinite

and unlimited. Do not limit yourself to your human understanding. Look to God for divine wisdom.

In all your ways acknowledge Him. There is that word *all* again—with *all* your heart and in all your ways. Believers are to acknowledge God or recognize His position and power over everything. Words, actions, and feelings are to be directed toward God in gratitude and praise. When we focus on God—who He is and how He works, we take our eyes off ourselves and others. He alone deserves our undivided attention, unwavering devotion, and unending praise.

And He will direct your paths. What a great promise! When we trust Him with all our hearts, seek Him with all our minds, and acknowledge Him with all our lives, He *will* guide us in His perfect ways. God has a perfect plan for your life that you can experience only when you give Him your all. You *will* know His will in His time and His way. So, trust Him with all your heart and all your life.

Rhonda Kelley

Prayer: *Do you have a life verse? If not, this Scripture would be a perfect guide for your life. Renew your trust in the Lord and give Him your all. Believe that He will direct your paths.*

Personal Reflection: ....

....

....

....

....

Discipline and Delight

Proverbs 3:11–18

"My son, do not despise the chastening of the LORD,
Nor detest His correction;
For whom the LORD loves He corrects,
Just as a father the son in whom he delights." (vv. 11–12)

Did your mother ever speak these words to you, or have you spoken them to your own child? "I am only punishing you because I love you." Your thoughts may have echoed mine when I heard them as a child: "I just wish you didn't love me so much!" Discipline is no fun whether you are giving it or receiving it. But, discipline is necessary for teaching, and it is actually an expression of love.

Proverbs 3 addresses the tough topic of discipline and instructs God's children in righteousness. "Chastening" (Hb. "*musar*") means training, discipline, or instruction. Verbal correction or physical consequences can help a child understand the guidelines and redirect behavior. Immediate discipline of smaller infractions can often prevent greater disobedience and more severe judgment. If the authority (parent or teacher) does not administer discipline, she becomes a part of the wrongdoing.

My mother was a fair disciplinarian. She never punished in anger and always levied consequences equal to my crime. However, I still did not like discipline. Often, I began crying before I was caught. I confessed my disobedience before receiving judgment. Ultimately, I understood her love for me hat necessitated her correction of me. While I did not like the discipline, I learned to love the disciplinarian.

God our heavenly Father loves us and must often correct us (Deut. 8:5; Heb. 12:3–12; Rev. 3:19). He is a loving God who gently redirects, not an angry God who vindictively punishes His children. Disobedience often requires discipline so obedience will develop into a faithful lifestyle.

444

When I was a teenager, I fell head-over-heels for an older boy at church. My parents did not approve because of the age difference, though he was a Christian. They told me not to see him or talk to him. I disagreed with them and was infatuated with him. While visiting my grandparents, I decided to write him a letter. My mother found out and disciplined me more severely because of my deliberate disobedience. I was fifteen, but she spanked me. I was angry and humiliated, though I realized that she meant what she said and wanted the best for me. Today, I am grateful that she disciplined me in love. She redirected my misbehavior and restored my obedience to God.

The psalmist David proclaimed the importance of trust in the Lord and obedience to His Word is Psalm 37. He also promised God's blessing to those who seek Him: "Delight yourself also in the LORD, and He shall give you the desires of your heart" (Ps. 37:4). What a precious promise! When you *discipline* yourself and *delight* in the Lord, He will give you the *desires* of your heart.

Rhonda Kelley

Prayer: *Thank the Lord for His love and discipline. Repent and turn away from your sins. Receive His love and discipline as you walk in Him.*

Personal Reflection: ....

....

....

....

....

Sleep in Heavenly Peace

Proverbs 3:19–26

"When you lie down, you will not be afraid;
Yes, you will lie down and your sleep will be sweet." (v. 24)

My husband says I have three spiritual gifts not listed in the Bible—talking, shopping, and sleeping. I do like all three activities and pursue them passionately. Chuck enjoys recalling the time I almost slept through the afternoon matinee of a Broadway show. I can fall asleep anywhere at any time. And, when I sleep, I sleep deeply. Once our dog jumped on top of my chest as I slept, and I did not wake up. That is sweet sleep, not just deep sleep!

In this passage on wisdom, children of God are assured that God is sovereign and on His throne in glory even when life is chaotic. He created everything and knows everything. That firm knowledge gives assurance to frail human beings who lack full understanding and see only the immediate problems of life. Deep conviction that God is all powerful, all knowing, all loving, and all wise helps control fear, gives peace, and enables sleep.

Fear is often described as False Evidence that Appears Real. While fear feels real at the moment of panic, a conscious reminder of God's presence and power should help dissipate fear. A moment of fear can be diverted to peace by confidence in Almighty God. He is real; your fear is not. So, rest in Him.

Sweet sleep is contrasted with fear in this proverb because inability to sleep is a common symptom of fear. Anxiety or worry causes the mind to race through different painful scenarios, often preventing sleep. Do you sometimes let worry get the best of you and lose sleep? Even when conscious thoughts are focused on the Lord, unconscious thoughts often return to the source of concern. The psalmist faced fear and focused on God: "I sought the LORD, and He heard me, and delivered me from all my fears" (Ps. 34:4). Jesus reminded His disciples: "Do not worry about your life . . . do not worry about tomorrow"

(Matt. 6:25–34). Paul confidently counseled: "Be anxious for nothing . . . and the peace of God, which surpasses all understanding will guard your hearts and minds through Christ Jesus" (Phil. 4:6–7).

Several years ago, I developed a fear of flying. For someone who travels for ministry, that can be a real problem. After several turbulent flights and one lightning strike on the wing outside my airplane window, I began to dread trips. I anxiously watched the weather as flight time approached. My heart began to race, my stomach churned, and my body got clammy as the plane took off. The Lord spoke directly to my heart: "Fear not, for I am with you . . . I will uphold you with My righteous right hand" (Is. 41:10). I memorized that verse, repeated it over and over during my next flight, and immediately fell into a deep sleep. God taught me not to fear but to have total faith in Him.

Sweet sisters, the Lord has you covered. He is sovereign and on His throne even when life is hard. You must trust Him, and let go of fear. Then, you can sleep in heavenly peace!

Rhonda Kelley

Prayer: *Do you face any fears? Are there worries that rob you of joy and peace? Focus on your faith, and God will help your fear fade away.*

Personal Reflection: ....

....

....

....

Love Your Neighbor Anyway

Proverbs 3:27–35

*"Do not withhold good from those to whom it is due,
When it is in the power of your hand to do so." (v. 27)*

I grew up in the city of New Orleans, where few of my friends were Christians. Many of my high school friends thought we Baptists could not do anything fun. They believed that Baptists "do not drink, do not smoke, do not dance." Honestly, I wish that Baptists were known more for our holy lifestyles today. I learned that my Christian witness was stronger when I extended love and grace to others without discussing the restrictions of my faith.

Many passages in the book of Proverbs warn about ungodly behavior toward a neighbor. While verses 27–31 each begins with "Do not," believers should avoid distraction by the negative commands in Scripture. Instead, understand the biblical teaching, applying its truth in your life and relationships. Consider the positive responses to the instructions of this passage:

1. *"Do not* withhold good from those to whom it is due" (v. 27); *do* pay for services and repay all loans. Money borrowed should be re-paid (Ps. 37:21); work rendered should be compensated (James 5:4); and personal needs should be covered (Ps. 82:3–4; 1 John 3:17).
2. *"Do not* say to your neighbor, 'Go, and come back, and tomorrow I will give it'" (Prov. 3:28); *do* respond to the need in a timely fashion. Responses to personal need should be immediate, not delayed according to convenience or a selfish timetable.
3. *"Do not* devise evil against your neighbor" (v. 29); *do* trust God to right the wrongs done against you. Retribution is not a godly response to wrongdoing. In His perfect time, God will judge the faults of others justly.

4. "*Do not* strive with a man without cause" (v. 30); *do* live at peace with others, avoiding quarrels. Depend on the Lord to live in peace during conflict. God will right the wrongs. Take the high road, not fueling the tension but calming the storm.

5. "*Do not* envy the oppressor, and choose none of his ways" (v. 31); *do* honor the Lord and follow His ways. Seek to follow God's plan and the wise counsel of His Word as you relate to your oppressors. Be careful not to become like the world, behaving like your enemies.

God expects more from His children—their unselfish love and concern for all people. Love and benevolence are strong themes throughout the Bible because God is love, and He commands His children to love. Kindness is not an option for believers; it is a fruit of the Holy Spirit (Gal. 5:22). Christian virtues should include sensitivity to the needs of others, willingness to share resources, and time given to meet those needs. Benevolent kindness is not reserved for your family or those who are lovable; love all people as does God. Extend love and grace even to the most undesirable. When your neighbor accuses you falsely or speaks to you harshly, love her anyway!

Rhonda Kelley

Prayer: *Pray for someone God has placed in your life to whom you must show His love. Ask the Lord to help you follow this challenging biblical advice.*

Personal Reflection: ....

....

....

449

Listen and Obey

Proverbs 4:1–4

"Hear, my children, the instruction of a father,
And give attention to know understanding;
For I give you good doctrine:
Do not forsake my law." (vv. 1–2)

The Bible is adamant about parents teaching their children to love the Lord and obey His instruction (Eph. 6:4). However, while our parents are to teach us, we as children, must listen and pay attention. When I was young, I remember getting into an argument with my mom. She asked if I was hearing what she said. I replied, "Yes," and she responded, "You may be hearing me, but you aren't listening." I must admit she was probably right. I zoned out during several lectures, but that sentence struck a chord in my brain. I can hear my mom tell me something repeatedly, but I must listen or pay attention to her to gain an understanding of what she is telling me. Hearing and listening go hand in hand. In other words, you cannot "give attention" to something you are not hearing. Proverbs 4 tells us to "hear" and to take it a step further and actually listen.

Do not stop there! Not only do we have the job to listen to our parents, but we also have the ability to decide to obey what we have been taught. It is important to recognize that listening is completely different than obeying. To listen is to acknowledge something someone has said or to pay attention to it. Obeying is taking what you heard and putting it into action.

Proverbs 4 tells us to listen and obey. Recently, something occurred within our family. I was reminded by my mom that while she and my dad have taught us how to follow the Lord and obey His commands, it is ultimately the decision of me and my sister to follow God in obedience. Our job is not to forsake God or our parents. Some of you may not have strong parental figures in your lives, and you may be asking: How does this apply to me? I'm so glad you asked!

Even though you may not have an earthly mom and dad, you have a heavenly Father who loves you more than any earthly parent ever could. God gave us His instruction and wisdom (vv. 1–2). We are to read and "give attention" to God's Word, and we are to choose to obey Him daily.

Have you ever heard your parents or someone close to you say, "I'm telling you this out of love" or "I'm doing this with your best interest at heart"? That is what Solomon is saying in verse 2. He gives us "good doctrine." The most important truth is that God, the same God who died for you and me, gave Solomon this "good doctrine." Anything God says is worth listening to, so give your attention to Him.

Rebekah Howell

Prayer: *Ask the Lord to open your heart and mind while you read His Word. Ask Him to help you listen and pay attention to what He and those whom He has placed in your life would like to tell you. Thank Him for giving you His Word and the ability to study it.*

Personal Reflection: ....

....

....

....

....

....

The Path from Knowledge to Wisdom

Proverbs 4:5–9

"Get wisdom! Get understanding!
Do not forget, nor turn away from the words of my mouth.
Do not forsake her, and she will preserve you;
Love her, and she will keep you." (vv. 5–6)

Have you ever gotten a new appliance or tool that you knew would do something very useful, but you did not know how to work it without the instruction manual? I know I have. You can have knowledge of something; but if you do not know how to use it, then it does absolutely no good. To put it another way, you and I both know that a violin makes a beautiful sound. However, if you were given a violin, you would not be able to play it, assuming you have no musical experience, without having someone show or tell you how to play it. Proverbs 4:5–6 says that knowledge without wisdom and understanding is like a violin in the hands of someone who cannot play it—useless.

Solomon gives a warning "Do not forsake her [Wisdom], and she will preserve you." In other words, using wisdom is beneficial, but refusing wisdom is deadly. Let's go back to our violin analogy to apply this principle. What if the violin came with a beginners' lesson book that contained everything needed to begin learning how to play the violin? The use of that book would introduce you to the beautiful capability of the instrument, but ignoring the book would not prove beneficial at all. The application of wisdom has the power to preserve you, while the neglect of wisdom leads to destruction.

Solomon further tells us that honor comes with wisdom (vv. 8–9). Take a minute and think about it. What is the opposite of a wise person? The Bible classifies one without wisdom as foolish (Prov. 1:7). This prods me to a second question. Have you ever met a foolish person, one who is lacking in wisdom and yet is truly respected and honored? I have not. If your answer to that question

is "yes," then I have one more question for you. Using what the Bible says about wisdom and the foolish person, does God honor someone lacking in wisdom? If we are honest, all of us would say, "No." God honors those who honor Him. Those who honor Him have wisdom and understanding.

My family has had a dog since my birth. Actually, we have always had a male Labrador Retriever. The first was a very hyper black lab named Spurgeon, and now we have a beautiful yellow lab named Amos. Both dogs obeyed because a reward was promised to them. They would roll over because they knew a treat would follow if they complied. I want you to understand that we should not have this mind-set with God. We should gain and keep wisdom to bring glory and honor to God, not because we want a reward for our compliance. The end goal is to bring honor to God. Remember that as you go about your day.

Rebekah Howell

Prayer: *Ask God to give you wisdom in every area of your life. Pray that you would honor God in everything you do. Ask Him to get your attention when you begin to turn away from wisdom.*

Personal Reflection: ....

....

....

....

A Hold on Wisdom

Proverbs 4:10–19

"When you walk, your steps will not be hindered,
And when you run, you will not stumble.
Take firm hold of instruction, do not let go;
Keep her, for she is your life." (vv. 12–13)

Have you ever tried walking or running in soft sand, whether on a beach or in sand dunes? If you have, you know that it is extremely difficult. The sand feels as though it is pulling on your feet, keeping you—or at least trying to keep you—from moving forward. Sin has that same affect. When you are living a sinful life, your sin holds on to you and tries to prohibit you from moving forward. Satan loves to keep you from God, and he does everything in his power to do so. He makes false promises and tries to tear us down. These verses give us assurance that wisdom helps us to go on without fear of Satan gripping our lives. However, we must utilize wisdom to keep from stumbling.

When my sister Abigail and I were little girls, our mom signed us up for piano lessons. Once a week Abi and I would each have thirty minutes with our piano teacher where we were taught everything about the piano and how to play it. When we utilized what we were taught, we could play something beautiful. We could play "Mary Had a Little Lamb," and it was the most beautiful rendition you have ever heard! Anyway, if we did not utilize what we were taught and relied on our own devices, I assure you that nothing beautiful was coming out of that piano. Wisdom is the same. For wisdom to guide us, we must utilize it.

Solomon makes a very important point in verse 13. He says regarding instruction: "Do not let go; keep her. . . ." Just as wisdom can be learned, it can also be lost. Think of this concept in terms of picking up a sport, hobby, or instrument. Learning that sport or hobby may be easy, but it is easier to quit, to let it go. I pray daily that God would give me wisdom and that I would listen

to it. Holding on to wisdom requires a daily commitment; it is not a one-time decision.

God has put many wonderful, God-fearing, wise people into my life. He has given me the Bible to study, meditate on, and memorize. I am surrounded by wisdom. However, without a personal decision to listen to godly wisdom, it is useless. I pray that you will make the decision to soak up wisdom from all the people God has put into your life. Most important, look to the Bible for wisdom. God has given you His Word for that specific purpose, but you must utilize it. I urge you to seek wisdom and instruction daily because "she is your life" (v. 13).

Rebekah Howell

Prayer: *Go to God daily and ask for wisdom and discernment. If you do not have a wise counselor in your life already, pray that God would bring into your life people who can share wise counsel with you.*

Personal Reflection: ....

....

....

....

....

....

Guarding the Heart

Proverbs 4:20–27

"Keep your heart with all diligence,
For out of it spring the issues of life." (v. 23)

I have often been told that what is down in the well comes up in the bucket. If the well contains dirty water, dirty water is going to come out. A bad heart will produce bad fruit. In other words, my character reflects the condition of my heart. My heart determines what I see, what I hear, and what I do: "Out of [the heart] spring the issues of life" (v. 23). If your heart is detrimental to your being, shouldn't you do everything you can to protect it? Yes, and Solomon tells us to keep our hearts diligently (v. 23). How do we do that? Solomon provides three specific areas for our attention.

First, we must guard our *tongues*. "Put away from you a deceitful mouth, and put perverse lips far from you" (v. 24). Lying, bad language, sarcasm, critical, and judgmental words all fall under this category. I have seen firsthand the damage of a bad tongue, but I have also seen the overwhelming good of a God-honoring tongue. Our words have the power to tear down or build up, to lead people to Christ or to turn them away. We need to be diligent every day to guard such a precious and powerful instrument.

Second, we must guard our eyes. "Let your eyes look straight ahead, and your eyelids look right before you" (v. 25). We do not want to be like Peter walking on water during the storm. When he got out of the boat, Peter had his eyes fixed on Jesus, and he was given the opportunity to do something no one else could do—walk on water. However, the second he focused his eyes on the waves around him, Peter began to sink. Eyes focused on anything other than Christ reflect a heart that is focused on anything but Christ.

Finally, we are instructed to guard our actions. "Ponder the path of your feet" (v. 26). Think before you act. Think about the consequences, good or bad,

that could result from what you want to do. The majority of bad decisions I have made in my life could have been avoided if I had just thought about what I was doing. Please do not make that same mistake. Think before acting!

Like the nucleus of a cell, your heart is the control center of your life. If you have a heart that is focused on anything but God, evaluate your life and ask yourself if you have ever experienced the heart change that God offers when He is Lord of your life. The external will not change until the internal changes.

Rebekah Howell

Prayer: *Ask God to give you a tongue that brings glory to Him, eyes that rest upon Him, and feet that follow Him. Pray that God would help you to focus on Him in all areas of your life, and ask that He give you a heart that reflects His glory.*

Personal Reflection: ....

....

....

....

....

....

....

Protecting Discretion

Proverbs 5:1–14

"My son, pay attention to my wisdom;
Lend your ear to my understanding,
That you may preserve discretion,
And your lips may keep knowledge." (vv. 1–2)

The book of Proverbs is a book of repetition. Repetition is not necessarily a bad thing. In fact, the repetitive nature of the book reminds me of the importance of the message engraved within. As I have studied the Bible, I have often found whatever is repeated more than once to be of even greater value.

Whenever my mom and dad are about to begin a "teaching moment" or a lecture, they sit my sister and me down, making sure that we are free from distractions so that our full attention is on them and what they are about to say. Abigail and I both know that something serious is coming our way. Solomon does the same thing here. He starts a serious passage by sitting us down and making sure that he has our full attention. He wants us to know that a serious subject is to be addressed and that not listening could have terrible consequences.

"Lend your ear to my understanding" (v. 1). Did you catch the word *lend*? This truth is important; so I am going to say it again. As believers in Christ, we can choose to read God's Word and obey it. We can choose to read God's Word and not obey it. Or, we can choose not to read God's Word at all. The choice is left to us. By using the word *lend*, Solomon is urging us to choose to listen and obey.

A few years ago, I had the privilege of traveling to Washington, D.C., for a leadership conference. While we were there, we saw the Constitution of the United States as well as the Declaration of Independence. How neat to see something so old and of such great value. However, due to the age of the documents,

they had to stay inside a climate-controlled box with thick, bulletproof glass to preserve the documents. Solomon says that we should listen to his words so that we may "preserve discretion" (vv. 1–2). We should gather up wisdom and instruction and surround it with bulletproof glass for protection.

As you go about your day, remember that you have a decision to make. You can either disobey or obey. The decision is yours. But, if you choose to obey and soak up wisdom, protect it with everything you have.

Rebekah Howell

Prayer: *Pray that you would choose to follow God in obedience daily. Ask Him to help you preserve wisdom and instruction.*

Personal Reflection:

Remaining Faithful

Proverbs 5:15–20

"Let your fountain be blessed,
And rejoice in the wife of your youth.
As a loving deer and a graceful doe,
Let her breasts satisfy you at all times;
And always be enraptured with her love." (vv. 18–19)

This passage means different things to different people. For one who is married, this passage clearly states that you should remain faithful to your spouse and abstain from adultery and other forms of sexual sin. On the other hand, this passage also applies to the single woman. Many single women will conclude: "Well, that doesn't apply to me, so I am going to skip over that one." If that is your mind-set, you could not be more wrong. While speaking to married women, the passage also have fundamental truth for singles. I encourage you to have an open mind while we study these few verses.

For starters, we are reminded to be faithful. The married woman should be faithful to her spouse, never looking at anyone other than him. The single woman should remain faithful to the commitment she made to God to abstain from sexual union until marriage. When you became a Christ-follower, you promised God to uphold His Word and His commands. These verses serve as a reminder of that promise.

The reader is also reminded to help our fellow believers remain faithful. You made a promise to Christ, and so did other believers. While they are responsible to keep their promises, we should not conduct ourselves in a manner that could encourage them to break their promises. Please do not misunderstand me. They are responsible for their actions. However, so are we; and if we conduct ourselves in a manner that might cause them to stumble, then we are also

sinning. Conduct yourself in a way that pleases the Lord and will not cause another to stumble.

Isolation is not the way to live. No need to go to that extreme. You and I both know the difference between God-honoring and sinful behavior. We know the difference between conducting ourselves in a sinful manner and godly manner. We need to use wise discernment. While you do not always need to wear a turtleneck sweater, you still need to be conscious of the way you are portraying yourself by what you wear. The picture you portray of yourself comes from what you wear, what you say, and what you do. All are important for conducting yourself in a manner that prohibits you from becoming a stumbling block to someone else. The keys of Proverbs 5 are faithfulness to Christ and the promise you made in choosing to follow Him.

Rebekah Howell

Prayer: *Pray that you would remain faithful to the promise you made to Christ. Pray that you would keep from becoming a stumbling block in someone else's life (Rom. 14:13). If you are married, ask the Lord to help you remain faithful to your spouse. Ask Him to give you eyes for your spouse and only your spouse.*

Personal Reflection: ....

....

....

....

....

461

Worldly Choices Lead to Eternal Devastation

Proverbs 5:21–23

"His own iniquities entrap the wicked man,
And he is caught in the cords of his sin." (v. 22)

A few weeks ago, I decided to sit outside and read. About fifteen minutes later a little mouse scurried by me, scaring me almost to death. I immediately informed my parents of this problem, and Dad said he would go to the store and get a trap on his way home from work. So, we put some food in the trap and waited. The next day, the mouse was in the trap, struggling to set itself free. The mouse got caught because it wanted the food in the trap, and it was unaware of what was waiting. Sin does the exact same thing to us. We fall into sin because we want something that we see dangling before us. It appears promising; but in the end, it leads to a trap from which we cannot free ourselves (v. 22).

How many times have you thought, "This one time won't hurt"? or "I'm just going to tell a 'little' lie this one time"? If we are honest, we have all been there. We think that one "small" sin will not hurt us. Unfortunately, we could not be more wrong. Every "little" sin pulls us further from God and closer to sin's deadly trap. Think of how a chain is made with linking together several smaller pieces of metal. Every time we sin against God, we are adding another link to the chain that holds us to sin.

Many believers make the mistake of comparing sins. If you have ever watched Olympic gymnastics, then you have seen how the judges score the gymnasts after each round. Numbers are held up to tell the gymnast if the performance was great or disastrous. I think we do the same thing with sin. If someone is a murderer, we give them a low score, but if someone has "only" told a "white lie," we score them higher. We are lying to ourselves when we follow this system. The truth is that all sin is equal in God's eyes. A liar is just as bad as

a murderer or thief. We should never think that our sin was not bad just because we measured it as "small." All sin adds a link to the chain of disobedience.

Fortunately for you and me, Christ came and died for our sins; He cut that chain and offers us forgiveness and freedom. He has given us the opportunity to have a personal relationship with Him. If you have not accepted His forgiveness and freedom, I encourage you to go to Him in prayer and do so now. Your life will never be the same.

Rebekah Howell

Prayer: *Ask God to break the chains holding you to sin. Pray that He will free you from a mentality of scoring sin. Ask Him to renew your heart.*

Personal Reflection: ....

....

....

....

....

....

....

Do You Have Potential?

Proverbs 6:1–11

"Go to the ant, you sluggard!
Consider her ways and be wise,
Which, having no captain,
Overseer or ruler,
Provides her supplies in the summer,
And gathers her food in the harvest." (vv. 6–8)

I grew up in a family with parents who raised each of us to be independent adults. Self-discipline was always stressed in our home. I hated it. When my father reprimanded us for a lack of self-discipline, he made us recite its definition: "Self-discipline is knowing what needs to be done and doing it without being told." When I was an unruly middle-schooler who did not enjoy making her room tidy, I loathed that quote, only reciting it in the most sing-song tone I could muster. However, now that I am a young adult, I have come to be ever so grateful for my parents.

The Bible says a lot about laziness, but no passage is more poignant. The person Solomon addresses has all the potential for success. He could *become* wise, but that is the irony about potential—it is everything you currently are not. The sluggard *could* "be wise," study the ant, and provide for himself. But he is not, and his potential wanes. Eventually, he is left with nothing but his potential, which doesn't put food on the table.

Scripture effectively gives us illustrations from nature that help bring to life biblical truths, and the ant is one of the best examples. A well-known leader said, "Everything rises and falls on leadership," but the ant disproves that theory. Ants have no leaders telling them what to do. They have a queen, but she does not tell her subjects what to do. The ants decide which tasks they are going to do. And boy, do they do it! They are always on the move, usually with something twice their size on their backs. When gathering food, attacking an intruder, or recovering their devastated anthill, they instinctively get to work.

People often blame leaders for any negativity that we experience. "It's this boss I have." "If only my husband. . . ." "I did not vote for him!" We complain about our leaders and expect them to fix our problems instead of imitating the ant and doing what is needed. What would our jobs look like if we worked hard without being evaluated by our bosses? What would our homes look like if we were more loving and respectful without a reason to love and respect? What would our world look like if we disagreed without hating or demonizing people with opposing views? What if we learned to work alongside others, to make our communities a priority, to witness to our neighbors without our pastors pushing us on the Great Commission? What would it look like if we went to the ant, considered her ways, and lived the principles we found at the anthill?

Sarah Bubar

Prayer: *Ask the Lord to help you make changes in your heart first, your home second, and then in your community. Make a difference where you live.*

Personal Reflection: ....

....

....

....

....

465

A Look Can Lead to a Life

Proverbs 6:12–19

"These six things the LORD hates,
Yes, seven are an abomination to Him:
A proud look,
A lying tongue,
Hands that shed innocent blood,
A heart that devises wicked plans,
Feet that are swift in running to evil,
A false witness who speaks lies,
And one who sows discord among brethren." (vv. 16–19)

I do *not* like leftovers! Even though I take food home, I will not actually eat the leftovers. They'll remain in my refrigerator because *one time* when I went to get leftovers, I had a bad experience. That one bad experience with leftovers ruined all other leftovers for me. But isn't that how it is sometimes? One bad experience affects the whole?

The wise king addresses the character of the worthless person with a list, seemingly disjointed and categorical, of things that God hates. At first glance, we can be tempted to judge ourselves according to this list and come out thinking we are not half bad! We do not sit around plotting wicked schemes, and we definitely have not killed anyone, let alone an innocent person. Does this passage apply to us or not?

A theme most definitely emerges in these verses. All the characteristics involved (eyes, tongue, hands, heart, and feet) constitute the whole person, scheming to ruin the lives of other people. The list is not meant to be exhaustive concerning all the things that God hates, but rather it presents general traits of a person tearing apart the lives of her family.

Attitude always precedes actions. A prideful look does not belong to the woman who is teachable in the presence of the Lord. The passage moves from her eyes to her mouth, and lies are quickly spilt. She pretends it is a prayer request and not a gossip fest. All these lies and looks further prove that her heart has hatred taking root: "Whoever hates his brother is a murderer" (1 John 3:15). But sin does not ever stop there. The sinful woman does not just head toward evil—she sprints to it, sowing disunity and division like garden weeds that grow up and choke the life out of the family she was called to love (John 13:35).

What about you? Are you harboring hatred in your heart against someone you have been called to love? Do you look for ways to put her down so that you feel better? Do you ever find yourself "putting her in her place" in front of a crowd? What would your eyes, feet, hands, and heart say about your whole person?

Sarah Bubar

Prayer: *Ask the Lord to forgive you for sowing discord or having a bad attitude. Humble yourself before Him and keep your eyes from being prideful.*

Personal Reflection: ....

....

....

....

....

Having a Heart of Obedience

Proverbs 6:20–22

"My son, keep your father's command,
And do not forsake the law of your mother.
Bind them continually upon your heart;
Tie them around your neck.
When you roam, they will lead you;
When you sleep, they will keep you;
And when you awake, they will speak with you." (vv. 20–22)

Obedience is the most challenging lesson to teach children. It is never-ending from infancy into adulthood. Once they learn it in one area, another area pops up. Lessons from a parent never really end. As children move into adulthood, those lessons become more like sage advice, but they are teachings nonetheless.

Why do parents teach their children to obey? Is it just because they want little minions to be at their beck and call all the time, carrying out menial daily tasks? No! A loving parent teaches her child obedience because she knows that someday the child is going to have to obey the voice of God. If the child develops a habit of disobedience, she will follow that pattern and not have a very happy life. But if the child develops a heart of obedience, her future is bright and successful.

The book of Proverbs pleads with its readers to obey. First, this passage appeals to the elementary stages of obedience: "Bind them continually upon your heart" (v. 21). Solomon emphasizes the great importance of a parent's initial teachings. He wants them to tie the commands down. A crafty woman would say, "'Gorilla Glue' that truth onto your heart!" Make it become a part of you. The writer then describes all the practical ways a parent's teaching can assist you in life. It leads you, keeps you, and speaks to you. Parental instruction

goes everywhere you go—from morning to evening, dusk to dawn, sleeping and awakening.

As a child, did you learn your lessons in obedience well? Have you made obedience to God's Word a priority in your heart and life? If you are a parent, what lessons are you teaching your children? Are you binding that truth on their hearts? Are you teaching them lessons like loving and obeying God and His Word above all else? Do you model for them an obedient life?

Sarah Bubar

Prayer: *Thank the Lord for this reminder to bind His Word to your heart. Learn these lessons of obedience and continue living in obedience. Be the kind of parent who raises her children well in light of eternity and not just in the frazzled moments of life. Seek wisdom to pattern your parenting after the way that God parents you.*

Personal Reflection: ....

....

....

....

....

....

Don't Be Caught without a Flashlight

Proverbs 6:23–35

"For the commandment is a lamp,
And the law a light;
Reproofs of instruction are the way of life." (v. 23)

Every year I go on a camping trip. Something about lying in a hammock all bundled up with a warm blanket under a canopy of stars is so relaxing. Last year, I took my two assistants on a "bonding" excursion for three days into the forestry of the Tampa woodlands. We had full bathrooms and laundry rooms available, but we were in the woods!

One particular night it was overcast with a new moon, so basically pitch black. I headed to the facilities, assuming my eyes would adjust. About 10 feet from our site I could not see a *thing*! I quickly fumbled for my phone. I could not use the flashlight because my battery was low; I could only use the light from the screen. I was a pitiful sight, groping around in the dark. Suddenly a small light pointed toward me, bouncing up and down in the air. As it drew closer, I realized that it was one of my assistants with a flashlight. "Headed to the bathroom?" she asked. "Yup." "Me too!" And on we walked together, her light leading the way.

God's Word is just like that flashlight. Without it in my possession, I was completely vulnerable to anything that came across my path. As badly as I wanted to get to that bathhouse, I could not see. Scripture is described as "a lamp to my feet and a light to my path" (Ps. 119:105). When God's Word is opened to a situation, it sheds light and illuminates what would otherwise remain unseen, unnoticed, and thereby unavoidable. Without the teaching of God's Word lighting the path, your progress in life would be constantly thwarted by distractions and unsubstantiated fears along the way.

While God's Word is a great source of comfort, it is not always comfortable. Sometimes God's Word can feel like a "sucker punch" to the soul, landing you flat on your back, the wind knocked out of you, wondering how you got to that point. But even in those "tough love" moments with God's Word, it never reproves you for reproof's sake. No, God wants you to live blamelessly (Phil. 2:15). Stay in the Word; keep His light before you to light your path.

Sarah Bubar

Prayer: *Thank the Lord for His Word, for its instruction and illumination. Seek His help to recognize your need for His Word in your life on a daily basis.*

Personal Reflection: ....

....

....

....

....

....

....

Be Wise; Your Life Depends on It

Proverbs 7:1–27

"My son, keep my words,
And treasure my commands within you.
Keep my commands and live,
And my law as the apple of your eye.
Bind them on your fingers;
Write them on the tablet of your heart." (vv. 1–3)

This chapter tells the story of the infamous adulterous woman, who, though married herself, lays waste to the propriety and virginity of the young stranger walking past her door (vv. 14, 19). This woman plans, plots, and pursues her victim like a vicious cat stalking its prey (vv. 10, 12, 15). She is bold and brazen. The young man seems not to have an avenue of escape. However, verses 1–3 indicate why he is vulnerable—his disregard for prioritizing wisdom in his life.

Wisdom is more than knowledge and good sense. Wisdom combines knowledge and discernment with Spirit-led decision-making tempered by humility, patience, and spiritual maturity. A wise woman sees clearly the appropriate and biblical path, making decisions graciously, quickly, and confidently.

The book of Proverbs urges its readers to have the highest regard for wisdom, protecting it like you would the "apple of your eye." The writer is saying that wisdom is to be treated as the dearest thing you can possess! Protect it. Desire it more than anything else.

Wisdom will be your lifeline in difficult situations (v. 5a). Wisdom will speak truth when the flattering lies are screaming (v. 5b). Wisdom will anchor you when that temptation is pulling you away (v. 13).

I have incorporated Scripture and Bible journaling into my daily quiet time to help me meditate on God's Word. Visual reminders of biblical truths are also set around my home to help me acquire godly wisdom. When I am asked

for prayer requests, wisdom is always my go-to request. Why? Because I need wisdom like I need air! Wisdom is indispensable to life, ministry, godly choices, and holy living. Chasing after wisdom needs to be the pursuit of my heart.

Wisdom is found within the precious pages of the Word of God. I find wisdom in my church when I am sitting humbly under the teaching of God's Word. I find wisdom in my community when embracing the advice of my godly counselors. Are you pursuing wisdom? Do you seek knowledge for knowledge's sake, or are you seeking the discernment to apply that knowledge to life?

Sarah Bubar

Prayer: *Thank the Lord for His Word and the godly wisdom found within its pages. Give Him the glory as you grow in His wisdom and seek His truth. Ask Him to teach you through His Word and His Spirit, adding His wisdom and knowledge to your own personal experience.*

Personal Reflection: ....

....

....

....

....

....

What Do I Value?

Proverbs 8:1–11

"Receive my instruction, and not silver,
And knowledge rather than choice gold;
For wisdom is better than rubies,
And all the things one may desire cannot
be compared with her." (vv. 10–11)

"To me, having money is the mark of maturity and independence, basically becoming an adult," one of my college girls blurted out as we were driving back from a fun day in downtown Tampa. We talked about the logic and faulty reasoning behind her thought processes as we drove back home.

According to the world, gaining money is the surest way to have comfortable and happy lives. Yet I look at some of the richest people in the world and wonder if they are any closer to fulfillment than the college kids to whom I minister. The writer of Proverbs affirms that the value of wisdom is far more precious than anything on which a price tag can be placed. However, since wisdom is not a material asset, its value may be hard to grasp. Doubters may ask, "But will wisdom pay the rent or put bread on the table or pay down that college loan?"

Money falls short of wisdom in many ways. For instance, money can be lost. Wisdom can only be gained and then kept. Money can be spent, while wisdom is inexhaustible. While money may help in some situations, as my college student attested, it cannot buy *all* things. Wisdom, on the other hand, is useful in every situation in which you find yourself. Wisdom brings understanding (Job 12:12), placing a guard on your mouth so only the best answer is given (Ps. 37:30). Wisdom will protect and watch over you (Prov. 4:6). Wisdom draws you closer to the Lord (Prov. 4:7; Col. 2:2–3). God generously gives wisdom whenever you ask Him for it (James 1:5); He does not make the same promise

474

regarding your request for more money. In fact, the love of money is considered "a root of all kinds of evil" (1 Tim. 6:10), while the pursuit of godly wisdom is "better . . . than [obtaining] gold" (Prov. 16:16).

What value do you place on things? Do you value financial security more than you value godly wisdom? Take a moment to look at how you are spending your day. How much time do you spend in searching God's Word, sitting alone with your Bible open and asking God to reveal to you more about Himself? Do you carve out moments in your busy schedule to sit before the One who organizes all things (Ps. 139:16)?

Sarah Bubar

Prayer: *Make a commitment to seek wisdom from the Lord. Seek to make decisions, rear your children in the Lord, and minister to those around you. See the value of wisdom, and do all you can to pursue it.*

Personal Reflection: ....

....

....

....

....

Who Are Your Friends?

Proverbs 8:12–13

*"I, wisdom, dwell with prudence,
And find out knowledge and discretion." (v. 12)*

"You can choose better friends," my mother told me. As a high schooler, I wholeheartedly disagreed with her thinking. I could no more choose my friends than I could my family. Then I grew up, and I realized that my mother was right. I should choose better friends. My friends did greatly influence my outlook and attitude about life.

The people with whom I surround myself have a large impact on my thinking, my goals, my aspirations, my priorities! Wisdom, personified as a wise woman in Proverbs 8, pinpoints specific attributes of those in close proximity to her: prudence, knowledge, and discretion.

Prudence. This synonym for "wisdom" includes the idea of caution. This woman plans her finances in a thrifty manner, calculating the outcome before making an expenditure. A prudent woman thinks before she acts. She is prepared for the inevitable and even, at times, the preventable.

Knowledge. The wise woman is humble and teachable. She knows to keep knowledge close to her. She does not just innately have knowledge; she searches for and acquires it in her life.

Discretion. Wisdom knows that discretion is like the steering wheel to knowledge's motor, the rudder to knowledge's sail. Discretion tells knowledge when to speak and when to be quiet, when to act and when to wait.

Wisdom, with knowledge and discretion, is equipped to make the best choices. She is influenced by those around her and takes on their attributes. She is now wisdom with caution and thoughtful thinking; she is wisdom with knowledge and discernment to be wiser!

Believers really must choose their friends! How have you chosen? When it comes to you and your life, what sort of influences have you chosen for yourself and allowed to have a voice in your decisions? Would you say prudence, knowledge, and discernment are in your life? Or are you looking toward feelings, society, and impulsiveness? Perhaps the sources of your problems are the "friends" you have around you. Ask the Lord to help you evaluate the voices in your life to see whether they are wise or foolish.

Sarah Bubar

Prayer: *Do you want to live a life marked by wisdom? Ask the Lord to help you live a life marked by wisdom. Let your decisions reflect His Word as being fleshed out and coming to life. Ask God to surround you with influences that add to your wisdom and discourage foolishness.*

Personal Reflection: ....

....

....

....

....

....

Who Is Your Disciple?

Proverbs 8:14–21

"Counsel is mine, and sound wisdom;
I am understanding, I have strength." (v. 14)

The Lord provided in high school and college a woman who was a mentor/discipler/counselor for me. Although my mother did counsel and disciple me, an additional person was in my life to be a sounding board when I needed godly wisdom. Now that I am in my forties, I have graduated from constantly needing someone else's advice for the decisions I make. Fortunately, God has given me the opportunity to be that counselor/discipler for the young women He is placing in my path. My students will graduate from the elementary walks of the Christian life, and the Holy Spirit will be their discipler. The Holy Spirit will help them know how to act, what to do, when to speak, and when not to speak.

Wisdom offers personal counsel to those who seek after it like a rare treasure (Prov. 2:4). It becomes our advisor, giving us the courage and strength to follow through on those decisions. Wisdom yearns to be found, and God reveals it. "If any of you lacks wisdom, let him ask of God, who gives to all liberally and without reproach, and it will be given to him" (James 1:5). I had never made the request for wisdom a priority in my prayer life. I thought gaining wisdom from wise people was easier than acquiring it myself. I now see that I was foolish. I had the Source of *all* wisdom just waiting to give me godly wisdom for any situation, and all I had to do was ask. So I began to pray intentionally for wisdom in my morning devotional time: "Wisdom. I need just lots and lots of wisdom." And do you know what began to happen? While I did not become any smarter, I did become more aware of the Holy Spirit's presence in my life.

Who is your discipler? Is it the Holy Spirit? When was the last time you asked God for wisdom? Who is your mentor or counselor? Do you have a godly

friend sharing truth with you? Make the request for wisdom a priority in your prayer life and see how God draws you closer to Himself and to the influence of other godly people.

Sarah Bubar

Prayer: *Ask the Lord for wisdom beyond your years and beyond your experiences. Allow His wisdom to guide you and His Spirit to lead you.*

Personal Reflection: ....

....

....

....

....

....

....

Hearing, Humility, and Happiness

Proverbs 8:22–36

"Hear instruction and be wise,
And do not disdain it.
Blessed is the man who listens to me,
Watching daily at my gates,
Waiting at the posts of my doors." (vv. 33–34)

Have you ever met "those people"—those who charge ahead with an answer without first hearing the entire question? They would rather ask a classmate what the assignment is than read their syllabus. They assemble Ikea furniture without even glancing at the instructions! I hate to admit it, but . . . (*cringe*) I am one of "those people," and it has gotten me in a world of trouble!

At the end of her speech, Wisdom closes with these final thoughts. She wants her children to hear, to have humility, and ultimately, to be happy.

Hear instruction and be wise. This call of Wisdom to listen to what she has to say, to heed her advice comes again in Proverbs 8. She is the good counselor (v. 14), shrewd and knowledgeable (v. 12), crying out to the inexperienced and foolish (vv. 1–5). She wants to keep them from the waywardness of folly (6:23; 7:5). She follows the call to "listen" (8:32) with the reward of wisdom: "Hear instruction" and, subsequently, you will "be wise" (v. 33). She is not wanting something for nothing. Her returns for your life are more cherished than gold or any wealth you could quantify (vv. 19, 21).

Do not disdain it. At the core of "those people" is a heart attitude that says, "I don't need (or want) anybody's help with this. I can do it quicker myself." I know better. I have been here before and figured it out eventually. The heart despises help because it has its own way. If this strikes a chord with you, please humble yourself before the Lord and others. Godly wisdom can have no part with the woman who thinks that she does not need wisdom outside herself.

Blessed is the man who listens to me. The end result of many of God's commands is happiness. God is our Creator, and He knows how we work and what will make us truly happy in life. He knows that our obedience to Him and surrender to His will bring us the most abundant lives.

Why do we fail to seek His wisdom? Some days we are all "those people," refusing to stop for directions, to ask for help, or to listen. At the core of each of us is a sin problem, which only the blood and the cross of Christ can remedy.

Sarah Bubar

Prayer: *Thank your heavenly Father for loving you so much and for His gift of salvation. Do not disdain His wisdom; embrace it. Allow God to break the pride in your heart and help you seek His wisdom. Let God make you a wise woman!*

Personal Reflection: ....

....

....

....

....

....

....

The Way of Understanding

Proverbs 9:1–6

*"Forsake foolishness and live,
And go in the way of understanding." (v. 6)*

Proverbs 9 sets before us two differing paths: the way of foolishness (Lady Folly) versus the way of understanding (Lady Wisdom). This passage makes abundantly clear that following wisdom leads you on the path to understanding; whereas foolishness leads you down the path of destruction. But, how do you gain understanding? And, what does "understanding" look like?

Proverbs 9:1–2 describes two methods for achieving understanding. First, be wise with your time. In a world where social media, Pinterest, and HGTV call out and beckon you to waste precious time and energy on shallow relationships and vain projects, you need to be resolved in evaluating every minute to ensure you are being fruitful with your allotted time. Wisdom is described as a woman who "built her house." She did not have time to crowd her schedule with things of no substance. Building a home, whether physically or metaphorically, is challenging. Those who idly sit will struggle to accomplish the task. Let's be women who strive to live each day solely focused on the tasks the Lord has given us and faithfully execute our assignment. Our days are certainly numbered, and I want to be faithful. Do you?

Wisdom is also needed for our reasoning. Lady Wisdom prepared a feast, arranged her table, and then invited the foolish to partake of her insight. Being a woman of wisdom does not come easily. It takes diligent preparation and then proper execution. Our families and churches need spiritually-minded women who are willing to go through the difficult task of researching the subject, grappling with information, and coming to conclusions and convictions through the lens of Scripture. When faced with a difficulty, we are tempted to take the

easier route, accessing Google instead of accessing God's Word. In doing so, we have obtained worldly knowledge but not true wisdom.

True wisdom is found only on the pages of Scripture. This conclusion is not popular. Our society, and even the church, confuses human knowledge and compassion with wisdom and godliness. We are fearful to call out the sin in our lives and in the lives of others because of the acceptance of relative truth. We are as one "having a form of godliness but denying its power" (2 Tim. 3:5). Ladies, return to the Source of faith and to the One who gives wisdom. Commit to being a woman who looks to God's Word as her basis for understanding instead of relying on the world to tell her how to live. Will you strive to be a woman of wisdom?

Amanda Walker

Prayer: *Solomon asked God for wisdom, and He gave it in abundance (1 Kin. 3:5–12). You do not have to go through life foolishly, but you can obtain wisdom. Ask the Lord to make you into a woman who seeks His Word before she seeks the counsel of others.*

Personal Reflection: ....

....

....

....

....

Avoiding the Terrible Twos

Proverbs 9:7–9

"Give instruction to a wise man, and he will be still wiser;
Teach a just man, and he will increase in learning." (v. 9)

Why don't you value and seek instruction instead of running from it? Oftentimes, I want to ask my children this question. The Lord has blessed my husband and me with three precious children; therefore, I have had the privilege and head-ache of walking through the "terrible/terrific twos." And, I have lived to tell about it! This season is filled with comments such as: "No!" "Mommy, I do it myself!" "I don't want to!" A once accommodating, teachable infant turns into an independent, disagreeable toddler, and that is a frustrating time for parents. However, this same attitude could describe some of us spiritually.

A wise woman realizes that she is not above mistakes or correction. Ladies, no matter our position or status in life, we are fallen individuals prone to all types of sin. A trend in my ministry is the avoidance of accountability and instruction. We enjoy attending church, sitting in Bible studies, getting a warm feeling, gaining a "tweet-able" truth, and then returning home proud of our efforts. This mentality is not spiritually healthy. God created the church—His body—for encouragement, fellowship, instruction, reproof, *and* accountability.

Paul instructs older women to be "teachers of good things" (Titus 2:3–5). He goes on to give a list of the disciplines they are to teach the younger women. However, if you look at the beginning of Titus 2:3, Paul gives specific instructions for the older women. You cannot expect to be a Spirit-filled teacher or mentor if you are blind to your own shortcomings and disregard wise instruction. Godly reproof and correction are not evil or mean-spirited. When confronted with an issue, a woman may find it easier to get her feelings hurt instead of looking for the nugget of truth held within that correction. She may become

like a toddler holding her hands over her spiritual ears and screaming, "I do it myself!"

Ladies, this attitude is not becoming of a woman running hard after God. If we put aside our pride and open our hearts and minds to wise instruction, there will be much wisdom and far fewer pitfalls. As a woman of God, I ask you: Do you value and seek instruction, or do you run from it? My prayer is that you would see correction and instruction as a breath of fresh air and not a millstone around your neck.

Amanda Walker

Prayer: *Do you have someone in your life who is unafraid to speak truth to you? If so, thank God for giving you that person. If you do not have someone, ask the Lord to provide you with someone who would hold you accountable and speak wise instruction into your life.*

Personal Reflection: ....

....

....

....

....

....

485

The Secret to Wisdom

Proverbs 9:10–12

*"The fear of the LORD is the beginning of wisdom,
And the knowledge of the Holy One is understanding." (v. 10)*

One of the opening verses to the book of Proverbs is: "The fear of the LORD is the beginning of knowledge, but fools despise wisdom and instruction" (Prov. 1:7). Actually, Solomon mentions "fearing the Lord" numerous times in his writings. Therefore, we can assume that God is trying to help us understand a connection between fearing Him and gaining wisdom/knowledge. What does it mean to "fear God"?

When I was younger, I heard sermons on fearing God. The pastor often said that to "fear God" means to respect, honor, and esteem Him. Though that is true, "fearing God" means so much more. The God we serve is the same Person who spoke creation into being (Gen. 1), parted the Red Sea (Ex. 14), brought fire down from heaven (1 Kin. 18), and used an army of three hundred to defeat an army of thousands (Judg. 7). He holds the power to lift His hand from this earth and send the universe into utter chaos. Ladies, our God is not someone who sits on a cloud surrounded by harp-strumming angels. Revelation 4 describes God's throne room as having fire, lightning, and thunder. He is the fierce Lion of Judah who deserves much more than awe and respect; He deserves a good healthy dose of fear.

Why is this "fearing God" so important? Solomon says that we must fear God to obtain wisdom. To be clear, He is a God of love, but He is also a God of perfect justice. For those who are followers of Jesus, God now relates to you as a loving Father. He can do that because Jesus, His only Son, took your punishment and bore the judgment of sin. Understanding the reality of who God is and relating to Him based on that knowledge will give you wisdom. No longer will

life be about your intelligence or your earthly accomplishments, but you will readily turn your face towards your Creator.

The most gifted person you know pales in comparison to our Heavenly Father. I am thankful that He is far above me and my understanding. Yet, the Holy Spirit living in me gives me the ability to comprehend great truths. No one compares to Him. Ladies, hear the often untold story of the God we serve. I want to challenge you to look at God the way Scripture defines Him, and then allow yourself to be overwhelmed by Him.

Amanda Walker

Prayer: *Do you have a healthy dose of godly fear, or do you think of God as only a "buddy"? If you have not thought of God in this way, ask Him to show you what it means to fear Him. Because of God's vast power and justice, He has great love for you.*

Personal Reflection: ....

....

....

....

....

....

The Foolish Woman

Proverbs 9:13–18

"A foolish woman is clamorous;
She is simple, and knows nothing." (v. 13)

Our time has been focusing on the traits of wisdom and how to gain understanding. Today, let's shift the focus. Proverbs 9 is an invitation from two opposing characters: Lady Folly and Lady Wisdom. Today's passage calls out the foolish woman and reveals her true nature.

A modern-day translation of this verse could read: "A stupid woman is loud, obnoxious, naïve, and does not know anything." Two characteristics are given to Woman Folly. The first characteristic describes her as being loud and obnoxious. She can also be described as someone who causes an uproar wherever she goes. You see her coming and cringe for fear of what she will say or do. American society praises women who act this way. Music and movies often idolize women who throw off what they conceive as patriarchal restraints, speak their minds, and put others in what they perceive as their rightful places. Admittedly, there is something tempting and even fleshly attractive about asserting power, but these attitudes and actions are far from how God desires His daughters to live. Instead, women should possess the "incorruptible beauty of a gentle and quiet spirit, which is very precious in the sight of God" (1 Pet. 3:4). This verse does not suggest that you should allow others to take advantage of you. This assumption is far from the truth. You can be a strong woman of valor and also treat others with respect and kindness. A godly woman relies on the Lord, and not on worldly validation, as the source of her strength.

A foolish woman is also naïve and stupid. This trait speaks nothing of her intelligence but refers to her heart's attitude. According to Scripture, you can hold a Ph.D. from an Ivy League school and still be described as a naïve woman. The opposite is also true. You can barely have a high school diploma yet be

known as the wisest woman at your church. Scripture says: "The LORD does not see as man sees; for man looks at the outward appearance, but the LORD looks at the heart" (1 Sam. 16:7).

Is your heart turned toward the Lord and His ways, or is it turned towards worldly endeavors? God made you for fellowship with Him and to be an example of hope and salvation to those whom you encounter. If you continue to insist on your own way, then your life will never mirror the heart of Christ. Accept the challenge to be a woman known for her wisdom and courage instead of her boisterous naiveté.

Amanda Walker

Prayer: *Would God describe you as a woman of wisdom or a woman of folly? Ask the Lord to show you what it means to be a woman of quiet courage and wisdom instead of boisterous naiveté. And then thank Him for giving you tenacity, and ask Him to help you use it for His glory instead of your own.*

Personal Reflection: ....

....

....

....

....

....

Love Her Anyway

Proverbs 10:1–12

"Hatred stirs up strife,
But love covers all sins." (v. 12)

Have you ever been around someone who seems constantly to stir up trouble? I think we all have experienced people who find great pleasure in causing division, casting doubt, and pinning one friend against another. Such an individual is exhausting to be around and even more difficult to control, especially when she is flesh and blood. You dread the holidays because you know she will be there and will have nothing good to say. The moment she enters the house, her insults, innuendos, and arguments begin. It is easier to avoid her than become another target for her fiery darts. Therefore, you sit in a corner, with your arms crossed, and roll your eyes the instant she begins to speak. But, as a Jesus-follower, is that how you are to handle a contentious person? How should you respond?

The answer is love. I realize this sounds mundane and simple, but love is the model God gives us. As humans, prone to pride and righteous indignation, the natural response is to take up for yourself. The hair on the back of your neck bristles; you sit straighter; and you bear down for a fight. There is just one problem. You play right into the schemes of such trouble-makers. They enjoy fighting and discord; it comes naturally. However, a contentious person rarely knows how to respond to genuine, godly love. She has become so conditioned to people reacting out of anger that a response of love throws her off balance.

God reminds us that "love suffers long and is kind; love does not envy; love does not parade itself, is not puffed up; does not behave rudely, does not seek its own, is not provoked, thinks no evil" (1 Cor. 13:4–5). When faced with a divisive person, Scripture says that we should respond with forgiveness instead of spite, pointing that person to Christ instead of focusing on our own self-righteousness. We should be patient with her and respond with a kind word instead of more insults or with sarcasm. Is this easy? Absolutely not! But, God never called us to an easy task.

Living and responding differently does not come naturally to us, and God knows this fact. Therefore, He promises to love the unlovable through us. Praise God, we do not have to do it alone. Actually, apart from the Holy Spirit living in us, we cannot show love in the midst of strife. But, God can. So, the next time you are with a group of friends or at a family gathering and *that* person enters, stand firm and love her anyway.

Amanda Walker

Prayer: *Ask God to fill your heart with love and compassion for the person who brings you the most frustration. If you have responded to her out of sarcasm instead of love, ask her for forgiveness and then commit to love her anyway. Be a person of peace.*

Personal Reflection: ....

....

....

....

....

....

Don't Be a "Bridge Jumper"

Proverbs 10:13–18

"He who keeps instruction is in the way of life,
But he who refuses correction goes astray." (v. 17)

My middle child Hannah is a natural follower; whereas her older sister is a cautious leader. Countless times I have wanted to ask Hannah, "So, if your friend jumped off a bridge, would you?" To be honest with you, I am a little afraid of her answer. Her number one goal in life is to have fun, which brings great joy and, at times, much difficulty. However, the same question could be asked of many of us. This proverb reminds me of us "would-be bridge jumpers."

Solomon commends the one "who keeps instruction" (v. 17). The picture is one of a guard protecting what is important to him. A guard normally stands with his body erect and his eyes facing forward, not easily distracted by the activity around him. He may appear statuesque, but he is keenly aware of everything going on around him. However, we are often sidetracked by the temptations of Satan. In reality, I know more truth than I actually obey. I know that God tells me to "love my neighbor" (Luke 10:27), but I do not want to sacrifice my time and emotional energy actually to show her love. I know Scripture tells me not to covet my friend's property (Rom. 13:9), but I want her nicer car, house, and clothes. The examples are endless.

The problem is that we do not protect our hearts from the temptations that can and do ensnare us. We jump on the bandwagon of busyness instead of slowing down, prioritizing our own lives rather than looking for opportunities to serve and love others. Some jump off the bridge known as *materialism*. Though all needs are met, they are dissatisfied with what the Lord has provided. They are not living in the fullness and freedom that Jesus died to give because they are focused on material things instead of spiritual realities. It is time to turn our hearts back toward the instruction God has given.

The second part of this verse says that turning away from instruction is to turn toward the path of destruction. To go *astray* means to wander off the clear path, which leads to eternal life, and stagger into what is unknown. Sure, "off-roading journeys" look adventuresome, but they are normally full of pit-falls and calamity. God, in His Word, has given you everything you need to live a life of contentment, fruitfulness, and godliness. Are you willing to heed His instruction? Ladies, we must stop this unholy obsession with "bridge jump-ing," for it will lead you to destruction.

Amanda Walker

Prayer: *Has God convicted you of being a "bridge jumper"? If so, confess to Him that you have wandered away from His instruction and then come back under His control. He is waiting with arms ready to receive you.*

Personal Reflection: ....

....

....

....

....

....

Holding Your Tongue

Proverbs 10:19–21

"In the multitude of words sin is not lacking,
But who restrains his lips is wise." (v. 19)

If you are known as a "talker," please raise your hand. Whew! I feel better knowing I am among friends. This verse is one of the most convicting ones for me. I love to talk, and no one has to be present in order for me to have a conversation. (Just ask my husband.) But, Solomon gives a warning I would like to explore.

If you are familiar with the story of Job, then you know that he was a righteous man who had everything—wife, children, land, and wealth. However, Satan was convinced that Job's righteousness was based solely on his external blessings. He asked God if he could test Job. God gave the permission, and everything, excluding his wife and his own life, was taken away. Upon hearing this news, Job's friends came and "sat down with him on the ground seven days and seven nights, and no one spoke a word to him, for they saw that his grief was very great" (Job 2:13). In this moment, Job's best friends modeled restraint and wisdom. Ladies, there are times when all a person needs from you is your presence. She needs you to sit with her and quietly intercede for her. Our problem, much like Job's friends, comes when we open our mouths.

After seven days, the men began to speak, blaming Job for his calamity. They accused him of not being a righteous man and relentlessly asked him to confess his sin to the Lord. But, Job had nothing to confess. Therefore, God's anger burned against the men, and He told them to have Job pray on their behalf (Job 42:7–9). As a pastor's wife, I often have women who want me to listen to them. At times, their stories are so complex and heart-wrenching that my first instinct is to fix them. I know the Lord has an answer for their hurting hearts, and I want to be the one to give them hope. Oftentimes, I run ahead of God's counsel and seek to give them good advice using soothing words as a

balm for their tattered souls. What is the result? They leave feeling unheard, more hurt, and even more confused about what God is trying to say or do in their lives.

God did not give you a tongue to use as you please. Instead, it should be used as an instrument for His glory. An unsanctified tongue is full of all kinds of evil. But, praise God, a mouth that has been given over to the Lord can be used to bring healing, restore hope, give encouragement, and proclaim the gospel of Christ (James 3:1–12). Lay your tongue on the altar of God's grace to be used by Him.

Amanda Walker

Prayer: *Ask the Lord to sanctify your tongue and give you words of wisdom and not death.*

Personal Reflection:

495

Choosing Righteousness

Proverbs 10:22–26

"When the whirlwind passes by, the wicked is no more,
But the righteous has an everlasting foundation." (v. 25)

Have you ever wondered why nothing bad ever seems to happen to those who choose sinfulness over righteousness? I have certainly had that thought! When I was in high school, many of my friends decided to enter the party scene. They began drinking alcohol (a lot) and engaging in premarital sex. The more they partied, the more popularity and dates they seemed to gain. Though I was not yet a Christian, I had a "holy fear" of my parents, which caused me to refrain from many of those bad choices. It did not seem fair that my "good" choices did not result in immediate blessings. However, soon after God captured my heart for Him, I saw the harsh reality of their situations.

Whirlwinds come in all forms. Whirlwinds can be financial distress, illness, wayward children, infertility, and broken relationships. Scripture is also clear that both the righteous and the unrighteous will eventually experience seasons of pain and unrelenting temptation. This verse gives a stark warning to those who choose to "do life" on their own. They will not be able to stand. I have watched as former friends have gotten married, started families, and enjoyed life. When the whirlwinds of life hit, they were not prepared. Without a relationship with Christ, they had no one to bring peace to their aching souls. It was devastating to watch their lives spin out of control as they refused to turn to the One who could bring them hope and stability. But, this story does not have to be yours.

Hannah was a righteous woman who felt the pain and stigma of infertility. Her pain would be doubled because her husband's second wife seemed to have no problem bearing children. Scripture says: "Year by year, when she [Hannah] went up to the house of the LORD, that she [Peninnah] provoked her; therefore

496

she wept and did not eat" (1 Sam. 1:7). Can you imagine being ridiculed and shamed in your own home? There was no outward peace for Hannah. However, instead of retaliation, she turned her request to God. She begged Him to give her a son, and then she waited.

Note how Scripture describes Hannah. After pouring out her heart to God she "went her way and ate, and her face was no longer sad" (v. 18). Months later she gave birth to Samuel, who became one of the greatest prophets in Israel (1 Sam. 3:19–20). Though she went through years of ridicule and pain, she never lost faith in God as her firm foundation. As a result, God blessed her far beyond her wildest dreams.

Amanda Walker

Prayer: *Are you in the middle of a whirlwind right now? Ask the Lord to give you courage to continue to put your hope and trust in Him. Do not lose heart! God is still in control!*

Personal Reflection: ....

....

....

....

....

....

The Fountain of Youth

Proverbs 10:27–32

"The fear of the Lord prolongs days,
But the years of the wicked will be shortened." (v. 27)

God promises blessings to the righteous. He says they will experience longevity (v. 27), gladness (v. 28), protection (v. 29), and an inheritance (v. 30). However, the unrighteous will experience a shortened life, failed expectations, destruction, and no inheritance. Moses set before the Israelites two paths: "I have set before you life and death, blessing and cursing; therefore choose life, that both you and your descendants may live" (Deut. 30:19). He goes on to tell them that if they choose life, then their days will be lengthened, and they will live in the promised land. But, if they choose to be disobedient, then they will be given over to foreign enemies. God offers to you the same choice—obedience and blessings or disobedience and consequences.

Several passages compare the wicked to the righteous. In every instance, God has shown that the wicked will eventually come to ruin. In the moment, the unrighteous may seem to have things together. But, underneath their façade they are in complete turmoil. A person apart from Christ is empty, depressed, hopeless, and hurting. If this describes you, however, there is hope.

"For God so loved the world [that includes you] that He gave His only begotten Son [Jesus], that whoever [including you] believes in Him should not perish [spend eternity separated from God] but have everlasting life [a home in heaven for all eternity]" (John 3:16). If you are not a follower of Jesus, I pray you realize that, apart from a relationship with Jesus, you are eternally dead in your sin (Rom. 6:20–23). No amount of doing good or righteous living can terminate your guilt. The penalty of your sin and my sin is that we deserve death and hell. The only way we can find forgiveness and total freedom is to confess our sins

498

to the Lord, repent of that sin, and then turn and choose life, which is found in Christ (Rom. 10:9–11).

Do you want to know the secret to the fountain of youth? Proverbs 10:27 gives the answer: Fear God and trust in Him. Undoubtedly, godly people may die at an early age, and some ungodly people live past 100 years. Those who choose the path of life have eternity in heaven awaiting them. Scripture describes heaven as a real place where there is no more death, tears, or heartache. Instead, God takes His righteous hand and makes all things new (Rev. 21:4–5). In light of eternity, I think I can endure a few more lonely days, painful circumstances, and uninvited hardships on earth. No amount of earthly pleasure is worth trading for the eternal glory of being with Jesus.

Amanda Walker

Prayer: *If you are not a Jesus-follower, I urge you to confess your sin, repent of that sin, and choose to follow Christ. He is so worth it!*

Personal Reflection: ....

....

....

....

....

....

The Wisdom of Humility

Proverbs 11:1–6

"When pride comes, then comes shame;
But with the humble is wisdom." (v. 2)

When I was in grade school, I saw a pair of glasses that changed one's entire depth perception. I watched as a fellow student comically attempted to take a few steps across a flat surface but looked as though he was about to lose his balance! Because the glasses had altered his vision, he was not able to see reality clearly. When you and I take on attitudes of pride, it is a little bit like looking through those glasses. We do not see life as it really is. Our perception does not align with the truth. What we believe about God, ourselves, the world, and even sin is out of focus.

Throughout Scripture, pride is described as deeply offensive to the Lord. The Lord detests a proud heart (Prov. 16:5). Pride led Satan to rebel against the Lord and oppose His authority (Is. 14:12–15). Pride led Adam and Eve to disbelieve God's character and disobey His command (Gen. 3). Pride led King David to commit adultery and then try to cover it up with murder (2 Sam. 11).

What is pride? At its core, pride is making much of yourself and less of God. It is an attitude that fails to acknowledge the Lord as your Creator and source of your being. We express pride in a myriad of ways, including arrogance, self-pity, self-righteousness, self-reliance, comparison, competition, and even people-pleasing. Each of these attitudes has one, simple thing in common: a focus on yourself!

Pride may have a devastating effect on our lives. A proud heart leads us to sin (Prov. 21:4). God wants to protect us from the downfall of prideful choices. Because He loves us and we are His children, God will not ignore patterns of pride in our lives. Instead, He will lovingly discipline us (Heb. 12:1–17).

Today's verse describes an attitude of pride, which never yields its desired result (Prov. 11:2). In fact, when you are prideful, you are headed for a foolish choice. After all, your perspective is distorted! Scripture notes that humility receives honor from the Lord. The woman with a humble heart will also have a right fear of the Lord, since she will see God as He truly is. The humble heart that fears the Lord will have God's wisdom (9:10).

Thankfully, God gives you a pattern of humility to follow: the life of Jesus. Jesus was God in the flesh. He did not consider His deity something to hang onto but made Himself nothing for our sakes. You are to have this same mind (Phil. 2:5–11). If you want to be lifted up by the Lord, you must learn the wisdom of humility. Then, by humility, you will find wisdom.

Katie McCoy

Prayer: *Ask the Lord to protect you from pride. Allow Him to teach you the wisdom of humility so that you may be truly wise.*

Personal Reflection:

Wandering Words

Proverbs 11:7–13

*"A talebearer reveals secrets,
But he who is of a faithful spirit conceals a matter." (v. 13)*

Are you a trustworthy woman, or do you reveal information that is not yours to share? Would it surprise you to know that the condition of your speech reflects the condition of your heart?

This focal verse highlights the difference between a faithful and an unfaithful person. The Hebrew word for *talebearer* is derived from the same word translated as *walk*, as in reference to a wanderer or a wayfarer. A talebearer has a similar spirit as a person who wanders, someone who cannot be depended upon to stay where she belongs. Perhaps you have met this kind of person, one who seems to wander throughout a family or a church and in the process reveals someone else's sensitive information. Such a person is undisciplined and unreliable or, as today's verse implies, unfaithful.

By contrast, the woman who is trustworthy with confidential information is considered faithful. She can be counted upon not to expose someone to embarrassment. She will not make a matter worse by sharing a secret. Both faithfulness and self-control are among the fruit of the Spirit and are marks of Christian maturity (Gal. 5:22–23). When we are faithful not to reveal that which is sensitive or confidential and practice self-control over our words, we are walking under the control of the Holy Spirit. Such a person can be trusted to act in the interest of others.

Discretion with information is not merely about our words. Our speech is connected to our spirit. Jesus said that our mouths speak what is from the overflow of our hearts (Matt. 12:34). Bringing your speech under God's control signifies that the rest of your body is under God's control (James 3:2). "No man can tame the tongue" (James 3:8). How true! Only the work of the Holy Spirit

can make you faithful and self-controlled in your speech! Truly, whether or not you are trustworthy in your words is a spiritual issue.

Proverbs 25:19 describes confidence in an unfaithful person in a difficult time as being like "a bad tooth and a foot out of joint," which hinder your progress and make things worse! Can you be trusted with someone's sensitive information? Do you want others to know what you know, or are you content as a faithful confidant?

Ask the Lord to make you a trustworthy woman, someone who is faithful not to reveal that which is confidential and who will speak and act with discretion. Remember, it is not just about your words; it is actually about your heart!

Katie McCoy

Prayer: *Do you desire to have a faithful spirit? Pray that you will be a woman whom others can trust. Ask the Lord to convict you the moment you begin to wander into sharing what you should conceal or revealing something about which you should simply remain quiet.*

Personal Reflection: ....

....

....

....

....

The Wisdom of Godly Counsel

Proverbs 11:14–15

"Where there is no counsel, the people fall;
But in the multitude of counselors there is safety." (v. 14)

Who are your advisors in life decisions? Upon whose counsel do you rely? Every woman needs at least a handful of people whom she trusts to give her wise insights.

One particular person in the Bible chose not to rely on trustworthy counsel, and the result was ruinous. King Solomon's son Rehoboam had just inherited his father's throne (1 Kin. 12). The new ruler decided to assert his power by demanding more from the nation's labor force. His father's advisors, men who helped Solomon rule with peace, strongly warned against the decision. In fact, they told Rehoboam that he had an opportunity to win the loyalty of the laborers by showing them kindness. But instead of following their advice, Rehoboam relied on friends whose perspectives were like his own. He only listened to people who told him what he wanted to hear. As a result, Rehoboam lost his kingdom.

God often confirms His will for our lives through other people. Listening to godly counsel is a mark of maturity and wisdom. Neglecting to consider the advice of others leads to hasty, foolish choices. God's wisdom is that we can avoid missteps if we have a multitude of counselors (Prov. 11:14).

How do you know whether or not someone has wise counsel? What are some qualities and characteristics to consider? First and foremost, your advisor should be someone who walks with the Lord. She should be a person of integrity and godliness in all areas of her life—family, occupation, speech, etc. Her Christian life should reflect godly virtues.

Also, your advisor should be someone who demonstrates the fruit of the Spirit and the fear of the Lord. A woman characterized by the wisdom of

meekness will be a strong, godly advisor (James 3:13); a woman known for having a reverent fear of the Lord will be a trustworthy source of wisdom (Prov. 9:10). Further, your advisor should be a woman who relies on God's Word in her own decision-making rather than on her emotions. If you ask her a question and she answers with Scripture, that is a sign of a godly advisor!

Finally, great wisdom is exhibited in finding advisors whose perspectives are different from your own. Just like the foolish king Rehoboam, you can easily fall into a pattern of consulting only those people who see things as you do. Finding an older, godly woman is valuable (Titus 2:3–5)! She will often consider questions you did not even know you needed to ask. She may have a depth of insight that comes from having lived through the very situation you are experiencing!

Katie McCoy

Prayer: *Ask the Lord to bring wise counsel into your life and thank Him for the people He has used to guide you in His will. Allow Him to teach you the wisdom of relying on godly counsel and protect you from trusting your own perspective.*

Personal Reflection: ....

....

....

....

....

The Power of a Gracious Woman

Proverbs 11:16–21

"A gracious woman retains honor,
But ruthless men retain riches." (v. 16)

Humanitarian and Nobel Peace Prize recipient, Mother Teresa, once said, "Kind words can be short and easy to speak, but their echoes are truly endless." In her eighty-seven years of life, she ministered to the poorest of India's poor, including the lepers and the homeless. Mother Teresa was known for being a gracious woman.

Graciousness is becoming a lost art. Being gracious requires inner strength and self-control. A gracious woman builds others up. She is invested in others and focuses her attention on them, rather than on herself. She avoids embarrassing others with her words or actions. Like the Proverbs 31 woman, she has the law of kindness on her tongue (v. 26).

God has a gracious spirit toward His children. Of course, we see God's grace through the death of Jesus on the cross for our sins. But He also has an attitude of grace—He is kind, loving, and compassionate. The gracious woman reflects this attribute of God to others when she chooses a gracious heart.

Many times, graciousness is not valued in our culture. Often, the world's value system sends a message that we will acquire a position of honor through everything but giving others grace. If a woman wants to advance in her career, she is often encouraged to cut others down or to be aggressive and harsh. Ironically, many women believe that finding a place of respect happens when they take on characteristically masculine attributes. In other words, sometimes women attempt to find honor by acting like men.

This proverb is likely one that draws a comparison, explaining that a gracious woman will retain honor just as ruthless men retain riches. The verse describes how certain it is that a woman known for her graciousness will hold

on to her honor. The broad claim made by this verse goes against worldly wisdom. A woman will receive honor not through being belligerent or hard but by being tender and gracious.

Notice the detail describing the position of the gracious woman. She *retains* honor. You may look around and feel as though this verse fails to live up to reality. Perhaps people who live in direct opposition to God's Word are apparently getting ahead. But the proverb does not merely describe how a woman finds honor but how she holds onto it. You must choose whose value system you are going to allow to guide your life.

Would the people closest to you describe you as a gracious woman? Are you known for words of kindness? If you want to be a woman of honor, well into your senior years, you must cultivate a gracious spirit. Become a woman who is known for her kindness and whose legacy of graciousness endures!

Katie McCoy

Prayer: *Ask the Lord to help you become a gracious woman and teach you to be like Him. He can make you a woman who is known for kindness and grace.*

Personal Reflection: ....

....

....

....

....

507

The Beauty of Discretion

Proverbs 11:22–31

"As a ring of gold in a swine's snout,
So is a lovely woman who lacks discretion." (v. 22)

How's *that* for a word picture?! I am quite sure that none of us would want to be described as a well-accessorized pig; yet that is the image Scripture uses to describe an outwardly beautiful woman who is indiscreet.

Cultivating the virtue of discretion has become a lost art among women today. What is discretion, and how can you develop it? To be discrete is also to be modest; it means to avoid drawing attention to yourself. When a woman is discrete, she can be relied upon to speak and act appropriately, to guard sensitive information, and to respect others. Discretion also avoids giving offense through your words or actions. She is prudent and wise. The woman of discretion is self-controlled, trustworthy, dignified, and diplomatic.

Abigail was a woman of great discretion (1 Sam. 25). When her foolish husband Nabal (his name literally means "fool") offended David, the future king, she and her whole household were at risk of his retaliation. When Abigail received word that David was coming to exact revenge upon Nabal, she intervened. She involved only those people who were needed for the solution, wisely concealing the matter from her foolish husband. Abigail acted with wise diplomacy and spoke well-chosen words. She diffused David's hot temper with grace and dignity. As a result, Abigail received honor; when her husband Nabal died, David took her as his wife. This future king of Israel recognized the value of a woman of discretion!

According to this proverb, a woman can have a lovely appearance but still lack discretion. She can have the right look, yet not have the right spirit. A beautiful woman without discretion is as incongruent as a pig wearing a gold ring in its nose—the two just do not go together! Elsewhere Scripture talks

about the value of a woman with "a gentle and quiet spirit" (1 Pet. 3:3–4). Rather than being known only for her outward beauty, the woman of God must also be known for her inner beauty, which is expressed through her virtues and exemplified with a spirit of discretion.

Would others consider you to be a discreet woman? Can you be trusted with sensitive information, or do you lack prudence? Do your habits of speech, dress, and conduct display discretion, or do you draw attention to yourself? If you find that discretion is a virtue you need to cultivate, start with the motivations of your heart. Ask the Lord to give you a tender heart, to change what you value, and to teach you self-control. No matter what your age or appearance, you, too, can cultivate the elegance of discretion.

Katie McCoy

Prayer: *Do you find it easy to become wrapped up in your outward appearance and neglect cultivating the virtue of discretion? Ask the Lord to keep you from emphasizing external beauty at the expense of your internal character. Seek to become a woman like Abigail, a trustworthy and dignified woman of discretion.*

Personal Reflection: ....

....

....

....

....

See Him; Hear Him

Proverbs 12:1–3

"Whoever loves instruction loves knowledge,
But he who hates correction is stupid." (v. 1)

At the moment of my writing, a mother with her daughter is sitting next to me. Her daughter is starving for attention, talking to her mother with no reply, calling her name, patting her knee, and even running across the entire room. I want to grab the mother's cell phone and tell her to look up, acknowledge her daughter, and *give her some attention*! I glanced at the little girl, trying to get her attention. "I see you," I am saying as I wave at her and she sneaks a peak around the corner. "I hear you," I am saying. Then, as the mother ends her phone-texting and Instagram-viewing, she gathers her child and leaves.

How many times have you been distracted like this mother? Maybe you are preoccupied for good reason, but still, you are distracted. Often you can miss guidance from others, direction from an unbiased outsider who can see a need, or even correction of a behavior you had not recognized as sin. On the flip side, you may relate to the little girl, who was hungry for instruction, awareness, and assurance from her mother. You fight against the grain and try not to be conformed to the world or the ways of ungodly people. Perhaps Jesus is saying, "I see you" and "I hear you"; but often we miss that still small voice. God is always ready to point you in the right direction, ready to provide friends who can invest in your life, soften your heart, and love you through the tough correction He must give. But you must see Him and hear Him!

This verse reminds the reader to love instruction and knowledge. The source of wise instruction and knowledge is God and His Word. When a child of God rejects His teachings, God must discipline the disciple. While correction is despised by most people, it is necessary for personal growth and spiritual maturity. "No chastening [discipline] seems to be joyful for the present, but painful;

nevertheless, afterward it yields the peaceable fruit of righteousness to those who have been trained by it" (Heb. 12:11). Children of God should seek to learn from Him and accept correction when needed.

Maggie Carter

Prayer: *Ask the Lord to slow you down and listen to the instructions from His Word. Be quick to listen and slow to speak. Accept instruction from the Lord and from those whom He places in your life to guide and lead you in His truth. Be aware of times when you are stubborn, rejecting His direction.*

Personal Reflection: ....

....

....

....

....

....

....

The Excellent Wife

Proverbs 12:4–9

*"An excellent wife is the crown of her husband,
But she who causes shame is like rottenness in his bones." (v. 4)*

A godly woman is rare and very hard to find. Your friends or even family members may lack godly virtues. You may not always be that "excellent" woman described here. An excellent wife, by God's standards, describes a woman of virtue, strength, vigor, wisdom, prudence, modesty, and diligence. Although this description may sound intimidating, God has written out the measurements for this unique woman clearly. He gives a path to guide our steps. In marriage, if a wife steps outside God's boundaries, she can hurt her witness as well as her husband. Marriage is to represent the relationship between Christ and His church (Eph. 5:22–24). If couples are daily growing in their relationship with Jesus and striving to honor God, these characteristics will grow and overflow into their marriages.

Marriage is a beautiful but challenging journey. It is real, and it can be raw. Marriage should not be built on expectations but on selflessness and sacrifice, on honesty and service. Some wives find it hard to serve their husbands selflessly. They may find it difficult to stay quiet or not express their opinions. If you are like me, you want to react instead of respond. Here, a wife's shame is described as "rottenness in his bones" (Prov. 12:4), which suggests that you are slowly killing your husband. This is not giving grace as Jesus does for you daily. Grace is needed in marriage!

Marriage is a gift from God. When your life honors the Lord, He can work things out for the good of those who love Him. God, in all His grace and glory, can change your heart, your mind, and even your mouth so that you honor Him. And, as you honor Him in all things, grace overflows into your marriage.

Be a woman of excellence, a virtuous wife who is the crown of her husband. Do not cause him shame or weaken him. The character of a wife will make or break her husband.

Maggie Carter

Prayer: *Allow the Lord to strengthen you daily so that you honor Him in all things, especially in your marriage. Ask Him to grow in you a heart of encouragement and support and pray for your husband (or future husband) daily. See your husband through the lens with which God sees him. Love and cherish him as you grow in grace.*

Personal Reflection: ....

....

....

....

....

....

....

Sin's Deception

Proverbs 12:10–14

"A righteous man regards the life of his animal,
But the tender mercies of the wicked are cruel." (v. 10)

During my college years, I naively moved into an apartment with a girl I had never met. Soon after this move, she and I developed a friendship for which I will forever be thankful. Whitney was not a follower of Christ when we first met. We had many nights of "faith talks" and "Jesus questions," which helped me grow and stretch my love for God and my ability to defend my faith. Her unbelief taught me more about my belief, challenged my faith harder than ever before, and prepared me for a life of ministry that I never saw coming. Whitney surrendered her life to Christ four years later. Whitney and I were cities apart; and through a handwritten letter, she declared her love and faith for Jesus in a way I had never experienced.

To this day, I remember the phrases she shared with me as she was seeking God in those college days. After talking about sin one night, Whitney expressed her despair: "I didn't ask for that—to be separated from God. That's not fair." What a good point! The reality is that we are separated from God by our depravity whether or not we think that is fair. A surrender of self was needed for the new life she was seeking.

You and I as Christians can easily be just like my lost college roommate, innocently justifying our hearts' desires and sometimes even our sin. Yet, God has promised His people forgiveness, new life, a future, and a hope. God's people can experience true joy even through the smallest things in life. On the other hand, no matter how tender the mercies of those who are not His children, they are still considered wicked.

King Solomon is emphasizing this same reality; no matter how "good" a person tries to be, no matter how "right" the person believes she is, the wicked

still are lost, broken, separated and in need of a Savior (v. 10). Does this sound fair? No, but God, by His grace, has given you the good news of His victory over the unwanted depravity of sin. In His righteousness, God can give you righteousness.

Paul declares, "There is therefore now no condemnation to those who are in Christ Jesus" (Rom. 8:1). By the blood of Jesus, we can be healed and made new in salvation. The Good News of Jesus Christ is truth, and He promises that this truth will set you free (John 8:32). While sin deceives, His grace abounds!

Maggie Carter

Prayer: *Surrender to the Lord. Lay down your pride; let go of yourself; and fully trust in Him today.*

Personal Reflection: ....

....

....

....

....

....

....

Playing with Fire

Proverbs 12:15–16

"The way of a fool is right in his own eyes,
But he who heeds counsel is wise." (v. 15)

My nephew is one for the books! He is the cutest and most innocent little boy I know, but he is innocent to the point of his own detriment. Just the other day, he was sitting around the fire pit with me and a few family members. His adult uncle thought it would be fun to wave his hand through the fire. While doing this quickly, the adult was unharmed. The children thought it was magic! My little nephew stared with eyes wide open, slowly standing to take his try at the act. Thankfully, his uncle was watching him carefully and explained how he accomplished this feat. He advised the little one to wait until he had bigger, quicker hands. The difference between my nephew and his uncle was the measure of knowledge. My nephew needed instruction to learn how to protect his little hands.

Many people are at times naïve like my nephew. In ignorance, we may be mesmerized and, yet, blindsided by this world. We are often attracted by this world, other people, circumstances and expectations so that we sit too long mesmerized, wide-eyed at something or someone who could lead us down an undesirable path. We all have a lack of wisdom, but God tells His children to ask for it (James 1:5).

Even in the midst of God's amazing gift of life, we must be aware that the enemy Satan is out to steal, kill, and destroy (John 10:10). Yet, God does not expect His children to walk through life filled with fear and anxiety, as if we are in a jungle on the lookout for a lion (2 Tim. 1:7). Satan is seeking to destroy us. We are to grow in the counsel of the Lord by understanding His promises and heeding the cautions presented in His Word, the Bible (Eph. 1:7), and through the godly, wise counsel of others (Prov. 19:20). Share in the riches that are

516

found in Christian brothers and sisters who counsel you in the Lord. Take care to align their advice and wisdom with God's Word. Then, count yourself safe from the enemy who tempts you to play with fire.

Maggie Carter

Prayer: *Listen to the advice and wisdom found in God's Word and through the wise counsel of other believers with pure and gracious hearts. Gain wisdom and glorify the Lord.*

Personal Reflection: ....

....

....

....

....

....

....

....

....

....

....

Piercing Perceptions

Proverbs 12:17–18

"There is one who speaks like the piercings of a sword,
But the tongue of the wise promotes health." (v. 18)

I will never forget the peace and joy I felt the moment I followed Christ. Nothing could diminish my joy, until I noticed a note that was left on my car one day. The note was filled with lies about not only my new life in Christ but also my personality, my appearance, and my future. I would soon find out that this was written by one of my closest friends who, at the time, resented my conversion to Christianity and responded to it with jealousy. Though nothing ever stole my joy, what I was "feeling" about my new life in Christ was quickly overcast by hurtful words of accusations and perceptions. What I did not realize then and now know is the difference between **feeling** new life and **knowing** this new life.

Feelings are inconsistent; they are not always your best friend and can be deceitful at times. What I learned then and continue to experience each day, is that my strength is found in the knowledge and understanding of who Jesus is in my life and what I am now to Him! Many of you can relate! It is easy to view our value through the piercing perceptions of others. Remember this next time you react rashly instead of responding wisely to someone's criticism. Reacting with a rash, hasty, unconscious word can harm the toughest heart, defame the purest intention, and cause the deepest wound. Discipline is required to control our tongues (James 3:1–12).

Words from the wise lead to the polar opposite responses of those already mentioned. Words of wisdom remind you of God's rich promises. In wisdom you can find truth, and the truth can set you free (John 8:32). Bring life to those around you by imparting wisdom in your speech. Do not conform to untrue words others speak to you, and do not respond quickly to the rashness of another's speech. Remember the truths of God and the value He has placed

on you. He gave His own life for you, and you are worth His life. Do not allow ignorant words of others or their piercing perceptions to define you. Respond and rest in God's wisdom.

Maggie Carter

Prayer: *Ask the Lord to help you control your tongue and respond wisely to others. Forgive those who have hurt you with their words, and allow the Lord to use His wisdom to guard you from the attacks of others.*

Personal Reflection: ....

....

....

....

....

....

....

....

Freedom in the Tongue

Proverbs 12:19–21

*"The truthful lip shall be established forever,
But a lying tongue is but for a moment." (v. 19)*

As I watch my nieces and nephew grow up, I realize how fast time flies. The moments I have enjoyed being their aunt seem to pass by quicker than I could imagine. The hugs, the kisses, the laughs, and even the cries are all precious to me. But there are also moments of correction that are difficult and bring twinkling eyes of disappointment. All children fight and fuss, picking on one another; they do not realize how deeply they hurt or harm their peers. Ladies, sometimes we are much like quarreling children. We find ourselves swinging, crying, fighting, and fussing with our words. We may attack our spouses, our friends, and even our family members, who tend to be the easiest to hurt. We may act behind closed doors or through a whisper to your co-worker in a "venting" session. Shamefully, we have all been there; but we do not have to stay there—in a critical mode.

Our choice of words determines our nature. Are we authentic or fake? They can affect the emotions, bring about unity, or cause division. One thing is true: our words can and will be judged. God has called His people to represent Him with the truths of His character through our love for one another (John 13:35). Have you shown love to those to whom you have spoken lately? Have you made sure your words are true? Loving words can make a lasting impression on others.

Every heart desires freedom from the effects of hate, sin, and pain. Much more than your actions, your words can either create the deepest wound or bring the greatest joy. On the contrary, the lying tongue is what, in just a moment, can bring division, hurt, bondage, and shame. The lying tongue can "ensnare" a person (Prov. 12:13). Yet, God has bigger and better plans for you.

520

Allow the truth to flow from your tongue through the words that you speak to others.

Maggie Carter

Prayer: *Ask the Lord help you to be "slow to speak" (James 1:19). Renew your commitment to think before you speak so that you may speak words of truth and grace. Speak with love to those who are the hardest to love.*

Personal Reflection: ....

....

....

....

....

....

....

....

....

....

Run to the Lord

Proverbs 12:22–24

"Lying lips are an abomination to the LORD,
But those who deal truthfully are His delight." (v. 22)

How discouraging to realize that a person about whom you care very much is being dishonest. A few years ago, the Lord had allowed a friendship to bud into a cherished relationship. As our friendship grew deeper, we began talking about the possibility of marriage. The sweet moments and fun times were happening often and were so enjoyable that I felt like a child trying to gather all the fall leaves in a pile, yet failing to grasp them all. In the midst of this exciting moment, I discovered a lie. In his life, there was someone else who had been there for a few months. His heart for me was waning, and he was quickly becoming just a friend again. Looking back, I am thankful for that journey and friendship. I am beyond blessed to see how God allowed me and my friend to have our own families.

Can you imagine the magnitude of pain we cause God to experience when we lie to Him? We praise His name, ask for His assistance, and pray for selfish wishes and God-sized miracles, while holding in the other hand personal sin. It may be alcohol, a friend, a boyfriend or girlfriend, an expectation in life, an affirmation, hard work, or anything in our lives we put above God. He desires our hearts and everything we have. He despises the fake façade of selfishly clinging to things of eternal insignificance while professing to trust and love only Him. If you have committed yourself to Him with all your heart and therefore claim to be His daughter, then let go of what you are pursuing for comfort, and rest in the provision of your King. Your surrender is what brings Him true delight.

This proverb is a powerful reminder of the hurt God feels when His children lie to Him and rebel against His commands. If you confess your sins, "He is faithful and just to forgive" you and cleanse you "from all unrighteousness"

(1 John 1:9). When you seek forgiveness for lying to the Lord, who loves you, you should commit to truthfulness. Your truthful words of devotion and honest lives of holiness are God's greatest delight (Prov. 12:22).

Maggie Carter

Prayer: *Run to the Lord when you question your value and purpose in life. Keep your eyes focused on Him and the truth of His Word. Keep your mind on things of the Lord as you journey through life with grace.*

Personal Reflection: ....

....

....

....

....

....

....

Unnecessary Deception

Proverbs 12:25–28

*"Anxiety in the heart of man causes depression,
But a good word makes it glad." (v. 25)*

Organizing trips can cause nightmares! You worry about choosing the right hotel that everyone will like, the right restaurant that all will enjoy, and the perfect destination that is close enough yet not too far away. The worries of trip planning are endless. Last year I organized a two-day trip for our church staff to attend a Catalyst One Day Leadership Conference. By the grace of God, all went well; everyone was comfortable, and there were no hiccups. Though my team seemed to enjoy the trip, it was still a stressful "vacation" time for me.

I am not normally an anxious person, but I wanted my staff family to be happy and relaxed as they were filled with new and challenging knowledge on how to lead people effectively within the kingdom of God. We were set to go and about to start the conference when a coworker made my day. He stopped, waited for the last few folks to find their seats, and simply said, "Thank you," and gave me the sweetest, most genuine hug. Though a simple act, the reassurance, appreciation, thankfulness, and kindness ironed out the stress and worry of the previous day. That small gesture led me to write him a letter of gratitude and ask him to coach my group leaders the following semester.

Life can be stressful. Most of the time we allow the pressure to rest on our own shoulders, missing precious moments of affirmation. We have a certain timeline for our lives (degree, job, family, children, grandchildren, retirement, etc.), and we consider ourselves failures when our plans do not work perfectly. Maybe you criticize yourself to others. For you to degrade God's masterpiece (that is you) with excuses of imperfection is to question the wisdom of God Himself. God tells us not to worry about today. We have no need to worry. If He provides for even the smallest of creatures like the birds or the

ants (Matt. 6:25–34), how much more He will provide for His people! He loves you and provides for you as a father for his children.

Maggie Carter

Prayer: *Give the Lord your worries as you face challenging circumstances in your life. Remember that He will help you in your time of need. Speak a good word about the Lord, and you will make Him glad.*

Personal Reflection: ....

....

....

....

....

....

....

Crafted Conversation

Proverbs 13:1–6

"He who guards his mouth preserves his life,
But he who opens wide his lips shall have destruction." (v. 3)

The stained glass studio was in a one-hundred-year-old, two-story row house reminiscent of a small-town main street but now filled with the bustling sounds of the interstate nearby. The tables were set in the middle of the main meeting room under tall ceilings with light provided by the leaded glass windows. Colored glass decorated the walls. Here, I would learn to cut and assemble an octagon-shaped stained glass window of pastel seashells for the upstairs bath in our home. Listening to the instructor, the other students and I proceeded slowly and with caution. Not only handling cut glass, but also using the tools—cutters, grinders, soldering irons—presented an opportunity for injury if care was not taken. To rush through a step or be unthinking would potentially harm another or myself. Thankfully, I was able to complete this project without a misstep. The resulting window is lovely and has been decorating our home for many years.

Just as I carefully held the sharp and extremely hot tools for crafting, so I must also take care in the crafting of my words. Many Scriptures caution against the careless use of our expressions through words. Words cannot be seen, but they have power that can be used for good or harm. How destructive are the harsh, sarcastic, forceful, or lewd words that are carelessly flung about, bringing harm to those in their path! Words have power to cut a heart in two, and to cut away lies that bind the heart. We must guard the use, strength, frequency, tone, and flow of our words. Wisdom promises that this care will preserve life. The wise speaker preserves her own life; the foolish talker encounters her own ruin.

The New Testament says that the "word of God is living and powerful and sharper than any two-edged sword, piercing even to the division of soul and spirit, and of joints and marrow, and is a discerner of the thoughts and intents of the heart" (Heb. 4:12). Isaiah affirms that God's Word will accomplish what He purposes (Is. 55:11). What if our words were shaped by the words of God? What if the teaching of the Bible influenced our minds and hearts so that the words we speak preserved life? What if God's love, truth, grace, and mercy were the guides for our speech?

The beauty of stained glass is seen when the light shines through it. May we guard our mouths, allowing Jesus Christ, the light of the world, to reveal His beauty through our words.

Karen Yarnell

Prayer: *Let the Word of God be the guard over your mouth. Ask the Lord to convict you when your words are displeasing to Him. Thank Him for His promise of life.*

Personal Reflection: ....

....

....

....

....

....

The Wisdom of Work

Proverbs 13:7–11

*"Wealth gained by dishonesty will be diminished,
But he who gathers by labor will increase." (v. 11)*

Surprisingly, the hardest person to teach the skill of playing a musical instrument is often someone with a musical "ear" who is able to hear a song and play it without having to see the musical score. These gifted musicians find it much easier to enjoy playing without the labor of learning to read the notes on the staff and decipher the rhythmic notation. Though truly a useful skill, playing by ear limits the scope of musical proficiency. Not learning to read the music limits your ability to a certain level. In other words, the musician's level of innate skill limits the accumulation of knowledge.

In a similar way, Proverbs contrasts two ways to wealth: one of ease and one involving work—i.e., wealth attained by *dishonesty* or by *discipline*. According to today's verse, the easy way of dishonesty, is not the wise way. *Dishonesty* translates the Hebrew word *hevel*, "a fleeting vapor or breath." Some versions translate this word as "hastily" or "by vanity." The connotation is that one who puts forth only minimal effort in his work is being dishonest. Maybe the dishonesty is toward God or self, as well as others. In any case, the effort is small and results are temporary.

In contrast, the disciplined woman who labors, gathering little by little, will have a lasting return. Proverbs 10:4 and 13:4 promise productivity for the hand that works diligently. As the woman of strength, who is praised in Proverbs 31, uses her hands to provide for her family and to help the poor and needy (vv. 19–20), she receives in return the fruit of her labor and praise for her work (v. 31).

How fulfilling to spend the time learning the notes and rhythms of a difficult piece of music, training the hands to move quickly across the keys,

producing a lovely melody! Work, though difficult at times, also brings joy. So many benefits come from being disciplined in our work: learning a new skill, investing in others, gaining knowledge, growing spiritually. Will you commit to being disciplined in the work God has given you to do?

Discipline develops little by little:

- spending a few moments in God's Word, day by day;
- growing in spiritual maturity;
- speaking with gentleness to a belligerent child, moment by moment;
- modeling godly character;
- spending time each day learning a skill for work;
- becoming more available to be used by God;
- showing kindness in small actions to those whom we love; and
- growing in love.

Karen Yarnell

Prayer: *Make a list of the tasks required of you today and talk about them with the Lord. Tell Him your specific concerns and needs for accomplishing these tasks. Thank Him for the opportunity to work. Ask His guidance and strength to complete the work (Eph. 2:10).*

Personal Reflection: ....

....

....

....

A Recipe for Life

Proverbs 13:12–18

*"The law of the wise is a fountain of life,
To turn one away from the snares of death." (v. 14)*

My mom makes the best cornbread! She has shared her recipe with ladies in the family, but none of us seems to make it quite like mom. Along with her well-seasoned iron skillet used for baking the cornbread, I think she must have a bit of magic that she sprinkles in the cornmeal. My cornbread turns out as tasty as hers only when she is with me in the kitchen cooking. She has a certain method that equals success.

The wise person has a certain "recipe" that equals success and leads to life. Their way of living is called "the law [Hb. *torah*, "instruction"] of the wise." (The first five books of the Old Testament are also called the Torah.) All of us have a kind of code for living that is evident in the choices we make, the words we speak, and the habits we form. Sometimes our behavior is based on the Word of God and sometimes on practical lessons we have learned in life or ideas passed down from other generations. These things become a kind of recipe for life, our law of living. Described as a "fountain," the law of the wise leads to life and protects from death. More than a man-made fountain, which recycles the water using a pump system, this fountain is a spring, a source of water giving life to others.

Visiting with a Samaritan woman at a well, Jesus spoke about "a fountain of water springing up into everlasting life" (John 4:14). He told the thirsty woman that if she would drink the water He offered, not only would she never thirst again, but she would also have a fountain of life within her (vv. 13–14). What an amazing promise! Jesus taught the woman that to worship the Father, one must worship "in spirit and truth" (v. 23). I can listen to the truthful words of God and

allow His Spirit to work in me so that I can know life. This fountain of life is not something I produce in myself, but a work of God within me.

Jesus makes another wonderful statement: "The Father is seeking such to worship Him" (v. 23). He is seeking you so that you may learn His words and receive that fountain of life. He does not want you to be snared by death. Though deceptively attractive at first, a snare entangles and leads to death. The good news is that God is actively pursuing you in love so that you can have life, an abundant fountain.

What is the law your life communicates? Do you know of other women who abundantly share the love of God? Do you have an older woman in the faith who models for you the way to life?

Karen Yarnell

Prayer: *Maybe you have entangled yourself in snares that are leading you to sin. Ask the Lord to set you free. Ask Him to teach you the law of wisdom. Ask Him for a spiritual mentor to instruct and encourage you.*

Personal Reflection: ....

....

....

....

....

Diligent Discipline

Proverbs 13:19–25

"He who spares his rod hates his son,
But he who loves him disciplines him promptly." (v. 24)

Many proverbs focus on the responsibility of the listener to receive instruction and obey. This proverb focuses on the responsibility of the parent to do the work of disciplining her children.

Discipline is a good thing. Discipline is training. Discipline is instruction. Discipline makes one able to make correct decisions. The goal of discipline is to lead the child into a right relationship with the Lord.

Mathematics is a great example. When learning math, the student receives instruction, works problems, receives corrections, and then is tested on the material. That which is incorrect is marked with a red pen and reworked, sometimes retaught so the student is able to grasp the concept. The student whose work is never corrected will never be able to learn math. What if a child's thinking and behavior are never corrected? We make sure a child has instruction in order to learn math. Why would we expect the same child to navigate life with any less instruction? In fact, withholding discipline is not love, but hate.

These suggestions may be helpful in this area of parenting:

- Discipline with love. Let love be the guiding factor in discipline.
- Ask yourself, "What is the biblical principle that my child is disobeying?" The most difficult part of parenting is connecting misbehavior with biblical instruction. The grievance is not that they have offended you but that they have disobeyed God.
- Seek the Scriptures to find a biblical correction or instruction for the child, but do not use Scripture as punishment. God's Word is good and

helps us walk the correct path. All of us need the correction of God (2 Tim. 3:16).

- Instruct the child in correct behavior. Punishment may be necessary if the child demonstrates a rebellious attitude.
- Encourage the child to ask God for strength to obey. Help her learn the Scriptures that apply to the situation. The ultimate goal for discipline is that the child will know the Lord and have a relationship with Him! We can only teach outward behavior. The Lord can change the heart. We want our children to have lifelong communication with the Father through Jesus and by the presence and power of the Holy Spirit.
- Pray for your child, and pray the Scripture. Ask the Lord to build godly character in your child. Ask the Lord for the strength to be consistent in your instruction.

Results may not be immediate. Time and hard work are necessary to change behavior; children are no different. Remember, results do not determine the discipline. Parents discipline in obedience to God's Word because His Word is true. God brings the change in the child.

Karen Yarnell

Prayer: *Bring each child before the Lord in prayer, your own biological child or a spiritual child you mentor. Ask the Lord to give you wisdom and commitment as you nurture them and to give your children close relationships with God.*

Personal Reflection: ....

....

....

Calling All Builders!

Proverbs 14:1–3

*"The wise woman builds her house,
But the foolish pulls it down with her hands." (v. 1)*

I love watching bricklayers at work. Their movements are so swift; you can hear the swishing of their trowel as they apply mortar, lay the brick, and mold the cement. Skilled bricklayers move with precision so that the structure formed will remain for years to come.

You need to build your house with the same precision and skill! Just as the outside structure of a home needs to be built, so does the inside, both literally and figuratively. The beds need to be made, meals prepared, decorations placed, encouragement offered, instruction given, and prayers spoken. The wise woman recognizes the need to invest time, skill, creativity, and love in the care of her home. The foolish woman neglects the needs of her home and, in so doing, tears it down as if with her own hands.

A good portion of Proverbs discusses the important role a woman has in the building of her home. Chapter 9 tells the story of two women—one wise and one foolish. Both are seen in the setting of their houses, and both are calling out with an invitation. The wise woman has prepared a meal and offered a place to find the Lord with the promise of life. The foolish woman offers stolen and secret pleasures; but those who enter her house find these pleasures end in death.

Another woman highlighted in Proverbs 31 is the woman of strength who makes linen garments, sells her goods, provides for the poor, and speaks with kindness. She is one busy woman! But the thing that is most striking about her is that all of her activity centers on the good of her home, her family, and those in her care. Dorothy Patterson has coined the term *family-obsessed*, suggesting a woman who applies her energy, creativity, and care to the loved ones in

534

her home and the people to whom she ministers through her home. The wise woman is family-obsessed.

Building a house involves investing in the lives of your children. By making the home environment a place where Christ is honored, you are giving your children an eternal gift. As they grow in the Lord, they will continue sharing the fellowship of Christ with others, even after you have gone. You are literally investing in the future as you build the lives of your own children or children you mentor.

How would you describe your "house"? Is it an apartment, a townhome, brick or wood, two-story? Do you share that space with a large family, multigenerational family, blended family, roommate, alone? However you describe your home situation, you have the unique opportunity to build your particular house so that the Lord is known and honored.

Karen Yarnell

Prayer: *Begin by thanking the Lord for your home. Be specific about the physical properties and about the people in your home. Dedicate all your resources to be used by God for His purposes.*

Personal Reflection: ....

....

....

....

....

Faithful or False?

Proverbs 14:4–9

"A faithful witness does not lie,
But a false witness will utter lies." (v. 5)

Telling the truth does not seem to be in high demand these days; people are comfortable with speaking lies. Misrepresenting facts so that the speaker is presented in a positive light, falsifying documents at work, and even lying in court are acceptable, perhaps encouraged, in modern culture. A lie is spoken with ease and without any reservation. This lack of integrity is a spiritual issue that affects the foundations of society.

The source of lies is seen in the beginning of time when the first woman was deceived by the serpent. Satan told Eve the opposite of the truth; he told her that God's Word could not be trusted. She and Adam believed the lie and ushered death into the world. Satan's words bring death (John 8:44). Christians believe the truth of Jesus, who is called the Word of God, and find life (John 10:10).

Proverbs 14:5 does not say: "One who does not lie is a faithful witness, and one who lies is a false witness." The telling of lies does not make one a false witness, nor does telling the truth make one a faithful witness. On the contrary, the character of the person determines the truthfulness of her words. When called to the stand, you can be sure that a faithful witness will speak the truth. A true witness will deliver souls who are falsely accused. A faithful witness can be trusted.

Also, the habit of lying reveals that a person's character is dishonest. The false witness speaks against a neighbor without cause in order to harm (Prov. 24:28) and is like a maul, sword, and sharp arrow (25:18). The false witness is listed among seven abominations that the Lord hates (6:19). God is serious about lying; the false witness will be punished (19:5, 9).

I have discovered something else about my words: They reflect what I believe about God. For example, if I say that God is good but continually complain, then my words are a false witness about the character of God. If I say that my marriage is supposed to proclaim the gospel, but I constantly speak ill of my marriage and do not support others in their marriages, then I have not rightly affirmed God as the Creator of marriage. What must I do? I must spend time with the Lord and ask Him to give me the faith to believe what His Word says is true.

Are you a faithful witness or a false witness? What do your words testify about God?

Karen Yarnell

Prayer: *Will you ask God to open your ears to your own words? Ask Him to help you see whether or not your words are a faithful witness of His character. Ask Him to give you the faith to believe and to speak words that are pleasing to Him.*

Personal Reflection: ....

....

....

....

....

....

Which Way?

Proverbs 14:10–14

"There is a way that seems right to a man,
But its end is the way of death." (v. 12)

My husband and I have two different Global Positioning Systems (GPS) on our phones. I prefer the readability of the maps on one of the systems. Recently, using this system, we headed to the airport in our metroplex. At an important juncture, we encountered construction not mentioned by our program—our exit was closed! And the next exit was closed. And the next. Getting to the airport that day was a bit more challenging than normal. If we had chosen the second GPS system and its descriptive instructions, we would have been warned of the construction zone and would have chosen a different route.

My life and your life have a destination—eternity. We are moving toward this destination and hopefully living abundantly on the journey. Yet, we must take into consideration the ending point of the journey, for it is the endpoint that determines the value of the journey itself. For example, if we use GPS and miss our flight because of construction, then the path chosen by our GPS is wrong; it does not serve its purpose. Our choices and decisions can seem correct to us at the time; but if, in the end, they produce death, then we have chosen the wrong path.

God's message in the Bible is the message of love that leads us to an eternal destination, life with Him. Because of our sin, we need His help to get there; and God sent His Son Jesus. Because Jesus took your place and my place, paying for our sin by His death on the cross, we have the hope of eternal life. Praise the Lord! By receiving Jesus as your Savior, you are on the path that is right, and that leads to the destination of life.

Scripture tells us that in salvation, we confess, "Jesus is Lord" (Rom. 10:9). Similar to listening to the specific directions of a GPS system when traveling

on a journey, we now listen to the specific directions of God as given to us in the Bible and taught to us by the Holy Spirit. You and I need God's direction for everyday life—not just with our eternal destiny.

If I could have a "do-over" for my life, I would change one thing: I would pray about everything. I would pray about situations that confused me, and I would pray even when I was sure I knew what to do. I would seek the Lord diligently concerning every decision and relationship, every hurt and need, home management and time management, conversations and jobs, thoughts and dreams. I would present these decisions to the Lord instead of depending on what I thought was right. I want to avoid the death of relationships, families, plans, and dreams. I want the guidance only God can give in my daily life.

Karen Yarnell

Prayer: *Give thanks to God for His love for you, for sending His Son and giving His Spirit to guide you. Dedicate every detail of your life to Him as Lord.*

Personal Reflection:

Is Your Nose Short or Long?

Proverbs 14:15–21

"A quick-tempered man acts foolishly,
And a man of wicked intentions is hated." (v. 17)

Difficult moments can stir up feelings, causing us to do and say things with intensity. Especially when anger is involved, we tend to release the emotion immediately. If we act on those feelings without waiting to think things through, we may end up with regret.

In Hebrew thought, anger is conveyed when one breathes heavily through the nose, much like the snorting of a bull. If you are quick to display your anger, then you have a "short nose," because the passage for your anger to reach its expression is short. In Exodus 34:6, the Lord describes Himself this way: "The LORD, the LORD God, merciful and gracious, longsuffering." The word *longsuffering* may be understood as "long-nosed." Because the Lord is slow to anger, the path to His expression of anger is very long. God's restraint of His anger allows time for us to repent before He judges. "The Lord . . . is longsuffering toward us, not willing that any should perish but that all should come to repentance" (2 Pet. 3:9). I am so thankful that the Lord has a "long nose"!

A recent study has shown that when we vent our anger, often with the excuse that we relieve the situation, we actually mentally enforce the emotion. Instead of getting over the negative thoughts, we actually get angrier! We say things that we later regret and pass judgment without having all of the facts. The Bible says that a wise person waits before expressing the anger. A wise person allows time to think through the situation and, most important, to pray. When we allow time for God to give us understanding and compassion, we act more like Him.

Just as acting in a rash way is foolishness, so planning to do evil is hated. A person of wicked intentions may not express his emotion of anger but allows it

to fester while devising a way to repay the transgression. He may not appear to be angry; but in his heart, he plans to act in a way that hurts another. To hold our tongues is not enough if we then hold onto a grudge!

What can you do to please the Lord in heart and action when a situation makes you angry? First, keep your thoughts to yourself if you are tempted to respond with intense, angry words. Second, take those thoughts to the Lord and seek His counsel and understanding. He cares about every situation you encounter and will give you wisdom to respond. And third, ask the Lord to help you forgive so that you will not harbor hurt feelings toward another person.

Karen Yarnell

Prayer: *Today, you may be put in a situation where you are tempted to respond with anger. Ask the Lord to prepare your heart to respond with grace. Only by the power of the Holy Spirit can you have control over your emotions. Ask Him to make your character a witness of His character: merciful, gracious, and longsuffering.*

Personal Reflection: ....

....

....

....

....

Protection and Provision

Proverbs 14:22–30

"In the fear of the LORD is strong confidence,
And His children will have a place of refuge.
The fear of the LORD is a fountain of life,
To turn one away from the snares of death." (vv. 26–27)

Believers tend to make God into their own image, what they want Him to be. But the fear of the Lord acknowledges God for who He really is. He is great and good, and He provides for and protects those who fear Him.

Greatness. Have you ever been to the mountains? I remember visiting the Appalachians as a young girl and being overwhelmed with the magnitude of the mountains. Even greater is God who made the mountains, the earth, and even the universe with just a spoken word. One day each of us will stand before the God of such greatness and power. He alone is worthy of honor and praise.

Goodness. This very same God is also the One who meets us in prayer at the beginning of every day. He is the One who has promised never to leave or forsake us. He is the One who not only created us but also has done everything needed to redeem us and invite us into His eternal presence. I do not want to do anything that would put distance between Him and me. His nearness is my good (Ps. 73:25–28).

Our response. Because of God's greatness, I realize that I owe Him the utmost honor and respect. Because of God's goodness, I realize that fellowship with Him is precious and to be protected, not broken by sin. Isaiah's response to being in God's presence was, first, recognition of God's glory and, second, recognition of his own awful sin (Is. 6). Proverbs teaches that the fear of the Lord is the beginning of wisdom, knowledge, and understanding as well as the reason to hate evil and pride.

Protection and provision. The news media often uses the term "refugee" to refer to someone who has fled a terrible situation, often escaping the threat of death. Refugees are looking for a place that will provide shelter, food, and care for themselves and their children. Similarly, we recognize the greatness of God and place our hopes for provision and protection in Him; we place our confidence in the Lord instead of ourselves and our circumstances. Our children see that we hope in no one else to meet our needs, and they begin to see that God can be trusted. He becomes for them a place to flee and find protection, a place of refuge. God not only protects us but also gives us life in abundance, as a fountain—a constant source of refreshing.

Because God is great, we must obey Him. Because God is good, we must love Him.

Karen Yarnell

Prayer: *Will you spend a few moments praying "the ABCs of worship"? Will you name at least one attribute of God for each letter of the alphabet? "God, You are amazing, beautiful, compassionate, etc." Thank God that He is great and good.*

Personal Reflection: ....

....

....

....

....

The Blessing of Righteousness

Proverbs 14:31–35

*"Righteousness exalts a nation,
But sin is a reproach to any people." (v. 34)*

My favorite Hebrew word is *chesed*. It is God's pursuing, faithful, kind, and covenantal love. Used often in the Old Testament, *chesed* is found in Psalm 63:3, God's "lovingkindness is better than life." Occasionally, as in Proverbs 14:34, *chesed* has a negative meaning, translated "reproach." Instead of a pursuing love, it is a pursuing shame, zeal *against* instead of *for* the people. God's relationship to a rebellious, sinful people is active opposition; even an earthly king punishes evil. "The king's favor is toward a wise servant, but his wrath is against him who causes shame" (v. 35).

What is the nature of sin? Sin is deceptive. One thinks that sin can go unnoticed, but in truth, sin is never hidden from God, even if done in secret. More like an investment than a one-time purchase, sin builds and forms a habit and then a lifestyle. Last, sinful living requires either payment or punishment.

Sin, even secret sin, molds the character of a nation. When righteousness is forsaken, a nation begins to fall apart; injustice becomes the norm, the poor and needy are oppressed, and chaos rules. People assume that military power, wealth, strong government, and other factors make a nation secure. When a nation is sinful, God works against that nation, regardless of military strength or form of government.

Similarly, in Psalm 2 the nations think they are free to sin and can avoid punishment. They blatantly defy the Lord; and in turn, He derides them. According to this psalm, the Father has set a King who reigns in righteousness, punishing evil and rewarding the faithful (v. 6). This prophecy concerns Jesus, God's only begotten Son. Those in opposition to the Son will be punished; those who trust Him will be blessed (v. 12).

The opposite of sin is righteousness. Based on the rule of God, righteousness is a moral quality that produces order in society. The children of God, called by His name, are to live under the authority of God. His church will be a light, revealing righteousness and influencing the culture of the nation. The upright living of God's people will invite the blessing of the Lord.

God is zealous to have a relationship with His people, zealous to bless us or to remove that which harms us—sin. Revelation tells us the culmination of history as Scripture declares: "The kingdoms of this world have become the kingdoms of our Lord and of His Christ, and He shall reign forever and ever!" (Rev. 11:15). From the mighty to the weak, every nation will one day recognize the authority of the kingdom of God. All will bow to the greatness of God.

Karen Yarnell

Prayer: *God's lovingkindness is zealous for you. Will you ask Him to forgive your sin and trust His Son Jesus as Savior (Titus 3:4–7)? Will you pray for our nation and our world? Pray that God's people will live in righteousness.*

Personal Reflection: ....

....

....

....

....

Think Before You Speak

Proverbs 15:1–2

"A soft answer turns away wrath,
But a harsh word stirs up anger.
The tongue of the wise uses knowledge rightly,
But the mouth of fools pours forth foolishness." (vv. 1–2)

In January 2013, the contemporary Christian band, Hawk Nelson, released their single "Words," which went on to hit number one on the Christian music charts. This poignant song reminds its listeners of the power of words. Words can make you feel like a prisoner or set you free—a criminal or a king. These beautiful lyrics echo the truths found in Proverbs 15 about how what we say can be used to lift others up or to tear them down. Words of truth can point people to the Lord.

The writer of Proverbs 15 notes several things about our speech:

- Gentle words can diffuse anger, but harsh words ignite anger (v. 1).
- Your words reveal something about your character—a wise person uses words full of knowledge, but a foolish person spouts foolish words (vv. 2, 7).
- Words can bring healing or hurt—the word for *wholesome* actually suggests healing, and the word for *perverse* literally describes crookedness and distortion (v. 4).
- Knowing when to speak and when to keep silent is important—words spoken at the right time can bring joy and goodness (v. 23), and the wise person "studies" or "thinks carefully" before speaking (v. 28).

Unfortunately, far too often I have stuck my foot in my mouth because I have spoken too hastily without thinking of the repercussions. Or, I have used

my words to harm and hurt people under the guise of sarcasm. My words have condemned me as foolish instead of wise.

In the New Testament, Paul recognized the importance of how believers speak to one another: "Let no corrupt word proceed out of your mouth, but only what is good for necessary edification, that it may impart grace to the hearers" (Eph. 4:29).

I am not sure who came up with the acronym "T.H.I.N.K." in regard to our words, but I have found it to be a very helpful tool to remember to use my words to honor God. Before I speak, I try to ask myself these five questions:

T—Is it true?
H—Is it helpful?
I—Is it inspiring?
N—Is it necessary?
K—Is it kind?

If I can't answer "yes" to all of these questions, then it is better to keep my mouth shut!

Candi Finch

Prayer: *Ask the Lord to help you use your words wisely today to encourage and uplift people.*

Personal Reflection: ....

....

....

....

The Gift of Correction

Proverbs 15:5–11

"A fool despises his father's instruction,
But he who receives correction is prudent." (v. 5)

Does correction seem like a gift? Has someone ever pointed out a sin in your life or a mistake and you thought, "Wow, that was awesome! I would like more of that!" When someone offers a rebuke, most people do not put that experience in the same category as opening Christmas presents; we rarely wait for correction with eager anticipation and excitement like a kid on Christmas morning.

However, repeatedly in Scripture, we are told that the wise person welcomes the gift of correction, and a foolish person rejects it. The writer of Proverbs 15 mentions this idea several times in the chapter:

- "He who hates correction will die" (v. 10)—Yikes!
- "A scoffer does not love one who corrects him, nor will he go to the wise" (v. 12).
- "The ear that hears the rebukes of life will abide among the wise" (v. 31).
- "He who disdains instruction despises his own soul, but he who heeds rebuke gets understanding" (v. 32).

If you survey the whole book of Proverbs, you will see this idea repeated over and over again. Heeding correction is the mark of a wise person; ignoring a rebuke or correction is just simply foolish.

If you work with kids, you understand the importance of correction. If a toddler tries to touch a hot stove, you correct him. Why? Because you are a mean stick-in-the-mud who is stifling his inborn curiosity and thirst for life? Of course not! You correct him because you know that touching a hot stove is going to cause him a lot of pain. If that young child is wise, he will listen

to you. One of the reasons God gave us the Bible is for our "correction" (Gk. *epanorthōsin*, "restoration to an upright position, made straight again," 2 Tim. 3:16). He wants us to be on the straight path because He knows that when we stray from His Word we are in dangerous "hot stove" territory. The fact that God corrects us is a proof of His great love for us (Prov. 3:12; Heb. 12:3–11). In addition, one of the most loving things another believer will do for you is to tell you when you are wrong. You may not feel that way at the time, but do not dismiss the "wounds of a friend" (Prov. 27:6). That friend may be the instrument God is using in your life to warn you about a hot stove you are getting ready to touch.

Candi Finch

Prayer: *Do you receive the gift of correction from the Word of God and fellow believers or do you harden your heart? If you struggle with receiving correction, would you consider asking God to help you receive correction with a glad heart, repent of sins and dangerous behaviors, and turn back to Him? Remember, the wise person receives correction as if it were fine gold (Prov. 25:12).*

Personal Reflection: ....

....

....

....

....

Whistle While You Work

Proverbs 15:12–14

"A merry heart makes a cheerful countenance." (v. 13a)

In 1937, Disney released the animated classic *Snow White and the Seven Dwarfs*, which had such memorable songs as "Someday My Prince Will Come" and "Heigh-Ho," and my favorite of all, "Whistle While You Work." Snow White sang that last song as she and a surprisingly large group of woodland creatures cleaned the seven dwarfs' little cottage. Forget the fact that somehow Snow White recruited rabbits and birds and squirrels to wash the dishes and dust; the most surprising thing in that scene is the upbeat attitude that Snow White displayed while cleaning. She was joyful! While cleaning! Now, you may actually enjoy cleaning; but if I am being honest, household chores do not make me want to whistle a cheerful tune.

Are there tasks that you do not enjoy—chores that make you want to grumble and complain instead of hum a happy tune? Are the circumstances of your life causing you pain? As believers, no matter our task and no matter our circumstances, we can have a cheerful attitude and a merry heart because our joy comes from the Lord and not our surroundings. Paul said he was overflowing with joy even in his afflictions (2 Cor. 7:4), that he rejoiced in his sufferings (Col. 1:24), and that a fruit of the Holy Spirit working in our lives is joy (Gal. 5:22). James encouraged his readers to consider it all joy when they went through difficult trials (James 1:2–4). Do not misunderstand these verses; they are not saying "grin and bear it" or "put on a happy face" when you feel like you are dying inside. They are pointing you to your Savior. God can turn your sorrow into joy. He can turn your grumbling attitude into a happy countenance.

The writer of Proverbs 15 knew this truth. Knowing God changes you and gives you a cheerful countenance (Prov. 15:13; see also v. 15). Proverbs 17:22a

encourages, "A merry heart does good, like medicine." If you are facing an unpleasant task or experiencing suffering or heartache, can I still encourage you to whistle while you work? The Christian version of that sentiment is to dwell on godly things, to remember who God is and what He has done for you. As Paul says, "Whatever things are true, whatever things are noble, whatever things are just, whatever things are pure, whatever things are lovely, whatever things are of good report, if there is any virtue and if there is anything praiseworthy— meditate on these things" (Phil. 4:8). By dwelling on these kinds of things, the overflow in your life can be a merry heart and a cheerful countenance.

Candi Finch

Prayer: *Are you facing a dreaded task or a difficult situation today? Spend a few moments reflecting on what God has done for you. Ask Him to give you strength and renew your joy as you face whatever today will bring your way.*

Personal Reflection: ....

....

....

....

....

....

Money Doesn't Buy Love

Proverbs 15:15–17

"Better is a dinner of herbs where love is,
Than a fatted calf with hatred." (v. 17)

During the mid-twentieth century, a shocking observation was made about some of the world's wealthiest people—many of them were committing suicide. Some millionaires, who looked as if they had everything, ended their lives in tragedy:

- Leon Fraser, the fifty-five-year-old president of First National Bank of New York, shot himself in the head in 1945. His suicide note said that he had been "depressed mentally and [had] suffered from melancholia that had gotten steadily worse."
- Jesse Livermore, a millionaire several times over, was one of the most successful market speculators in the history of Wall Street, yet he committed suicide in 1940.
- Ivar Kreuger, a Swedish businessman who founded Kreuger and Toll, a multi-billion-dollar match conglomerate, shot himself on March 12, 1932.

Money, as the saying goes, cannot buy happiness.

Do you remember Ebenezer Scrooge in *A Christmas Carol* by Charles Dickens? He invested his life in acquiring more and more wealth. At the climax of the story, as Scrooge reflects on his life, he realizes that his overworked and underpaid sales clerk Bob Cratchit has had a fuller and more joyful life than he has. Scrooge learns that acquiring money has not made him happy.

In Proverbs 15:17, the writer says that a meager "dinner of herbs" or small bowl of vegetables is better than a grand feast, if you have love. In verse 27, the greedy person is warned that his lifestyle will bring trouble to his house. Please

do not get me wrong; money is not a sinful thing. In fact, God can use money to do incredible things for the kingdom. However, the problem comes when money controls and drives us, creating an insatiable hunger for more. We were meant to steward our money, not to be slaves to it. Paul warned Timothy about "the love of money" because it could cause all sorts of evil to take hold in his life (1 Tim. 6:10). Our only master is the Lord and Savior Jesus Christ; yet some believers are trying to serve both God and money.

Jesus urged us to let our treasure be in heavenly things and not earthly things that will not last (Matt. 6:19–21). Then He warned, "No one can serve two masters; for either he will hate the one and love the other, or else he will be loyal to the one and despise the other. You cannot serve God and mammon" (i.e., "riches or wealth"; Matt. 6:24). Are you trying to serve God and wealth? Do you think more money will solve your problems? Sister, that dead-end road that leads to disaster. Determine today to serve God alone.

Candi Finch

Prayer: *What place does money hold in your life? Are you driven by the need for more or do you view money as a resource given to you by God to manage wisely? Ask God's help to be a good steward of the resources He has given you.*

Personal Reflection: ....

....

....

....

Are You Always Looking for a Fight?

Proverbs 15:18–27

*"A wrathful man stirs up strife,
But he who is slow to anger allays contention." (v. 18)*

Irritable. Crabby. Cantankerous. Quarrelsome. Belligerent. Argumentative. Aggressive. Does anyone come to mind when you read those descriptive words? Maybe you have a coworker whom people avoid because she seems a bit too eager to stir up controversy. Or perhaps the older gentleman who only seems pleased when he is knee-deep in a heated argument comes to mind. Hopefully, you did not think of yourself when you read those words!

The Bible warns about being known as a person of anger. The word *wrathful* in this proverb literally means "burning, intense anger and rage," as if picturing boiling, molten lava that is getting ready to erupt. Trouble follows this type of hot-tempered person; she leaves a wake of controversy. Yet, the person who is able to control her anger, a cool-tempered person, is like a healing balm, soothing disputes and calming quarrels.

What is the danger of being hot-tempered? I heard a great illustration of a dad who tried to teach his son this very lesson. His son had a temper problem and would "fly off the handle" quickly. The dad took his son out to the backyard where they had a sturdy wooden fence and gave his son a bag of nails and a hammer and said, "Son, every time you get angry and react, I want you to come out here and pound a nail into the fence."

By the end of the first day, the son had pounded over thirty nails into the fence, but in the ensuing days and weeks, the nails were pounded with much less frequency. The young boy slowly learned to control his anger until finally the day came when he did not have to pound any nails in the fence. The boy was so excited that he could not wait to tell his dad. As father and son surveyed the

fence, the father suggested that the son now remove a nail each time he made it through the day without giving into his anger.

Weeks and months passed, but the day finally came when all the nails had been removed. This time, as father and son surveyed the fence, the dad said, "Son, I am proud of you for learning to control your anger. However, look at the fence. Do you see all the holes left by the nails that you pounded into it? That fence will never be the same. I want you to remember that when you let your anger get the better of you, you can leave scars in people just like those nails have scarred our fence."

In the same way, when we let anger control us, we can scar people. God urges us to be slow to anger because He knows the damage our anger can bring to us and to the people around us.

Candi Finch

Prayer: *Ask the Lord to help you be a woman who brings peace and not one who brings conflict.*

Personal Reflection: ....

....

....

....

....

555

Rejecting "Selfitis"

Proverbs 15:28–33

"The fear of the LORD is the instruction of wisdom,
And before honor is humility." (v. 33)

In 2014, a fake news website circulated a story about a fictional mental disorder, purporting that the board of the American Psychiatric Association (APA) had discovered and classified a new disorder—"selfitis." They defined this mental disorder as the obsessive compulsive desire to take photos of oneself (i.e., a "selfie") and post them on social media as a way to make up for the lack of self-esteem. According to the story, there are different levels of this psychosis: borderline, acute, and chronic "selfitis," depending on how often you take a picture of yourself and act on the urge to post the picture on social media. While there is no cure currently for "selfitis," the story did recommend different forms of therapy to help a person cope.

Although this story was completely false and no such disorder as "selfitis" has ever been minted by the medical community, there is a hint of truth to it. We do live in a culture with a "me-first" mentality, which is probably why so many people believed the fake news story; it seemed so believable. Whether you call it "selfitis," the "selfie syndrome," a "me-first mentality," or just plain, simple selfishness or self-centeredness, such thinking and attitudes are prevalent in today's world. However, the Christian worldview is diametrically opposed to such a self-focused mind-set. Christianity is others-focused. We are called to deny ourselves, to die daily to our own desires, and follow Christ's desires for us (Luke 9:23).

The biblical way to combat the selfish mind-set is for one to honor the Lord and obey Him (Prov. 15:33). If a person is seeking recognition or honor, she is approaching life the wrong way. Before honor comes humility, and humility is the cure for "selfitis." Jesus modeled this approach to life. He did not seek honor

or His own self-interests. Instead, Jesus (the God of the universe, Creator of the heavens and earth) humbled Himself, died on the cross, and rose again so sinful men and women could have a relationship with Him (Phil. 2:5–11). Jesus was not thinking of Himself first as He died upon the cross; He was thinking of you and me. Christ was others-focused and modeled true humility. It has been said that "true humility is not thinking less of yourself but thinking of yourself less."

Living an "others-focused" life can be difficult in our "me-first" world. The culture calls out to us to think of ourselves, seek honor for ourselves, and promote ourselves. But, my friend, that is stinkin' thinkin'!

Candi Finch

Prayer: *Do you ever struggle with selfishness or self-centeredness? Consider reading Philippians 2:5–11 and meditating on Christ's example of humility. Then, ask God to help you model an others-focused mentality. Pray for an opportunity to serve someone today, not for recognition but simply as a way to honor God.*

Personal Reflection: ....

....

....

....

....

....

Steady My Heart

Proverbs 16:1–2

*"The preparations of the heart belong to man,
But the answer of the tongue is from the LORD." (v. 1)*

"This wasn't in the script," I whispered. I had always thought that my mom was going to be the one to trace her finger over the white lace detailing of the store-window wedding dresses and help me pick just the right one for my special day. I had planned that she would cradle my newborn baby with her familiar lullabies and teach me all the things a new mommy needs to know. I even dreamed of our future together as mother and daughter on the front porch sipping ice-cold lemonade while chatting about the rain, recipes, and raising daughters. That was my plan. But our family would find out that my mom had a rare terminal illness that would take her from us sooner than we dared to imagine.

Isn't it like us to hold to our plans so tightly? If you are like me, planning and dreaming of the future gives me confidence. I know what to expect, minimizing the risk of embarrassment, failure, and regret. But holding on to our plans when they are not God's plans is an effort to take control and causes us to miss the lessons that come from depending on Him. God created us to depend on Him so *He* could be the one to steady our hearts.

When you bring your plans before the Lord and reflect on who He is, something happens in your heart. You recognize that His thoughts are not your thoughts (Is. 55:8–9). "His way is perfect" (Ps. 18:30). His timing is right on schedule (Eccl. 3:11). His plans are always for your good, giving you a hope and a future (Jer. 29:11). He simply asks you to trust Him (Prov. 3:5–6).

Women of God must learn to call on His name, trust in His sovereignty, and depend upon His promises. When we let go of our heart's longings and trust His divine will, we can confidently open up our closed fists and with outstretched palms whisper, "Your way, Lord. Your timing, Lord. I will trust You."

Then He steadies our hearts and strengthens our spirits for the expected and the unexpected, for the mountain tops and the valleys, and for the harvests and the storms.

As I have learned to give my dreams of a young adult life with my mom into the Lord's hands, I can confidently and gently assure you that His plans and timing are always best. While you do not know what tomorrow holds, you can confidently rest in the One who holds tomorrow.

Melissa Meredith

Prayer: *Ask the Lord to show you what plans need to be surrendered to His control. Write them down, giving those plans over to the Lord one by one, saying: "Lord, help me to trust You with these. Your plan and timing is perfect. Make known Your path for me."*

Personal Reflection: ....

....

....

....

....

....

Thy Will Be Done

Proverbs 16:3–6

"Commit your works to the LORD,
And your thoughts will be established." (v. 3)

How many times do we let the lies of Satan silence our work as women? How many times do we stand paralyzed in fear instead of moving with faith? How many times do we panic, make hasty decisions, or give up instead of walking in truth? The words of today's focal verse give power in the face of lies, strength in the face of fear, and a plan in the face of doubt.

To commit is not just a decision made in your heart but also involves the actions necessary to carry out that decision. When we purpose in our hearts to center our lives on God's Word and commit our works to the Lord for His glory, God receives the praise and expedites the plan. Sometimes that plan is to sanctify us to be more like Him. Other times that plan is tangible, seeing the fruitful harvest around us and lives changed for the kingdom. Regardless, He always has a purpose.

How can you center your life on His Word and commit your works to Him, especially in light of Proverbs 16:2: "All the ways of a man are pure in his own eyes, but the LORD weighs the spirits"? Recall what God has done for you and bow before Him, examining your heart in His presence and lifting up your concerns and desires to Him. He prepares your hearts to wait on Him, listen to Him, and obey Him. He purifies your heart and aligns your desires to His, making room for gratitude, humility, and willingness to obey. As you commit your activities to the Lord, these promises are yours in Christ Jesus:

- "The LORD . . . is the One who goes before you. He will be with you, He will not leave you nor forsake you; do not fear nor be dismayed" (Deut. 31:8).

- "The secret of the LORD is with those who fear Him, and He will show them His covenant" (Ps. 25:14).
- The God of peace will "make you complete in every good work to do His will, working in you what is well pleasing in His sight, through Jesus Christ" (Heb. 13:21).

In those moments of truth, the desire, strength, and joy to carry out God's will for your life comes to life. The Lord's promises to "those who fear Him" overrides the lies, fears, and doubt (Ps. 103:11, 13, 17). We can say with commitment: "Thy will be done in and through me, Lord."

Melissa Meredith

Prayer: *Is anything holding you back from committing your work to the Lord? Write these lies down, then meditate on Hebrews 13:21, and pray this verse: "Make me complete in every good work to do what You have called me to do, working in me what is well pleasing in Your sight, through Christ Jesus." Amen!*

Personal Reflection: ....

....

....

....

....

Please Him Alone

Proverbs 16:7–15

"When a man's ways please the LORD,
He makes even his enemies to be at peace with him." (v. 7)

In my personal and professional life, relationships have wounded me and caused me pain. And, I have also been a woman who has walked outside the will of God and have wounded other women. Why do women wound, and why do we seek the approval of women rather than pleasing God who loves us (1 John 3:1)?

Since we live in a fallen world and have the complexities of personalities, conflict is often unavoidable. When conflicts erupt, we often limp around unprepared, dodging women who wound, trying to play peacemaker—sometimes at the detriment of our relationship with God and our relationships with others. How do we stop people-pleasing, love women who wound, restore broken relationships, and become women who please the Lord?

Today's focal verse holds a key to unlocking the mystery. Women who have accepted God's gift of salvation and who desire to walk according to His plan can trust the Lord to deal with their enemies. We can concentrate on pleasing the Lord and stop focusing on pleasing, for example, Wynonna two desks down, Carrie two pews back, or Miranda two arguments ago and counting. Scripture calls us to please only the Lord.

When we confess our sins, ask for His forgiveness, and turn from our ways, our hearts are reconciled to God, and we are made pure before the Lord. When we live, move, and breathe from His strength made known in our weakness, He receives the glory. And when we serve from the joy of our salvation, we only have room in our hearts for God's approval. When we shift our eyes from our need for affirmation and the satisfaction of depending on the Lord, our hearts are ready to love the ones who are hard to love, extend grace to those who wound, ask for forgiveness, and make room in our hearts for God to work.

An unbelieving woman once wounded me deeply. During one of our conversations, I saw her change from an out-of-control frenzy to a calm and peaceful person. She confessed her role in the conflict (I also confessed my role since I was not blameless) and began taking steps toward reconciliation. I saw the Spirit working in her life and mine! The Lord's work in our relationships will be sweeter and His Name will be magnified!

What about you? Do you allow people-pleasing to rule your relationships with others and harm your relationship with God? Purpose today to please the Lord alone, and watch Him act in your life as well as in the lives of friends and foes.

Melissa Meredith

Prayer: *Humbly come before the Father today. Ask Him to reveal any broken relationships in your life. Evaluate your own behavior in the broken relationship, and ask God to show you the next steps. Give that person over to the Lord. Set new boundaries, and confront in love.*

Personal Reflection: ....

....

....

....

....

....

More Precious Than . . .

Proverbs 16:16–21

"How much better to get wisdom than gold!
And to get understanding is to be chosen rather than silver." (v. 16)

Recently I drove to my maternal grandparents' home, affectionately known as the "Old House." As I drove up to the Old House, I was pleasantly surprised to see the honeysuckle bush where my grandma taught the girls how to suck honey from those little yellow flowers. Around that honeysuckle bush I learned some of my first lessons about wise living from the women in my family: discerning between good and evil, receiving God's instruction, and exercising good judgment. The flowers and leaves had fallen, but the lessons I learned as a little girl around that bush are still tucked deep in my heart.

God gave Solomon wisdom, insight, and understanding (1 Kin. 4:29). Solomon is described as wiser than everyone (v. 31)! And, his reputation extended to all the surrounding nations (v. 31). When a man who is given wisdom and said to be the wisest in all the land speaks, I want a front-row seat!

Solomon indeed tells us what, above all, to pursue. We should be at the edge of our seats, ears perked, pens pointed to paper, and hearts wide open to receive a good word! Can you hear the urgency in his voice as he says: "Get wisdom—how much better it is than gold! And get understanding—it is preferable to silver" (Prov. 16:16). Can you hear the assurance in his comparison? It is better to get wisdom than gold; it is better to get understanding than silver!

What do you desire the most? If you are honest with yourself, you might be thinking of your earthly treasures. Jesus said, "Do not lay up [collect] for yourselves treasures on earth . . . but lay up for yourselves treasures in heaven. . . . For where your treasure is, there your heart will be also" (Matt. 6:19–21). Scripture teaches an important truth: Knowing God is more valuable than anything, including gold and silver. Need more proof? Check these verses out:

- The beginning of wisdom is "the fear of the Lord, and the knowledge of the Holy One is understanding" (Prov. 9:10).
- The blessing of wisdom is happiness (Prov. 3:13).
- The beatitude of wisdom is experiencing "the depth of the riches" of God (Rom. 11:33).
- The beseeching for wisdom is our birthright as daughters of the King (James 1:5).

Let the honeysuckle bush remind you that nothing is more precious than knowing and following the Lord.

Melissa Meredith

Prayer: *Praise God for His character and His works: "Lord, You are more precious than _____. Lord, You are more beautiful than _____." Ask Him for wisdom and understanding in faith—He promises to give to you generously (James 1:5).*

Personal Reflection: ....

....

....

....

....

A Drop of Honey

Proverbs 16:22–26

"Pleasant words are like a honeycomb,
Sweetness to the soul and health to the bones." (v. 24)

My mom was known for her gracious words and handwritten notes. She kept a desk drawer with cards and stamps, and her address book was up-to-date. After her quiet time with the Lord each day, Mom prayed that God would bring someone to mind who needed encouragement. She would spend her early mornings sending little drops of honey through the mail. As a child, I received a handwritten note in my lunch box each day. As I grew older and moved away from home, on Fridays, I could count on seeing her familiar handwriting on a brightly colored envelope in my mailbox.

Today's focal verse is such a powerful reminder and inspiring challenge for women who profess to be followers of Christ! In and of ourselves, there is no good thing apart from Christ. We learn through our study of His Word the cost of grace, the free and unmerited favor in the Lord. As we mature in Christlikeness, our values and very lives begin to reflect Him, including our words, which become a reflection of the precious gift of grace we have received.

Our words are likened to a honeycomb, sweet to the taste and health to the body. "Out of the abundance of the heart" our mouths speak (Luke 6:45). Words overflowing from a heart that recognizes the grace, mercy, forgiveness, and love that we have abundantly received from the Father are naturally sweet, pleasing to the receiver, treasured and savored.

Pleasant or gracious words are also healthy to the body. Words saturated with truth and light are life-giving to all who hear them. Words—whether written down and mailed in colorful envelopes, shared over mochas in a coffee shop, or whispered in a hospital waiting room—can be a healing balm to a hurting soul and satisfying to the dry, parched, and thirsty spirit.

Sadly, every woman has had times when she used her words for evil. Harsh words are anything but pleasant and cause us to question our worth, doubt our giftedness, and bring disharmony and destruction to relationships. This verse challenges all of us who desire to be godly women to walk in the fear of the Lord and speak words of love.

The words of my lunch box notes and weekly notes are still life-giving to me every time I read them, as well as a reminder to me to share the grace that I have received from Christ to others and to be intentional about praying for and creating opportunities to share that grace through my words with others.

Melissa Meredith

Prayer: *Examine your heart before the Father. Are your words life-giving or life-draining to those women He has placed around you and under your influence? Confess your sins before God and ask for His forgiveness. Ask Him to bring someone to mind, and send a note of encouragement to her, practicing Proverbs 16:24.*

Personal Reflection: ....

....

....

....

....

....

Trees of Righteousness

Proverbs 16:27–33

"The silver-haired head is a crown of glory,
If it is found in the way of righteousness." (v. 31)

I have been blessed by the lives of many godly women whom God has planted beside me for certain seasons of my life. During a particularly hard season, the gracious Lord set my feet on solid ground with the help of three precious gray-haired women. They were my spiritual mothers and my life-giving mentors. One mentor was reserved in nature, with a gentle and quiet spirit, and used her spiritual gift of mercy to serve me in tangible ways. She listened to the concerns of my heart and pointed me to the Father. One mentor was very artistic, with a sense of humor that left me in stitches, and she used her spiritual gift of encouragement as balm for my heart on difficult days, pointing me to the Father. And one mentor was bold and courageous, whose discerning eyes saw through me. She used her spiritual gift of wisdom to challenge and strengthen my faith, pointing me to the Father. All three were very different personalities but each shared life with me, sharpened me, and served me. I have purposed in my heart to be just like them someday.

These three spiritually-seasoned women had made decisions to follow Christ and determined in their hearts to live godly lives. Their prayer was "That they may be called trees of righteousness, the planting of the LORD, that He may be glorified" (Is. 61:3). I lovingly referred to these ladies as my "trees of righteousness," my "grove." Though each had experienced her own tragedy, all were women who chose to walk with God each day. They were known as women clothed with strength and dignity who laughed at the days to come (Prov. 31:25). When they opened their mouths, wisdom and loving instruction were on their tongues (v. 26). They were women who truly feared the Lord (v. 30).

At lunch one day, I asked one of my mentors to share the secret for righteous living. Her answer: "I don't want to go a day without opening my Bible and spending time in my Father's presence." Oh, friends, why do we make it so difficult when God simply calls us to saturate our lives in His Word and delight in His presence? God used three gray-haired women to teach me the way of righteousness: waking up each morning, opening the Word, spending time with our Father, and letting my life reflect that time spent with Him. Learn wisdom from the "tree of righteousness" in your life.

Melissa Meredith

Prayer: *Are you following the way of righteousness? Seek God's face, and ask Him to reveal a spiritually mature woman with whom you can meet regularly to grow in your relationship with Him.*

Personal Reflection: ....

....

....

....

....

....

Peace That Surpasses All Strife

Proverbs 17:1–3

"Better is a dry morsel with quietness,
Than a house full of feasting with strife." (v. 1)

After a long week of work, I was in the kitchen cooking Friday dinner for my husband and me despite the unrest in our house, which predictably included quite a bit of bickering. Our household was far less than peaceful. I decided to make a nice dinner in hopes it might clear the tension. We got the twins down to bed; I set the buttery green beans and steaming sweet potato on a plate next to the freshly roasted chicken breast. My husband prayed for our meal, and I pushed the food around with a fork while an awkward silence hung in the air. The strife was not healed by the delicious meal; only talking things out and forgiving one another could restore the peace in our household.

A dry piece of toast and laughter with my husband would have been better than the fancy meal in the midst of fighting. No material thing can erase incongruous situations that arise with loved ones. No matter what car you drive, where you live, or the brand of clothes you wear, no material possessions will fix a difficult situation with someone you love. It is true: money cannot buy happiness. The writer of Proverbs conveys this point (v. 1). The health of our relationships with one another can turn any situation into beauty or misery.

The emphasis in this verse is not actually on the meal itself. This illustration draws a comparison between living in peace or strife. How much better to live in harmony with those around you! I know, personally, my life is much easier when I am getting along with the people I love.

If you and a loved one have been dealing with strife, think about how you can make the situation better. The only person you can fix is yourself. Ask God to reveal to you where you have gone wrong and seek His direction on how to proceed with mending any broken relationships. Go to your husband or

daughter or sister or friend and ask for forgiveness. Sometimes when we feel like we have been wronged, we throw ourselves a pity party instead of finding a way to reconcile. Lay down your pride, and allow God to work out your relationships. Nothing can replace the joy of happy times with those you love. If you are not dealing with any conflicts right now, remember this Scripture the next time you struggle with someone in your life.

Dominique Richardson

Prayer: *Ask the Lord to help you live in peace and remove any strife within your family and circle of friends. Seek forgiveness when you cause strife; live in harmony with one another.*

 Personal Reflection: ....

....

....

....

....

....

It's the Small Things That Make a Difference

Proverbs 17:4–5

"He who mocks the poor reproaches his Maker;
He who is glad at calamity will not go unpunished." (v. 5)

I did not want to look directly at the homeless man as my car stopped where he stood. The wrinkles dotting his face and the tattered clothes he wore showed a hard life. His cardboard sign read: "Hungry. Anything helps. God bless." I knew immediately what I had to do. I rarely carry any cash, but I rummaged in my purse, desperately hoping I would find something to give him. I found several dollar bills and rolled down my window to get his attention as the light turned green.

Horns from cars behind me honked, but I remained stopped to hand over my cash. He thanked me with a toothless grin, and I accelerated my car while the drivers to my rear continued their raucous disapproval of my delayed start. I did not intend to offend any of the drivers behind me, but I needed to do what was right. How could I have ignored this man?

Seeing the man as the traffic light turned red, I had initially hoped my car would not end up right next to him. I was in a hurry, running late to an appointment, and I did not need to add any distractions that might slow me down. On the inside, my hurried state had me feeling more like the person who was honking behind me. Honestly, I was not thinking of how I could show the love of God to someone else, but I am thankful I made the right decision. The man on the side of the road is a beautiful creation of God. If I had looked away and kept my window closed, without giving him a second glance, I would have forsaken the warning of Proverbs 17:5.

It is not easy to do the right thing in such moments, but realizing that everyone on this planet is a dearly loved creation of our Maker prompts us to step outside ourselves and serve others. I never want to be in a situation where

I inadvertently reproach God. But, it can happen if I am not intentional about my actions.

This verse also warns against thinking and saying things like, "They got what they deserved" or "Good, they deserve what is coming to them." Even when people are suffering the consequences of their own wrongdoing, we should not rejoice in their misfortune. The proper response is to show empathy and pray for those who are dealing with calamity, even if they brought it on themselves.

Dominique Richardson

Prayer: *Are you aware of those around you who are in a situation less fortunate than your own? Pray for those who are suffering, and never rejoice in another person's calamity.*

Personal Reflection: ....

....

....

....

....

....

The Generational Blessings of Family

Proverbs 17:6–8

"Children's children are the crown of old men,
And the glory of children is their father." (v. 6)

Whenever Grandma comes over, I can see the joy written all over her face when she spends time with my twin boys. I like to watch from the kitchen as they play in the living room. It brings me happiness to hear the three of them having fun. Grandparents brag about the fun grandkids bring. Grandchildren are the real crowns in their lives. Grandparents experience satisfaction to see their legacy continue through their grandchildren.

In a similar way, I love to watch my husband with our sons. My little boys adore their daddy. When he gets down on the floor and pushes cars around with them or helps them go down the slide at the park, the little smiles on their faces could light up a city block. Every time he comes home from work, they simultaneously cry out, "Daddy!" as they run to greet him. Their dad really is their glory.

Proverbs 17:6 captures three generations. You clearly see how children are a blessing to a family. Grandparents get to rejoice in seeing their legacy carried on. Children find their glory in their parents (especially when they are young, struggling as teenagers, and in adulthood). Psalm 127:3 declares: "Children are a heritage from the LORD, the fruit of the womb is a reward." As a mother of young children, I know this job of parenting can be a thankless one at times. When the monotony of changing diapers, folding laundry, and cleaning dishes sets in, I remind myself of how blessed I am to be the mother of these two sweet boys.

Motherhood is not easy! It is a tough job, but the reward is great in the long run. The work is hard now but will continue to pay dividends in the generations to come. Whenever you find yourself in the trenches of the sleepless nights and

the constant correction, remember God's intent for families. Our families are a blessing from the Lord, from children all the way up to the grandparents.

The focal verse also captures beautifully God's picture for the family unit. If you are a mom, rejoice in your children when they are young, even though it can get difficult at times. Celebrate the children—whether in your personal family or church family—as they grow, despite the reality that they will never be small again. And be proud of their accomplishments as they move through the different stages of their lives. If one day you are blessed with little grandbabies, revel in this gift from the Lord.

Dominique Richardson

Prayer: *Thank the Lord for your family. Remember the blessing of children and your parents. Cherish these precious gifts from God.*

Personal Reflection: ....

....

....

....

....

....

Forsaking Gossip for Love

Proverbs 17:9–13

"He who covers a transgression seeks love,
But he who repeats a matter separates friends." (v. 9)

Whenever I stand in grocery store lines, I glance at the headlines on the magazines dotting the aisles. Who has broken-up with whom, who is pregnant now, which celebrities got into a fight. This type of gossip glares at you, unavoidable like a bad-hair day. Other types of gossip can also sneak up and quietly ensnare us.

Everyone has experienced those moments after a particularly bad disagreement with a friend, where you want to run to anyone else who will listen to your side of the story on how you have been wronged. When the friend learns of the gossip—because it always comes back around— the situation is far worse than when it started. What started as a small disagreement blossoms out of control because you did not keep it to yourself. Now, something that started out small has grown into a chasm as wide as the Grand Canyon.

I have learned that it is better to keep my mouth shut about issues I have with my friends. As the focal verse notes, this response really is the loving thing to do. Jesus tells us to go to one another in love and reconcile our differences (Matt. 18:15–17). He does not instruct us to announce our grievances at the city gates or to discuss them with every person we know. He admonishes us to address the matter directly with the person who has been offended. While uncomfortable at first, the outcome is always better when we address a situation head-on, rather than indirectly through others. When we continually rehash an argument with others, we are not genuinely forgiving our friend.

Proverbs 17:9 presents the two choices for dealing with offenses with our friends. The first approach encourages love and can actually strengthen the friendship. The second choice can dismantle a relationship, even your

relationship with your spouse. Rather than discuss every little disagreement between my husband and me with my friends or family, the better choice is to forgive my husband instead of dragging my family and friends into the conflict. I will get over it and move on after the disagreement is over. By choosing to forgive, I have responded in a loving manner.

The next time you are offended by someone, choose to work it out with her and her alone. Forgive her and watch how the Lord grows your friendship. Do your absolute best to refrain from carrying the burden with you and discussing it with others. Cover the transgression with your love.

Dominique Richardson

Prayer: *Seek to be more loving toward your friends, forgiving them when you are offended. Keep your tongue quiet instead of discussing your problems with others. Ask the Lord to help you reconcile with your friend, heal the relationship, and become stronger when everything is said and done.*

Personal Reflection: ....

....

....

....

....

....

Stopping the Flood before It Happens

Proverbs 17:14–16

"The beginning of strife is like releasing water;
Therefore stop contention before a quarrel starts." (v. 14)

Few people would describe me as the quiet mouse sitting in the corner. I like to be part of the action, speaking my mind when I have something to say. Yet, there have been moments when I wish that I had held my tongue, choosing not to speak or speaking words of peace in a tense situation. I am not contentious, but I can be quicker to speak than to listen at times. In those moments, I may be hastening the way to anger and potential quarreling.

This verse describes the way an argument begins "like releasing water." The imagery here is not that of a small trickle from your faucet; rather, the description is of "a flood" (CSB), which tends to happen quickly. Someone is offended, one sharp word is said, the argument escalates, and harsh words pour out like water through a broken dam.

The writer of Proverbs 17 urges believers to stop a fight before it breaks out. Jesus addresses this topic in the Sermon on the Mount: "Blessed are the peacemakers, for they shall be called sons of God" (Matt. 5:9). Are you a peacemaker? Keeping the peace is something that will not just benefit you but will also benefit many others around you. Being a peacemaker is not being a pushover, allowing someone to walk all over you. It is choosing to walk in love and kindness, seeking unity in all situations.

The next time you are in a situation where tension is rising, try to find ways to bring calm back into the situation. If you were the one who was offended, try to remind yourself that the other person is not your enemy. The person's intent is most likely not to hurt you. If you gently let her know that what was said hurt your feelings, you are likely to see your friend soften her approach to the discussion.

Likewise, if you realize you might have offended your friend, be quick to apologize and take responsibility for your words. Whether or not your intent was to offend, you should apologize and ask for forgiveness as quickly as you can.

Seek to keep peace even when you have a difference of opinion with someone else. Learn to fight fair, forgive quickly, and be slow to anger. Stop the flood of arguments before it ever starts.

Dominique Richardson

Prayer: *Do you have trouble holding your tongue? Be quick to forgive, slow to anger, and patient to listen. Be aware of others around you and conscious of how your words might be affecting someone else. Seek to be a peacemaker, living your life according to God's way.*

Personal Reflection: ....

....

....

....

....

....

....

Friendships for the Hard Times

Proverbs 17:17–23

"A friend loves at all times,
And a brother is born for adversity." (v. 17)

When I was pregnant with my twin boys, the doctor walked solemnly into the room at my twenty-four-week appointment, gently seated herself on the stool, and slid over in front of my husband and me. She explained the need to admit me to the hospital on complete bed rest until the babies were born. It was a terrifying situation with many unknowns as we left her office to check into the hospital. After a five-day inpatient stay, I was allowed to serve my bed rest time from the comforts of my couch at home.

Without the friends and family who regularly visited me, brought me meals, and cleaned the house, it is highly likely that I would have descended into madness sitting on my couch all day. While it was not easy to survive those three months on bed rest, the love poured out by everyone sustained me. New friendships budded and old friendships blossomed during that difficult time.

Friends are there for you not just during the good times; often the difficult times reveal the depth of a relationship. My husband and I were astonished by the acts of kindness showered on us. We learned through that experience how friends become family and are meant to be there for adversity (v. 17).

Supporting people is easy when life is fun and games, but it is far more challenging when they need you to show up during the tough times. Look for opportunities to be the light someone needs when darkness is closing in on them. Be the sister that is born out of adversity.

When a friend has a newborn baby, take her a meal. Or if she is taking care of an elderly parent, offer to run errands or mow the lawn or clean the house. If you have not heard from a friend in a while, call and check on her. You never know what someone could be going through if you do not ask.

Be on the lookout for ways you can help others who are struggling. Show the love of Christ by loving at all times, especially when things are hard. While I remember fun times with people, the friends who have joined my family circle are ones who have been by my side during the most difficult times in my life. They are the friends who have become like sisters to me, and I am grateful to God for their presence in my life.

Dominique Richardson

Prayer: *Thank the Lord for the amazing people in your life. Thank Him for giving you loving friends to walk through difficult times. Look for opportunities to be there for your friends and to love at all times, especially when they need it most.*

Personal Reflection: ....

....

....

....

....

....

....

Keeping Our Eyes on God

Proverbs 17:24–28

"Wisdom is in the sight of him who has understanding,
But the eyes of a fool are on the ends of the earth." (v. 24)

I took a class on productivity recently. The instructor asked us to write down everything we did daily in fifteen-minute intervals. While the task was tedious, the results were revealing. I spent far more time watching television and aimlessly scrolling through Facebook than I expected. Time slips away quickly if you are not careful with how you use it. This experiment helped me realize the imbalance in my leisure time between worldly and spiritual things. Quite frankly, I was embarrassed by the discrepancy. Why hadn't I spent a higher percentage of time on Bible reading and prayer? I was investing my time in earthly things instead of focusing on the things of God.

If you have had a long day at work, you are tired and just want to do something to relax. You turn on the TV and hours pass without realizing your mind is being affected by what you watch, read, or hear. "And do not be conformed to this world, but be transformed by the renewing of your mind" (Rom. 12:2). The more time you spend with the things of this world, the more likely you are to be conformed to it. My timesheet was a wake-up call for me, helping me see my need to spend more time practicing personal spiritual disciplines so my mind can be transformed rather than conformed.

How about you? Have you taken a look at your schedule recently to see how you are spending your time? One trick I learned for reducing the amount of time spent on social media is to move those apps to a different location on your phone. Putting a Bible or devotional app where they were located can remind you to get into the Word of God whenever you habitually look for the time-draining apps.

Consider praying while driving to work in the morning. Take fifteen minutes to do a Bible study on your lunch break; or better yet, invite a friend from work to join you in that study. When you get home from work, instead of turning on the television, spark your creativity by putting on some worship music; grab colored pencils with a piece of paper, and script a verse of Scripture. Making small adjustments like these in your daily routine will quickly help you spend more time focused on the things of God. By doing so, you will obey the teaching of today's verse. You will have understanding and find wisdom because you are seeking God first; you will not be ensnared by the world like the fool who keeps his eyes turned toward it.

Dominique Richardson

Prayer: *Keep your eyes fixed on the Lord, seeking His wisdom. Ask Him to help you find ways to spend more time with Him. Find areas in your life where you can adjust your schedule so you can be focused on Him throughout your entire day.*

Personal Reflection: ....

....

....

....

....

....

....

....

What Is Your Heart's Desire?

Proverbs 18:1–4

"A fool has no delight in understanding,
But in expressing his own heart." (v. 2)

When the word *heart* is mentioned, what thoughts fill your mind? Valentine cards with lace and flowers? A doctor's appointment for an electrocardiogram (EKG)? Or perhaps an evaluation of your own heart in light of Scripture? As women seeking to please our heavenly Father, we should be concerned with both our physical heart and spiritual heart.

The physical heart provides nourishment, sustenance, and energy throughout the entire body. If a weakness, either by breakdown or disease, occurs within the heart, it could lead to weaknesses in the rest of the body.

The spiritual heart is the center of thinking and reason (Prov. 3:3; 6:2; 7:3), the emotions (15:15, 30), and the will (11:14, 20)—whatever affects our speech (4:24), sight (4:25), and conduct (4:26–27). The condition of your spiritual heart determines your spiritual health and ultimately controls how you respond to life's circumstances (4:23).

The book of Proverbs teaches that everyone has either a foolish heart or a wise heart. The foolish heart despises correction (5:12), is proud (14:14; 18:2, 12), lacks discretion (12:23; 19:3), and is hardened (28:14). Standing in stark contrast is the wise heart, which receives commands (10:8), has wisdom and understanding (14:33), seeks knowledge (15:14), and learns and grows (16:23).

Proverbs 18:2 paints a graphic word picture of an individual with a foolish heart. Regrettably, I regularly encounter women who display the characteristics described in this verse. They have both a closed mind (they do not "delight in understanding") and an open mouth (insist on "expressing their own heart"). Such women stand in stark contrast to the description of Mary, who sat at Jesus' feet to absorb His wise teaching (Luke 10:39). She took advantage of her ability

to spend time with her Lord, so that she would be better prepared to serve Him effectively. Mary teaches us that when we choose to delight in gaining godly wisdom, significant results can occur:

- We are guided by God's Word (Ps. 119:105).
- We linger in sweet prayer (1 Thess. 5:17).
- We commit to memory His life-changing Word (Ps. 119:11).
- We meditate on things of the Lord (Ps. 119:97).
- We view life's circumstances through the lens of servanthood (John 12:26).
- We are ready for each day's special assignment (Phil. 3:13–14).
- Our words reflect a heart of wisdom (Prov. 31:26).

As you consider the truth of Proverbs 18:2, will you ask your heavenly Father to help you desire to develop a wise heart? Choosing to do so will potentially yield significant eternal results.

Pat Ennis

Prayer: *Thank your heavenly Father for loving you, redeeming you, and giving you a new heart (Ps. 51:10). Ask Him to help you consistently desire a wise heart that is reflected in your conversation.*

Personal Reflection: ....

....

....

Are Your Words Tasty Trifles?

Proverbs 18:5–9

*"The words of a talebearer are like tasty trifles,
And they go down into the inmost body." (v. 8)*

English trifle is the tasty pudding, cake, and fruit dessert that has graced tables for more than four centuries. Frequently a trifle is the crowning touch to holiday dinners. Proverbs 18:8 speaks of another type of "tasty trifle," a glamorous description for a challenge frequently experienced by women—the desire to bare tales or gossip. Drawn from a Hebrew word meaning "swallowing greedily," this trifle is considerably more damaging than a large serving of English trifle rapidly consumed. Like food being digested, gossiped news is assimilated into the depths of one's body, often retained, frequently with damaging results.

Spiritually, James 3:3–5 teaches that even though the tongue is small, it has the power to control a woman and everything in her life. Isaiah 6:1–8 relates the account of how God called Isaiah to become a prophet. He did so by first giving Isaiah a vision of His awesome holiness and then by sanctifying the prophet's tongue. Isaiah realized, after catching a glimpse of the purity of God, that his tongue needed to be purified (Is. 6:5–8).

Early in my Christian walk I recall reading the account of a family living in North Dakota in a small town that was destroyed by a tasty trifle. The mother had not been well since the birth of her second baby, but everyone knew that she did all she could to create an atmosphere of love in her home.

One day a village gossip whispered that the man was being unfaithful to his wife. The story was entirely without foundation, but it began to spread. Eventually it came to the wife's ears. Because of her weakened condition, it was more than she could bear, and a few weeks later when her husband returned home, no one met him. The coldness and quietness of his home sent a chill of fear over his heart. Soon the awful truth became apparent. His wife, sick and in

despair, had taken her own life and those of her two children! Later the lie was exposed, but it had already done its deadly work.

At the end of the age, believers will be judged by how we have used our tongues. Matthew 12:36 teaches that "for every idle word men may speak, they will give account of it in the day of judgment." Talebearers are quick to start or repeat gossip. As Christians, we must be careful never to be guilty of the devastating sin of transmitting tasty trifles in our conversations. Rather, may our words always be comparable to the lingering lusciousness of a serving of English trifle (Prov. 16:24; 25:11).

Pat Ennis

Prayer: *Ask your heavenly Father to give you the desire and strength of character to make Psalm 19:14 a criteria for your speech. Speak only words of sweet encouragement.*

Personal Reflection: ....

....

....

....

....

....

What Is the Source of Your Security?

Proverbs 18:10–13

*"The name of the Lord is a strong tower;
The righteous run to it and are safe." (v. 10)*

If you walk into a room and the conversation stops, what is your assumption? Is your reflex reaction fear of rejection because you thought they were talking about you or trust in your heavenly Father who loves you unconditionally and promises to be "a strong tower" (v. 10) in the midst of potentially challenging situations (John 14:27)?

Fear is defined as "a distressing emotion aroused by impending danger, evil, pain, etc., whether the threat is real or imagined."* We live in a fear-dominated world—serious illness, financial reversal, old age, death, and rejection are all categories of fear that cause a focus away from God's character and toward the circumstance. Fear is real and not always negative—when you sense danger, fear usually stimulates you to fight or flee. However, the fear of rejection (Prov. 29:25) is a negative reaction because you are actually reversing "the royal law" described in Matthew 22:36–40 and placing more focus on loving people (Lev. 19:18) than on loving God (Deut. 6:5).

As an introverted college/seminary professor, each semester I have the choice of allowing the fear of rejection to affect my classroom performance. Though I have many years of successful teaching experience, the most challenging part of starting a new semester is the potential that this group of students will not accept me. I have two options: I can either choose to focus on my heavenly Father's previous faithfulness and rely on Him to be my security in this situation (Prov. 18:10), or I can allow negative thoughts to plunge me into despair. By "bringing every thought into captivity to the obedience of Christ" (2 Cor. 10:5) and "running to my heavenly Father's strong tower" (Prov. 18:10), I continue to excel in the classroom.

The only positive fear recorded in Scripture is the fear of God (Prov. 1:7). This fear is a reverence of God's majesty, power, and greatness. If you choose to embrace the fear of God, the fear of rejection will likely dissolve. As you run to the Lord's strong tower, peace and security fill your heart and mind (Ps. 119:11; Eph. 6:10–20). When you do so, may I encourage you to use the strategy I began many years ago. Purchase a journal and inscribe it with Psalm 103:1–2. Daily record only God's blessing to you. Weekly review the blessings; and as your journal expands, return to the blessings of the previous year. I am confident that you will find that the remembrances of running to God's "strong tower" will replace fear of rejection in your life as it has in mine.

Pat Ennis

Prayer: *Scripture teaches that your "adversary, the devil walks about like a roaring lion, seeking whom he may devour. Resist him, steadfast in the faith" (1 Pet. 5:8–9). Pray that you will remain steadfast in your faith by running to your heavenly Father's "strong tower" when fear threatens your spiritual security.*

Personal Reflection: ....

....

....

....

....

Random House Webster's College Dictionary, 2nd ed., s.v. "fear."

Am I a Spirit Breaker?

Proverbs 18:14–18

"The spirit of a man will sustain him in sickness,
But who can bear a broken spirit?" (v. 14)

What mental pictures fill your mind when you hear the word "broken"? An assortment of images cross mine, including fractured, damaged, weakened, rejected, and despairing people or objects. Clearly the word lacks positive associations.

The Hebrew word for "broken" (*naka'*) in this verse suggests being stricken or distressed. It describes people who have been battered by events in their lives, causing them to be depressed and defeated. The word can also refer to a heart that has been crushed by affliction. "A broken spirit" can sap all our strength, leaving us weak and sickly both emotionally and spiritually. There is an undeniable connection between our emotional and physical health (v. 14).

Women have the ability to break the spirit of others with a very small part of the body. Can you guess what it might be? The New Testament teaches us: "If anyone does not stumble in word, he is a perfect man, able also to bridle the whole body. . . . Even so the tongue is a little member and boasts great things. See how great a forest a little fire kindles!" (James 3:2–5). In the Old Testament, Moses' sister Miriam serves as a graphic illustration of the impact of a sharp, complaining tongue (Num. 12:1–15). The entire nation of Israel was delayed for seven days because she chose to use her tongue in an inappropriate manner. As I read the account of her life, I am challenged to examine my own life. The best way to do that is to collect and record some basic information:

- Determine the approximate length of my tongue.
- Record my height in inches. Calculate the ratio of my height to tongue length in percentage form (my tongue length is 2.5" and my height is 66"—2.5 ÷ 66 = .03 or 3%).

- Pose a probing question, "Am I going to allow something that is 3% of my body height to control me?"

Research reveals that it takes a minimum of two, and perhaps as many as five, positive remarks to offset a negative one. Consistent negative remarks can break the spirit of others. Will you choose to use your words to inspire others with renewed courage, spirit, and hope? Proverbs 25:11 teaches us the fruit of affirming words: "A word fitly spoken is like apples of gold in settings of silver." Marvea Johnson's thoughts provide poignant motivation to apply this proverb daily in our lives, "Kind words are jewels that live in the heart and soul and remain as blessed memories years after they have been spoken."*

Pat Ennis

Prayer: *Ask your heavenly Father to help you control your tongue so that it affirms and encourages others rather than breaking their spirits.*

Personal Reflection: ....

....

....

....

....

*Marvea Johnson, *The Beauty of Friendship* devotional calendar (Siloam Springs, AR 2007), October 9 entry.

591

Do You Choose to Build Bridges or Barriers?

Proverbs 18:19–21

*"A brother offended is harder to win than a strong city,
And contentions are like the bars of a castle." (v. 19)*

Aunt Jan is not attending the family holiday celebrations this season because last year she was offended by a remark John made about her "famous deviled eggs." After moving to her son-in-law and daughter's home and funding the construction of her own granny flat, Ellen moved out four years later because the contention within the family was so intense. The root cause of both scenarios? Failure to practice the *unending* forgiveness taught in Matthew 18:21–35 and Luke 17:3–4 when relational challenges occur. Commenting on Proverbs 18:19, John MacArthur writes, "There are no feuds as difficult to resolve as those with relatives; no barriers are so hard to bring down. Hence, great care should be taken to avoid such conflicts."* What is true in biological families is equally true in the body of Christ. Whether offended, provoked, or wounded, Scripture is adamant that relational difficulties are to be dealt with biblically and quickly (Ps. 4:4; Eph. 4:26). Failure to do so opens the door to sinful reactions (Rom. 14:13).

Forgiveness is the foundation of all relationships—especially behind the closed doors of our homes and among our brothers and sisters in Christ. Though the actions of others will at times disappoint us, from a biblical perspective we are consistently to offer unconditional forgiveness. It is a sobering thought to realize that barriers are erected rather than bridges built if we refuse to forgive.

When our sinful reactions collide with another person's opinions, anger often results. Anger breeds an unforgiving spirit, bitterness, and damaging relationships. To avoid that heartache, Ephesians 4:26 calls us to deal with broken relationships before we lay our heads on the pillow at night. Matthew 5:43 teaches that to forgive is the most God-like action possible. God by nature is a forgiving God. We reflect His character when we choose to forgive (Eph. 4:32; 1 John 1:9). When Peter generously offered to forgive seven times, Jesus corrected his faulty reasoning by suggesting that he was to forgive at least 490 times! Holding a grudge is an unrighteous act. Unresolved conflict may erect relational barriers that are "like the bars of a castle."

The injuries and injustices that others commit against us are trials God uses to perfect us. Choosing to realign reactions to them and viewing them as tools by which our heavenly Father makes us more like Christ, is a godly response (2 Cor. 12:7; James 1:2; 1 Pet. 5:10). When we respond biblically to relational challenges, our spiritual stamina increases because God's strength is perfected in our weakness (2 Cor. 12:9–10). Can you imagine the outcome if Aunt Jan and Ellen had viewed their situations through this biblical perspective?

Pat Ennis

Prayer: *Ask God to help you choose to build bridges rather than barriers in all your interpersonal relationships.*

Personal Reflection: ....

....

....

....

*John MacArthur, *The MacArthur Study Bible* (Nashville: Word, 2000), notes at Proverbs 18:19.

Are You a "Good Thing"?

Proverbs 18:22–23

*"He who finds a wife finds a good thing,
And obtains favor from the Lord." (v. 22)*

As a Christian woman, trained as a Family and Consumer Scientist, I never expected to be single past my mid-twenties. However, the Lord had a much different plan for me and has gently matured my attitude toward singleness, as well as increasing my understanding of the purpose of marriage. Rather than seeing marriage as only providing an intimate, nurturing relationship, I understand that a man and woman should marry only if their united lives would be more effective for the Lord than either of them as singles. As I meditate on Proverbs 18:22, the Holy Spirit motivates me to focus on becoming a woman "worth finding,"—one who is "complete in Christ" (Col. 2:10).

Ruth is my greatest role model for this focus. She was consumed with the responsibility for sustaining life for her and her mother-in-law rather than flirting with the young men in the harvest field (Ruth 2). Boaz's evaluation of her character suggests that she was a "good thing" (Ruth 3:11).

The wise woman's choice to pursue completeness in Christ eliminates the temptation to look at other people and other situations to meet her needs. Only spiritual maturity—not professional achievement, marriage, children, or ministry—will stimulate spiritual completeness and joy in her life. Several concepts of completeness emerge as the "wise woman in progress" views life from the "good thing" perspective:

- Her growth commences by "holding fast" to Christ (John 17:3; Eph. 2:1; Col. 2:19; and 1 Pet. 1:23).
- She is capable of doing what God has called her to do (2 Tim. 3:17).
- She acknowledges Christ as her authoritative Head (Eph. 1:22–23).

- Her strength to deal with Satan's temptations develops (Eph. 6:10–20; 1 Pet. 5:7–9).
- Her completeness in Christ and effective ministry occur with the combination of divine assistance plus personal responsibility (Phil. 4:13)!
- Her knowledge of God reminds her that He will not take second place and achieve His completeness in her (Deut. 10:12–13; 30:6; Matt. 22:37–39; Mark 12:29–31).
- She acquires a humble faith as the process is carried to completion (Col. 2:20).
- She is confident that as she walks uprightly there is no good thing that her heavenly Father will withhold from her (Ps. 86:11).

Regardless of your marital status, you are essentially involved in a courtship relationship that culminates with the return of your forever Bridegroom, the Lord Jesus (Rev. 19:7). Will you purpose to embrace a lifestyle that prepares you for that ultimate union? Choosing to do so will undoubtedly allow you to be classified as "a good thing" as you daily seek completeness in Christ.

Pat Ennis

Prayer: *Seek direction from your gracious heavenly Father and be consumed with your eternal courtship with Him. He will create in you the desire to mature in completeness in Christ so that you qualify for the description of a "good thing" rather than living as the "foolish virgins" (Matt. 25:1–13).*

Personal Reflection: ....

....

....

Are You a Velcro Friend?

Proverbs 18:24

"A man who has friends must himself be friendly,
But there is a friend who sticks closer than a brother." (v. 24)

When I read this focal verse, my training as a Family and Consumer Scientist immediately kicks in—from my perspective, this verse clearly describes the resulting union when the two sides of Velcro are joined. Velcro fasteners consist of two mating components: hook and loop. When pressed together, the resulting closure is adjustable and highly secure. Just as there are varied applications of Velcro— from plant ties to fasteners securing equipment in a spaceship, so multiple forms of "Velcro relationships" are possible. May I share with you two found in Scripture?

The classic description of a Velcro friendship recorded in Scripture is that of Jonathan and David (1 Sam. 18:1–4; 23:16; 2 Sam. 1:17). Their relationship models some important qualities:

- **Initiation.** Jonathan's initiation of his friendship with David reflects a willingness to cross social barriers and personal agendas to develop a genuine relationship (1 Sam. 18:1).
- **Sacrifice.** Unselfishness is always necessary to practice true friendship. Each individual must be willing to give up something treasured; in Jonathan's case, he willingly surrendered his rightful position as king (1 Sam. 18:4; 23:16–17).
- **Promoting the best interests of the other.** Jeopardizing his own safety and relationship with his father, Jonathan sought to alert David to potential danger (1 Sam. 19:1–2), to defend him, and to cultivate a spirit of reconciliation between Saul and David (v. 3–7).
- **A willingness to take the brunt of another person's circumstances** (1 Sam. 20:24–33).

My friends should sense a spirit of trust and confidence in the shared relationship. As a friend, when I consider the characteristics of trust and confidence that comprise a Velcro friendship, I am reminded that Elizabeth's life is another example of the model I desire to follow (Luke 1:39–56). She teaches much about trustworthiness and confidence in her response to Mary, her cousin and friend, who was experiencing personal challenges:

- Mary had confidence that she would be welcome in Elizabeth's home. Mary had no way of alerting Elizabeth of her intention to come for an extended visit (vv. 39–40).
- Mary chose to share her situation freely with Elizabeth, a relative as well as an older woman. This action suggests that Mary trusted Elizabeth to believe the best rather than the worst about her (v. 40).
- Elizabeth waited for Mary to share the reason for her visit rather than immediately interrogating her or preempting the situation by sharing her own good news (vv. 40b–41).
- Elizabeth was a clean vessel that the Holy Spirit could use to affirm the Lord's work in Mary's life (v. 41).
- Elizabeth offered extended hospitality to Mary (v. 56).

Friendship is one of God's most precious gifts to us. Evaluating your life against these models, would you conclude that you are a Velcro friend?

Pat Ennis

Prayer: *Ask the heavenly Father to help you to be a woman who nurtures her friendships regardless of the circumstances.*

Personal Reflection:

Actions Speak Louder Than Words

Proverbs 19:1–8

*"The foolishness of a man twists his way,
And his heart frets against the LORD." (v. 3)*

"Actions speak louder than words" is truer than most of us probably realize. According to researchers, our body language communicates 90 percent of what we are thinking and our words only 10 percent. If you really want to know how someone feels, learn to interpret body language!

My dad practiced this principle well even without higher education. He would tell me, "Do as I say, not as I do!" He knew his actions were speaking louder than his words. He wanted to be sure I had a clear understanding of what I was to follow—his words!

Most people know that eating chocolate will cause weight gain. So why, when we are on a diet, do we still eat chocolate? Our knowledge and actions are not lining up. Why? Because we want the chocolate! The battle begins between knowledge and action.

Living the Christian life sometimes presents the same tension. What we know and what we do are not always in agreement. Paul speaks to this issue in Romans 7:13–25. We want our lives to be ours. Basically, we want the "chocolate" and spiritual growth at the same time.

A woman may want to lose weight with her whole heart; but until she puts into practice healthy nutrition, regular exercise, and the rules of weight loss, desire alone will never be enough. Accordingly, desire alone will never be enough to live your life pure, holy, and blameless in the sight of the Lord.

Recently I met a young woman who had just lost 110 pounds. She came in the chapel early. All of the other women were eating a wonderful French toast breakfast. I asked whether or not she had eaten. She said, "Yes," and began telling me her weight loss journey. French toast was her favorite breakfast, and

she knew that lingering in the cafeteria would only lead to eating more than was healthy. She left the temptation and came into the chapel. Her knowledge, words, and actions were working together and paying off in a big way.

Our spiritual life is much the same. When what we know about God's Word changes our actions and words so that they speak the same, we are spiritually healthier and the world gets a wonderful picture of Jesus in our lives (James 2:18).

Will it always be easy? No. We may still want the "chocolate" even though it is the very thing that leads us astray. Loving God is not just what we know in our heads, but it is how we live our lives. That discipline means being in God's Word everyday regardless of everything else on our to-do list. Choose to honor God in every aspect of your life, and remember that "he who keeps understanding will find good" (Prov. 19:8).

Gayla Parker

Prayer: *Ask God to speak to and through you!*

Personal Reflection:

This Hurts and It's Not My Fault

Proverbs 19:9–13

*"The discretion of a man makes him slow to anger,
And his glory is to overlook a transgression." (v. 11)*

Recently my youngest son, Jesse, was in a minor car accident in Philadelphia. The other driver put fault on Jesse, though he was innocent. When the police and insurance company talked to Jesse, they asked these questions: "Were you in your lane?" His response, "I think so." "Can you say without a doubt that you were in your lane?" "I can say I'm 99 percent sure. I'm driving a small car, which helps with these narrow lanes." Unfortunately, Jesse's insurance had to pay the claim because he would not commit to 100 percent certainty. Jesse was not happy with the decision because he felt that he was being blamed for something that he did not do. I am grateful that Jesse was honest in his statement. While Jesse may not like the decision of the insurance company, he can know that God is 100 percent pleased with his decision to be 100 percent honest.

One of the hardest things to do is to overlook the offense of another, but it shows great spiritual strength. The Bible includes accounts of spiritual giants such as Joseph, who was sold into slavery by his brothers. Thirteen years later, when his brothers were in need, he met their every need and then some (Gen. 45:15). He overlooked their offense, showing great virtue. Balthasar Hubmaier, an Anabaptist pastor who baptized as many as six thousand in one year, when accused of heresy, refused to recant on his faith. Before he was burned at the stake in 1528, he said: "I forgive all those that have done me harm."* In his death, he showed great virtue. In more recent history, a radical Islamist group kidnapped missionary Martin Burham, who was serving in the Philippines. He was held in captivity for an entire year, praying daily for the protection of his kidnappers. He was more concerned with their salvation than his kidnapping. Martin was killed in a rescue attempt.

Jesus Christ is the greatest example of a sacrificial life. He was wrongly accused of many things in the course of His earthly life. Eventually, He would die on a cross for crimes He never committed for the sake of our salvation.

Is it easy to overlook an offense? No! Does it demonstrate Christ in us? Yes! God's insight, understanding, and strength give us courage to forgive "seventy times seven" times (Matt. 18:22).

Gayla Parker

Prayer: *Ask the Lord to help you forgive those who have hurt you. Trust Him to handle their transgressions against you.*

Personal Reflection: ....

....

....

....

....

....

*William R. Estep, *The Anabaptist Story: An Introduction to Sixteenth-Century Anabaptism*, 3rd ed. (Grand Rapids: Eerdmans, 1996), 103.

What Is Your Legacy?

Proverbs 19:14–17

"Houses and riches are an inheritance from fathers,
But a prudent wife is from the LORD." (v. 14)

When my father-in-law passed away in January 2011, I had the privilege of sorting through his personal possessions while my husband sat by his father's bedside until his homegoing. Many tears were shed and a few giggles were voiced as I went through the memorabilia representing the life of Everette G. Parker.

One treasured discovery was his diary from WWII in which he wrote about the first time he saw my mother-in-law, who preceded him in death. I found a 1943 article from his hometown newspaper reporting details he had never shared with us. He had mailed his monthly army check to the church to help build a new worship center debt-free. I found copies of sermon notes and commitments he pursued to know Christ. His Bible was still on the table opened to the next day's devotion, as well as canceled checks from decades of giving to Olivet Baptist Church. On the meager salary of a carpenter, my father-in-law gave his tithe and additional dollars to foreign missions while my husband and I were serving in the Philippines. That kind of sacrificial giving continued even when his only income was Social Security. My husband now has those treasures in his office.

My father-in-law's eight-hundred-square-foot home was located in a modest middle-class neighborhood. As the years passed, his neighborhood declined. Our family spent countless hours urging him to move. He responded, "This house is fine, and it is paid for!" As I read through canceled checks, contribution statements, and articles about his generosity, I felt overwhelmingly ashamed that I had challenged him to leave a lifestyle that allowed him to do so much for the kingdom of God!

My husband and his brother inherited that small house, located in a very undesirable neighborhood. The house is worth little, but the lifestyle of the

man who had lived there and the huge testimony he left behind are so valuable that their worth cannot be measured in dollars. To be prudent is to show care and thought for the future. My father-in-law showed care and thought for the eternal future of others.

My prayer is that our family will inherit his commitment to be a faithful servant of the Lord. His testimony certainly challenged me to consider the "things" I will be leaving behind for my children. Will they find the same testimony I found? Do my "things" tell the story of one who gives sacrificially to the cause of Christ? Do my "things" tell the story of one who fervently loves God? Do my "things" tell the story of one who shares the story of Christ at all costs? Do my "things" tell the story of one who is prudent so that God can be glorified in the generations to come?

Gayla Parker

Prayer: *Claim eternal life through faith in Jesus Christ as a joy that is forever! Ask the Lord to make your legacy that of a prudent woman—one that leads others to life eternal.*

Personal Reflection: ....

....

....

....

Crossing Home Plate

Proverbs 19:18–22

*"Listen to counsel and receive instruction,
That you may be wise in your latter days." (v. 20)*

The batter hit the ball to the center field fence. The runner on first base ran to home plate, scoring a run. The batter ran to first base and . . . stopped. "Run!" the coach yelled. The batter, assuming the coach was yelling the instruction to his teammate, joined in yelling, "Run!" The batter had no idea the instruction was for him. My son was the batter in his first high school varsity baseball game.

Having just returned from fourteen years in the Philippines, my son could not wait to play baseball, which is non-existent in the Philippines. To our surprise he made the team and was a natural hitter. His skill, however, did not get him across home plate that day. The thought of his mistake still horrifies him. His problem was not inadequate skills but his lack of knowledge of the rules of the game.

Both skill and knowledge are required to finish well. My son learned the difference between hitting a homerun and scoring a homerun. As Christian women, our desire should be more than hitting the homerun; we should seek to cross home plate. We must listen to counsel and receive instruction, especially when it comes from the Lord, even when it does not make sense.

Have you received God's instructions, which did not make sense at the time, but which then yielded results that far exceeded what you could have ever imagined? The Bible is His rulebook to help you play this game of life. So how do we play the game of life well all the way to home plate?

First base: Know your purpose.

Jesus said, "Go . . . make disciples . . . teach. . ." (Matt. 28:19–20). That command defines our purpose: going to the lost and the needy, introducing

others to Christ, teaching them to hear God's call, and training them to follow in His footsteps.

Second base: Know your resources.

Jesus also tells us that He will be with us even "to the end of the age" (Matt. 28:20). He has all the resources we need!

Third base: Keep running!

Paul said: "I run . . . not with uncertainty" (1 Cor. 9:26). Paul ran for the prize, with purpose. That requires intentionality, focus, and diligence.

Home plate.

Like Abraham, we find ourselves on "the Mount of the Lord" (Gen. 22:14), where He provides and says, "Well done, good and faithful servant" (Matt. 25:21).

Gayla Parker

Prayer: *Ask the Lord to give you wisdom, and follow Him across home plate.*

Personal Reflection: ....

....

....

....

....

Fear That Controls

Proverbs 19:23–29

"The fear of the LORD leads to life,
And he who has it will abide in satisfaction;
He will not be visited with evil." (v. 23)

As a child I was more often than not afraid to go to bed. During my early years, I lived with my grandmother and her adopted sons, who were big fans of scary movies. I was not! Every Saturday morning they watched scary movies. In one of those movies, a woman was abducted by aliens, taken to their planet, injected with strange medications, and brought back to earth. She had no memory of the event, but over time she turned into a giant woman who destroyed her hometown. For months I went to bed measuring where my feet were so I would know if I were growing into a giant.

However silly, these events set a pattern for fearing sleep. When I accepted Christ at sixteen, I never went to bed fearful again. Why? I had His salvation, and nothing could ever take that away (John 10:28). Before Christ, my fears were in the wrong place. When our fear is in the wrong place, it can and will prevent us from allowing Christ to rule and thereby conquer the giants in our lives. Fearing the Lord enabled me to give Him control of my life.

"Let us go up at once and take possession, for we are well able to overcome it" (Num. 13:30) are Caleb's words after going into a land God had shown Moses. Twelve spies went into the land where they saw the giants. When they returned, they advised Moses to stay away because they were fearful. Fear of giants rather than trust in God controlled their decision. Only Caleb and Joshua recommended moving forward to take the land. These two men did not fear the giants; they feared the consequences of ignoring God's call. The Israelites ignored Caleb's advice, and they spent years wandering in the desert instead of enjoying milk and honey.

Giants are in the land today—illness, shyness, sin, past hurts, problems . . . and the list goes on. Giants may be anything that keep us from moving forward in God's will and taking possession of the "land" (our lives) that God has shown us. They are the things we allow to control our lives rather than trusting God. Caleb knew that with God, any giant could be conquered. There will always be giants, but they should never bring the kind of fear that brings spiritual paralysis, keeping us from fulfilling God's will. God has given us all unique gifts that are perfect for conquering our giants and sharing God's love.

Gayla Parker

Prayer: *Ask the Lord to be with you, enabling you to love the lost, conquer the giants, and follow His mandate to "Make disciples!"*

Personal Reflection: ....

Danger! Danger!

Proverbs 20:1–2

"Wine is a mocker,
Strong drink is a brawler,
And whoever is led astray by it is not wise." (v. 1)

Several of my family members dealt with addictions to alcohol, nicotine, and prescription pain medications. As a result, I have been an avid advocate for total abstinence from these substances. I know firsthand what an addiction can do to a family emotionally, financially, physically, and spiritually. Through the years, the view of alcohol consumption has taken many forms—from total abstinence to moderate drinking and everything in between. One thing remains the same: Acceptability does not take away the dangers of alcohol, and it does not change what the Bible says about "strong drink."

Drinking alcohol will always have the potential of leading to drunkenness and addiction. One drink holds the potential to change a life forever. Solomon encouraged his audience, including future generations, to flee from alcohol lest they find themselves in a drunken state—a condition he describes as marked by sorrow, complaints, wounds, and red eyes (Prov. 23:29); as wasting most of our time either looking for a drink or lingering over one (v. 30); as living in a fantasyland by glorifying the properties of drink (v. 31). He summarizes by describing the one who drinks in excess as "not wise" (20:1).

The Bible identifies several characters who were not wise in the midst of their drunkenness! Some of them may surprise you. Noah was seen naked by his son while passed out from drinking too much alcohol (Gen. 9:21–22). Belshazzar unwisely drank from a gold goblet and worshiped the gods of gold and silver. He died under the influence of alcohol before the night was over (Dan. 5:1–30). The clergy of Ephraim wallowed in their vomit after getting drunk (Is. 28:7–8). Lot had sexual relations with his daughters while drunk

(Gen. 19:30–38). Amnon was killed by Absalom while drunk (2 Sam. 13:28–29). These horrific accounts illustrate the impaired judgment of being drunk.

As a believer, I want to be great in the sight of the Lord and give Him glory. That is reason enough for me to avoid alcohol. I want to live as a wise woman so that others may see in me Christ, "in whom are hidden all the treasures of wisdom and knowledge" (Col. 2:3). When God sees me, I do not want Him to find me hiding in conformity to the world; I want Him to see me as "a living sacrifice" (Rom. 12:1), "set apart" (Ps. 4:3), making "ready a people prepared for the Lord" (Luke 1:17) for the sake of His glory.

Gayla Parker

Prayer: *Seek wisdom from the Lord and avoid drunkenness. Glorify Him through your holy life.*

Personal Reflection: ....

....

....

....

....

....

Does It Matter in Eternity?

Proverbs 20:3–4

*"It is honorable for a man to stop striving,
Since any fool can start a quarrel." (v. 3)*

As a mother, I have had times of success and times of failure. One of those failures came in my attempt to resolve a dispute between my second born (Nathan, eight) and third born (Jesse, five). Just as I entered the dispute, I found Nathan ready to punch Jesse in the arm. They knew my first question would be: "Does this argument matter in eternity?" On a good day that question was enough to stop a fight. Not this day. I mustered up all the motherly wisdom I could and threatened: "If you hit your brother, it will cost you this week's allowance." Nathan cherished his allowance; so I was positive this would stop the fight immediately. He stood there a few seconds, hit his brother on the arm as hard as he could, went to his room, and came back with money in hand. Mom failed! I did not even come close to my desired outcome. To this day my sons cannot remember why they fought. Evidently, it did not matter in eternity.

Quarrels are like that; the details are rarely remembered. A moment of uncontrolled anger can bring great hurt. When a dispute can be resolved, a beautiful picture of God's grace and forgiveness is painted. While serving as a missionary in Asia, I had the privilege of seeing this work of God firsthand and the revival that followed.

Muslims and "Christians" experienced disputes for centuries. Vigilantes on both sides of the disputes have committed horrible crimes and great atrocities for the sake of "religion." In 1999, a powerful Muslim leader became a believer under the godly influence of his wife. In that same year, an influential leader on the "Christian" side became a follower of Christ. Some months later, both men attended a secret meeting for believers interested in serving as missionaries to the Muslims. Fear, concern, and worry were evident as the two

made their way to the platform during an altar call. In front of 125 believers, these two men confessed their sins to one another, asked for forgiveness, wept, hugged, and prayed for one another's people groups. Never in all of my years of ministry have I seen such a powerful testimony of God's grace and forgiveness. These sinful men were laying aside their dispute to serve alongside one another as brothers in Christ. A revival ensued in the regions these men called home.

Quarrels come easy for women in the midst of mood swings and on bad days when feelings can be easily hurt. But does a quarrel matter in eternity? It does when it keeps another from experiencing the forgiveness of Christ (Col. 3:13). God's wisdom and grace can help resolve the conflict and spark revival—if not in our nation, at least in our own hearts where revival begins.

Gayla Parker

Prayer: *Consider any conflict in your life and confess it to the Lord.*

Personal Reflection: ....

....

....

....

....

....

Truth or Fiction?

Proverbs 20:5–6

"Counsel in the heart of man is like deep water,
But a man of understanding will draw it out." (v. 5)

The word *deep* refers to heart motives. When my sons were small and said, "Mom, you are the best cook ever," a request for cookies was on the horizon. Although the compliment was sweet, it came with an ulterior motive—getting homemade chocolate chip cookies. Understanding is more than the dictionary meaning.

One of the most difficult tasks of a missionary is learning the unspoken meaning of the second language. We received a notice that a package had arrived, and we were certain it was the long-awaited Christmas package. Arriving at the post office with all three sons in tow, I did not get the response I was expecting. The worker politely informed me that I was too busy to get the package. First of all, how would she know how busy I was? Second, why would I leave without the Christmas present for my sons? After a long discussion, the postal worker finally took us back to the customs inspector. Only then did I understand our conversation. The employee had been trying to tell me that the unscrupulous customs agent was on duty that day. He demanded a payment of $200 to retrieve my package, an amount of money that not only did I not have but was also more than what the contents of the package were worth! I left the post office with three very sad boys and no package in hand. I failed to heed the counsel of the postal worker because I did not dig deep enough to understand the situation.

Jesus was the master of drawing out the intent of the heart to understand actions and words. He knew what to ask the Samaritan woman: "Go, call your husband, and come here" (John 4:16). He was drawing out the truth of her life and helping her recognize her sin. Looking religious is easy; surrendering to

Christ is hard work. Jesus challenged the rich ruler to look past his easy life: "Sell what you have . . . and come, follow Me" (Matt. 19:21). This young man found it easier to pursue a life of good works than a life lived by faith—just as it is today.

A spiritual checklist of good works does not require a 24/7 commitment to Christ. The works mentality recognizes one day of being kind and giving to the poor as fulfilling the religious requirements. Jesus wants much more than a checklist!

Gayla Parker

Prayer: *Ask the Lord to bring you into relationship with Him to "serve Him with a loyal heart and with a willing mind" (1 Chr. 28:9).*

Personal Reflection: ....

....

....

....

....

....

....

Clean Is in the Eye of the Beholder

Proverbs 20:7–9

*"The righteous man walks in his integrity;
His children are blessed after him." (v. 7)*

Spring means spring-cleaning! Our three boys love getting their bikes out, but spring-cleaning bedrooms is not their idea of fun. Before the bikes come out, the rooms must be cleaned.

The boys have different understandings of clean. The dictionary definition of *clean* suggests "free from dirt or impurities; unsoiled; unstained; recently laundered; having no obstructions." Yet that meaning of "clean" is of little interest to my three sons. I can assure you that their rooms were not free from dirt or impurities, unsoiled, newly laundered, or free of obstructions on the floor.

A smell coming from a boy's room lingers no matter how much air freshener is used. My boys are blind to clutter, dust, and dirt. They believe that cleanliness is in the eye of the beholder; and, according to my sons, the clutter and smell in their rooms is just fine.

Despite their messy rooms, I love my boys dearly. They have brought much joy into my life. As we tease in our family about spring-cleaning and our varying definitions of clean, I wonder how my definition of a clean heart must differ from God's. "Who can say, 'I have made my heart clean; I am pure from my sin'?" (v. 9). Like my boys, have I been blind to the dust, clutter, and dirt that is in my heart (Mark 8:18; 2 Pet. 1:9)? Do I cover up sin like they cover up messy sheets (2 Sam. 12)? Is my heart free from impurities and obstructions (Matt. 5:8)? Am I one who lives with integrity and righteousness (Ps. 7:8)? Or, do I leave a "sweet-smelling aroma" from a Christ-like attitude (Eph. 5:2)? "Children

are blessed" when their parents are righteous. My boys needed clean rooms, but even more, they need clean hearts in Christ!

Gayla Parker

Prayer: *Ask yourself: "Am I radiating a spirit that comes from having a clean heart?" As you clean your home, clean your heart, allowing His brightness to pierce the darkness in this lost world.*

Personal Reflection: ....

....

....

....

....

....

....

....

Little Becomes Much!

Proverbs 20:10–13

"Even a child is known by his deeds,
Whether what he does is pure and right." (v. 11)

God made both our ears and our eyes, to hear and to see (v. 12). Perhaps what we see speaks louder than what we hear, especially when words are backed up by actions. Scripture encourages believers to keep actions and words in alignment as a spiritual act of worship—an act of worship that knows no boundary of age.

A few years ago a group of students in a Caribbean country gathered for a weekend retreat. The programming looked much like a retreat in America: time for worship, Bible Study, break-out sessions, and prayer. The difference was the communist influence in this country, the hot weather without air conditioning, uncomfortable backless benches, and one out-of-tune guitar for worship. None of those distractions mattered; the students enjoyed the fellowship with believers worshiping and praising God.

During a prayer time, the students were challenged to pray for a mission effort in Asia. The missionary appointee needed prayer for protection, his ministry, and specific project funding. The students were so moved by the need that they wanted to give to this mission effort. Without any prompting, one by one students came to the front of the room, emptying their pockets of all their money. Those without money placed their shirts, socks, and shoes in the offering plate. The students gave the equivalent of $200.

Their complete surrender caused me to weep and question my own level of commitment. Would I be willing to put my favorite sweater in an offering plate knowing it could not be replaced? Would I be willing to give up my one and only pair of shoes in order for someone else to be the beautiful feet of Christ taking the good news to the lost (Rom. 10:15)? Do my actions show my life in complete surrender to Christ like these students (James 2:22–25)?

In the homeland of those students there is poverty and communism. Missionaries are few, but God is bigger than it all (Luke 1:37)! What started as little is now much. God does not need megabucks or megachurches to change the world, He only needs complete surrender. In a non-Christian country, that group of students who own very little can take Christ to the nations. Their actions are speaking loudly!

Gayla Parker

Prayer: *Ask God to use your life to make a difference in eternity. Make your actions show Christ in you. Let God multiply your little effort into His big work.*

 **Personal Reflection:** ....

....

....

....

....

....

....

617

Is It Worth the Cost?

Proverbs 20:14–19

"Plans are established by counsel;
By wise counsel wage war." (v. 18)

Captain C. B. Sullenberger, after an emergency landing of his commercial airplane in the Hudson River, said, "There are events that divide our lives into before and after. While they may be unexpected, we owe it to ourselves to be prepared for whatever comes our way." On January 15, 2009, three minutes after take-off, the engines on US Airways Flight 1549 went silent after a massive bird strike. Sullenberger, along with copilot Jeffrey Skiles, glided the plane successfully into the Hudson River. All 155 people on board survived. The success of that landing was no accident. The skill of the pilots made the difference. In just a few minutes, costs were considered and decisions were made. The cost? An airplane. No life was lost.

Most people will never land a plane in the Hudson, but we do need to be prepared for making life decisions. Without weighing the costs, the end results can be tragic. Jesus described the manner in which kings decide to wage war (Luke 14:31–32). I seem constantly to wage war on the laundry! In reality, I am in a war every day. Will I choose the will of God or my own? What is the cost? What will be the results?

The term *wage war* is used in reference to weighing the costs (Prov. 20:18). The cost is determined by asking questions. What kind of toll will this new job take on my family? Who will be neglected if I finish my to-do list? Will this purchase create a financial burden? What is the "after" of this decision?

After a long day at work, I came home to find my son and new daughter-in-law enjoying a movie. Clutter was everywhere. I wanted to bark orders and get that disaster area cleaned up, but the Holy Spirit reminded me of the impact on my relationship with my very new daughter-in-law for the years to come. In

a brief second, I weighed the cost of my angry words and took a deep breath, politely excusing myself, to bed. The next morning my oldest son, Allen, was cleaning the disaster area: "Don't worry, Mom; I've got this. Sorry we left such a mess." I was grateful that I controlled my emotions and heard the sweet apology of my son. There is a cost for words and actions. Like Captain Sully, I want all the people on my watch to "live," which requires me to prepare, seek counsel, and know when to wage war.

Gayla Parker

Prayer: *Be prepared for war by knowing God's Word (Eph. 6:17). Seek counsel through prayer (Phil. 4:6). Ask the Lord to help you choose carefully what wars to wage.*

Personal Reflection: ....

....

....

....

....

....

....

Exposed

Proverbs 20:20–30

"The spirit of a man is the lamp of the LORD,
Searching all the inner depths of his heart." (v. 27)

Have you ever noticed that light often exposes things? At times I have finished polishing or dusting furniture and then opened the windows for natural light, only to see streaks or dust particles left behind. What about the lighted makeup mirrors? The light surrounding the mirror can expose the tiniest blemish on your face. Light has a way of exposing things unseen by the naked eye.

The sayings of Proverbs 20 touch on topics such as drunkenness, quarrels, laziness, cheating, and discerning the behaviors and intentions of others. These themes are very similar to those you hear in many country music songs. However, although verse 27 starts with a sobering tone, much wisdom and truth abound from its words.

The human mind and creation are quite remarkable topics to consider. In verse 27, "the spirit" (Hb. *neshamah*, "breath") refers to a person's breath or life. Figuratively, the word may signify the mind or intellect. Romans 1 teaches that every man is accountable to God because His "eternal power and Godhead" are "clearly seen" in creation. However, God allows for you and me to choose between accepting God's existence, and thus modeling our lives after God, or rejecting God completely. To accept God is more than just mental decision; it is complete devotion manifesting itself in the heart. For this reason, God is concerned only with actions resulting from a heart with pure motives. God alone knows the "inner depths" of our hearts and determines if we are truly serving Him or merely using Him (vv. 27, 30).

Hebrews 4:12 likewise teaches that God's Word is able to discern the "inner depths" of our hearts: "For the word of God is living and powerful, and sharper than any two-edged sword, piercing even to the division of soul and spirit, and

of joints and marrow, and is a discerner of the thoughts and intents of the heart." As your Creator, God knows your thoughts, attitudes, and desires just as a lamp can illuminate or reveal what is in darkness. Because He knows you intimately, your innermost places are not hidden from the Lord. Similar to the way breath fills your bodies and gives you life, so, too, does the "lamp of the Lord" search your heart and reveal your every thought.

Jessica Pigg

Prayer: *Ask God to shine light on the "inner depths" of your heart and reveal them to you. Repent of your sins, whether known or unknown, and ask for forgiveness. Take active steps to change your behavior and allow the Holy Spirit to guide you and move mightily through you as you serve Him.*

Personal Reflection: ....

....

....

....

....

....

....

Sand Castles

Proverbs 21:1

"The king's heart is in the hand of the LORD,
Like the rivers of water;
He turns it wherever He wishes." (v. 1)

After countless trips of gathering sand and water, my sand castle was finally standing tall. But, I quickly noticed that the ocean waves were coming increasingly closer to overtaking it. With great panic, I quickly began building a wall-like barrier around the sand castle hoping that the rushing waves would not be triumphant. Much to my dismay, my sand castle was washed away so quickly you would never have known it was standing tall just seconds before. You know what I learned on the beach that day? No matter how quickly I move or how hard I try, I will never be in control. Unlike God, I cannot tell the waves of the sea to stay put at the shoreline. Even though I could not hold back the rushing waves that sought to destroy my sand castle, the Creator can "turn" the waters wherever He wishes.

In Proverbs 20, the focus is on the king's powers of discernment and judgment. However, in chapter 21, the emphasis is on the greater purposes of God and His desire for integrity (vv. 1–3). The figure of speech used in verse 1 alludes to an ancient method of irrigation in which several channels were formed from one stream so that the worker could direct the flow of the "rivers of water" with little effort. This figure of speech clearly illustrates the Lord's power and control over His creation. During this time, rulers were considered most powerful because of the absolute control they had over others. Yet, God in His sovereignty had unlimited control over the king's heart without interfering with the king's free will. Much like the grains of sand and "rivers of water" are not out of His reach, so, too, will the king's heart follow the directives of God to establish His purposes. The theme of this verse re-echoes these words: "The preparations of the heart belong to man, but the answer of the tongue is from the LORD" (Prov. 16:1). Dependence upon the Lord is contrasted with personal understanding.

The idea of God's infinite rule and sovereignty over our lives is not only challenging to grasp, but it is also difficult to trust. When the unpredictable waves of life come crashing into the shoreline of your situation, how do you react? Do you become frantic and go into a panic mode, or do you remain calm and trust in a sovereign God who cares for you?

Jessica Pigg

Prayer: *God holds authority over us, and we owe Him our allegiance for one simple reason—He is our Creator. Thank God for loving you so much that He cares for the small details of your everyday life.*

Personal Reflection: ....

....

....

....

....

....

Heart Check

Proverbs 21:2

"Every way of a man is right in his own eyes,
But the LORD weighs the hearts." (v. 2)

Let's face it: As humans, we are lovers of measurement. If you were to look in your pantry, every carton would display the weight and value of its contents. Your gas gauge tells you how much gas is in your tank. Your budget tells you how much you can spend. Your social media account measures your circle of friends. However, there is One whom we cannot measure. The God of the Bible is infinite—immeasurable, unquantifiable, and uncontainable. We cannot comprehend the vastness and full measure of Him, no matter how hard we may try (Job 11:7–9; Ps. 145:3).

This proverb links your actions to the heart that directs you. Proverbs 16:2 is similar: "All the ways of a man are pure in his own eyes, but the LORD weighs the spirits." As creative as we are in justifying our own ways and believing that we are "right," the Lord alone determines an accurate measure of its true intentions. Proverbs 20:5 compares the intentions of the heart to "deep water." Although the wise can bring it to light, there are limits.

God is infinite, but we are not. On the day you were born, the doctor inscribed on your birth certificate your weight and length. This small record of measurement is the first evidence that you are not God. Long before your first act of disobedience, the chasm between who God is and who you are was already established by the simple fact that you are measurable. This same infinite God is able to weigh the hearts of all humanity and look deep into the dark crevices, where no one else can see. Why? Because He is God, and we are not. The Lord alone can determine what is known and what is hidden from a person's own self-perceptions. Proverbs 21:2 reveals the importance of relying and depending on the Lord in contrast to looking to our own understanding.

What is your heart's intention? Sit for a moment and ask the Lord to search your heart, like David did in Psalm 139. He wanted to be cleansed even of His hidden faults and motives that were impure and self-centered. You may be surprised, but you sin even when you do not know you are sinning, and you need to be cleansed of those sins (Ps. 19:12–13). Sister, we are utterly in need of the gospel of Jesus Christ at all times. We need His blood to overflow into all areas of our lives, even the hidden areas. How beautiful would it be if we all bowed before our King with no one watching and no one knowing other than Him?

Jessica Pigg

Prayer: *Pray a bold prayer to God as the One who is infinite and boundless. Search your heart and confess all of your sins to God, for He is forgiving and merciful.*

Personal Reflection: ....

....

....

....

....

....

....

Super Powers

Proverbs 21:3–8

"To do righteousness and justice
Is more acceptable to the LORD than sacrifice." (v. 3)

If you could have one super power, what would it be? I think my top three choices would be mind-reading, the ability to fly, or the power to become imaginary. But, what if you could choose the ability to know the pure intentions and attitude of a heart? Let's be honest for a second—that would really terrify some people. Why? Because the heart is the source from which everything else flows, the dwelling of our wicked and sinful human desires.

Within Proverbs 21:3, the focus moves from the intentions of the heart to the actions it directs. Everyday deeds that are done in "righteousness" and "justice" are "more acceptable to the LORD" than special actions such as "sacrifice." The proverb affirms that the Lord has had plenty of experience with people who believed that sacrifice was enough (Prov. 21:27; Jer. 7:1–11).

Psalm 51:16–17 explains this concept of sacrifice in further detail. Old Testament law did not prescribe any sacrifices for such sins as murder and adultery. Therefore, the one who committed these sins could only cast himself on the mercy of God (2 Sam. 12:13–14). The sacrifice of your selfish will is the ultimate sacrifice God desires. He accepts and forgives those who are honest with Him and dependent on His grace. No matter what you do in His name, without a right spirit, no sacrifice you offer is pleasing to the Lord.

David had all the resources and wealth he needed to bring many sacrifices to the Lord, but he knew that his meager sacrifices would not please the Lord or wash away his sins. David was not denying the importance of the validity of the Jewish sacrificial system (Ps. 51:16). Instead, he was affirming the importance of a repentant heart and a spirit yielded to the Lord. Isaiah

57:15 states that "the High and Lofty One" makes His dwelling with those who have "a contrite [Hb. *dakka'*, "crushed"] and humble spirit."

Ritual ceremony and tradition are not ways into the presence and favor of God. Jesus is the only path to God. The righteousness of Jesus, not our own actions, is what earns us right standing with God. What are the motives of your heart? Do you seek to do righteousness and justice or do you seek to be seen and praised for your efforts?

Jessica Pigg

Prayer: *Ask God to forgive you of the times when you have walked through the motions of a relationship with Him without having a heart that was truly focused on Him.*

Personal Reflection:

Uber Driver

Proverbs 21:9–18

"Better to dwell in a corner of a housetop,
Than in a house shared with a contentious woman." (v. 9)

Over the years, my husband and I have had some memorable conversations with our Uber (on-demand private transportation) drivers. By far the craziest experience we have had was when we were in Boston last fall. After we made it through the introductory small talk, we asked the middle-aged man why he chose to work for Uber, driving people around in the middle of his day. He quickly responded, "Man, my wife is crazy; I just had to get out of the house!" He went on to explain that he only drives for Uber if he comes home from his full-time job to a nagging wife.

Much like our Uber driver, the husband depicted in this proverb prefers to "dwell in a corner of a housetop," exposed to harsh conditions, rather than to share a home with his wife, a "contentious woman." Three of the five proverbs that describe the contentions (Hb. *midyan*, "quarrel, controversy, strife") of a wife underscore the domestic despair of her husband (vv. 9, 19; 25:24). A wife's constant complaining and criticizing can make the atmosphere of her home so unpleasant that her husband might prefer being alone more than being with her.

So, what are the characteristics of a contentious wife? First Peter 3:1–6 outlines the behaviors a wife *should* have when interacting with her husband. As emphasized in the earlier verses of Proverbs 21, Peter also reminds the reader that a woman's inward character, not her outward appearance is primarily what matters to God. In this passage, Peter uses two descriptive characteristics to further explain the internal beauty of a wife: gentleness and quietness (1 Pet. 3:4). Being "gentle" (Gk. *praos*, "meek, humble") is a mark of strength rather than weakness. Aside from including the quality of gentleness in the Beatitudes

("meek," Matt. 5:5) and "fruit of the Spirit" (Gal. 5:23), Jesus described His own disposition as "gentle" (Matt. 11:29). "Quietness" (Gk. *hēsuchiou*) does not mean being totally silent. Instead, the idea is "self-control" and "trust," closely connected with meekness. Both of these characteristics of a godly woman are described as "precious in the sight of God" (1 Pet. 3:4).

The quiet and gentle woman will be admired by her husband and by those who observe her behavior. In obtaining "the incorruptible beauty of a gentle and quiet spirit," she will be approved by God for her faithfulness in living according to His original design. What kind of woman are you? Do your words and actions speak life into your home (1 Pet. 3), or do they tear down (Prov. 21)?

Jessica Pigg

Prayer: *An ideal wife is described in Proverbs 31:10–31. Read this passage and pray that God will mold you to be a woman who follows His design, building up your husband and children and making your home a safe refuge to those who enter.*

Personal Reflection:

Wilderness Living

Proverbs 21:19–31

*"Better to dwell in the wilderness,
Than with a contentious and angry woman." (v. 19)*

When you think of a garden, what comes to your mind? To many, a garden is often associated with beauty and provision. At the beginning of creation, "God *planted* a garden" in which Adam and Eve were to dwell (Gen. 2:8). God established the home before other institutions, including civil government, communities, and worship assemblies. God created the home first to show how crucial the family is as the foundation for community and order. Every home should be a place of shelter and delight, an Eden. A home should be the opposite of a "wilderness."

For the husband to "dwell in a corner of a housetop" (Prov. 21:9; see Day 311) was not enough. Proverbs 21:19 takes it one step further. It is "better to dwell in the wilderness." Seriously, the wilderness? Living with "a contentious and angry woman" is so awful that one must forsake the house entirely for solitary existence in the "wilderness."

Proverbs 21:19 intensifies the illustration by adding the characteristic of being "angry" (Hb. *ka'as*, "provocation, vexation") to the description of the "contentious wife" (v. 9). Proverbs 31:10–31 provides God's paradigm for a woman who desires her house to thrive. She fears the Lord, which is the foundation for wisdom (v. 30). The importance of a woman being "wise" is addressed again in Proverbs 14:1, which states: "The wise woman builds her house, but the foolish pulls it down with her hands." The verb "builds" (Hb. *banah*, "cause to prosper") is also used in Genesis 2:22 in the account of God's creation of the woman. Women who can be called "wise" are those who focus their energies on modeling their households according to God's original plan and design. Being "wise" (Hb. *chokmot*, "discriminating between good and evil, receiving

instruction, exercising good judgment") is used here in a spiritual sense as a perspective found only in those who seek the Lord. The "foolish" woman does the opposite by pursuing what she wants at the expense of God's purposes for her family.

If you are married, you have the ability to create an Eden in which your husband and family dwell, grow, and flourish. What steps are you taking today in order to create this atmosphere for your family and those who enter your home? Are you growing in wisdom and thriving in your relationship with the Father, or are you more consumed with nagging, instigating arguments, and driving your loved ones into the wilderness?

Jessica Pigg

Prayer: *Ask God to teach you to walk in the fear of Him so that you can have the wisdom needed to create an "Eden" in your home.*

Personal Reflection: ....

....

....

....

....

....

One Thing Money Cannot Buy

Proverbs 22:1–3

"A good name is to be chosen rather than great riches,
Loving favor rather than silver and gold." (v. 1)

Did you know that there are some things that money cannot buy? Money cannot buy everlasting joy. Money cannot buy a closer walk with God. Also, money cannot buy you "a good name."

While growing up I noted that my parents used to remind me how important it was to behave correctly in public because I was representing them. Then, after I accepted Christ, my parents said that I was not only representing them, as evidenced by my last name, but also I was associated with the name of Jesus. I believe that my parents were trying to instill within me the awareness of living in such a manner as never to tarnish my reputation or that of those whom I loved the most.

Your name reflects on your family, character, and walk with God. Presumably, Solomon recognized the great value of having a good name since that is to be more desirable than having "great riches" (v. 1). The proverb is not condemning the accumulation of wealth but is merely comparing wealth to something far greater—one's reputation and untarnished character. A "good name" is the result of a life that is disciplined by choosing wisdom and walking in the fear of God daily.

However, there is real tension in this verse as we consider the allure of great riches on our hearts. The author utilizes the modifier "great" to indicate an abundance too numerous to count. The author is communicating that an untarnished character ("good name") is more valuable than a storehouse of riches too numerous to count. Wealth is viewed as being of secondary importance compared to the value of a "good name."

Solomon started off well with prosperity and influence, but he ended his life with compromised convictions and loss of the esteem and trust of his people and the Lord (1 Kin. 11:1–13). Perhaps you are wondering if your name can ever be recovered and be considered as good? There is good news: God's specialty is in mending the brokenness of our lives. Nothing you are doing, have done, or will do renders you ineligible for the good news of the gospel. Accept the love and forgiveness of your heavenly Father. Strive to live a godly life. Remember that a "good name" is one thing money cannot buy!

Jessica Pigg

Prayer: *Take a moment to call upon God, who specializes in healing your brokenness. Ask Him to establish your name through your pursuit of His righteousness.*

Personal Reflection: ....

....

....

....

....

....

....

Humbly Rich

Proverbs 22:4–5

"By humility and the fear of the LORD
Are riches and honor and life." (v. 4)

In this modern era, everyone thinks he knows the answer or secret to a well-lived life. Books upon books are devoted to making you successful in thirty days; thousands of blogs promise you happiness if you follow just a few simple steps; and talk-show hosts spend an hour each day trying to convince you that they have all the answers to your challenging circumstances. In the rare occurrence that you cannot find the answer to your question, in just the touch of a button, you can ask a computer-operated "woman" named Siri. One thing is for certain: Everywhere you turn, some guru somewhere claims to have the secret to wealth, wisdom, and well-being.

Solomon provides two directives that are guaranteed to provide you with "riches and honor and life." Some Bible translations make the interpretive choice to say that riches, honor, and life are the rewards that come to a person who is humble and walks in the fear of God. It is fitting for Solomon to begin with "humility" and then mention the "fear of the LORD." Humility is one's proper disposition toward a God who is omnipotent, and we should approach God in personal humility.

What does it mean to have humility? The New Testament provides a beautiful description of genuine humility (Phil. 2:5–11). Paul explains that humility is the complete submission of one's life to the plan and purpose of God as He works salvation in the lives of those around you. Paul uses Jesus Christ Himself as the perfect example of humility and obedience because Jesus set aside heaven in order to come to earth to procure salvation for humanity. In this passage, Paul calls believers in the city of Philippi to live in accordance with and to imitate the attitudes and actions of Christ.

Solomon describes the action that humility produces by using the phrase "the fear of the Lord," which appears numerous times throughout Proverbs. It serves in at least four ways as the key to unlocking the different aspects of spiritual maturity:

- First, "the fear of the Lord" unlocks knowledge (Prov. 1:7; 2:5).
- Second, "the fear of the Lord" unlocks the ability to resist evil (Prov. 8:13).
- Next, "the fear of the Lord" unlocks wisdom (Prov. 9:10).
- Finally, today's focal verse shows that "the fear of the Lord" unlocks "riches and honor and life." When we fear God rightly, we recognize Him for who He is—the God of no limits.

Jessica Pigg

Prayer: *Take a moment to confess to God the areas where you are not humble, and ask God to help you to walk in reverent fear as you serve Him.*

Personal Reflection: ....

....

....

....

....

The Prodigal's Parents

Proverbs 22:6–16

"Train up a child in the way he should go,
And when he is old he will not depart from it." (v. 6)

One of the saddest situations in life and ministry is the heartbreak of godly parents crying over their wayward son or daughter. The story of the prodigal son (Luke 15:11–32) emphasizes the graciousness of the father rather than the sinfulness of the son. The father in this account does not seek out his son, but the son's memory of his father's goodness brings him back home through repentance and forgiveness. This parable notes the similarity between the prodigal's reconciliation with his father and our coming to the heavenly Father through Christ. No matter the wisdom, love, and spiritual guidance the father gave throughout his years of rearing his son, ultimately the son chose the path he wanted to take.

Today's focal verse is a proverb well-known to parents grappling with a child's rebellion. Although traditionally considered a promise to parents who have conscientiously and faithfully nurtured the spiritual development of their children, many godly parents experience the heartbreak and disillusionment of watching their children veer away from what they were carefully taught in the home and church.

Consider these three factors when applying this verse:

- First, God has given each individual the free will to make his own choices. Despite the preparation and guidance poured into their lives by parents, children are still able to make their own choices.
- Second, Satan targets godly families in order to derail their faith and keep them from serving Christ. Unfortunately, through the craftiness of Satan, this situation happens all too often.

- Third, parents must remember that their hope is not to be grounded in the actions of a child but in their own obedience to God. Despite the future choices a child may make through his lifetime, parents still have the high calling and responsibility to teach their children biblical truths and to model God's instruction in their own lives.

If you are a parent, do you spend as much time praying for your children as you do worrying and thinking about them? How often do you make your children aware of what you are praying for them?

If you are not a parent, perhaps you can come alongside a mom in praying for and encouraging the spiritual growth of her children. Perhaps you can pray for and with a family grieving the choices of a prodigal, reminding them that their hope and faith are rooted in the Savior, not in the actions and choices of a wayward son or daughter.

Jessica Pigg

Prayer: *Spend time in prayer for a prodigal child—your own or one you know. As you intercede, ask God to bring to that person's memory His goodness and readiness to forgive.*

Personal Reflection: ....

....

....

....

Live Out His Word Daily

Proverbs 22:17–18

"Incline your ear and hear the words of the wise,
And apply your heart to my knowledge." (v. 17)

I have a bad habit of tuning out and not hearing a word anyone says when I am watching one of my favorite television shows. Due to my intense focus, the fire alarms could go off, a hurricane could approach, or an intruder could barge into my home, and I would have no clue. In that moment, from nine to ten at night, I incline my ear to one thing only, *Madam Secretary*, a popular television series.

In Proverbs 22:17, as in other proverbs (2:1–2; 4:20; 5:1), the author gives three imperatives that make up a charge: "Incline your ear"; "hear the words"; and "apply your heart." This charge is part of the "words of the wise," parallel with "my knowledge," identifying this teacher as one of the wise or someone who teaches using words. This section exhorts the readers to listen (22:17), then gives two reasons why (vv. 18–19). The author reveals that to " keep . . . within you" the teacher's words and knowledge is "a pleasant thing . . . so that your trust may be in the LORD."

The focal verse opens with the demand to "incline your ear" and "hear the words." The phrase "incline your ear" vividly depicts careful listening as turning the ear toward a speaker. Listening with this kind of intensity conveys both having interest in and giving attention to the wise words.

To "apply your heart" is a beautiful picture of actively learning, understanding, and then applying the truths to your heart and life, which simply means that we are not only to listen to the Word of God but also submissively to obey it as well. To know the Bible is not enough. Believers must hear God speak through His Word and gain wisdom to become more like Jesus. Gaining knowledge and wisdom without personal application will never amount to transformation.

A woman must not only incline her ear and study God's Word but also apply the truths to her life. Are you guilty of reading and studying Scripture, then turning and doing the same old things? After spending time in the Word, do you leave changed? Let's be women who do not merely go through the motions in our daily quiet time. Allow the Word of God to pierce your heart and change your life.

Jessica Pigg

Prayer: *Ask God to give you a heart for Scripture memory and for studying the Word with diligence and purpose.*

Personal Reflection: ....

....

....

....

....

....

....

The Wise Mentor

Proverbs 22:19–23

"Have I not written to you excellent things
Of counsels and knowledge,
That I may make you know the certainty of the words of truth,
That you may answer words of truth
To those who send to you?" (vv. 20–21)

Nothing is more beautiful than a mentoring relationship, two people pouring themselves into each other's lives and sharing words of truth and wisdom all for the sole purpose of glorifying God. Dorothy Patterson once said, "Mentoring relationships among women were ordained by God as a profoundly effective way to transfer from generation to generation biblical instruction and spiritual applications." Although Titus 2:3–5 is one of the most recognizable passages about mentoring, a similar mentoring relationship is displayed right before our eyes in Proverbs 22:20–21.

In these verses, the author was serving as the mentor and teaching wise counsel so that the learner could "answer words of truth to those" who were sent to him. The primary purpose of verse 20 is to introduce these "written" sayings of "counsels and knowledge." For the first time in Proverbs, oral teaching has given way to teaching by means of written text. "Counsels" here is a plural noun, the means by which "knowledge" is transferred from teacher to learner.

The goal for teaching "the certainty of the words of truth" is to prepare one with reliable words in order to answer those who send to you (v. 21), a reference that brings to mind earlier sayings about messengers both bad and trustworthy (Prov. 10:26; 13:17). In teaching these "words of truth" to the learner, the reader is instructed in the truth and thereby molded into a reliable person who is prepared for service. Through such strenuous preparation, we can conclude

that one function of these teachings is to prepare a young man for some sort of diplomatic service. When representing a king or official, one must be prepared to give an answer, knowing what to say not only in terms of content but also in terms of style and speaking with eloquence.

Do you have a mentor? Have you surrounded yourself with godly women to provide wise counsel as an investment in your life? Over the years, we have glamorized what it means to follow Jesus. We think it happens on public stages and on printed pages, but mentoring really happens around dining room tables, in small groups, and in living rooms. I imagine the top three people who have changed your life were eye-to-eye, across from you, investing time in your life. Who were they? What is holding you back from investing in the life of someone else?

Jessica Pigg

Prayer: *Ask God to surround you with godly women who will pour into your life and speak truth to you. Then, ask God to reveal to you someone in whom you can invest and whom you can mentor.*

Personal Reflection: ....

....

....

....

....

Set in Stone

Proverbs 22:24–29

*"Do not remove the ancient landmark
Which your fathers have set." (v. 28)*

Growing up, I was the absolute worst partner for playing the game of Tag. Everyone gathered together and established the rules and location of the main base. The base acted as "home"—a place of safety, security, and rest when one needed it throughout the game. However, when I was about to be "tagged" or needed to rest while too far away from the official base, I would just create my own base, ignoring the rules and simply doing what would benefit me in the moment. You can imagine the frustration and confusion such self-centeredness caused in our game.

Much like the base in the game of Tag, a stone marker was put in place as a boundary to one's property or territory. In effect, anyone who moved such a boundary stone was stealing land. The personal pronoun "your" implies that the person on the other side of the property line is a relative. Ancient landmarks and boundary stones are mentioned and explained elsewhere (Prov. 15:25; 23:10–11).

The prohibition against moving the boundary stone stands alone, with no accompanying motivation or reason (22:28). The reason is given in Proverbs 23:10–11. The "ancient landmark" was important to the widow and "fatherless." "Their Redeemer" (Hb. *go'ēl*, "one who buys back, kinsman-redeemer," Ruth 4:4, 6), God Himself, will not tolerate encroachment on the vulnerable and will protect their borders (Prov. 23:11). Furthermore, Proverbs 15:25 states that the Lord will "establish [Hb. *natsav*, "cause to stand firm"] the boundary of the widow." Scripture consistently recognizes that widows and orphans naturally fall prey to thieves and those more powerful than they. The book of Ruth illustrates a widow's typical loss of protection, security, and provision. Because

of her vulnerability, the Lord Himself made a point to guard and defend her "boundary."

In both of these cases, to move a boundary stone was to attempt to seize land secretly. However, more is involved here than real property. The boundary stone represented the ancient constitution of Israel, and to violate that rich heritage was to undermine the distinctive character of the land in Israelite society.

Just like I removed and replaced the base to benefit me in a game of Tag, what things have you removed or eliminated from your faith or doctrine to benefit you? Now, more than ever, women need to be unwavering in doctrine and practice. Women must be devotedly fearless and doctrinally faithful to share the gospel and equip others to do the same.

Jessica Pigg

Prayer: *Take a moment to renew your commitment to faithfully share the gospel with others and guard doctrine in your personal life.*

Personal Reflection: ....

....

....

....

....

....

Spending Less, Living Wiser

Proverbs 23:1–4

"Do not overwork to be rich;
Because of your own understanding, cease!" (v. 4)

Have you ever said, "If only I had a million dollars. . . ." In our pursuit of "if onlys," we have found ourselves chasing after "the pot of gold at the end of the rainbow" or looking for "a silver lining" in the clouds. One major chase I have discovered is the race to have it all. A song from my past says: "The more we get the more we want, can't settle for less . . . But the best God has for us if we'd only trust and obey His will, then it will lead to life."

A local business owner and I discussed this focal verse: "Do not overwork to be rich." She responded by saying, "I do not work to become rich, just to make a living" because "money never replaces purpose." My friend had discovered, after many years, contentment: "Now godliness with contentment is great gain" (1 Tim. 6:6). The apostle Paul further warns his protégé Timothy concerning the "temptation" and "snare" that accompany the desire of those who long to become rich (v. 9).

After graduating from college with a promising medical profession, I began to make assumptions about my future. After seventeen years of work in my career, I began to break even. I resigned my position for six months to reorganize my priorities and family commitments. I spent less and lived wiser, making Jesus first in all my spending. Twenty years later I have never returned to the work force. I discovered the great gain of godliness with contentment as well.

For more than fifteen years, I have adopted these words: "Give me neither poverty nor riches—feed me with the food allotted to me" (Prov. 30:8). According to my local business-owner friend, my true God-given purpose was fully realized within the confines of my daily allotment. Riches were no longer

significant. I found it all "in the Master's hand." When we no longer work for money, God will make money work for us!

Paul shares another promise: "For you know the grace of our Lord Jesus Christ, that though He was rich, yet for your sakes He became poor, that you through His poverty might become rich" (2 Cor. 8:9). We have everything we need because Christ gave everything for us. To know Christ and to love Him are worth more than gold.

Remember "that the genuineness of your faith, being much more precious than gold that perishes, though it is tested by fire, may be found to praise, honor, and glory at the revelation of Jesus Christ, whom having not seen you love. . . . receiving the end of your faith—the salvation of your souls" (1 Pet. 1:7–9).

Elizabeth Luter

Prayer: *Express thanksgiving to the Lord, acknowledging His provision for your needs. Tomorrow morning, ask Him for your daily bread (Matt. 6:11).*

Personal Reflection: ....

....

....

....

....

Discipline's Reward

Proverbs 23:5–12

*"Apply your heart to instruction,
And your ears to words of knowledge." (v. 12)*

Have you ever cut corners on a well-established recipe? Was the outcome a delight or a disaster? When cooking, I choose to follow my own way because recipes always seem to have too many ingredients. In addition, my pantry does not contain many of the required resources. Just the other day, I discovered an old recipe book and stayed up late reading every page. I discovered that all the ingredients were basic and found in my kitchen.

Discipline is required to follow instructions. Most, if not all, of us have struggled following biblical instructions. Old Testament instructions seem too complicated, especially when delivered during Moses' life. On Joshua's inauguration day, God said, "This Book of the Law shall not depart from your mouth, but you shall meditate in it day and night, that you may observe to do according to all that is written in it. For then you will make your way prosperous, and then you will have good success" (Josh. 1:8).

The reward for spiritual discipline then and now is "good success." So what is the problem? Who in this day and time has the space on her calendar to meditate day and night on the words of God? Better still, who can live out all that is written in God's Word? Jesus was confronted by a lawyer who asked, "Teacher, which is the great commandment in the law?" (Matt. 22:36). This Pharisee was looking for simplification of the instructions previously given by God to Moses and the Prophets. "Jesus said to him, 'You shall love the LORD your God with all your heart, with all your soul, and with all your mind'" (v. 37).

After the death, burial, and resurrection of Jesus Christ, the ability to follow instructions was simplified by the imparting of the Holy Spirit to all believers. "This is the covenant that I will make with them after those days, says the

LORD: I will put My laws into their hearts, and in their minds I will write them" (Heb. 10:16).

My failings were many before receiving the Lord Jesus Christ as Lord and Savior of my life. Meditating on the Word of God both day and night and following the Spirit's lead have indeed yielded good spiritual success. Spiritual disciplines will guarantee a favorable outcome almost every time. Stick to the recipe because your own way will lead to disaster.

Jesus came to earth in bodily form to demonstrate the successful adherence to the law. He lived and died always obeying His Father with great discipline. To the natural eye, His outcome was disastrous. Yet, His life of discipline, culminating in His death and resurrection, was a substitute for our lack of discipline.

Elizabeth Luter

Prayer: *Look no further for successful outcomes in this life. The instructions, if you are a believer, are written on your heart and mind. Yield to the Spirit's lead, and you will have success every time.*

Personal Reflection:

Discipline's Rescue

Proverbs 23:13–16

"Do not withhold correction from a child,
For if you beat him with a rod, he will not die.
You shall beat him with a rod,
And deliver his soul from hell." (vv. 13–14)

Have you ever watched the dreadful end of a rebellious person and wondered if correction was ever applied? With so much emphasis on methods of correction, the purpose for correcting becomes obscure. Discipline has served as a mighty tool for believers, saving us from the ills of society and the highway leading to the pit. Yes, godly discipline has a goal in mind—to rescue us from a life of sin and a world of destruction. With so much at stake, we must continue to give careful consideration to this matter of discipline.

While growing up in a household of eight children, notable defiance and rebellion was on every hand. After careful observance of the correction applied to the older siblings, the younger siblings required less intervention. Eventually, each of us had a healthy fear of our parents. Some disobedience and disrespect continued but never in their presence. Chastisement gained its desired outcome: "Now no chastening seems to be joyful for the present, but painful; nevertheless, afterward it yields the peaceable fruit of righteousness to those who have been trained by it" (Heb. 12:11).

In this temporary world, with eyes set on temporary goals, believers can miss the training necessary to give us great eternal outcomes. When we cross over to an eternal focus, we recognize chastisement on another level. We know that there is a rescue in mind: "My son, do not despise the chastening of the LORD, nor be discouraged when you are rebuked by Him; for whom the LORD loves He chastens, and scourges every son whom He receives" (Heb. 12:5–6). Our greater rebellion against God, His will, and His way, was cause for our

Savior Jesus Christ to suffer: "But He was wounded for our transgressions, He was bruised for our iniquities; the chastisement for our peace was upon Him, and by His stripes we are healed" (Is. 53:5).

My earthly father guided and corrected his children until we were adults and no longer under his authority. My heavenly Father was leading and guiding me long before I knew He existed. As a mature adult, His discipline continues: "For they [human fathers] indeed for a few days chastened us as seemed best to them, but He [God the Father] for our profit, that we may be partakers of His holiness" (Heb. 12:10). The holiness of God is beyond our comprehension, but possible through the blood of Jesus. Now we are safe; our pathway and destination is sure!

Elizabeth Luter

Prayer: *Thank the Lord for the chastisement that drove you to His side. Pray for continuous discipline to stay on the narrow road of obedience. Be grateful for the love and correction of the Lord, which brings you back when you go astray.*

Personal Reflection: ....

....

....

....

....

Envy's Distraction

Proverbs 23:17–18

*"Do not let your heart envy sinners,
But be zealous for the fear of the LORD all the day." (v. 17)*

Have you ever stared at the abundance of the wicked with a deep longing in your heart and a question on your tongue? The psalmist Asaph knew firsthand the struggle you and I face: "For I was envious of the boastful, when I saw the prosperity of the wicked" (Ps. 73:3).

I admit feeling a little disheartened to serve God and live life with limited resources. On the other hand, it is even harder to witness the accumulation of those who do not acknowledge, serve, or worship God our Father. However, time spent in that dreamland can rob the believer from seeing the many resources of God. This distraction keeps us focused on ourselves rather than revering a Holy God. As we begin to fear God daily, He becomes larger than anything else in life.

Job's fear of God provided great stability in the time of severe loss and devastation. "There was a man in the land of Uz, whose name was Job; and that man was blameless and upright, and one who feared God and shunned evil" (Job 1:1). God Himself validated the character of Job to Satan, Job's accuser and adversary. Job was "a blameless and upright man, one who fears God and shuns evil . . .[holding] fast to his integrity" (Job 2:3). The ultimate outcome for Job's life included much more than temporal resources: "For surely there is a hereafter, and your hope will not be cut off" (Prov. 23:18). The same promise was given to Israel during their time of great tribulation: "For I know the thoughts that I think toward you, says the LORD, thoughts of peace and not of evil, to give you a future and a hope" (Jer. 29:11).

Our abundance comes from the hand of the true and living God. He is the Father of our Savior, the Lord Jesus Christ, who said abundant life is His reason for coming into the world: "I have come that they may have life, and that they

may have it more abundantly" (John 10:10). So the next time you look at the advantage of the wicked and ask why their abundance is greater than yours, just know that your view has been distorted.

Keep your eyes on "Jesus, the author and finisher of our faith, who for the joy that was set before Him endured the cross, despising the shame, and has sat down at the right hand of the throne of God" (Heb. 12:2).

Hold on! Your seat in Heaven awaits you! (Eph. 2:4–7).

Elizabeth Luter

Prayer: *Thank the Lord for the day He transformed you from a sinner to saint when you repented of your sins, believed in His death on the cross and His resurrection from the grave. Accept the abundance from God's hands, knowing it is greater than any wealth earth can provide.*

 **Personal Reflection:** ....

....

....

....

....

....

Finding Wisdom's Way

Proverbs 23:19

"Hear, my son, and be wise;
And guide your heart in the way." (v. 19)

Have you ever feared the next step when you were uncertain? Every wise parent works hard to direct her children down the right paths. No loving, God-fearing parent would deliberately lead her children down a road to destruction. The average parent spends a large amount of money on education to eliminate a negative, nonproductive future. On graduation day, parents stand proudly with a sense of accomplishment.

"I have taught you in the way of wisdom; I have led you in right paths" (Prov. 4:11). Unfortunately, parents can walk with their children only so far, and then the children must choose for themselves to continue along the right path. Most of us fear when true independence comes: Will the next step lead me to rise or fall? When we walk with God, He is a consistent Guide: "But your eyes shall see your teachers. Your ears shall hear a word behind you, saying, 'This is the way, walk in it,' whenever you turn to the right hand or whenever you turn to the left" (Is. 30:20b–21).

As Christians, our struggle is to have a consistent walk with God. Shortcuts and detours are so appealing when the road of life seems difficult or longer than we anticipated. Although I joined Jesus on "Wisdom's Way" a long time ago, I still struggle when the road turns. My "natural man" (1 Cor. 2:14) still fights for control to follow a pathway that is simple and clear, with no rough terrain. Jesus says, "And where I go you know, and the way you know . . . I am the way, the truth, and the life" (John 14:4, 6). There are no missteps when following close behind Jesus. The songwriter penned, "I want Jesus to walk with me all along my pilgrim journey." If you ever miss a step, causing you to stumble and fall, the experience will remind you to pay attention when you walk: "See then that

you walk circumspectly, not as fools but as wise, redeeming the time, because the days are evil. Therefore do not be unwise, but understand what the will of the Lord is" (Eph. 5:15–17).

From this day forward, what will you do with the wisdom that was imparted to you? Will you run speedily in the direction of "Wisdom's Way" or will you flounder on misguided paths? If the Lord Jesus Christ is not your guide, make a U-turn. Ask for directions to "Straight Street," then walk up the "King's Highway." You will never regret this decision for one moment. Your best life is up ahead!

Elizabeth Luter

Prayer: *Because the road to eternity is so confusing at times, ask the Lord to renew your commitment to stay close to Him and never fall away from His truth.*

Personal Reflection: ....

....

....

....

....

....

Dead-End Delights

Proverbs 23:20–21

"Do not mix with winebibbers,
Or with gluttonous eaters of meat;
For the drunkard and the glutton will come to poverty,
And drowsiness will clothe a man with rags." (vv. 20–21)

Have you ever cried aloud inside, knowing that someone dear to you was hanging with the wrong crowd? When I was growing up, the words *drunkard* and *glutton* had little meaning. When I was old enough to see the outcome of these excesses, I became concerned for those I knew with substance abuse. "Do not mix" or associate is a mandate that sounds harsh until you witness the destruction of all who are affected by a loved one's excesses. The words *dead end* are carefully hidden from the one who will not heed the "Do Not" sign. The enemy of our souls is aware of the destruction that is headed our way: "Woe to those who rise early in the morning, that they may follow intoxicating drink; who continue until night, till wine inflames them" (Is. 5:11)! *Woe* is a sign of grave trouble, but it is carefully tucked away from the mind of someone who deliberately runs the stop signs: "They have struck me, but I was not hurt; they have beaten me, but I did not feel it. When shall I awake, that I may seek another drink?" (Prov. 23:35).

In our overindulgence, have we considered the depletion of our souls? We have each underestimated the life we have been given and the warning manual that comes with it. A solution was provided many years ago: "And she will bring forth a Son, and you shall call His name JESUS, for He will save His people from their sins" (Matt. 1:21). Yes, God has a remedy for whatever ails us. To disassociate is not to condemn but to have a posture of readiness to rescue when duty calls. On a daily basis, someone is out of control from overeating or drinking.

The crowd has such an alluring pull, who can resist its influence? Only those who will look to Jesus for their salvation and heed the "Do Not" signs.

> Therefore let us not sleep, as others do, but let us watch and be sober. For those who sleep, sleep at night, and those who get drunk are drunk at night. But let us who are of the day be sober, putting on the breastplate of faith and love, and as a helmet the hope of salvation. For God did not appoint us to wrath, but to obtain salvation through our Lord Jesus Christ, who died for us, that whether we wake or sleep, we should live together with Him. (1 Thess. 5:6–10)

Elizabeth Luter

Prayer: *Ask the Lord to show you the "Do Not" signs. Praise Him for rescuing you from your flesh and giving you strength to say "no" to temptation. Ask Him to help you rescue others who have already succumbed to the "Dead-End Delights."*

Personal Reflection: ....

....

....

....

....

The True Value of Parents

Proverbs 23:22

*"Listen to your father who begot you,
And do not despise your mother when she is old." (v. 22)*

Have you lived long enough to wish that you had valued the wisdom of your parents? Parenting is one of the hardest jobs in life. The responsibility for molding and shaping another life is very challenging. Without the Word of God and the fear of God, parenting is basically trial-and-error.

Although people can offer suggestions on how to raise a child, only God can give the wisdom necessary to complete the task successfully. Children struggle with obeying the rules of their parents and sometimes later despise the methods their parents used to teach them. To listen is to obey, and there are grave consequences for choosing to do otherwise. "Children, obey your parents in the Lord, for this is right. 'Honor your father and mother,' which is the first commandment with promise: 'that it may be well with you and you may live long on the earth'" (Eph. 6:1–3).

Obedience is a crucial element. The ability to submit and follow without clear understanding is very valuable, especially when following Christ. Good parents live for the day when their children and their children's children are successfully navigating this thing called life. Although unable to take credit for the successful outcome, a parent can know that following God pays great dividends and yields generational rewards. "The father of the righteous will greatly rejoice, and he who begets a wise child will delight in him" (Prov. 23:24).

The apostle Paul takes note of the genuine faith of Timothy, his son in the ministry, who attributes his faith to a generational succession: "I thank God . . . when I call to remembrance the genuine faith that is in you, which dwelt first in your grandmother Lois and your mother Eunice, and I am persuaded is in you also" (2 Tim. 1:3, 5).

Someone might argue that their parents' skills were limited due to a lack of education. Although my parents lacked extensive education, their true value was seen in the wisdom they gained as they encountered everyday experiences. Their greatest wisdom came after choosing to follow Jesus Christ as their Lord and Savior and becoming obedient to Him and His commands. Even though my siblings and I did not recognize their true value while growing up, we have all lived long enough to discover the value, especially, of their decision to follow Jesus: "Though He was a Son, yet He learned obedience by the things which He suffered. And having been perfected, He became the author of eternal salvation to all who obey Him" (Heb. 5:8–9).

Elizabeth Luter

Prayer: *If you have taken your earthly parents for granted, pray for an opportunity to tell them you appreciate them. If you have taken for granted the wisdom imparted by your heavenly Father, repent and ask Him to help you experience the fruit of obedience.*

Personal Reflection: ....

....

....

....

....

Run from Evil!

Proverbs 24:1–2

"Do not be envious of evil men,
Nor desire to be with them;
For their heart devises violence,
And their lips talk of troublemaking." (vv. 1–2)

These verses should be read through the lens of what wisdom is not. A wise person lives a righteous life and flees from wicked, evil people to avoid the destruction and drama such people inevitably bring.

Wise women are not to crave, desire, or covet such unwise relationships; instead they are to seek connections to righteous and wise women. Women have an innate desire to be included and feel loved. We need to be careful not to desire to be part of a crowd that is not God-honoring in their conversations and actions. These relationships may lead us to compromise our convictions and hurt our witness (Matt. 5:13). There may be times when you desire to be part of a "group" but continue to feel rejected. God may be protecting you from potential harm and painful consequences. Wise and godly relationships are marked by peace and righteousness instead of trouble and turmoil.

Verse 2 describes evil or unwise men: "Their heart devises violence, and their lips talk of troublemaking." The book of Proverbs continually warns believers against being in fellowship with evil people (see Prov. 4:14–16). These commands are bold and repetitive, leaving little room for confusion. Being around such people can become our downfall because we tend to mimic those who surround us. When an evil person is punished, the consequences will be so all-encompassing that if you are in their company, you will be affected as well. Be warned: If you join with such men or women, you, too, are a partner in their sin. A wise woman will desire "the paths of righteousness" accompanied by light and peace (Prov. 2:20; 3:17; 4:18).

As women, our mouths can get us into trouble! Our words can cause a fire, which has been ignited by the forces of hell, destroying relationships, families, and churches. Our mouths can literally steer a conversation in righteousness or evil (James 3:3–6). A wise woman who seeks to know God and honor God will flee from such destruction in her own life and flee from the unrighteous conversation of others. A woman who continually speaks destruction assumes an opposite approach from David in his prayer: "Let the words of my mouth and the meditation of my heart be acceptable in Your sight, O Lord, my strength and my Redeemer" (Ps. 19:14).

DeeDee Williams

Prayer: *Ask the Lord to help you see the difference between His wisdom and ungodly evil. Then live and speak His truth.*

Personal Reflection: ....

....

....

....

....

....

Wise Home-Building

Proverbs 24:3–4

"Through wisdom a house is built,
And by understanding it is established;
By knowledge the rooms are filled
With all precious and pleasant riches." (vv. 3–4)

Proverbs 24:1–2 describes how wisdom steers us away from evil and destruction. Verses 3 and 4 explain that wisdom brings about forethought and preparedness. As I am writing this devotion, it is not a coincidence that my husband and I are purchasing a home. We have prayed for wisdom, examined our finances, planned for potential renovations, and sought guidance from godly counselors. This morning I prayed that our home would reflect His divine order, that His beauty would be on display, and that our home would reflect our eternal hope. God's glory is on display through redeeming the most chaotic situations in my home.

The Hebrew word for "house" (*bayith*) in this verse means "home or dwelling." Simply put, we need wisdom in the management of our homes. Although the main application is focused on the physical nature of our homes, the secondary application is helpful. The Hebrew verb for "built" (*banah*), referring to the building of our physical homes, is used differently in other verses focusing on the building of our households. In Proverbs 9:1, wisdom is personified as a woman who "builds" her house, preparing and establishing it. The same is true in Proverbs 14:1 where "build" is used for the wise woman's investment of time in her home.

Women need wisdom to build our physical homes, but we also need just as much wisdom to build our households. We are to build our homes "through wisdom." Wisdom can be personified in our homes no matter how big or small, elaborate or simple. Wisdom is known through God's Word. A wise woman

seeks to run her household and raise her children by holding fast to wisdom, not following worldly measures and standards.

A house is also "established" (Hb. *kun*) by understanding, suggesting keeping yourself in a continual state of "understanding." A wise woman will continually spend time in prayer and Bible study, seek to honor God with her home, and use it to minister to her family and to others. God is described as the One to whom "counsel and understanding" belongs (Job 12:13). Therefore, the woman seeking to establish understanding is seeking Him first—continually, desperately, imperfectly, and by grace through faith in Jesus (Eph. 2:8). Only then, through the abundant love of Christ, will the Lord use our feeble earthly efforts to create a picture of the divine. By God's grace a wise woman can fill the rooms of her home with "riches" of eternal value.

DeeDee Williams

Prayer: *Dedicate yourself to understanding God's Word. Ask Him to help you display your understanding of His ways in how you operate and manage your household.*

Personal Reflection: ....

....

....

....

....

This Means Wars

Proverbs 24:5–9

"For by wise counsel you will wage your own war,
And in a multitude of counselors there is safety." (v. 6)

Wisdom is powerful enough to win wars. You may be asking yourself, "What 'war' am I waging that calls for this kind of wisdom?" Readjusting your perspective to see your daily battles is important. A believer's war always begins in the spiritual realm. She has a constant enemy, requiring continuous warfare. No matter the "face" of your current battle! You must know the real enemy: "For we do not wrestle against flesh and blood, but against principalities, against powers, against the rulers of the darkness of this age, against spiritual hosts of wickedness in the heavenly places" (Eph. 6:12). Our battles may take on different forms in each season of life, but wisdom is necessary for victory.

What is "wise counsel" and who is in the "multitude of counselors"? A counselor is an advisor or deliberator, one who considers action and purpose, one who gives good, godly advice. Wise counsel suggests steering in the right direction. Godly advisors, counselors, and mentors will help point you in the right direction through their godly wisdom.

The importance of seeking "wise counsel" is reiterated throughout Proverbs (e.g., 11:14; 15:22; 20:18). Repetition in God's Word is a call to take note of the message. The purpose in these verses is to praise the success that wisdom brings when we as God-fearing women are obedient to seek out godly advice, rather than being content to live as a "lone-wolf" Christians.

The opposite of this truth is also presented in Proverbs—the path of a fool—to highlight the benefits of seeking wisdom in a more tangible way (Prov. 18:1). Women who seek godly counsel are looking beyond themselves, not being preoccupied with their own opinions on matters. Isolation is not God's plan for believers. Rather, He admonishes us to seek wise counsel.

The approval of a predetermined path may be desired more than sound guidance. Position yourself around godly believers and seek their advice. Some of your social circles and intimate friendships may need to be changed. There is great value in making these adjustments, asking yourself these hard questions, and seeking godly wisdom. Do not wage war without seeking wise counsel.

DeeDee Williams

Prayer: *Examine your heart and ask God if you are being obedient to this truth. Do you have any strongholds that need to be brought to light? Is pride making you afraid to ask wiser women for help?*

Personal Reflection: ....

....

....

....

....

....

....

Do Not Cry "Uncle"

Proverbs 24:10–12

*"If you faint in the day of adversity,
Your strength is small." (v. 10)*

Life can be downright hard and exhausting. That's what makes the hope of heaven even sweeter as I age. As a woman, wife, mom, and pastor's wife, I am often overwhelmed with the insurmountable battles. Sometimes I feel like throwing the covers over my head and saying, "I don't want to be an adult today!" The Lord has great compassion as we experience stress and face adversity, but He does not want us stay there. He has more work for us to do, which requires that we get up and engage again. Proverbs 24:10 speaks to believers who choose to stay curled up in the fetal position of their situation rather than trusting in the daily supernatural strength and grace of God.

Trusting God is easier when life is going smoothly; but when "life happens" and the days are hard, trust falters for most. Exhaustion and discouragement may be the result. Most women juggle a multitude of responsibilities and handle the typical stress of everyday life with amazing skill. However, a crisis may be "the straw that breaks the camel's back." Adversity causes extra pressure and will either tear a relationship apart or make it stronger. Proverbs 24:10 offered good advice to the Israelites who needed to get up and do the hard thing. God had already promised the victory; they just needed to take hold of it! We must choose to move ahead in faith when life gets tough, not give up and cry "Uncle."

What does the proverb mean by "your strength is small"? Strength is your capacity to act, in both physical and figurative terms. A woman who is strong in the Lord when facing adversity has confidence in the wisdom of God and hope in the future He has secured. As honey is to the lips, so wisdom is to the soul (v. 13). Wisdom gives satisfaction in the face of adversity and joy in knowing how to confront the challenge.

Do you remember the cartoon character Popeye the Sailor, who gained extraordinary strength when he ate spinach? I wish I could just eat a can of spinach and gain strength to overcome the things that seem daunting and over-whelming in my life. But what is the real source of great strength? Believers grow stronger by relying on God's strength, exercising faith and thereby gain-ing godly wisdom. God displays His strength in you most clearly "in the day of adversity." When facing difficult situations, God does not call you to be super-human; He asks you to trust His supernatural strength!

DeeDee Williams

Prayer: *Do you find yourself in a difficult situation, feeling powerless even after asking God to strengthen you? Exercise faith and claim His strength for the weary (Is. 40:29). Even when you feel empty, you must move obediently, knowing God will often do the impossible through you.*

Personal Reflection: ....

....

....

....

....

....

"Nana-Nana, Boo-Boo"

Proverbs 24:15–22

"Do not rejoice when your enemy falls,
And do not let your heart be glad when he stumbles;
Lest the LORD see it, and it displease Him,
And He turn away His wrath from him." (vv. 17–18)

Sometimes a child chants "Nana-Nana, Boo-Boo" to a childhood "enemy" when she gets what she "deserves." Most adults have matured enough not to stick out their tongues—or at least not until the enemy has turned her back. God's Word warns about rejoicing when your enemy gets what's coming to her, and such an attitude is not to be taken lightly. The prohibition is rooted in the fear of the Lord (vv. 17–19). The fear of the Lord is the beginning of knowledge (Prov. 1:7); therefore; wise women do not gloat or rejoice when an enemy falls.

Let's begin by defining the "enemy." The book of Psalms, the books penned by the prophets, and the book of Proverbs all speak of the joy and celebration resulting from the destruction of God's enemies (Prov. 11:10). Likewise, people today rejoice when terrorists are stopped because of their slaughter of God's people. However, the enemy mentioned in Proverbs 24:17 is not God's enemy but a personal enemy. "Your enemy" is one who causes personal hurt to you or your family. The most difficult challenge of this proverb is to love your enemy, a consistent theme throughout God's Word (Prov. 25:21; Matt. 5:44; Rom. 12:20).

The prohibition uses two negative verb phrases: "Do not rejoice" and "do not let your heart be glad" (Prov. 24:17). The first warning addresses the external behavior of expressing excitement when your enemy falls. The first warning seems a bit easier to obey since most people have more control over *how* they rejoice than over the feeling of gladness in their hearts. However, in the second warning, God focuses on the heart. God is leveling the playing ground; both heart and actions are to be obedient and pure. Inner thoughts are the substance

666

of our character and will be manifested in our actions. God does not desire plastic people who are doing the right things on the outside while their hearts are far from Him. God yearns for us to have a right heart in dealing with our enemies.

Why is God angry when we enjoy the suffering of our enemies? As a mother, I do not like to punish my children when they have done something wrong. I get even more upset when one of my children enjoys the punishment of the sibling. Sometimes I get so angry, I send the punished child out to play and scold the rejoicing sibling. Do not be concerned with how God deals with your enemies; be focused on the Lord and His plans for you.

DeeDee Williams

Prayer: *Ask the Lord to help you obey Him and love your enemies.*

Personal Reflection: ....

....

....

....

....

....

First Things First

Proverbs 24:23–34

"Prepare your outside work,
Make it fit for yourself in the field;
And afterward build your house." (v. 27)

Wisdom gives order to our lives. God desires organization and peace for His children, which can only be achieved through heeding His wisdom. God teaches us how to order our priorities: "Seek *first* the kingdom of God and His righteousness, and all these things shall be added to you" (Matt. 6:33). "*First* remove the plank from your own eye, and then you will see clearly to remove the speck from your brother's eye" (Matt. 7:5). Married women must put their husbands first—over parents and children—to promote a healthy marriage (Eph. 5:22–24). When God speaks to the ordering of priorities in our lives, he guides us in how to start.

God's people are warned to prepare their outdoor work in the field *first* and "afterward" to build their house (Prov. 24:27). "Make it fit" in this context means to prepare or make ready. Before provision and purchase, there must be preparation. What does a "fit" field look like in society today? A source of income must be established before purchasing a home. The ability to support a family within the home is required as well. First do the work to provide the income; then you will be able to plan for your future in a God-honoring way. Do not make purchases beyond your income.

A consumer-driven culture has believed the lie: "You can have it all, and you can have it now." Though enticing, the myth is a snare. God's ways are different and will lead to peace, not bondage. Having it now comes with a big cost—debt. Debt causes undue stress and anxiety, as well as potential marital strain. God's Word teaches the virtue of contentment (1 Tim. 6:6). Godliness comes from dependency on Christ, not on self-sufficiency through worldly

means (1 Tim. 6:7–10). Sufficiency enables believers to live beyond the material gain or sometimes the lack of it. Every believer is challenged to learn this lesson. Many of us have made both wise and unwise choices with our money. We may experience the consequence of not putting first things first, or we may experience the blessing of doing things according to God's provision.

By doing the work God provides for us to do, by asking God to direct us in our financial planning, and by learning to be content within our means, our plans will be stable. God longs to bless His people when they live according to His order and His way. Wisdom says to work, plan, and prepare. Then wisdom says to "build." In all things, God reminds us to "keep first things first."

DeeDee Williams

Prayer: *Do you rely on the Lord, not yourself, for provision? Keep first things first; then He will bless you.*

Personal Reflection: ....

....

....

....

....

....

Please Wait to Be Seated

Proverbs 25:1–7

"Do not exalt yourself in the presence of the king,
And do not stand in the place of the great;
For it is better that he say to you,
'Come up here,'
Than that you should be put lower in the presence of the prince,
Whom your eyes have seen." (vv. 6–7)

A *proverb*, which is classified as wisdom literature, is a short, catchy saying designed to be easily remembered. The writer/speaker seeks to convey a specific meaning or admonition to the reader/listener. Many proverbs are expressed using "like" or "as" comparison statements. For the next few days we will look at focal verses from Proverbs 25.

Many sayings that have been passed down from generation to generation flourish in families and can be traced back to the book of Proverbs. I remember my mother asking my grandmother, "Now, Mother, which one of the Proverbs is *that*?" The proverbs contained in Scripture were inspired by the Holy Spirit and thus are considered to be the Word of God, profitable for those who seek to live in a way that pleases God. Biblical proverbs possess moral value and provide spiritual guidance. Proverbs should be approached with the same reverence and obedience reserved for the other sixty-five Bible books.

Exalting yourself is always a personal and spiritual train wreck! The Bible is filled with people and situations that prove the truth of the proverb in this focal verse. Satan acted it out in the garden of Eden and led Adam and Eve down a sinful path. Being first in line is an honor, not a given. God honors "foot washers" who serve others. Jesus is a perfect example (John 13:1–7).

Jesus told a parable (a proverb in story form) to some leaders of the Pharisees who were seeking the seats of honor at the Sabbath meal. True to His

trademark "last-shall-be-first" reasoning, Jesus closed His parable with these words: "For whoever exalts himself will be humbled, and he who humbles himself will be exalted" (Luke 14:11). Next time someone sits in your favorite pew at church, greet her warmly, smile, and find another pew.

Proverbs 25 is part of a unique section of this book. Verse 1 tells us that these are proverbs of Solomon, son of David, king in Jerusalem. These particular proverbs were compiled and recorded by the servants of King Hezekiah. Solomon reigned just after David (c. 970 BC). Hezekiah reigned approximately 250 years after Solomon (c. 715 BC). The Word of God stands the test of time, then and now.

Becky Brown

Prayer: *Ask the Lord to remove any desire in you to be first, top, and best. When you place Him first, the needs of others will cross out self-exaltation.*

Personal Reflection: ....

....

....

....

....

....

Crush, Slice, Pierce

Proverbs 25:8–18

"A man who bears false witness against his neighbor,
Is like a club, a sword, and a sharp arrow." (v. 18)

In Exodus 20, God gave Moses the Ten Commandments for the people of Israel. The ninth commandment foreshadows today's proverb: "You shall not bear false witness against your neighbor" (v. 16). To *bear* has the sense of "reply, transfer, or announce." *False* is the opposite of *true*. *Witness* refers to one's testimony from personal knowledge. To "bear false witness," then, is to lie or deceive, to give a false or distorted report, to accuse wrongfully.

Against means in opposition. "Your neighbor" can be the folks next door, a friend, or basically any fellow human being. The key phrase here is God's command, "You shall not." With this commandment nestled in between "You shall not steal" (Ex. 20:15) and "You shall not covet" (v. 17), God magnifies the fact that our word is our bond, requiring truth in all encounters.

God commands His children not to bear false witness. Our word is our bond and certificate of authenticity as a child of God. We are required to live the truth and speak the truth. God knows how words can either encourage growth or destroy character. Jesus Himself was mocked and falsely accused. He was crucified physically after being crucified verbally. Words can be building blocks that encourage and edify. Words can also be weapons that wound and destroy. Failure to denounce a falsehood can be as detrimental as refusing to tell the truth. Silence in the face of the need to speak truth aloud can damage character as well.

Bearing false witness against someone else wounds as if you had used a weapon. Three weapons are mentioned in the focal verse: "a club, a sword, and a sharp arrow." All three of these weapons inflict wounds that involve the shedding of blood and can literally take life. The club is used to crush; the sword is

used to stab, slice, and divide; the well-placed, sharply-honed arrow point can pierce. Character can be crushed, sliced, and pierced, sustaining a potentially mortal wound. Recovery is complicated.

In the biblical language, our proverb for today has this word order: "Club / sword / arrow / sharp / man / answer / against / neighbor / witness / deception." Providing painful emphasis, the verse begins by listing the weapons! When you choose to bear false witness against someone, you are walking in with weapons drawn for the kill!

Becky Brown

Prayer: *Consider how your words impact others. Lay down your club, sheathe your sword, and leave your arrow in the quiver as you lay down your bow. Give the Lord your life and your words.*

Personal Reflection: ....

....

....

....

....

....

673

Toothaches and Toenails

Proverbs 25:19–20

*"Confidence in an unfaithful man in time of trouble
Is like a bad tooth and a foot out of joint." (v. 19)*

Eventually, in the living of this life, we find ourselves caught between the pro-verbial rock and a hard place with no visible means of support or escape. Today's proverb tells us who *not* to trust: the treacherous, "unfaithful" person. Times of trouble, distress, and calamity will come in life and are bad enough. We should not make matters worse by placing our trust in folks who are deceptive and who do not have our best interest at heart. Only God is our true help in time of trouble. In His grace, God provides good friends to journey through life with us, but God loves us best!

Do you find it hard to concentrate on anything else when your tooth hurts or your foot is sore? When your tooth hurts and your toe hurts, everything in between your head and your foot is in pain. When you cannot eat without pain and you cannot walk without pain, very little else is right until you get some relief.

On a medical mission trip to Mexico, our team was tasked with helping the doctor with procedures. One lady needed a tooth pulled due to a terrible infec-tion. The tooth was on the top, right in front. Her smile was about to be severely affected. The doctor said, "We can leave the smile, but she would have to keep the pain!" The decision was made when the doctor said, "If we do not pull this tooth, she could die of the infection." The next day, she came with painless gratitude to thank us, and we were able to tell her about Jesus. This doctor had her best interest at heart, physically and spiritually.

Solomon, assisted by the scribes of King Hezekiah, is pointing toward the best Source of help in troubled times. "Truth" and "wisdom" express the char-acter of God in this book. Trust in God is not mentioned here in verse 19 but

is implied as Solomon is using these verses to point back to God as the most valuable Helper "in time of trouble" (Pss. 27:5; 37:39).

The word *confidence* means the act of taking refuge or finding security. The someone or something in which you take refuge or find your security reveals where you invest your personal hope. When you find yourself in a time of calamity or distress, squeezed into a narrow, inescapable place by your current circumstances, your hope must be in God. He is the beginning of the end of your troubles. God is your answer.

Becky Brown

Prayer: *Seek the Lord when you find yourself in a narrow place of deep need. Allow Him to help you to have confidence in Him as your true Source of help.*

Personal Reflection: ....

....

....

....

....

....

....

Love Your Enemies

Proverbs 25:21–24

"If your enemy is hungry, give him bread to eat;
And if he is thirsty, give him water to drink;
For so you will heap coals of fire on his head,
And the Lord will reward you." (vv. 21–22)

My grandmother taught us to treat everyone with kindness no matter how we had been treated. She would say, "You can catch more flies with honey than with vinegar!" I often wondered why in the world anyone would want to catch flies. Through the years, I have come to understand what she meant. In almost every situation, people will respond positively to kindness.

A believer's goal is not simply to "win friends and influence people." Our "go-mission" is to make, repair, and sustain relationships. We are to make friends, not enemies. In Exodus 23, God tells Moses to make sure the people secured and returned the stray livestock that belonged to their enemy. Elisha reminded the men that they were to treat prisoners of war (sworn enemies) with respect (2 Kin. 6:22). In Deuteronomy 32, Moses wrote a song for the people. One verse describes the Lord's plan for those who have been wronged by their enemy. The Lord says vengeance belongs to Him and that He will repay (v. 35). Paul quotes this song lyric (Rom. 12:19). Kindness to enemies carries over from the Old Testament to the New Testament.

Today's proverb repeats the formula for how to treat enemies: Feed them if they are hungry; give them water if they are thirsty; meet their needs; be their friend; pour on the kindness. "Heaping coals of fire" has come to mean giving your enemy reasons to feel blessed and even guilty so that the wall between you will possibly be torn down and a path potentially opened for reconciliation. As believers, we are to do our part and leave the results to God. Our part is never to seek our own vengeance.

Jesus is the ultimate example of how to treat enemies. He told us to love our enemies (Matt. 5:44), and He also wore His crown of thorns willingly. He could have called for legions of angels to rescue Him from those enemies, but He did not (26:53). Jesus literally turned the other cheek as He was struck with blows by Roman soldiers (5:39; 26:67). One of His own disciples was His betrayer (Luke 22:3–6, 47–48). In the face of accusations, He kept silent (Matt. 27:12–14). Even the centurion at the foot of the cross was amazed (Mark 15:39).

Some enemies chose to remain enemies of God and His people, but one day God will use His enemies as a footstool for His feet (Ps. 110:1; Heb. 10:12–13). Until then, as God's children we must love our enemies.

Becky Brown

Prayer: *Pray for God to give you the grace to treat your enemies as Jesus treated His enemies. Make a commitment not to seek vengeance for yourself but to leave those matters in God's hands.*

Personal Reflection: ....

....

....

....

....

"Kool-Aide"

Proverbs 25:25–29

"As cold water to a weary soul,
So is good news from a far country." (v. 25)

This proverb was written long before telegraph, telephone, or the Internet. The news channel of the day must have been "Camel News Network" (CNN) since messages from the "far country" were carried and then hand-delivered by hired runners or transported via caravans. When the news courier arrived, people were excited. Good news would certainly be refreshing like a cup of cold, clear well water. Sad news would simply be . . . sad.

My parents were missionaries to Israel for eight years. Their term of service occurred prior to the Internet and e-mail. Our only method of contact was "snail mail," along with one-way radio phone calls at the rate of $2.00 per minute. We learned to write letters (which we have kept and still treasure) and talk quickly, and only when necessary, by phone. Hearing those voices was the cup of cold water for this weary soul, especially in the initial stages of the Gulf War, which impacted the region of the Middle East where my parents were located.

At one point, there were four separate "family member units" scattered across the globe on three separate continents. Waiting for news from each of them was excruciating at times. Meanwhile, they devoted their days to giving a cup of cold water in the name of Jesus to the locals in their respective mission fields.

Finally, I was able to visit all of their locations to see how the Lord was using them in their various cultural contexts. My eyes were opened as I saw the locals arrive at the missionary homes after walking miles and miles in heat or rain or cold. Every culture had a customary "greeting," which involved sitting down together for talk and food. In all cultures except ours, time was never a factor. A beverage was offered to relieve thirst. In West Africa, I learned

the meaning of "Kool-Aide" as I watched visitors arrive dehydrated from the heat and depart filled and refreshed for the return journey. The colored water was "kool" and the refreshing beverage provided much needed "aide" to weary guests.

After each trip to the far countries, I realized that these indigenous people groups were thirsty for so much more than a cup of cold water. They desperately needed "living water" found only in a relationship with Jesus Himself (John 4:1–26). Waiting for the news courier to appear over the horizon was one thing. Having missionaries follow the call of God to cross the ocean to deliver the good news of the gospel was another thing altogether: eternal hope.

Becky Brown

Prayer: *Ask the Father to help you keep an empty cup ready to be filled with the good news of Jesus Christ; then share the "Kool-Aide" with those who are thirsty.*

Personal Reflection: ....

....

....

....

....

....

A Time for Silence and a Time to Speak

Proverbs 26:1–9

"Do not answer a fool according to his folly,
Lest you also be like him.
Answer a fool according to his folly,
Lest he be wise in his own eyes." (vv. 4–5)

Social media has become a popular form of communication in our lives. Many times social media is a wonderful vehicle for connecting families and friends, disseminating information, and even providing ministry a virtual environment. Unfortunately many people sitting safely shielded behind a computer screen find it easier to express uninhibited thoughts, feelings, and beliefs they otherwise would have kept to themselves or would have shared with only a trusted friend. An unhindered post on social media can lead to hurt feelings, misunderstandings, misjudgment, and even harsh criticism. Social media has become a place where fools play and folly flows freely.

How do Christians respond to this challenge? Wise women need to know how to deal with fools. Today, social media supplies an arena where women feel free to remove all filters and reveal the foolishness of their hearts. Discernment is needed to know when to keep silent and when to speak. Proverbs 26:4–5 can help.

Sometimes a wise woman must shake her head and move on when seeing or reading something foolish. If the fool boasts, and we boast back, are we not also the fool? If she tells a lie or half-truth and we do the same, we are just as guilty. If she exaggerates, we can be tempted to counter with a similar exaggeration. Perhaps the better response, if she communicates sarcastic criticism, is not to respond in like fashion. When we answer a fool in the language of a fool, nothing more is accomplished than to make ourselves a fool just like her. As much as we feel the need to retaliate, we do not need to engage in every

680

argument, misstatement, or foolish posting on social media, lest we be considered fools as well. Rather, ask yourself, will my response teach, convict, redeem, or rescue? If the answer is no, then keep silent.

On the other hand, there is a time to speak. When a fool's folly is harmful to herself or to others, a wise woman will share what she knows to convict, redirect, or even teach the fool, especially those with whom she has a relationship. If there is hope of redemption, correction, or protection, then speak.

Resist temptation to engage in all conversations on social media today. Avoid answering "a fool according to his folly" (v. 4). Be a wise woman, knowing when to be silent and when to speak.

Terri Stovall

Prayer: *Ask the Lord to give you the discernment to know when to keep silent and when to speak. Have courage to engage the foolish when it means the rescuing of a soul who has lost her way.*

Personal Reflection: ....

....

....

....

....

....

Don't Be a "Know-It-All"

Proverbs 26:10–19

"Do you see a man wise in his own eyes?
There is more hope for a fool than for him." (v. 12)

A "know-it-all" is someone who acts as though she knows everything and dismisses the opinions, comments, or suggestions of anyone else. A "know-it-all" may be called a smarty pants, braggart, or even windbag. Notice that this label does not have anything to do with how much she knows but rather with the attitude that she exudes. I do not want to be known as a "know-it-all."

The first verses of Proverbs 26 discusses the fool and how to respond or not respond to her (vv. 4–5). In the focal verse, Solomon exposes a particular type of fool, one who is so enmeshed in her own overconfidence that she refuses to learn from the experience of others. The person who is wise in her own eyes is even more hopeless than the common fool because she spurns learning, confident that she knows it all without recognizing her own foolishness.

A "know-it-all" with her self-conceited heart has even less hope than the common fool. A fool typically knows she is a fool. A "know-it-all" does not even see the error of her ways, nor is she open to correction, rebuke, or instruction. Often she becomes opinionated, dogmatic, and dismissive.

A religious "know-it-all" is just as desolate. There is more hope for a sinner who knows she is hopeless than for the proud Pharisee who considers himself perfect (Matt. 21:32; Luke 15:7; 18:14). Many believers are hindered from being truly wise because they are blind to the truth, assuming that they know-it-all and declaring their own wisdom. A God-fearing woman has a reverential awe and loving devotion for God (John 9:35–41).

Only as we become a fool in our own eyes do we receive the wisdom of God (1 Cor. 3:18). Only as we recognize our own worthless and hopeless state without Christ, do we find an everlasting, unshakable hope. Avoid being a

"know-it-all" who shuns even the instruction, rebuke, and discipline of the Lord. Rather, live as one who is wiser than a hopeless fool, embracing the fear and admonition of God.

Terri Stovall

Prayer: *Ask God to reveal to you any areas where you are arrogant and boastful. Ask Him to help you be a lifelong learner who is open to learning from those around you. Thank the Lord for His loving instruction, discipline, and direction and ask Him to help you learn at least one thing each day.*

Personal Reflection: ....

....

....

....

....

....

....

Swallowing Lies

Proverbs 26:20–26

*"The words of a talebearer are like tasty trifles,
And they go down into the inmost body." (v. 22)*

What a joy to gather around a holiday table, with family and friends enjoying each other's company while eating all the wonderful family recipes you do not get to sample at any other time. If you have a sweet tooth, the holiday season may present temptations beyond your resistance. Have you ever consumed some special treat so quickly and in such quantities that it tasted so good going down, but soon found yourself feeling miserable? What you so eagerly consumed turned sour in your stomach, causing extreme discomfort. Proverbs 26:22 paints a similar picture.

The message of a talebearer equates to the words of a gossip, the one who has news to tell or "the latest" from the infamous grapevine. And you may find yourself devouring the gossip like tasty holiday trifles. You willingly and ravenously consume them, and they go to the very depths of your soul.

A fire needs wood to burn and charcoal to serve as starter (vv. 20–21). Similarly, a contentious man or talebearer is needed to kindle strife. He need only find a willing party who will consume the lies he determines to share.

Many quarrels are either resolved or fueled by words. The destruction of character is often attributed to gossip and the retelling of lies and half-truths. Just as fire must have a constant fuel source to keep burning, the talebearer or gossiper is only effective if she keeps finding someone willing to consume the tasty tidbits she is offering. If there is no one to swallow the lies of the talebearer, then the destruction stops.

Rules of good nutrition suggest wise choices for the food consumed. Most nutritionists say that a bite of sweet now and again is fine. But to eat blindly any and everything placed before us may not be the best. The same is true with the

words, information, and stories that we are told. We have to evaluate them, use discernment, and ask ourselves if they are words of a talebearer or are words of truth.

Terri Stovall

Prayer: *As you are privy to information, stories, and the latest news, ask the Lord to help you have discernment about when to feast and when to walk away. Seek to be a woman who uses words that resolve quarrels rather than the talebearer who fuels discord.*

Personal Reflection: ....

....

....

....

....

....

....

And Words Can Sometimes Harm Us

Proverbs 26:27–28

"A lying tongue hates those who are crushed by it,
And a flattering mouth works ruin." (v. 28)

Do you remember the classic children's rhyme: "Sticks and stones may break my bones, but words will never harm me"? I remember a time in grade school when I yelled those words at a group of girls who had said mean things about me and criticized my appearance. I walked away with tears running down my cheeks, even though I did not believe that words would never hurt, because they did. Those girls were not my friends, and they never would be. While the words stung, the scars left were shallow. The deeper wounds are reserved for words of betrayal uttered by those whom we trust. Those words hurt; they cut deeper than any other pain and can cause wounds from which some never recover.

Proverbs 26:28 speaks about two kinds of lies and the power of the tongue to hurt and destroy. First, there is the lie that slanders. These words are openly hostile, spoken from a heart of hatred, and their intent to hurt is clear. Their blows are offered and felt in plain sight, and we can often see them coming, guard against them, and even slough them off before the words cut too deep. The second lie is much more damaging; it is the flattering lie. These lies of betrayal are often spoken by those whom we trust, love, or respect. Sometimes the lies are clothed in artfully crafted words, which at first seem complimentary. Then we discover that those flattering words conceal hatred, hostility, and an intent to ruin. And as we look into the eyes of the person we trusted, the betrayal cuts deep.

Have you ever been on the receiving end of a flattering lie that cut so deep, the wound still bleeds? Perhaps the time has come to forgive the person who spoke those words and pack the wound with words of healing and truth from God's Word. Or perhaps you are remembering a moment when the words that

flowed from your mouth were a cleverly crafted lie that was meant to put someone in her place or to get a last jab with a final word in a quarrel.

Are you guilty of openly slandering someone in order to hurt her? What if your words have left wounds in the heart of someone who loved you and trusted you? Is it time to seek her out and ask her to forgive you?

Terri Stovall

Prayer: *Ask the Lord to help you only to speak words that build up rather than words that crush and ruin. Ask God to give you the courage to go and seek the forgiveness of anyone who has been harmed by your critical words. If there are open wounds in your own heart caused by sharp words, seek to forgive the one who wielded those words.*

Personal Reflection: ....

....

....

....

....

....

....

Living in the Present

Proverbs 27:1–4

"Do not boast about tomorrow,
For you do not know what a day may bring forth." (v. 1)

As a little girl, one of my favorite pastimes was to play house. I had a toy kitchen with everything I needed to prepare and serve a delectable gourmet meal. My guests were my stuffed animals and well-worn dolls, who always raved about how much fun they had at my dinner parties. I also had a baby doll bed that once belonged to my mother, a little rocking chair, and two especially favored baby dolls. As I rocked these "babies," changed them, and fed them, I dreamed of the day I would have my own children. I just knew that I was going to have two children, both boys; and I knew exactly what I would name them.

Years passed, and life moved on, graduating from high school, then college, and finally graduate school. I met the man I married, and we began to set up our home and family together. But, I still dreamed about the day we would welcome our own children into the world. I even found myself thinking, *When we have children, then. . . .* That day never came.

Proverbs 27:1 reminds us not to boast about tomorrow because we never know what today will bring. This proverb is not meant to discourage you from planning for the future. We are wise to prepare for whatever may come. This proverb underscores the importance of living with purpose every day and embracing the present season of life.

Do any of these phrases sound familiar?

"When I get married, then I will be . . ."
"When we have children, then . . ."
"When I can buy my own house, then . . ."
"When I get that job, then . . ."

Although we can voice our hopes, dreams, and desires, believers are wise to speak of tomorrow with submission to the will of God. Focusing on tomorrow can lead to anxiety and worry today (Matt. 6:34). Putting off until tomorrow what God has asked you to do today is a sin. You have no idea what will happen tomorrow and may be unable to fulfill what God has asked you to do (James 4:13–17). Submitting our tomorrows to the Lord and living in obedience in the present allow God to do His work, often carried out behind the scenes and in ways that we may not even see (Eccl. 11:5–6).

Boasting about tomorrow and keeping our eyes on a day that may never come causes us to miss the opportunities and blessings right in front of our eyes. If my focus were still on the dream of tomorrow, I would miss the many spiritual daughters God has placed in my care for a season. And, oh, what blessings I would miss!

Terri Stovall

Prayer: *Ask the Lord to help you live in the present, speaking of tomorrow with hope and expectation but remaining submissive to God's will.*

Personal Reflection: ....

....

....

....

....

When the Truth Hurts

Proverbs 27:5–8

"Open rebuke is better
Than love carefully concealed.
Faithful are the wounds of a friend
But the kisses of an enemy are deceitful." (vv. 5–6)

During a difficult season of my life, someone about whom I cared was making poor decisions with some damaging consequences that I could see coming. I did not know what to do until a trusted friend asked, "Do you care enough about her to confront her?"

No one likes or enjoys confrontation. Having those difficult conversations and speaking hard truths are risky, emotional, painful, and intense. But, at the end of the day, I would much rather risk hurting the feelings of my friend than to let her continue to cause harm to herself and those around her because I love her and only want the best for her.

Proverbs 27:5–6 is a reminder that it is much better to offer an open, honest correction than simply to ignore the matter. Carefully concealing love means taking the easy and almost cowardly way of ignoring the need for rebuke, hoping it will all go away. Speaking the truth in love is seldom easy and may appear to jeopardize the friendship, but such accountability is one of the most important ingredients in a true friendship (Eph. 4:15).

A faithful friend corrects the faults of one whom she loves. A wise woman receives reproof from someone she trusts has her best interest at heart even if it hurts and cuts to the quick. The "kisses" or flattering praises are more dangerous. They are kisses of betrayal and deceit from one who may appear to be your friend but is not.

Consider two kisses of betrayal found in Scripture. During a tumultuous time in the reign of David, Joab met his half-brother Amasa on the battlefield.

Joab approached Amasa to give him a brotherly greeting and kiss but then killed him. Unresolved conflict led to an unexpected kiss of betrayal (2 Sam. 20:8–10). Judas Iscariot, one of the twelve disciples, deceitfully planned to betray Jesus with a kiss. As he did, Jesus, his friend, openly rebuked Judas saying, "Judas, are you betraying the Son of Man with a kiss" (Luke 22:48)?

Confrontation is not easy, but a true friend does not shy away from the hard things of friendship. When I nervously and prayerfully confronted my friend, at first she was not receptive, even pushing me away. But the pain of that experience was worth it as I continued to pray and pursue, eventually seeing her receive the truth given and take giant steps of growth in the faith.

Terri Stovall

Prayer: *Ask the Lord to give you the courage to confront when a friend or loved one needs to hear hard truth. Likewise, ask God to help you hear the loving rebuke of a friend who graciously and faithfully confronts you.*

Personal Reflection: ....

....

....

....

....

....

Sweet Friends

Proverbs 27:9–12

*"Ointment and perfume delight the heart,
And the sweetness of a man's friend gives delight by hearty counsel." (v. 9)*

Nothing is sweeter than a friend who has been with you through thick and thin. Especially sweet are those friends whom you may not see often; but when you do, you immediately pick up where you left off as if you had just seen her the day before. Those friendships serve as a balm to the heart and soul.

Several decades ago, the term "bosom buddy" was coined to refer to the closest of friends. "Bosom," referring to the chest area where the heart is located, intimated that a "bosom buddy" is closest to your heart, a person who knows you and your innermost being. "Bosom buddies" are so close to you that they know your hopes, dreams, fears, and struggles. The term is associated with a nurturing, close, and affectionate relationship. Having a friend who is a bosom-buddy with whom you can speak and act freely, with whom you can communicate on the deepest level, and from whom you seek counsel, is a good thing. Just as ointment soothes, so, too, does a friend who makes our burdens lighter, offers faithful advice, and gives hearty counsel. As a special bottle of perfume can evoke delight, an out-of-the-blue phone call from such a friend can instantly make your heart soar.

Today, women struggle to have deep, lasting friendships. Because women are busy, on the move, and guarded, true friendships are few and far between. However, this proverb is a reminder of the importance and benefits of a genuine friend. First, great pleasure is experienced with a true friend. Friends bring joy and delight to your heart. I have shared my longest, most satisfying, tear-streaming laugh with a "bosom buddy" friend. There is just something so very sweet about time with a special friend.

Second, friendships are advantageous and helpful. During hard times, days of calamity, and difficult circumstances, a true friend gives advice, help, and hope. True friendships rest more in heavenly counsel than in hearty laughter. Difficult days come "where the rubber meets the road," as the expression goes, and we learn the identity of our true friends.

A faithful friend is a rare find. She can make your life richer, bringing delight to your heart, and joy to your soul.

Terri Stovall

Prayer: *Thank God for the sweet friends in your life. Recount to Him the blessings you have experienced from the hands of the friends who delight your heart.*

Personal Reflection: ....

....

....

....

....

....

....

Annoying Dripping Faucets

Proverbs 27:13–16

*"A continual dripping on a very rainy day
And a contentious woman are alike;
Whoever restrains her restrains the wind,
And grasps oil with his right hand." (vv. 15–16)*

I was in a hotel room, trying to adapt to unfamiliar noises when I heard it—the distinct, rhythmic dripping of water. As much as I tried, my ear focused only upon the drip, drip, drip. I arose from my bed to seek out its source and found the culprit—a leaky shower head. I tried everything I could to stop that dripping, all to no avail. Knowing that I would not be able to ignore the sound and wishing for much-needed sleep, I blocked it by shutting the bathroom door and playing music so I would not have to hear it anymore. But, I knew the annoying drip was still there.

Houses in Old Testament times were typically small squared structures with flat earthen roofs. Because they were not sloped, water easily pooled on the roofs when it rained. The construction materials of the roofs were prone to leaking, especially during heavy rains. The scene depicted in Proverbs 27:15–16 is set in such a home on a day when heavy rain has caused a troublesome, uncomfortable, and impossible-to-get-away-from leak. Those leaks were impossible to repair until the rains stopped and the roof dried. The homeowner was forced to endure the constant drip, drip, drip.

The proverb here likens the irritating dripping of a leaky roof to the actions of a contentious woman. In every reference to the contentious woman in Proverbs (see 19:13; 21:9, 19; 25:24), a sense of endless annoyance and nagging are implied. The proverb for today implicitly compares the experience of a homeowner who simply had to endure the endless annoyance of a leak to the experience of anyone who must endure the habitual negativity of a contentious

woman. Changing or at least curbing this woman's impatience, discontent, and expressions of her ill-tempered outlook seems impossible. She is the ultimate pessimist.

Look at the analogy. We cannot pour oil into our hands and expect to hold it there without its seeping out. Nor can we hold back the wind and its power to destroy. Similarly, a contentious woman cannot be restrained with any effectiveness. Only God, who made the wind and provides the oil, can change her into a woman who is loving, encouraging, and cheerful. Just as I tried to do everything I could to stop that dripping faucet, so, too, would I do anything to stop the dripping of contention from my heart and mouth. I pray that God will continually work on me so that I will never be like that annoying dripping faucet.

Terri Stovall

Prayer: *Ask God to help you see areas of contention in your own life. Ask Him to forgive you for any habitual negativity and to renew your heart, mind, and tongue so you can be a woman who provides contentment, not contention, to your home and family.*

Personal Reflection: ....

....

....

....

....

695

The Honing Rod

Proverbs 27:17–27

"As iron sharpens iron,
So a man sharpens the countenance of his friend." (v. 17)

Have you ever wondered why a dull knife is more dangerous in the kitchen than a sharp knife? A dull knife requires the use of extra force and effort. When it does cut, a dull knife tears and rips rather than slicing through material cleanly and easily. A dull knife can cause injury when, as the extra resistance is applied, it suddenly slips and slices or gouges fingers instead of the food. Cuts and other such accidents can still happen when you use a sharp knife; but the wounds from a dull knife cause much more damage, take longer to heal, and leave more significant scars.

Any good chef starts each day sharpening knives so these tools will do what they are supposed to do. The best, most efficient way to sharpen a knife is with a honing rod—a long rod, usually made of steel. A knife is lightly placed on the rod, and as it glides along the steel, the honing process produces a sharp blade edge. First, when a knife is "honed," small deformities in the blade are abrasively removed. Second, as the knife is "steeled," the rod realigns the blade's edge, which may have curled a bit due to use. Steeling does not remove any material from the blade; it merely reshapes what had become misshapen.

With the above picture in your mind, consider the meaning of Proverbs 27:17. A honing rod and a knife are made of like material. Iron upon iron is the best method for sharpening. Similarly, a man—or better still a friend—is of the same nature as his friends. The two encounter one another through daily life, leaving each other better for the task at hand. Friend-to-friend is the best method for one person to sharpen another.

Iron tools are made sharp and fit for use by rubbing them against the file or the steel rod. People are made sharper and more fit for use by provoking

one another to love and good deeds (Heb. 10:24). Sometimes one friend helps another to sharpen by honing her life, helping her identify those weaknesses that need to be removed for better service. Other times, friends will merely help redirect or reshape areas of a life that has become distorted, distracting from the task at hand.

Who plays the role of a honing rod in your life? Are you being sharpened daily to be fit for use by God? Do not get caught trying to use a dull knife to do work requiring the sharpest of blades. You just might end up causing more damage, exerting more effort, and experiencing unintended consequences.

Terri Stovall

Prayer: *If you do not have in your life a friend who can be your honing rod, pray today about developing a friendship with someone who can sharpen you. Ask God to allow you to be a honing rod in the life of another.*

Personal Reflection: ....

....

....

....

....

....

Protecting the Poor

Proverbs 28:1–8

*"One who increases his possessions by usury and extortion
Gathers it for him who will pity the poor." (v. 8)*

My children enjoy making what we call "homeless bags." Often they make them in one of their classes at church, but we have also put them together at home. The concept is very simple. We gather gallon-sized plastic bags and fill each with essentials and non-perishable food items like crackers, socks, a water bottle, tissues, soap, mouthwash, a poncho, Bible, etc. We keep the "homeless bags" in the car and look on the side of the road for men or women who could use the bag. This concrete and practical gift helps less fortunate people and involves our family in ministry.

God commands His children to love others, especially poor or underprivileged persons. Part of loving someone is protecting him, caring for him, and helping to provide for him. God's love is not dependent on life's choices or circumstances. We are to love the homeless, too. In our family's season of life, the best way I know how to do that is through giving away these simple little bags of provisions.

The opposite of loving someone in need is exploiting him. Exploitation means to make unethical use of someone or something for one's own profit. If a person's goal is not to love others but to love self, then she will act in whatever way necessary to promote and increase her own wealth and power. Unfortunately, the most susceptible people to this manipulation are those who are poor and, therefore, unprotected from their evil ways.

God is aware of this abuse and neglect. He wants to make very clear through the wise words of Solomon that whether here on earth or in eternity, those who take advantage of the poor for their own personal gain will experience consequences for their sin. God is emphatic about this because

exploitation goes against His very nature. God is love, and the mistreatment of defenseless people is not consistent with His character of love.

Believers who are saved by God's grace and have committed their lives to serving Christ must exercise love on a daily basis, not only avoiding the exploitation of the poor, but also defending the innocent from abuse by others. We can help to provide for and to protect those less fortunate so that they will be less vulnerable and susceptible to the cunning vices mentioned in Proverbs 28.

Melanie Lenow

Prayer: *Thank the Lord for loving you and giving you the charge to love others. Find ways in your community to help those who are less fortunate. Reject selfishness in managing the money God has provided for you.*

Personal Reflection: ....

....

....

....

....

....

....

No More Hiding

Proverbs 28:9–17

"He who covers his sins will not prosper,
But whoever confesses and forsakes them will have mercy." (v. 13)

"Can you find me?" my son yelled as he hid behind the curtains. Hide-and-seek was one of his favorite games as a toddler. His favorite hiding place was either behind the couch or behind the curtains. His sisters or I would lovingly play along, the moment made more charming because it was quite evident where he was hiding. A chubby leg or arm would be sticking out for anyone to see. But that did not matter to him. In his world, he was completely hidden and would squeal in delight when we pounced upon his hiding place.

In the garden, Adam and Eve knew they had sinned, and the first thing they did was cover and hide (Gen. 3:8). When we try to hide from God because of our sins, we are acting as a child trying to hide behind the curtains. We think we are completely covered, but the signs of our sin show everywhere. Of course, God was not fooled and pursued Adam. When we try to conceal our sins from God, we only hurt ourselves. Instead of a thriving relationship with the One who created us, we enter into a dark web of deceit, leading to further separation from God. God has other plans for us. In the Old Testament, God hid His face from His people when they were in direct rebellion toward Him. He longs to show His face to us and cleanse us with His Spirit. "'And I will not hide My face from them anymore; for I shall have poured out My Spirit on the house of Israel,' says the Lord GOD" (Ezek. 39:29).

When you sin, do you not try to hide and live in darkness? Instead, you should allow God to pour His Spirit upon you as you confess that sin. Come clean. Find mercy. The psalmist says: "Purge me with hyssop, and I shall be clean. Wash me, and I shall be whiter than snow" (Ps. 51:7). Just like cleaning a wound may be painful at first, after it is cleaned the healing process can

begin. Healing can never begin in the darkness. Only after you confess your sin and repent can God cleanse you with His love and start you on the process of redemption.

Hide-and-seek is a fun game as a child, but hiding your sin from God only causes discouragement and stunted growth. Trust God and confess your sins to Him; for He is trustworthy, gracious, and ready to forgive.

Melanie Lenow

Prayer: *Confess your sins to the Lord. Do not hide or run away anymore. Thank Him for pursuing you despite your disobedience. Seek the Lord first and do not fall prey to the temptations of this world.*

Personal Reflection: ....

....

....

....

....

....

....

Faithful Pursuits

Proverbs 28:18–21

"A faithful man will abound with blessings,
But he who hastens to be rich will not go unpunished." (v. 20)

I work with juniors and seniors in high school in their post-graduation pursuits. Some students want to go to college immediately; some want to work for a few years, studying on the side. Each ultimately has the goal of accomplishing success. Businessmen from the community are invited to come and speak to my class on how to accomplish this goal of success. Without fail, most of the businessmen describe the key to success as being a strong sense of character and fortitude rather than the path you study or the accolades you accrue. People in every stage of life have dreams of trying new things and chasing new pursuits. Developing the character trait of faithfulness will always bring blessing to your life.

Faithfulness means persevering even when it is hard, being the last to quit and the first to try. It means never questioning where God has led you and staying where He has put you until He clearly tells you to move. Faithfulness allows you to develop lasting relationships and see the fruits of your labor as people grow and mature in the Lord because of your influence in their lives. Faithfulness allows you to see a job completed and rejoice unto the Lord for the great work He has done. These blessings are waiting in the wings for the faithful one.

Sadly, people who want a quick path to riches will miss out on these blessings. The quest for wealth often blinds them to the needs of others, and they will miss the joy in the journey because of the fixation on their destination.

Punishment is not a result of the wealth itself. Wealth is not a sin, and the most faithful sometimes become wealthy. No, the punishment is a result of the pursuit of wealth by ignoring things that are so much more important

in the economy of God. The faithful one is in the journey for the long haul. In contrast, the one in a hurry to get rich is quick to arrive on the scene and quick to leave.

God wants to use us in each stage and situation of life. Just as those wise businessmen in my class challenge my students, let us choose faithfulness to what God calls us to do. Focus on God's eternal investments and not the world's temporal rewards.

Melanie Lenow

Prayer: *Ask the Lord to help you choose faithfulness. Seek His vision for your life, and invest in others for His glory.*

Personal Reflection:

Trusting God in a Sinful World

Proverbs 28:22–25

"Whoever robs his father or his mother,
And says, 'It is no transgression,'
The same is companion to a destroyer.
He who is of a proud heart stirs up strife,
But he who trusts in the Lord will be prospered." (vv. 24–25)

Conflict. Greed. Destruction. Unfortunately, these conditions are all around us in this sin-tainted world. One thing brings me comfort: "There is nothing new under the sun" (Eccl. 1:9). While we may be surprised, the sin of this world does not surprise God. He is grieved, saddened, and angered by sin today just as He was in the days of the Old Testament. How should believers react to the sin around us? Solomon's observations in Proverbs 28:24–25 suggest three guidelines that we can follow.

1. **Call sin "sin."** When we refuse to acknowledge sin and skirt around the problem, we only add to the pain that the sin causes. Denying sin can destroy the society around us because right and wrong become relative to interpretation. Moral relativism is a close friend to destruction. When we point out the truth and share the redemption of Christ, healing begins and personal growth continues.

2. **Be a peacemaker.** A greedy person serves self, whether through money, food, possessions, or accolades. Greed is the gathering of possessions for personal use and enjoyment at all cost. Because greed is a means of self-promotion, it often causes conflict with others. In fact, greed enjoys conflict because when people are tearing each other down, the greedy person looks taller. In contrast, the peacemaker builds people up, pursuing peace for the benefit of others. She gains nothing except

the knowledge that her reward is in heaven and her pursuits please God. Serving others instead of self brings peace to a society.

3. **Trust in the Lord and prosper.** Nothing can separate believers from God's perfect plan for their lives. Yes, sin abounds, but God is bigger, and He wins in the end. We as believers must lift our heads and choose hope each day. We must work to battle evil, but ultimately we must trust God to continue His work in our lives and in the lives of those around us. Praise God, He is still on His throne, and nothing can change that. The more we trust God for who He is, the more we will prosper in the things of the Lord. We will become more loving, more patient, and more long-suffering toward others who might not know Him.

Melanie Lenow

Prayer: *Praise the Lord because He will ultimately win against the sin of this world. Keep your eyes fixed on Him and not on the world around you. Identify areas where you can be an influence by speaking His truth in love.*

Personal Reflection: ....

....

....

....

....

Trusting the One Who Can Save

Proverbs 28:26–28

*"He who trusts in his own heart is a fool,
But whoever walks wisely will be delivered." (v. 26)*

Everywhere you go, you hear these messages: "You can do it!" and "Follow your heart." The ideas of self-reliance and independence are woven into American culture. Unfortunately, we have become our own mini-gods, trusting in ourselves to accomplish whatever we wish. The true danger comes when you trust your own goodness to establish and sustain a relationship with God and secure your eternal salvation.

The problem with trusting in ourselves is that we have a sin problem. We are incapable of conjuring enough goodness within us to overcome that fact. Paul gives us this accurate picture: "For all have sinned and fall short of the glory of God, being justified freely by His grace through the redemption that is in Christ Jesus" (Rom. 3:23–24). Every person has sinned and, therefore, comes short of the requirements for having a relationship with God, for He is holy and perfect. No matter what we do, we cannot forge the bond of that relationship ourselves.

However, do not be discouraged! Someone made a way for that relationship. Look at the second part of the passage in Romans: We are "justified freely by His grace." No, we cannot achieve a relationship with God by working for it in our own strength, but He freely gives it to us. His grace is a gift offered to everyone who has a mind to understand and a heart to receive. How is God able to offer us this gift so freely? Salvation is accomplished only through the redemption that is found in Christ Jesus. Jesus came to this earth and lived a perfect and sinless life. When He died as a punishment for our sins and then rose from the dead as a sign of defeating even death itself, He made the way for us to have a relationship with God. Not only are we given the gift of enjoying a

personal relationship with God while we are alive, but we are also given the gift of eternal life with Him.

When we trust in ourselves to provide the fullness of a relationship with God, we are fools. The job is too big, and the requirements are impossible to attain. But there is One who offers redemption freely to us. God wants us to walk in wisdom and be confident of our relationship with Him. We can faithfully depend on God for our eternal salvation and not fall prey to the folly of self-reliance.

Melanie Lenow

Prayer: *The heavenly Father has made a way for you, a sinner, to have a personal relationship with Him. Seek His forgiveness when you rely on yourself for salvation and protection. Trust Him, for only He is righteous and powerful to save.*

Personal Reflection: ....

....

....

....

....

....

707

The Effects of a Leader

Proverbs 29:1–10

"When the righteous are in authority, the people rejoice;
But when a wicked man rules, the people groan." (v. 2)

History fascinates me! I once studied history as a series of great events, but now I enjoy learning what happened between the times of the great events that molded and shaped the way history unfolds.

Proverbs 28 and 29 contain a series of verses that discuss the effects of righteous leaders and wicked leaders. From the time it was written, we can see the truth these verses play out all through history, even until the present day. Four verses all come together to speak two specific truths (28:12, 28; 29:2, 16).

1. **The character of leaders greatly affects the character of the people.** As a general rule, the actions of the followers tell a great deal about the character of the leader. Is there great rejoicing among the righteous? If so, the leadership shows signs of good character and encourages right behavior. However, are the wicked prospering? More than likely, wickedness is being encouraged and aided by corrupt leadership. This correlation rings true in any area of leadership—business, ministry, or government. The character of a leader infiltrates the people who are being led.

2. **People will be affected by the leadership of those in authority.** History demonstrates that no one is immune to the events of the world. The effects of current events may not be felt immediately, but over time the decisions of leaders touch our lives. When events in the world seem overwhelming, many want to run off to an isolated island and live only with people they love, but we all know that cannot happen. Therefore, to understand that all events affect us and see them as opportunities

to affect the lives of others around us is beneficial. Proverbs 29:16 explains that "When the wicked are multiplied, transgression increases." Believers must understand that a time is coming when rebellion will be all around. How will we react? What are we doing today that might help build our character so that we can do the right thing when the situation arises? Persecution may arise, and believers may suffer greatly. What decisions can you make today to strengthen you and your family to stand for Christ when that time comes?

The stories of individual people greatly affect history. Whether our leaders are righteous or wicked, we have the choice of acting in ways that help or hurt those around us. We can embrace the character of the leaders, or we can continue to pursue righteousness and goodness for God's glory.

Melanie Lenow

Prayer: *Ask the Lord to orchestrate those in leadership for His purposes. How can you glorify God in your neighborhood, city, business place, or ministry? No matter who has authority over you, choose righteous behavior so that you might point more people to the Lord.*

Personal Reflection: ....

....

....

....

Keeping Anger in Check

Proverbs 29:11–19

"A fool vents all his feelings,
But a wise man holds them back." (v. 11)

An ongoing theme throughout Proverbs is the comparison of the foolish person to the wise person. Believers, with the Holy Spirit living within, should strive to grow in wisdom, casting foolishness to the side. Now the wisdom of God sometimes looks like foolishness in the eyes of the world. The actions Solomon denounces throughout Proverbs are applauded in our culture. However, fearing the Lord and growing in our knowledge of Him leads to godly wisdom, which, in turn, leads to righteous behavior and sanctification. A beautiful cycle brings us, ultimately, to become more like Christ.

This particular verse addresses self-control in the venting of anger. Anger, in and of itself, is not what is being condemned. Throughout Scripture, righteous anger is permissible for the believer. As God's people, injustices and evil in this world should cause us to rise up in anger. However, we dare not sin in expressing our anger. How is this possible? Our anger should move us to action. We should take that emotion and funnel it into working purposefully to end the injustice or protect the persecuted. Anger that leads to sin is no more useful than a toddler who pitches a fit. The situation is not helped and may be worsened by adding sin upon sins. When you practice self-control and hold your anger in check, you can be more productive in producing change.

As I strive to be more like the wise man, I am working to put my fleshly desires under the authority of Scripture. When I might want to "fly off the handle" and spew my anger over my adversary, I must work to control myself. God never planned for us to handle these frustrations alone. He has sent us a Helper who will come alongside with divine assistance. Jesus said, "And I will pray the Father, and He will give you another Helper, that He may abide with

you forever" (John 14:16). When we ask God to help, He has promised that His Holy Spirit will come alongside and teach us how to control the fleshly nature inside us. All it takes is a willing heart that wants to grow, casting aside foolish ways and learning to be wise.

Melanie Lenow

Prayer: *Seek forgiveness from the Lord when you have chosen the foolish way. Remember that His Holy Spirit is within you to help you grow in wisdom. Denounce your fleshly desires and submit to Him a tender and moldable heart.*

Personal Reflection: ....

....

....

....

....

....

....

Avoiding Pride's Pitfalls

Proverbs 29:20–27

"A man's pride will bring him low,
But the humble in spirit will retain honor." (v. 23)

Once again, Solomon gives wise counsel that directly contradicts the modern culture's way of thinking. In a culture that encourages people to fight for the upper hand and make sure their voices are heard, the reminder that "a man's pride will bring him low, but the humble in spirit will retain honor" comes as a shock (v. 23). How do you avoid falling into the trap of pride? Jesus' parable in Luke 14:5–10 identifies truths that help keep a position of humility:

1. **Acknowledge that there are others more important than you** (v. 5). When you are in a group setting, acknowledge the importance of those around you. Even if they are not higher in stature or rank, acknowledge their roles in society or the home and consider their work important.
2. **If you do not humble yourself among others, they will do it for you** (v. 9). As embarrassing as it might seem, we do have the habit of thinking higher of ourselves than others might. Keeping a humble spirit makes this less likely.
3. **Be content among others** (v. 10). Everyone likes to be special. Retail stores give special perks to loyal customers. We like to be the first in line in order to receive our preferences. However, we need to grow content in staying among others, not singled out for special privileges. For it is among the masses where we can have great influence for God's kingdom. He wants us among His people.
4. **With humility, accept honor** (v. 10). Receive any personal honor with grace and appreciation. Develop within yourself a truly thankful heart for those who see God's work in your life enough to acknowledge it.

Great accomplishments and prestigious roles of leadership are not bad things. The charge that Solomon makes in Proverbs 29:23 is a reminder to keep a humble spirit. Whether we accomplish great things or small things, we should give all honor and glory to God who made us and purposed within us to do good works. Let us not steal His glory but always remain thankful that God chose to use us.

Melanie Lenow

Prayer: *Thank the Lord for using you and for creating you to glorify Him with your actions and words. Ask Him to forgive you when you do not give Him glory but take some of the glory for yourself. Allow the Lord to create in you a clean and contrite heart so that all glory and honor and recognition will go to Him.*

Personal Reflection:

When Words Matter

Proverbs 30:1–6

"Every word of God is pure;
He is a shield to those who put their trust in Him.
Do not add to His words,
Lest He rebuke you, and you be found a liar." (vv. 5–6)

Agur describes his speech as an "utterance" (Hb. *massa'*, "burden or load," figuratively "what is heavy on you," v. 1). Most translations read as if he is delivering this message to his sons, friends, or students. However, some Jewish commentators suggest that these words—*Ithiel* (Hb., "God is with me") and *Ucal* (Hb., "devoured, weary")—are his own statement of despair: "I am weary, God, and perishing."

You, as I, can identify with weariness. You may be overwhelmed with mundane duties—tasks such as preparing, serving, and cleaning up meals; doing laundry, putting it away, only to have it soiled and returned; cleaning bathrooms—truly the "necessary room" most often in disarray! The entire day is interrupted again and again without time for enriching and celebratory moments or satisfying accomplishment!

What can you learn from Agur, who sought and valued wisdom and whose wisdom was sought by others?

- Even the wisest cannot *master* wisdom (v. 3).
- Those deserving honor and esteem still face the uncertainties of life and struggles of faith (v. 4).
- Even women who are set apart unto the Lord for leadership and ministries cannot understand and ultimately explain the mind of God (v. 4; Is. 55:8–9).

- Agur opens his speech in despair and self-deprecation (attitudes all of us have experienced), but he moves to a clear statement that only the one true God can bestow on the heart heavenly knowledge and truth, which are found in the words of God (Prov. 30:5; see also Ps. 119).
- With life-enriching, God-anointed blessing comes human-directed responsibility: We as hearers and recipients must not add anything to the words of God, which would suggest that our words are the essence of wisdom independent of God (Prov. 30:6).

You may experience the cycle of trials and difficulties, joys and celebrations, suffering and pain, achievement and recognition. Only God knows what is ahead; He can take you by the hand and lead you through; and He is the faithful rearguard, coming behind, restoring and renewing even when you personally have failed and stumbled with misspoken words or unaccomplished tasks or when you have gone through a season of suffering and pain that has kept you from doing the most important tasks of life and ministry.

Dorothy Kelley Patterson

Prayer: *For the understanding of knowledge and the discernment of wisdom as you walk through the challenges of life, let God's Word be a "shield" to those who will listen and embrace its truth. Be sure that your own human understandings do not override what the Lord has clearly said and given to you through His written Word.*

Personal Reflection: ....

....

....

A Prayer of Restraint

Proverbs 30:7–10

"Remove falsehood and lies far from me;
Give me neither poverty nor riches—
Feed me with the food allotted to me." (v. 8)

This chapter has a series of numerical sayings (Prov. 30:7, 15, 18, 21, 24, 29), literary devices that draw the reader's attention to important information. Focus on Agur's appropriate conclusion to his speech—the only prayer in the book of Proverbs (v. 7). He has rightly determined that all wisdom comes from God, and only that wisdom is reliable and protective. What are the components of this simple prayer? Can such a template be helpful to you?

The prayer begins with unusual requests, especially for those focused on entitlement and personal whims:

- Agur is aware of his own frailty and inadequacy. He asks the Lord to protect him from lies and a false witness (v. 8a).
- He is more concerned about character and wisdom than he is about poverty. To seek divine favor, Agur wants neither to punish himself with deprivation nor to enhance his own wealth (v. 8b).
- He is asking God for the necessities of life, as Scripture admonishes (v. 8c; Matt. 6:11). Agur recognizes that to accrue excessive wealth can move one to over-confidence in her own abilities, but he also realizes that a fixation on poverty can draw attention to one's own ability to develop holiness before God simply by personal deprivation.

What then can be learned from Agur for women who want the blessings of God in order to become conduits of His blessings upon their families and others? Affirm with the wise sage Agur that God is infinitely wise beyond your human understanding and powerful enough to work through your human frailties to accomplish His purposes in your life and through you in the lives of others. Before God uses you, He prepares you to recognize Him as the one and only God who alone has the wisdom and power to prepare you for life. In your human limitations, once you bow before Him, He then will guide you with the wisdom of His Word to accomplish His purposes not only for your own life but also for those who cross your path.

Reading a section of Scripture daily and adding devotional insights arising from that text of Scripture is one way to saturate yourself with the Word of God, to begin filling the reservoir of your heart with His unfathomable wisdom. Then as Agur shared what he learned from his personal relationship with the one true God, you can do the same with your friends or in your Bible study group, growing together in the knowledge of God's truth and finding ways to use that wisdom in the living of life.

Dorothy Kelley Patterson

Prayer: *Ask the Lord to open your own heart to His wisdom; to prompt needed restraints in your life so that you can focus on His Word; to give you the courage to stay true to His Word whatever the cost; and to use you as salt and light to draw others to Him!*

Personal Reflection: ....

....

....

....

A Generation with Evil Intent

Proverbs 30:11–17

"There is a generation that is pure in its own eyes,
Yet is not washed from its filthiness." (v. 12)

How can anyone bearing the name "Christian" pursue a path of evil intent? In our corrupt culture, the definition of *evil* has been blurred, an effective ploy of the devil when operating within the Christian community.

"Generation" (Hb. *dor*) here refers to a "group of people" with common characteristics. These four generations are described in a metaphorical sense, implying their common moral and spiritual character. They are marked by evil intent, beginning with how they relate to parents in the home (v. 11) and moving to the public community with attacks on the weakest in society (v. 14). Such generations have always been with us. Evildoers are found even within the congregations of faith!

What are the characteristics of these evildoers?

- They are disrespectful to their parents through words or deeds (v. 11).
- They are determined to follow their own way, whatever the cost (v. 12).
- They embrace an inflated view of themselves, leading to open contempt of others (v. 13).
- They are cruel and contemptuous toward the most vulnerable in their communities (v. 14).

The *leech*, a bloodsucking worm, depicts the insatiable appetite of the evildoer who focuses on personal desires (v. 15). Death (finality of the grave), the infertile woman (longing for a child that does not come), land without water (parched earth that refuses to produce), raging fire (destructive force that

cannot be stopped)—these represent deep human desires that cannot be satisfied (vv. 15–16).

So, how can you escape the clutches of these evil desires that creep into the human heart? Wisdom is found throughout the book of Proverbs, but some clues on how to use God's wisdom to overcome the evil impulses that pursue the human family are in this passage.

Reverse characteristics of the evildoer by honoring parents (Ex. 21:17), by cleansing yourself of evildoing and determining to go God's way (Prov. 3:5–6; Is. 1:16–17), by humbling yourself before the Lord and acknowledging your own weakness, by reaching out to the needy with tender mercy and compassion (Mic. 6:8). Give attention to your own testimony and lifestyle and make yourself an example of all that is good and godly because your children will be like you (Prov. 30:15; Jer. 31:29).

Dorothy Kelley Patterson

Prayer: *Clean out the filth of evil thoughts and desires in your own heart. Seek divine wisdom and a heart to do what the Lord demands in every decision you make and in every step you take.*

Personal Reflection: ....

....

....

....

....

Wonderful Things

Proverbs 30:18–23

"The way of an eagle in the air,
The way of a serpent on a rock,
The way of a ship in the midst of the sea,
And the way of a man with a virgin." (v. 19)

God is amazing—no doubt about that! "The way [Hb. *derek*] of . . ." points to the wonder found in the movement of the eagle, the snake, and the ship—all moving along a path with virtually no trace, smooth and graceful in the process. "The way of a man with a virgin" (Hb. *'almah*, "a young woman of marriageable age, yet under the care of her parents and thus hidden from the public")—illustrates the mystery of love. Solomon wrote a book on it (see Song of Solomon). These metaphors all suggest a mystery—something beyond human comprehension.

The numerical saying describes "four" evils with this in common: Something is obviously and radically wrong, and someone is so out of place that the earth itself is affected. How appropriate for the upside-down world in which we are living! Someone may be elevated to a higher station in life for which she is not prepared or gifted. A servant reigns as a king (v. 22); a fool eats with lack of restraint (v. 22); a woman behaves in a hateful manner—whether rejected by her husband or the victim of her own misdeeds (v. 23); a maidservant finds a way to ingratiate herself to her master so that she supplants her mistress (v. 23). These metaphors serve as warnings appropriate for every household.

Wise women will guard their households from contention and unpleasantness by taking special note of the two women described in verse 23 lest their husbands and children suffer (cp. 19:13). The emphasis in these metaphors is not so much on immorality as on the fact that there will always be people who attain what they do not deserve, and often a person can be utterly at ease

in making and executing sinful choices. Perhaps those in this series could be described as "too big for their britches"—or in Texas, "their boots"!

What is the lesson from these numerical sayings so carefully selected for our edification? We must above all seek wisdom that only God can provide. As we put feet to follow that path of wisdom, we must be content with even the most challenging—and sometimes disappointing—path; yes, we must be willing to endure restraint and even self-denial, making our choices not on what is easy and self-fulfilling but clinging to the ways of the Lord so that nothing will mar our testimony or bring shame to His name!

Dorothy Kelley Patterson

Prayer: *Ask the Lord to grant protection from the evils of this world—all that would appeal to your senses in unholy ways! Plead for courage to stay the course—the way of the Lord, to walk faithfully in that path with a determination to bear your witness even in an upside-down world.*

Personal Reflection: ....

....

....

....

....

....

Foot-and-Mouth Disease

Proverbs 30:24–33

"If you have been foolish in exalting yourself,
Or if you have devised evil, put your hand on your mouth." (v. 32)

Sometimes size suggests weakness and lack of the ability to function effectively. Teachers present many examples of the strength and power of the smallest child. Even the tiniest creature can and does make a difference in the Creator's world. A numerical metaphor describes four small but clever creatures:

- *Ants* without physical strength work diligently and faithfully without a leader (v. 25; Prov. 6:6–8). They show initiative, preparation for the future, and diligence with the knowledge that they may be crushed underfoot anytime. Provision is their goal.
- *Rock badgers* are "feeble" but clever enough to find sanctuary among the cliffs secure from their enemies (30:26). They have foresight; they recognize and accept their weakness.
- *Locusts* are committed to their community, moving as an army with order and discipline without a commander (v. 27). They are unselfish, not caring who gets credit. They move forward, refusing to be pulled off course.
- *Spiders* can find a way into any dwelling—even the palace of a king (v. 28). They show patience, perseverance, and ingenuity.

These creatures show that wisdom is superior to size or strength; each is unique even though all are committed to the same goal. The Creator has given each the means for provision, defense, and safety.

Physical prowess or prominent position or place of dwelling should not be your driving force. Weakness is a driving force in faith. Look for ways to use who

you are and where you have been placed as springboards for bringing glory to your Creator God. No creation of God is insignificant! No woman should be too proud to learn or too indifferent to be sensitive to heeding divine mandates in preparing for what is to come.

The last numerical metaphor speaks of four animals noted for their majestic way of moving within their respective spheres:

- The lion has immense strength and a great roar (v. 30).
- The greyhound has speed (v. 31).
- The male goat has courage to climb up the rockiest cliff (v. 31).
- The king—at the climax of this metaphor—has his troops with him (v. 31). He inspires devotion because he embodies all of the above!

Words can bring into the public arena power and destruction, especially in the sense of being hurtful to others. You may not be able to prevent the thought, but you can "put your hand on your mouth" to restrain the unleashing of that hurtful thought into the public sector from which it cannot be retrieved. Especially is this admonition important with the rise of social media, the invasion of false news, and the unrestrained flow of verbiage without any thought for the "unintended" consequences of those words. Discipline your thoughts, guard your speech, and restrain your words!

Dorothy Kelley Patterson

Prayer: *Ask the Lord for a humble heart. Focus on retraining your speech to bring peace and encouragement to those who cross your path.*

Personal Reflection: ....

....

Mother Knows Best

Proverbs 31:1–9

*"The words of King Lemuel,
The utterance which his mother taught him." (v. 1)*

These inspired words were transmitted from the heart of God into the hands of a loving and devoted mother, who imparted to her son King Lemuel wisdom concerning his choice of a wife. Simultaneously the words extend to every woman throughout the generations, inspiring all —wife, mother, daughter—to work toward high and lofty goals.

The "utterance" (Hb. *massa'*, "pronouncement, speech" or more precisely, "burden, load") suggests that which is heavy on a person (v. 1). Her message must have come from a heavy heart burdened for her son and his work in guiding a kingdom. She set the scene with sharing her deep affection, using carefully chosen epithets to describe her relationship to her son from his birth through nurturing his development into manhood (v. 2).

These initial words of wisdom are directed as personal instruction from a mother to her son. She certainly addresses his social or kingdom responsibilities—what he does in the public sphere of his work. However, she does not forget to admonish him concerning distractions and caution him against the temptation to yield to fleshly appetites, which might pull him away from his duties to God and kingdom (vv. 3–7). She presents her case carefully and passionately, knowing that the opportunity has come for her to teach her son.

The teaching method she used is not simply sharing facts. Rather she "taught" (Hb. *yasar*, "instruct, bind, correct, reform, improve"). This mother was literally chastising her son with words; her message was of such importance that she intended for her correction to be a tool to enhance the learning experience. God's discipline intends to change lives and to move His children to obedience. This method of transmitting instruction with the determination

to bring obedience is fleshed out by a diligent mother, who is an inspired messenger—even to her adult son, who happens to be the king!

A godly mother's counsel to her son is linked with the son's respectful receipt of that wisdom. The mother was no longer prominent in the life of the king—perhaps no longer living; yet he recognized her wisdom and blessed her for this investment in his life. Her message did not reach the public audience from her lips but came from her son, making this message more impressive to the succeeding generations. This principle appears again in verse 31 as the works of this woman of strength will be praised by those who profited most—her husband and children. The bookends appear beginning with the mother imparting wisdom to her son (v. 1) and ending with her works/fruit as a tool of praise (31:31).

Dorothy Kelley Patterson

Prayer: *Your prayers for every child whom God sends to cross your path should begin with your own longing to mold a life in consecration to the Lord. If the Lord blesses you with a child formed in your womb, knit your heart to hers as you embrace great joy and heavy responsibility.*

Personal Reflection: ....

....

....

....

....

A Heavenly Appraisal

Proverbs 31:10–12

"Who can find a virtuous wife?
For her worth is far above rubies." (v. 10)

This acrostic poem uses a literary tool to set apart this paradigm for biblical womanhood, elevating its words to one of the most valued and treasured passages in Scripture. What kind of woman should a man choose to marry? What kind of wife should a woman aspire to be? What should a mother want her son to find in a wife? In the Hebrew text, each of the twenty-two verses begins with a successive letter of the Hebrew alphabet (Prov. 31:10–31), not only setting it apart as a literary masterpiece but also making the verses easier to commit to memory.

Undoubtedly the passage does not describe a particular woman but rather provides a prototype of what God envisions in His design for the woman. Her identity is not important, but her character and focus of life and ministry are to be carefully studied and emulated. Every godly woman I have personally known and admired is linked to this description, although no one is fashioned exactly as this woman of strength.

Perhaps most impressive is her commitment to biblical priorities. Her relationship to her husband and children and the ways in which she reached beyond the family circle to her community and world are inspiring. Certainly her gifts are impressive, but more meaningful is the diversity of those gifts. I can see myself and even encourage my students with the assurance that every woman with a heart for God can find herself in these epithets describing the many opportunities open to women who want to serve their families and the Lord.

Another benchmark for this passage is the theme of wisdom. The discerning grasp of God's wisdom for life is woven within the passage and crowned with

the essence of wisdom from God's perspective, i.e., her fear of the Lord. She balances relationships with responsibilities, keeping central her primary commitment to the Lord and His truth as the basis for managing time, giftedness, and opportunities for service (Matt. 6:33).

The emphasis is not so much the rarity of this woman of strength as her value. Such a woman is often overlooked and ignored. Her humility of person and dedication of energies to serving family and others may hide her talents and accomplishments from the world. I have chosen to translate the descriptive phrase identifying this woman as "woman of strength" since the Hebrew word *chayil* often refers to strength—physical prowess, great wealth, personal character, intellectual abilities. The emphasis is on the virtues of character that sustain a woman even in the midst of suffering and trials and enable her to overcome obstacles and challenges in order to accomplish her God-given task.

Dorothy Kelley Patterson

Prayer: *Praise the Creator God for making you a woman and for placing you exactly where He wants you to be. Seek every day to attain God-honoring character in your life and to do God-assigned work within your family and community.*

Personal Reflection: ....

....

....

....

....

727

Willing Service

Proverbs 31:13–20

". . . And willingly works with her hands." (v. 13)

This verse pops out of an ancient setting with a relevant summary. The woman described is seeking "wool and flax" to weave her own cloth—few women today even sew their own clothing! Remarkably this woman is not portrayed as a saintly recluse, refusing mundane tasks to pursue holiness of character as did those who locked themselves away in religious retreat. Rather she pursued even her mundane tasks with energy and creativity in behalf of her family. She secures the materials needed, puts her own hands to the task, arises early, and remains busy until late in order to manage her household.

Even more amazing is her sensitivity to those employed in her household and those less fortunate outside her family circle. The lamp burning through the night is not just an ancient night light; rather the metaphor suggests that she is alert to the needs of her household around the clock.

This "woman of strength" is marked by her commitment to watch over her household, whether supervising others or actually doing the task with her own hands. A certain satisfaction and even delight comes when you invest your time and energy in those whom you love the most.

One Christmas I determined to make something for every family member with my own hands. This task was daunting since I have no skill for sewing or crafts. Our Christmas theme was "A Beary Merry Christmas!" I selected needle-point and sought instruction on how to do this work. I purchased twenty-five "bear imprints" to prepare one for each family member. What an overwhelming burden that became!

For a novice to pursue such a project was quite foolish. Nevertheless, I finished with help from my young daughter, who mastered the craft much more quickly than I. Then I paid a small fortune to have an expert add the necessary

fabric backing and stuffing to complete Christmas ornaments. Despite my regret that the work was not at the level I would have liked and the investment was far beyond what I had expected, I had a sense of satisfaction in "working willingly with [my] hands" to produce a personal gift for each of those so very dear to me!

To this day, I take delight when I prepare food, care for clothing, clean an area used by one I love—knowing that in this season of life I can still perform the mundane tasks that make life easier for those whom I love! Whatever the conveniences or lack thereof, my heart is to serve those dear to me.

Dorothy Kelley Patterson

Prayer: *Ask the Lord to provide opportunities for you to give "hands-on" attention to those whom you love. Depend on the Lord to give you joy even in the most mundane task. All you do should be "as unto the Lord."*

Personal Reflection: ....

....

....

....

....

....

Queen for Life

Proverbs 31:21–25

"Strength and honor are her clothing;
She shall rejoice in time to come." (v. 25)

This amazing woman is marked by the fact that she is not overcome by the daily cares of life. With a large and productive household, she faced difficulties and challenges and even some despair and failure over the years. Yet she is not only portrayed with happiness in her present circumstances, but she also is noted as one who rejoices (literally, "laughs at" what is to come; v. 15).

One outstanding characteristic is the establishment of priorities. Those who are in her household are foremost in her thoughts, and her first and freshest energies are invested in them. She is not only giving attention to providing them with "food" (v. 15), but she also prepares their clothing to protect them even in a severe winter. She understood well the importance of preparing the next generation. Clearly this mother was proactive in protecting her children not only from inclement weather but also from those forces that would attempt to pull them away from the Lord!

Beyond providing for her family, this woman of strength also recognizes the importance of personal care so that she represents well her husband, who sits "in the gates" (v. 23). The Lord does not frown upon feminine beauty, nor does He denigrate the woman who dresses attractively. Determining the limits within this area of life is not easy. The highest goal is modesty, and ultimately nothing is truly aesthetically beautiful if it does not fall within the appropriate boundaries of holiness. Nor should money be pulled from family necessities just to meet some level of expectation in personal appearance. True elegance of form begins in the heart with a humble spirit and with the desire to represent family and the Lord well, even with one's outer appearance.

The section's climax comes with a reference to the woman's clothing. She represents Him well with appropriate dress but even more with a heart that reflects the sensitivities and God-anointed priorities of a woman of strength (v. 25). She was not recognized merely for her clever creativity or successful marketing of household products or for the wealth and position of her husband. Rather she reached this pinnacle of praise because she was truly bathed in the joy of the Lord, and her attractiveness is a worthy testimony of her commitment to Yahweh God! Her inner confidence enabled her to pursue a path of excellence in serving her household. Such a woman is not merely queen of her household for a day, but she assumes the role in her own right—and that for a lifetime of service to the King of kings!

Dorothy Kelley Patterson

Prayer: *Seek the Lord's help in covering your children for their spiritual protection and in giving attention to your appearance so that you represent your family and the Lord in the best possible way!*

Personal Reflection: ....

....

....

....

....

Right Talk Leads to Right Way

Proverbs 31:26–27

*"She watches over the ways of her household,
And does not eat the bread of idleness." (v. 27)*

What comes from the mouth reveals the heart (v. 26). "Wisdom" (Hb. *chokmah*) is part of the opening/closing or bookends of this wonderful book of Proverbs. We are led on a search for wisdom through the book, which culminates in the unveiling of this extraordinary, flesh-and-blood, virtuous woman who fears the Lord (vv. 10–31).

This woman does not indulge in gossip or slander or lies. Rather she goes the second mile to hold her tongue until she can find a way to speak with "kindness" (Hb. *chesed*, an extraordinarily vivid word used often throughout Scripture as God's signature). When associated with God, this word is most often translated "lovingkindness," linking together love in the heart with deeds and setting these apart in covenant. To express another way, this woman is looking for ways to share an encouraging word with those in her household or beyond (see James 3:2).

Words indeed can be a balm for human sorrows and hope for difficulties. This tool of godly speech is an outward evidence of feminine excellence, bearing testimony to the "gentle and quiet spirit" described as precious to the Lord (see 1 Pet. 3:4–5). Her outer attractiveness was enhanced by the disciplines of a gentle and quiet spirit within. Making reference to this discipline as a "law" underscores its importance not only in human relationships but also as evidence of spiritual discipline.

Words are not this woman's only tool. She works hard to exercise good management of her household. She takes responsibility for molding and edifying through her actions. There is no better defense against the evils of a fallen world than a noble woman who is overflowing with good words and deeds. As

this busy woman manages her household, she is not lazy or idle (Prov. 31:17). The magnitude of her responsibilities and the excellence with which she does her work call for vigorous work and consistent activity. She sees value even in the most mundane tasks in her household. Although she obviously has helpers who provide a work force under her supervision, she does not hesitate to put her own hands to the work. She is above reproach and exemplary even in her own household. She is adept at managing her time, resources, and the giftedness God has given to her so that her family is well served and the Lord is glorified!

Dorothy Kelley Patterson

Prayer: *Let us not forget to pour our energies and creativity into making our homes a haven of comfort and spiritual formation for our families. We must remind ourselves to guard our speech and use our time wisely.*

Personal Reflection: ....

....

....

....

....

....

A Woman Blessed and Praised

Proverbs 31:28–29

"Her children rise up and call her blessed;
Her husband also, and he praises her." (v. 28)

What an honor to be praised by those who see you at your worst as well as your best! I immediately think of my own mother—Doris Weisiger Kelley. She embraced this paradigm with a determination to live her life selflessly and to invest faithfully in her husband and children and others beyond her household. We as a family gathered to celebrate her entry into the heavenly court—not to weep and wail, although each of us felt a keen loss of one who had been for us strength and joy over the decades; rather, we called her "blessed" (Hb. `ashar`)! Although this word never comes from the lips of God, the word includes not merely happiness but more a state of bliss, an offering of congratulations for a job well done.

Some mothers pass Mother's Day wondering if their sacrificial labor and investment in the lives of their children has even been noticed, much less appreciated. Perhaps these words embedded in this chapter devoted to biblical womanhood admonish you to take every opportunity to express appreciation for your mother if she is living. If she is no longer on this earth, you can still acknowledge to succeeding generations her investment in your life just as my siblings and I share the legacy of our mother.

Second, mothers can take heart in knowing that whether or not those words of appreciation fall upon our ears in this world is not nearly as important as knowing that God Himself is watching the ledger and noting our continued investment in the lives of our children. At "the judgment seat of Christ," believers will lay these "blessing crowns" of their children at the Lord's feet. Third, we dare not neglect the responsibility of presenting wise counsel and loving discipline as a holy example unto Christ since we are constantly on display before

our children. There is no better way for us to "bless" the Lord and express our gratitude for the opportunity to partner with Him in bearing and preparing the next generation.

Praise is given to a wide array of women who have done well, but there is a double or repetitive use of the key word "chayil" (Hb.) in the passage, mentioned first in verse 10 ("virtuous" or "noble" or "excellent") and then twice in verse 29 ("well" or "excellently" and then "excel" or "surpass"). The use of this word at the beginning and end of this passage sets it apart as bookends do for a group of volumes on your desk. What a precious tribute for husband and children to present the wife and mother of their household as a woman who excels even beyond the most talented women!

Dorothy Kelley Patterson

Prayer: *Only the Lord can prepare our hearts for this awesome task of managing a household in such a way that our children and husbands will invoke blessing upon us and offer praise for our efforts!*

Personal Reflection: ....

....

....

....

....

"The Failsafe Key"

Proverbs 31:30–31

*"Charm is deceitful and beauty is passing,
But a woman who fears the LORD, she shall be praised." (v. 30)*

Are charm and beauty descriptors of good or evil? Many consider charm and beauty as inappropriate traits of biblical womanhood; yet there is no denigration of charm and beauty in Scripture (cp. Prov. 4:7–9; 1 Sam. 25:3; Job 42:15; Song 2:14). Nevertheless what is most important is the heart commitment of devotion to the Lord, which overwhelms all else (cp. 1 Pet. 3:4)—not dependent upon charm or beauty.

To be charming means kindness even in the midst of rude treatment by another, patience even when treated unjustly, graciousness even when you have been wronged. Occasionally I feel that I have been pushed too far. I then "put my charm into a bag" and push forward with whatever it takes to get results—not a godly response. Indeed charm is an outer veneer and can be revoked on personal whim or disrupting circumstance.

Beauty, too, is often illusive. We have all watched the mirror as the years go by with wrinkles coming, hair thinning, pounds added—aging is not all it's cooked up to be! And most of us have seen a loved one in the agony of pain and suffering, watching the tragic change in her countenance as the disease or injury ravages her body. Beauty does pass as we move through the seasons of life.

Yet even when charm is put away out of frustration and beauty fades because of the trials of life and passing of years, a godly woman still has the failsafe key available for her use. She can seize upon the divine challenge and embrace "the fear of the LORD."

The fear of the Lord makes you aware that the Lord is watching everything you do and listening to what you are saying, even reading your thoughts before

you verbalize them. This awesome discovery awakens a measure of self-restraint that is beyond mere human politeness. To embrace this challenge means giving up your own desires and turning away from going your own way (cp. Prov. 3:5). You become overwhelmed with a desire not to do anything to displease the Lord, to beware of disappointing or hurting Him because you are conscious of His loving investment in you. You love Him above all others and are committed to honoring Him as never before with every deed, word, and thought!

Such an attitude of heart goes beyond emotional feelings or even godly intuitions. For you to live is to devote yourself to the Lord's ways and to pleasing Him! You humbly receive His rebuke and correction in your life. You begin a diligent search for understanding His ways (vv. 5–7), which begins with understanding the holiness of God (Prov. 14:26).

Dorothy Kelley Patterson

Prayer: *Spend time in prayer seeking intimate conversation with the heavenly Father, calling for His strength and wisdom to help you remain steadfast in life's journey.*

Personal Reflection: ....

....

....

....

....

A Woman's Looking-Glass

Proverbs 31:10–31

*"Give her of the fruit of her hands,
And let her own works praise her in the gates." (v. 31)*

This praise is impressive—not just because it happens "in the gates" where the leaders of the community gather to make decisions and celebrate occasions but also because the praise originates from the work of the woman's own energies and creativity! The discipline of setting priorities for managing time, resources, and giftedness cannot be maintained without the intervention and divine direction of God Himself. This journey begins with fearing God and obeying Him whatever the cost. Responsibilities and relationships are intertwined without wasted time or frivolity. This woman is satisfied and blessed by that to which she puts her hand and by those whom she serves.

These beautifully crafted words describe a woman as both charming and beautiful. However, what sets her apart is inward beauty and spiritual discipline—her commitment to God and His ways (see Matt. 6:33). She is not worthy of this level of honor and commendation because of her actions. Many women have generated good deeds and done work worthy of recognition. Yet the selflessness and expressions of lovingkindness of this "woman of strength" are not in response to what has been done for her or because of goals she hopes to attain personally. She ministers to her husband, nurtures her children, looks after her household, and reaches beyond her home with a hand of mercy as unto the Lord. She seeks no public stage for unfolding her good deed. Although she is most definitely a "public blessing," the Lord alone is the audience before whom she does her work and lives her life.

This woman is not insulted by the necessity for mundane tasks, but she embraces the most insignificant work as important and worthy of the investment

of her time. Duties to her husband, children, and even her household helpers are important, demanding the highest level of commitment on her part.

Commentator Matthew Henry referred to this passage as a "looking-glass for ladies," challenging every woman to approach it as a useful mirror before which to stand, taking care to note if you are clothed according to the paradigm preserved throughout the generations. Its place in Holy Scripture and the literary device that presents its important message in an alphabetic code are tools to ensure that every woman is challenged by its words:

- Note the connection between inner commitment of heart and outer conduct of life.
- Do not miss the happiness and bliss that naturally accompany the life lived according to godly admonitions.
- Search with diligence to find the requirements for being rightly related to the Lord and pleasing to Him.*

Dorothy Kelley Patterson

Prayer: *May the Lord call out women to follow this pattern of godliness in the home and family relationships, reaching beyond to the community and to the ends of the earth with godly example and influence. Let this prayer be yours.*

Personal Reflection: ....

....

....

*Charles Bridges, *An Exposition of Proverbs* (Grand Rapids: Zondervan, 1959), 629–32.

Co-Editors

Rhonda Harrington Kelley is the president's wife and adjunct professor of women's ministry at New Orleans Baptist Theological Seminary. She is also a Christian author and speaker. Formerly the director of speech pathology at Ochsner Medical Center, Dr. Kelley has a Master of Arts in Speech Pathology from Baylor University, a Doctor of Philosophy in Special Education from University of New Orleans, and additional studies in Women's Ministry from New Orleans Baptist Theological Seminary. She lives in New Orleans, Louisiana, with her husband Chuck, who has been president of New Orleans Baptist Theological Seminary since 1996.

Dorothy Kelley Patterson, a homemaker, helps her husband Paige Patterson, president of Southwestern Baptist Theological Seminary, by serving as professor of theology in women's studies. With graduate and post-graduate degrees in theology, Dr. Patterson teaches, speaks, and writes for women. She is a member of the Evangelical Theological Society, serves on the Advisory Board for the Council for Biblical Manhood and Womanhood, and attends Birchman Baptist Church. The Pattersons reside in Fort Worth, Texas, but travel extensively throughout the world. Their children Armour and Rachel Patterson as well as Carmen and Mark Howell, with their daughters Abigail and Rebekah, live in Texas.

Contributing Authors

Chris Adams is the retired Senior Lead Women's Ministry Specialist at LifeWay Christian Resources. She is also an adjunct professor in the Women's Certificate Program at New Orleans Baptist Theological Seminary, where she received her undergraduate degree in Christian Ministry from the seminary's Leavell College. She was Executive Editor of *Journey*, a women's devotional magazine, until her retirement and has compiled several Women's Ministry resources for LifeWay. She currently is an author and speaker, as well as a consultant for women in leadership. She and her husband Pat live in Nashville, Tennessee.

Karen B. Allen is the wife of Midwestern Baptist Theological Seminary President Jason Allen. In addition to her responsibilities as the president's wife, she also oversees the Midwestern Women's Institute. She received her undergraduate degree from the University of Mobile. She is the mother of five children: Anne-Marie, Caroline, William, Alden, and Elizabeth. The Allens live in Kansas City, Missouri.

Monica Rose Brennan is associate professor of Women's Leadership in the Department of Church Ministries and Christian Leadership as well as the director of the Center for Women's Leadership at Liberty University. She holds an advanced women's studies certificate from Southeastern Baptist Theological Seminary plus a Master of Arts in Religion and a Doctor of Ministry from Liberty Theological Seminary. Dr. Brennan and her husband Michael are parents to five-year-old Elizabeth and twenty-month-old Johnluke, live in Madison Heights, Virginia, and serve with The Oasis Church.

Becky Brown is an author and composer through her ministry Little Brown Light. She has a Bachelor of Arts in History and English from Louisiana College, a Master of Arts in Student Personnel Administration from Northwestern State University, and a Master of Arts in Christian Education from New Orleans Baptist Theological Seminary, where she served in administration for a number of years. She enjoys writing devotionals and teaching women in retreat and conference settings. She lives in Richland, Mississippi.

Sarah Bubar is the dean of women for Word of Life Bible Institute at their extension campus in Hudson, Florida, overseeing the spiritual needs and discipleship of the women. She received a Master of Divinity with concentrations in Women's Studies and Biblical Languages from Southwestern Baptist Theological Seminary. She has taught a biblical womanhood class and is actively involved in the college ministry at her church. Her passion has always been the discipleship and biblical education of the women God places before her.

741

Maggie Carter is growth groups director at Venture Church in Hattiesburg, Mississippi. She holds a Bachelor of Arts in English from the University of Southern Mississippi and a Master of Divinity in Christian Apologetics from New Orleans Baptist Theological Seminary. Maggie and her husband Coby reside in Purvis, Mississippi, with their two dogs, and they are expecting their first child. In addition to her ministry responsibilities across Venture Church campuses, she also oversees the writing of Bible curriculum and women's counseling at her church.

Emily Dean is coordinator of Women's Programs and adjunct professor at New Orleans Baptist Theological Seminary, where she earned her Master of Divinity and Doctor of Philosophy in Christian Education. She and her husband Jody, along with their two precious children Lydia and James Robert, live in New Orleans, where Jody serves as assistant professor of Christian Education at NOBTS. Passionate about training women to study and teach God's Word, Dr. Dean has served in various capacities in the local church, writing curriculum and Bible studies for women of all ages, as well as leading girls' discipleship.

Pat Ennis is distinguished professor of Family and Consumer Sciences at Southwestern Baptist Theological Seminary. Dr. Ennis has authored and coauthored several books, including *The Christian Homemaker's Handbook* with Dorothy Patterson. Her life's mission is to love her Lord with ALL of her heart (Matt. 22:37), walk worthy of her calling (Eph. 4:1–3), and train the younger women to fulfill the Titus 2 mandate so that God's Word will not be discredited (Titus 2:3–5). She lives and serves the Lord in Fort Worth, Texas.

Candi Finch serves as assistant professor of theology in women's studies at Southwestern Baptist Theological Seminary where she received a Master of Divinity with a concentration in Women's Studies and a Doctor of Philosophy in Systematic Theology and Church History. She is a published author and widely used speaker. She has a heart to see young women come to know the Lord and become mature disciples of Christ. Dr. Finch lives in Fort Worth, Texas.

Donna Gaines is a teacher/speaker who loves to help the Bible come to life for women at conferences and Bible studies. She is the founder and president of ARISE2Read, a nonprofit that partners with churches and businesses to boost reading proficiency in public schools. Donna has authored three books, gives leadership to the SBC Pastors' Wives Conference, and serves on the Executive Committee of the Ministers' Wives Luncheon. She has been married to Dr. Steve Gaines, pastor of Bellevue Baptist Church, Memphis, Tennessee, since 1980. They have four grown children and ten grandchildren. Donna has a Bachelor of Science from Union University and a Master of Education from Texas Woman's University. She is passionate about missions and discipleship.

Susie Hawkins received her Master of Arts in Christian Leadership as well as a Master of Arts in Theology from Criswell College. She is married to O. S. Hawkins, president of GuideStone Financial Resources of the Southern Baptist Convention. They have two married daughters and six grandchildren. She has been actively involved in teaching, speaking, and writing for women's ministry and ministry wives. The Hawkins family lives in Dallas, Texas.

Tamra Hernandez has a Master of Divinity with Biblical Languages and a Doctor of Philosophy in Systematic Theology from Southwestern Baptist Theological Seminary. She has one son, David, who is a long-term survivor of pediatric cancer, and a wonderful daughter-in-law, Katie. Dr. Hernandez lives in Fort Worth, Texas, where she serves on the faculty of Southwestern Baptist Theological Seminary and actively serves in the Hispanic ministry of Wedgwood Baptist Church.

Carmen Howell is a pastor's wife and mother to two beautiful girls. Her favorite pastime is her family, and her passion is God's Word and her home. She loves to teach, mentor, and write. The Howell family lives in Plano, Texas, where her husband Mark is pastor of Hunters Glen Baptist Church.

Rebekah Howell is a pastor's daughter and a high school student. She enjoys playing her guitar, writing her *Me . . . Plain and Simple* blog, and serving in the children's ministry at church. She lives with her family in Plano, Texas.

Ann Iorg is the wife of President Jeff Iorg of Gateway Seminary of the SBC. They have been married for more than thirty years and have three grown children. She has a Bachelor of Behavioral Science from Hardin Simmons University and a Master of Arts in Educational Leadership from Gateway Seminary of the SBC. She has also served as a preschool director and teacher at various churches for more than thirty years. At the seminary, she enjoys being a hostess and teaching women about the practical aspects of life and ministry.

Lauren Johnson received her Master of Divinity with a concentration in Women's Studies from Southwestern Baptist Theological Seminary. Her husband is Dr. Chris Johnson, pastor of First Baptist Church of Van Buren, Arkansas. They have four children and two Labradors that keep them on their toes. Lauren loves to serve alongside her husband and especially enjoys teaching and discipling women.

Melanie Lenow is the wife of Dr. Evan Lenow and mother of four children ranging in age from five to twelve. She received an undergraduate degree in psychology and Christian studies from Mississippi College as well as a Master of Biblical Counseling from Southeastern Baptist Theological Seminary. God has called her first to minister to her family and, second, to serve the ladies of her local church and Southwestern Baptist Theological Seminary. She has a passion for teaching God's Word as she leads Bible studies and writes for the *Biblical Woman* website. The Lenows live in Fort Worth, Texas.

Elizabeth W. Luter, a pastor's wife, mother, grandmother, and retired pharmacist, has a passion for women in the areas of spiritual growth and divine calling. She graduated from Xavier University College of Pharmacy and has also taken several courses at New Orleans Baptist Theological Seminary. She is Director of Women's Ministry at Franklin Avenue Baptist Church in New Orleans, Louisiana, and serves as an intercessor/counselor for LifeWay Women's Events. She annually teaches women at the LifeWay Conference Center in Ridgecrest, North Carolina. She and her husband, Pastor Fred Luter, Jr., have two adult children—Kimberly

(son-in-law Howard) and Fred, III, "Chip" (daughter-in-law Jasmine)—as well as two grandchildren, Fred Luter, IV ("Drew") and Zoe Grace.

Katie McCoy serves as assistant professor of theology in women's studies at the College at Southwestern. She is also the editor of *Biblical Woman*, a women's issues website from the Women's Programs at Southwestern Baptist Theological Seminary. Katie holds a Doctor of Philosophy degree in Systematic Theology from SWBTS, where she wrote her dissertation on Old Testament laws and women's dignity. Dr. McCoy is also an accomplished harpist.

Melissa Meredith serves as director of the Horner Homemaking House at Southwestern Baptist Theological Seminary, where she also received a Master of Divinity in Women's Studies. She is passionate about gathering and discipling women as well as writing. Among her greatest joys is equipping women to savor and share the hospitality of the Lord in their hearts and homes. Melissa also lives in Fort Worth, Texas.

Diane Nix is the founder and director of *Contagious Joy 4 Him*, a network of encouragement to ministry wives around the globe, as well as an author, speaker, and blogger. Her husband, Dr. Preston Nix, is professor of evangelism and evangelistic preaching at New Orleans Baptist Theological Seminary. Serving in ministry together for thirty-four years, they have two biological daughters, two grown spiritual daughters, two sons-in-law, and two precious grandchildren. She lives in Abita Springs, Louisiana.

Denise O'Donoghue is the director of women's life and assistant professor at Southeastern Baptist Theological Seminary, where she earned her Master of Arts in Biblical Counseling and Doctor of Education. Dr. O'Donoghue has served as Women's Ministry Coordinator at Bay Leaf Baptist Church. She has two married daughters and seven grandchildren. Denise and her husband Rod live in Raleigh, North Carolina.

Gayla Parker is currently serving as a pastor's wife and women's ministry leader at Lifeway Baptist Church in Little Rock, Arkansas. She has also served as an International Mission Board missionary in the Philippines, Woman's Missionary Union executive director/women's consultant for the Baptist Convention of Maryland/Delaware, and missions innovator specialist with WMU. Gayla is a published author, guest blog writer, and women's event speaker. She holds a Bachelor of Science degree in Social Work from Jacksonville State University, Jacksonville, Alabama, and will soon receive her Master of Divinity in Biblical Studies from Southwestern Baptist Theological Seminary. Gayla and her husband have three sons.

Monica Patrick has loved Jesus for as long as she can remember. After serving in Nicaragua with the International Mission Board and then in the oil and gas industry, she married her best friend Charles. They live in Fort Worth, Texas, with their four children—Susanna, ten; Josiah, eight; Nathaniel, six; and Seth, four. Charles serves as Vice President for Strategic Initiatives and Communications at Southwestern Baptist Theological Seminary, and Monica is working toward a Master of Theological Studies at the seminary. She feels incredibly grateful to be able to be a homemaker and serve her husband, homeschool their children, and care for their home. She and Charles are members at Birchman Baptist Church, and she takes great delight in talking about Jesus and His faithfulness, as well as podcasts, crockpot meals, and a host of other things.

Jessica Pigg is a contributing writer for the *Biblical Woman* website and enjoys serving in ministry alongside her husband Timothy, who is pastor of First Baptist Church Immokalee. She received her Bachelor of Science in Biblical Studies from Southwestern Baptist Theological Seminary, where she is currently pursuing her master's degree. She is passionate about sharing biblical advice about the home and hospitality. She lives in Immokalee, Florida.

Dominique Richardson is a Bible study leader with a passion for sharing the hope and life-changing power of Jesus Christ with women. She is a contributing writer for the *Biblical Woman* website and is pursuing a Master of Divinity

from Southwestern Baptist Theological Seminary. She served on staff as the director of connections at Idlewild Baptist Church before taking on the role of "Stay-at-Home-Momma" when her twin boys, Mason and Gavin, were born. She loves serving alongside her husband Luke, and they most recently taught in the college-age ministry together. They live in sunny Tampa, Florida, ran a marathon together last year, and go on as many outdoor family adventures as possible.

Terri Stovall is the dean of women's programs at Southwestern Baptist Theological Seminary, where she oversees the academic programs for women as well as the various women's organizations on campus. She has earned two master's degrees and a doctorate from SWBTS. Dr. Stovall has also served in several churches in women's ministry and has co-authored books about women's ministry. She and her husband Jay live in Arlington, Texas.

Courtney Veasey is the director of Women's Academic Programs at New Orleans Baptist Theological Seminary as well as a communicator for events for women and teen girls. She holds a Master of Theology in New Testament from Gateway Seminary of the SBC and a Master of Divinity in Biblical Languages from New Orleans Baptist Theological Seminary, where she is currently pursuing her Doctor of Philosophy in Biblical Interpretation. She lives in New Orleans, Louisiana, where she loves walking with Jesus and fulfilling her small role in the greater ongoing story of His glory and renown.

Amanda Walker is the author of *Discovering God's Design: A Journey to Restore Biblical Womanhood* and a contributing writer for the *Biblical Woman* website. She enjoys serving alongside her husband Chris, who is a college and missions pastor. She has a Master of Arts in Christian Education with a concentration in Women's Studies and Biblical Counseling and a Doctor of Educational Ministry in Educational Leadership from Southwestern Baptist Theological Seminary. She has three children—Makaylan, Hannah, and Aaron—and is passionate about training women to fulfill God's calling in their lives. She lives with her family in Ruston, Louisiana.

Joy Martin White is the president's wife at Cedarville University as well as an adjunct professor and Bible study leader. She has a Master of Divinity in Women's Studies and a Master of Theology from Southeastern Baptist Theological Seminary. She enjoys serving alongside her husband Thomas, homeschooling their two children—Rachel and Samuel, and discipling college students. She lives in Cedarville, Ohio.

Kim Whitten is the managing editor of the *Biblical Woman* website and a current student at Southwestern Baptist Theological Seminary. She is pursuing a Master of Divinity with a concentration in Women's Studies and serves as an intern in Women's Programs at SWBTS. Prior to the Lord's call to seminary, she served in full-time ministry at her church in Tampa, Florida. She has a passion for understanding God's Word and loves all people! Her greatest desire is to connect others with the truth of God's Word so that they can change their little corners of the world.

Janet Wicker is a pastor's wife at First Baptist Church Naples, Florida, where she and her husband have served for twenty-five years. She received her Bachelor of Arts in Music Performance and Education from Tift College and her Master of Religious Education from Southwestern Baptist Theological Seminary. She also serves as a teacher for the RefresHer Women's Bible Study at her church. She has three children who love the Lord and five grandchildren who delight her heart.

DeeDee Williams is a pastor's wife and mother of three precious children ranging in ages from four to ten. She serves alongside her husband, Andrew, who pastors Galilee Baptist Church in Zachary, Louisiana. DeeDee's two decades of experience working with girls and women demonstrate her passion for teaching and equipping women to understand God's Word. She has completed her Master of Divinity in Biblical Languages through Southwestern Baptist Theological Seminary and is pursuing a Doctor of Philosophy at New Orleans Baptist Theological Seminary focusing on Biblical Interpretation. Beyond her accomplishments and passions, her greatest joy is being found in nothing other than Jesus, purely and authentically.

Hongyi (June) Yang is assistant professor of theology in women's studies and the director of a translation project at Southwestern Baptist Theological Seminary, where she received a Master of Theology in Biblical Studies and a Doctor of Philosophy in Systematic Theology and Missions. Dr. Yang has served in women's ministry for many years and has a passion to help women know and experience the great love that God lavishes on them.

Karen Yarnell is a Bible study leader and ministers to women through teaching. She has a Master of Divinity from Southeastern Baptist Theological Seminary and is pursuing a Master of Theology at Southwestern Baptist Theological Seminary. She enjoys spending time with her five children and serving alongside her husband Malcolm. She lives with her family in Fort Worth, Texas.

Kristin Yeldell teaches women about the transforming power of the Word of God and serves alongside her husband Eric, who is a Worship Pastor at First Baptist Church Naples. She has a Master of Divinity with a concentration in Women's Ministry from Southern Baptist Theological Seminary. Kristin and Eric have four children and live in Naples, Florida.

Acknowledgments

Sincere gratitude is expressed to many people who have labored diligently "behind the scenes." Appreciation is conveyed to Stephanie Cline and Julie Stewart of the New Orleans Baptist Theological Seminary for their support and encouragement. Special thanks are extended to the Southwestern Baptist Theological Seminary team—Tamra Hernandez, Candi Finch, Kim Whitten, Awa Key, and Hannah Roberts, who have provided excellent skills and expertise.

Working with Heather Nunn, associate publisher of Women's Books, B&H Publishing Group, has been a joy. We are also thankful for the continued support of the entire B&H Publishing team, especially Jennifer Lyell, who has shared our vision for this tool.

Our families have provided overwhelming encouragement in our commitment to develop excellent Bible study resources for women. We are especially grateful for our parents, who have prayed for us and taught us to love God's Word. Rhonda is grateful to her husband Chuck Kelley, who encourages her in the pursuit of her ministry calling and lovingly supports her personally, while maintaining the many responsibilities as president of the New Orleans Baptist Theological Seminary. Dorothy is grateful for her children Armour and Rachel Patterson; Mark and Carmen Howell (and her granddaughters Abigail and Rebekah); and most of all for her husband Paige Patterson, who generously offers guidance and wisdom and the loving support that made such a project possible, while serving as president of the Southwestern Baptist Theological Seminary.

Daily Bible Reading

Daily Bible reading plans have been developed to familiarize readers with God's Word through a systematic reading of portions of Scripture every day. Many different daily Bible reading plans are available to assist Christians in developing the spiritual discipline of Bible study. This specific plan includes the reading of five Psalms and one chapter from Proverbs each day of the month. Systematic reading of the Bible provides a broader biblical context and insight into the whole counsel of truth.

755